Law and Medicine in Revolutionary America

Studies in Eighteenth-Century America and the Atlantic World

co-sponsored by
The Lawrence Henry Gipson Institute for Eighteenth-Century Studies, Lehigh University

General Editor: Scott Paul Gordon, *Lehigh University*

Publishing rich, innovative scholarship that extends and enlarges the field of early American studies, *Studies in Eighteenth-Century America and the Atlantic World* embraces interdisciplinary work in eighteenth-century trans-atlantic literature, history, visual arts, material culture, religion, education, law, and medicine.

Titles in This Series

Linda Myrsiades, *Law and Medicine in Revolutionary America: Dissecting the Rush v. Cobbett Trial, 1799*

William A. Pencak, *Contested Commonwealths: Essays in American History*

Dorothy T. Potter, *"Food for Apollo": Cultivated Music in Antebellum Pennsylvania*

James P. Myers, Jr., *The Ordeal of Thomas Barton: Anglican Missionary in the Pennsylvania Backcountry, 1755-1780*

Heikki Lempa and Paul Peucker, eds., *Self, Community, World: Moravian Education in a Transatlantic World*

Priscilla H. Roberts and Richard S. Roberts, *Thomas Barclay (1728-1793): Consul in France, Diplomat in Barbary*

Sarah Fatherly, *Gentlewomen and Learned Ladies: Women and Elite Families in Eighteenth-Century Philadelphia*

Jewel A. Smith, *Music, Women, and Pianos: The Moravian Young Ladies' Seminary in Antebellum Bethlehem, Pennsylvania (1815-1860)*

Jean R. Soderlund and Catherine S. Parzynski, eds., *Backcountry Crucibles: The Lehigh Valley from Settlement to Steel*

Charles K. Jones, *Francis Johnson (1792-1844): Chronicle of a Black Musician in Early Nineteenth-Century Philadelphia*

Steven Craig Harper, *Promised Land: Penn's Holy Experiment, The Walking Purchase, and the Dispossession of Delawares, 1600-1763*

http://inpress.sites.lehigh.edu/

Law and Medicine in Revolutionary America

Dissecting the Rush v. Cobbett Trial, 1799

Linda Myrsiades

LEHIGH UNIVERSITY PRESS
Bethlehem

Published by Lehigh University Press
Co-published with The Rowman & Littlefield Publishing Group, Inc.
4501 Forbes Boulevard, Suite 200, Lanham, Maryland 20706

10 Thornbury Road, Plymouth PL6 7PP, United Kingdom

British Library Cataloguing in Publication Information Available

Library of Congress Cataloging-in-Publication Data

Myrsiades, Linda S.
Law and medicine in revolutionary America : dissecting the Rush v. Cobbett trial, 1799 / Linda Myrsiades.
p. cm.
Includes bibliographical references and index.
ISBN 978-1-61146-102-2 (cloth : alk. paper) — ISBN 978-1-61146-103-9 (electronic)
1. Rush, Benjamin, 1746–1813—Trials, litigation, etc. 2. Cobbett, William, 1763–1835—Trials, litigation, etc. 3. Porcupine's gazette. 4. Trials (Libel)—Pennsylvania—Philadelphia—History—18th century. I. Title.
KF228.R85M97 2012
346.7303'4—dc23

2012008375

∞™ The paper used in this publication meets the minimum requirements of American National Standard for Information Sciences—Permanence of Paper for Printed Library Materials, ANSI/NISO Z39.48-1992.

Printed in the United States of America

Contents

List of Illustrations

Acknowledgments

This study is indebted to the support of my home institution, West Chester University, which in many ways—grants of research support, talented library staff, supportive colleagues—has provided the best possible climate for teaching faculty invested in scholarship.

I appreciate the cooperation of the following societies and collections for their kindness and assistance during my studies at their sites and for their help in locating images, providing copies of images, and granting permission to use images from their holdings: The Historical Society of Pennsylvania, The Library of Congress, The National Library of Medicine, The College of Physicians of Philadelphia, The Boston Public Library, and The New York Historical Society.

I express with this book my deep affection for the premier member of team Myrsiades, my husband Kostas, who has been my rock and my comfort over my career.

Prolegomena

This study provides a textual reading of an important and largely unstudied eighteenth-century libel trial, *Rush v. Cobbett*, together with a cultural analysis in terms of how it affected or was affected by trial law, medicine, the press, and religion as they informed the trial, trial strategies, and the roles of Benjamin Rush and William Cobbett, the plaintiff and the defendant in the trial. The case arose out of the events of the 1797 yellow fever epidemic in Philadelphia and Cobbett's attacks in *Porcupine's Gazette* on Rush's heroic bleeding practices, practices that were as controversial in the medical community as they were widely adopted.

Rush was a leading republican in Philadelphia and a signer of the Declaration of Independence, which made him a prime target for a federalist journalist like Cobbett, who saw in Rush a figure who posed a danger to the health of the city as a medical man and to the health of the body politic as a political figure. Cobbett's preferred mode of attack was satire, a weapon he used to ridicule Rush relentlessly and which left him open to a libel charge by his victim. Rush's response was to file a civil action against the journalist, taking advantage of the opportunity to have the case heard by the prestigious Pennsylvania Supreme Court sitting *en banc* as a trier of the facts.

A rash of libel suits clogged Philadelphia courts at the time and was deplored by Rush's prosecution team and the presiding justices Edward Shippen, Jasper Yeates, and Thomas Smith. Libel suits were an issue of concern to legal figures, politicians, and the public at large for their tendency to fuel feuds and duels and to lead to mob actions, undermining the efficacy of the legal system and confidence in it. At the same time, the liberty of the press upon which Cobbett relied was itself threatened every time a publisher was taken to court for assailing government officials or private reputations, giving rise to unpopular prosecutions aimed by federalists at the republican press at a time when the new republic was struggling to establish itself as a new nation.

The critical political events of the last two decades of the eighteenth century—Jay's Treaty with England of 1795, diplomatic efforts to negotiate with the French in 1798 that resulted in the XYZ Affair, and the Alien and Sedition Acts of 1798—were all implicated in the issues addressed in the trial. *Rush v. Cobbett* occurred just at the cusp of the presidential election of 1800 and at the acme of the frenzied decades that produced the development of political parties, a partisan press, and political consolidation of the new republic. The trial embodied the republican-federalist contests of the period, pitted liberty of the press against the privacy interests of individuals, and engaged in the debate between Anglophiles and Francophiles whereby the two sides tried to drag America into the war declared by France against England in 1793. It raised questions about an emerging free enterprise medical marketplace that led to medical malpractice issues that would come to a boil with the turn of the century. The trial occurred at a time when American law had not yet become established as a unique entity distinguished from English common law, a particular problem for the Pennsylvania Supreme Court which had as well to address popular outrage against its adherence to the English law on libel, the very issue it was to try in the Rush case.[1] The case was, moreover, a stellar example of the rhetorical flourish and oratorical eloquence to which the late eighteenth century subscribed. It expressed the shift the nation was experiencing from a religious culture of biblical jeremiad and the evangelism of the Great and Second Awakenings to a secular culture of civic jeremiad and the political development of an American national identity. In every sense, the case was thus a crucible for testing critical issues of the times, even as it presented itself as a contest between the rights of individual reputation (on Rush's side) and first amendment rights of the press (on Cobbett's side) in the young republic.

As for the trial itself, *Rush v. Cobbett* was published in transcript at a time when American court records were not routinely collected. When they did appear they did so as abbreviated trial reports that preserved a judicial opinion.[2] Trial transcripts containing proceedings, like *Rush v. Cobbett*, were rare enough—they largely appeared with more sustained and extensive newspaper trial coverage after 1800[3]—and a trial taken down by a court reporter who ascribed his name as author was the rarest of all. Trials in the seventeenth and eighteenth centuries had been recorded by clergymen as exemplars (conversion or execution narratives, for example, as well as the Salem witchcraft trials) and in the nineteenth century by printers for popular consumption, but a trial transcript presumably taken down by a lawyer and intended for use by lawyers, rather than mere lawyers' notes, was not a common practice until court reporters began to be assigned by legislatures.[4] Massachusetts did so in 1804, but Pennsylvania delayed until 1845.[5] We are thus presented with a rare opportunity to access an important eighteenth-century trial through a period text that preserves not only the judge's charge to the jury and a record of the evidence and witness testimony, but legal arguments by six prosecution and defense counsel in a text that is sixty-seven pages in length. Such a text allows us to provide a focused analysis of *Rush v. Cobbett* that interrogates the trial in detail.

This study answers questions about the legal text and about its setting. Questions are raised about the provenance of the trial transcript, so that considerations related to how it was taken down, by whom, and to what purpose are addressed, as well as its status as a legal text. The study answers questions about the legal issues the transcript takes up, the body of law to which they belong, and how those issues were argued. How the legal subjects in the trial were constituted in the text is questioned in terms of how defense and prosecution arguments framed them. The jury's role in the trial and the jury's relationship to the community raise questions about the construction of the arguments and the conduct of the trial from the perspective of jurors as a target audience. Even as the study raises such questions, it does so by querying the themes, images, and language that make up the legal narrative and how the trial operated rhetorically as a persuasive modality.

In terms of the larger setting, this work raises questions about the critical inputs that inflected the trial and the informative outcomes that emanated from it. As a cultural study, the work anatomizes the trial from multiple disciplinary perspectives, asking what kind of statement discourses as different as law, medicine, religion, and politics offered and how the trial acted as a crucible to shape the convergence and divergence of disciplinary narratives. The conflicting vectors of libel law, medical malpractice, and the rights of the press detail the framing that emerged from medicine, religion, and the press. The study asks how developments in American legal practice affected the roles of counsel, the judge, jury, and accused; and, given that political parties and the partisan press had their origins in the same decade as the trial, it asks how they affected the trial as they emerged and grew. In the process of dissecting the trial and placing each of its organic parts, the study asks what serves as a connective tissue to give coherence to the whole. In what way did the role of medicine prove dispositive to the prosecution's argument and to its preemptive defense of Rush's medical practice? What did the alternative healing fiction of fever sermons contribute to the jeremiadic narrative and the greater civic myth used to explain and justify the plaintiff and how did the cultural artifacts—visual and verbal editorializing through prints, satires, and doggerel—add to our understanding of the reputations of the litigants and recriminations against them over their feuding?

The troubles began when William Cobbett, having emigrated from England, was drawn into a doctors' war over the treatment of yellow fever during the fever epidemic of 1797. The battle of words played out in pieces published in his newspaper *Porcupine's Gazette*, which he had begun in Philadelphia in that year. Together with the American John Fenno, publisher of another federalist paper *Gazette of the United States*, he began ridiculing Benjamin Rush's system of bloodletting and his attempts at puffing, a form of quackery or self-advertisement. He wrote a series of satiric letters about a tavern keeper turned bleeder, which clearly mocked Rush, and compared him to an infamous fictional bleeder, the Spanish physician Sangrado from Alain Rene Le Sage's novel *The Adventures of Gil Blas of Santillane*. Cobbett's accusation that Rush slew more patients than Samson slew Philistines had more bite than perhaps Cobbett intended, as it led to the charge that he had libeled Rush as a murderer. These were the pieces that provoked Rush to file charges in October 1797 against both Fenno and Cobbett, only to drop the charges against the American publisher.[6]

THE TRIAL TRANSCRIPT

Rush v. Cobbett was called for trial on December 13, 1799, in the Pennsylvania Supreme Court.[7] The court called the case as the first trier of fact under the *nisi prius* system then in effect whereby this appellate court also acted in selected cases as a trial court.[8] A transcript of sixty-seven pages was taken in shorthand by T. Carpenter, a clerk either acting as court reporter or assigned to the trial by the printer W. W. Woodward, who announced his publication of the transcript within days of the trial.[9] Cobbett, who had secreted himself in New York and neither attended the trial nor was present in Philadelphia in its aftermath, charged that the transcript—which he called the "report of the trial"[10]—had been organized and published by Thomas Bradford, a republican printer with whom he had a contentious relationship and whom he considered Rush's friend. Whereas it is possible Bradford published the transcript while Woodward only printed and advertised it, there is no evidence of Bradford's involvement nor is there a second transcript that could be linked to Bradford. Neither is there a link to the court itself, for example as part of a collection of judges' or lawyers' notes of cases such as those published by Alexander Dallas, Jasper Yeates, or Alexander Addison.[11] Woodward, having printed his announcement just six days after the verdict, thereby laid claim to the transcript that does exist.

The fact that Cobbett was not in Philadelphia, and therefore not immediately knowledgeable about what was being published, might account for his assertion that Bradford published the transcript. In any case, Cobbett raised a number of objections to the objectivity of the report, attacking it as "the most infamous bundle of libelous falsehoods that ever was published in the world"[12] and claiming that "they"—presumably Rush's republican acolytes, to whom Cobbett referred as "Rushites"—"have published a 'report' of the trial, not badly calculated to justify themselves and to deceive the world."[13] Nevertheless, in an extensive response that appeared in five issues of a newspaper he called *Rush-Light*, Cobbett treated the transcript as standing—however askew—for what occurred at the trial. The falsehoods he objected to, as a result, were just as likely a reference to the prosecution's case as they were a statement about the reliability of the transcript as a trial record. Cobbett engaged directly the arguments as the transcript presented them without further comment on the quality or accuracy of the transcript itself other than to say that "*The Narrative of the judicial proceedings* in the cause of Rush, furnishes . . . a series of facts [that] demand an ample exposure."[14]

The transcript does appear to privilege the prosecution case in several ways. For one, it prefaces the legal arguments with presiding justice Edward Shippen's charge to the jury, in which his commentary proves seriously prejudicial to Cobbett. It is worth noting that the republican press was highly congratulatory of Shippen's charge, isolating it for attention when the verdict was announced. On the very day of the verdict, for example, the *Constitutional Diary*[15] represented Shippen's presentation as "elegant, sensible and pointed upon the doctrine of libels and the press . . . a bold and decided opinion." In the same issue, Cobbett was described in less adulatory terms by a correspondent who remarked, "Porcupine, we are happy to find, will be *bled* and *purged* to some tune."

The transcript restricted itself almost exclusively to the presentation of the legal arguments by counsel. It did provide for reference the main exhibits of the trial (a selection of attacks on Rush printed in Cobbett's *Porcupine's Gazette*), a truncated version of an examination of one witness, a description and excerpt of an examination of a second, and a deposition from a third. The respective amount of time devoted to prosecution and defense arguments were clearly disproportionate: the former was accorded little less than two thirds of the transcript (thirty-six pages) and the latter one third (twenty pages), suggesting either a bias on the clerk or printer's part toward the prosecution or a clearly inadequate representation by the defense.

Even before the transcript was published, the general consensus was that *Rush v. Cobbett* was an important trial for republicans, in line with which the verdict was enthusiastically embraced by the Rush-friendly crowds that attended the trial, a crowd described in the press as having expressed its satisfaction "in a manner (unprecedented in the Courts of this city) [*sic*] by a universal clapping of hands."[16] The jury itself was referred to, given its republican verdict, as "enlightened and honest." The importance of the trial was testified to not only by the press's reference to the jury's "important and just decision" and by Woodward's notice announcing a transcript of "the whole of this important trial,"[17] but by the transcript's title, "Important Trial of the Supreme Court of Pennsylvania."[18] Jared Ingersol, closing for the prosecution, defined the case "as one of the most important ever entrusted to a jury of this country,"[19] while even Cobbett acknowledged the perception: "They call it an *important* trial, and I shall certainly endeavour to make it so in its effects."[20] Indeed, Cobbett felt that in some way this case had not only sealed his fate in America, but that its notoriety, indeed in his view its infamy, expressed the republican nature of the city itself and the dangers of popular democracy: "The Philadelphians, in the hey-day of their malignant exaltation, called the decision against me an *important* one, triumphantly publishing the names of the jurors, and as their publication never was, and never will be, read, these jurors ought to thank me for snatching their names from oblivion."[21]

CONSTRUCTING THE PLAINTIFF

As a plaintiff, Benjamin Rush was a legal subject of considerable complexity and mythic proportions. Broadly conceived, his self-presentation organized around two constructions: a physician who modeled the best and worst of his profession; and a unique figure around whom controversy swirled and from whom leadership was expected. Benjamin Rush's trial exemplifies the subject authoring himself for future memory, his professional narrative shaping his personal story, and thereby his personal identity, so that he informs the cultural practices through which he will be defined even as institutions define individual existence. It is through his cultural narrative that Rush will be understood as a person and as part of a people. As Priscilla Wald says in her study of narrative and culture, parties compete "to forge narratives that instantiate their visions,"[22] visions that represent cognizable cultural identities, that create boundaries, and that establish a past for the future to remember. It is a struggle of considerable cultural anxiety, of risk-taking strategies, and of competing and conflicting practices.[23]

Work has already begun on constructing yellow fever, Benjamin Rush, and the eighteenth century, work which this study will take into account as it considers Rush as a legal subject. We find, for example, that Etta Madden constructs Rush in terms of his ambition to "make a figure" in the practice of medicine and in medical literature.[24] She focuses on rhetoric and the social construction of science as truth, contending that Rush figured his culture as much as it figured him. Whether Rush was aware of his self-construction is another matter, although Colleen Terrell's comparison of Rush with Benjamin Franklin suggests Rush was unlikely to have been conscious of such an effort.[25] In any case, Madden makes clear that Rush was energetically engaged in "performing" his identity both privately and publicly, following Bruno Latour in developing the notion that "the assertion of self . . . describes an essential part of scientific writing."[26] For our purposes, the "expanded clearing" such a view suggests culminated in the Rush-Cobbett trial.[27]

Extending Madden's constructivist view of Rush, Jacquelyn Miller considers that coping with fear and grief in the yellow fever epidemic was itself a feature of the construction of middle class identity in the eighteenth century, an offshoot of the ability to control one's passions that was regarded as a central element of middle class actors like Rush.[28] Indeed, she contends, "the fact that the majority of those who died during the epidemic were poor, seems to have lent credibility to the belief in a connection between disease and a lack of self-control."[29] Lack of self-control is very much the thesis embraced by Leon Eisenberg who tells a therapeutic story of Rush that constructs him as a man who thought himself infallible.[30] As Eisenberg puts it, Rush was so convinced that he was right, "he attributed each new instance of improvement to the efficacy of his treatment and each new death in spite of it to the severity of the disease. I tell this story of Rush's *furor therapeuticus* as a cautionary tale. Sympathy for the afflicted and service at personal risk do not ensure good outcomes. Conviction must be tempered by awareness of fallibility."[31] Paul Kopperman, looking at Rush purely from the perspective of physical medicine, would have endorsed Eisenberg's diagnosis, having himself concluded that Rush "did not concede that his therapy failed to save any patients whose case was not yet formed. As he saw it, the method was virtually infallible."[32]

Rush's sense of his own infallibility was complemented by what Colleen Terrell calls the manufacture of republican virtue by way of the eighteenth-century image of the machine. She casts Rush's work in terms of his assertion that it is "possible to convert men into republican machines,"[33] placing him at the center of mechanical imagery inscribed in eighteenth-century thought. Collateral images of moral improvement and the perfectibility of man define for her Rush's conflation of religion and science as they informed his rational views of medicine and his understanding of political operations and the machinery of government. Thus, Terrell contends, "the concept of a machine perfectly analogizes the fundamental tension between order and liberty at stake in the new republic,"[34] with reference not only to Cartesian philosophy but to Herman Boerhaave's mechanical view of the body, a system Rush studied under the tutelage of William Cullen in Edinburgh. Wade Williams, by comparison, goes beyond issues of self-control to treat Rush as a uniquely positioned witness, as "a site of reception," that is, not in terms of his person so much "as an embodiment of the transformations occurring in a host of rhetorical discourses."[35] Rush's use of rhetoric constitutes for Williams a cultural case study or a sociology of rhetoric, placing him at the crossroads of Great Awakening theology, enlightenment science, and eighteenth-century republicanism. At the confluence of the three, Williams finds that "Rush republicanizes and Christianizes the body: he makes it an instrument for external forms of political and religious authority."[36]

In the context of such unique positioning, the extent to which Rush has been addressed as a legal subject leaves something to be desired. Overdetermined as a physician, he has attracted significantly less attention for his willingness to put his medical reputation in play as a litigant testing libel law in the courts. That he was not only willing but determined to do so provides the opportunity to consider Rush's medical practice in relation to his libel case and to regard the *Rush v. Cobbett* trial in terms of contemporaneous medical liability and malpractice law. Before we take up the legal issues, however, it will be useful to review, as we do in the first chapter, Rush's medical practice in the context of the yellow fever epidemics of the 1790s, the doctors' wars provoked by his treatments, his position relative to quackery of the period, and the devastating cultural effect on the medical profession that resulted from the controversies and conflicts in which he was engaged.

THE REPUBLICAN NARRATIVE

The legal themes of Rush's trial team did not occur in a vacuum, but, rather, responded to and applied the larger republican narrative of the 1790s and exemplified the religio-secular jeremiad. The time period of the 1790s constituted dark days for the republicans, but it was the years 1797–1801 with the run-up to the passage of the Alien and Sedition Acts of 1798 and the presidential election of 1800 that would ultimately find federalists on the wrong side of history. Campaign politics would flood over into the streets, parties would bump heads over the "quasi-war" with the French,[37] and the politics of the Alien and Sedition acts would play themselves out, as Jefferson would write in 1799, "as powerful sedatives of the X.Y.Z. inflammation."[38] These years represented both the worst stress and the greatest opportunity for the republican press, which appeared likely to collapse in 1798 only to find itself in the midst of a turn-around by mid-1799.[39]

All of these events were bound to affect the Rush trial, particularly in light of Cobbett's incendiary political commentary that tied federalism to the British and the Jeffersonian narrative strategy that saw 1798 as an analogue to 1776.[40] Tellingly, Jefferson would write that this period was "the most eventful ever known since that of 1775, and will decide whether the principles established by that contest are to prevail or give way to those they subverted."[41] That analogy worked itself out in several ways. It related to the repression of the republican press by contending that its freedom was critical to civil liberty so that the struggle over the Alien and Sedition Acts was a paradigm for the central meaning of the American Revolution. That is, a free press was essential to an American defense against British tyranny and the destruction of the republican press represented no less than the subversion of the revolutionary principles of liberty and equality that it defended and expressed. In terms of generating self-conscious Americanism—a pillar of republicanism in the 1790s—the analogy forged a link between 1776 and 1798 that provided "a clear and compelling definition of American national identity."[42] Associating federalists with the English (a negative definition of American identity) and separating themselves from the French (inoculating themselves against the Francophobia of the late 1790s), gave republicans the high ground as true Americans who resisted foreign influence.[43] In this regard, Jefferson would speak of the possibility of a war with France in terms that made clear republican identification with the American nation above all others: "It is our duty still to endeavor to avoid war; but if it shall actually take place, no matter by whom brought on, we must defend ourselves. If our house be on fire, without inquiring whether it was fired from within or without, we must try to extinguish it."[44]

The republican narrative made its own use of the dominating myth of revolutionary history to suggest a replay of the war for independence in 1798 over the repressive alien and sedition attacks by the English place-holders, the federalists.[45] It was so successful that Jefferson referred to his campaign and election as "the revolution of 1800," capturing a sense of the nation's rebirth in a second revolution meant to reaffirm the promise of the first.[46] Through the image of the revolution, Jefferson signaled to republicans that they were passing through a crisis. The period of the 1790s, as a result, was one of pessimism that, like the jeremiad, threatened disunion; 1800 would optimistically promise hope by inoculating the new nation against threats and making the first step to a millennium.[47] In this sense, the language of nationhood was myth-making and magical, a gospel of republicanism[48] leading to a unified American people with a oneness of spirit and a self-consciousness that could be called American.[49]

In many ways this was the narrative that the Rush trial would adopt. The principles were the same (liberty and nation); the enemies were the same (the federalists as English place-holders); and the rescuers were the same (republicans as true Americans). The scenario was one of holding steady to a vision that would preserve the union. As Jefferson would express it, "A little patience, and we shall see the reign of witches pass over, their spells dissolved, and the people recovering their true sight, restoring their government to its true principles."[50] If Cobbett was of the party of witches, Rush was inadvertently implicated in Jefferson's view of a "doctor" who would restore unanimity: "This disease of the imagination will pass over, because the patients are essentially republicans. Indeed, the Doctor is now on his way to cure it, in the guise of a tax gatherer. But give time for the medicine to work, and for the repetition of stronger doses, which must be administered."[51] The excesses of a doctor whose purging doses of taxation would make the citizenry good republicans again might have been intended as a gibe at federalists, but the medical imagery gave up Rush as well. Rush, after all, set the standard for punishing treatments at the extreme end of the therapeutic continuum. Capitalizing on a hyperbolic prosecution of his federalist nemesis Cobbett, he would mimic the federalist tax collector and risk the very cause he intended to support. To his good fortune, Rush would be rewarded with a more propitious verdict than the "taxing" doctor would receive.

Rush had yet other issues with the republican narrative as a gospel,[52] among them his position on the press. Rush found himself in the position of attacking a free press when it was a question of a federalist (Cobbett) attacking a republican (Rush), whereas republicans presumed that freedom of the press was a verity and that the republican press was the target of federalist legislation (the Alien and Sedition Acts). In yet another twist, republicans argued that civil liberty required an uncorrupted public and that a free press was the means of preserving an enlightened people. Rush would argue, by contrast, that a licentious press, meaning Cobbett, undermined the prospect for individual freedom, personal integrity, and privacy. Both agreed that relief for the republican press and the destruction of the federalist press would liberate the people from federalist tyranny. Rush was thus caught in the conflicted position of attacking freedom of the press even as he supported freedom of the press. Moreover, he had to navigate staying within the republican narrative, which attacked the Alien and Sedition Acts, even as he found himself wandering off the republican reservation by arguing that Cobbett was an alien and applying the acts to his own use.

In terms of the themes of threat and hope and of historical ties to contemporary events, Rush found himself in more compatible territory. The pessimism of the republican narrative originated in a federalist administration whose legislation threatened republican values, at the same time that the smell of electoral vindication was very much in the air. In another pairing of optimism and pessimism, the troubles for the republic were over insofar as the nation had gained its independence (liberation from England), but only so long as it did not slide back to a position of undue English influence (infection by federalists). The solution was to return to first principles, those of the American Revolution. For Rush, first principles took him back to the Puritan jeremiad and forward to a secular millennium. The transformation of republican pessimism of 1797 into the optimism of 1799 and 1800 would parallel Rush's movements within exactly the same time frame: Cobbett's attacks and Rush's choice to prosecute would occur from 1797 to 1798; Rush's vindication would come at the end of 1799. The two moves mirrored each other significantly, without fitting neatly into the same trajectory. Rush would profit from the change in climate that led to the republican victory in 1800, while he would contribute to reinforcing the surge in republicanism by being pilloried and then by choosing to prosecute in the midst of the formative discussions that led to the Alien and Sedition Acts. His vindication would converge with the ascendancy of republicanism in the verdict of December 1799 and the election of 1800. The themes mutually exploited would as well demonstrate convergence. Rush's reliance on the theme of American exceptionalism mirrored that of a virtuous republican people. The danger of pollution reflected Cobbett's pernicious foreign influence. Rush's redemption was no less than resurrected republicanism. The epic contests of good and evil, foreign and native, alien and domestic, as well as those of the epochal and timeless struggles of a people and a nation, of a millennialism that made Rush and republicans models for mankind, all spoke to an overall narrative in which pessimism reverted to optimism, attacks to vindication, and the trial, intentionally or not, became a republican response to antirepublican laws, tracing the distance traveled from 1797 to 1800 in Rush's individual history and the history of the party as a whole. Rush might not have chosen to prosecute because of his politics rather than his person, but once in trial, and representing a prominent exemplar of republicanism, Rush capitalized on trial language that unerringly refracted the rays of republicanism to his own use, as if pent-up political energy had breached the walls that held it in. Federalist laws would be turned against federalists in an apt metaphor for what was happening in the larger political contest where the repressive "taxation" doctor, as Jefferson had put it, would overplay his hand and leave an opening for republican themes of liberty to link back to their origin and reverse this reversal of the revolution.

The political jeremiad became a secular fiction that would address the afflictions that had descended upon the nation and explain the nation's future prospects. It was a way of experiencing Americanism that the prosecution in *Rush v. Cobbett* would find immediately attractive and immanently exploitable as a tool to create a community of feeling that would unite the jury in its support of Rush's legal position. Joining the jeremiad to the republican perspective, the idea of a truly American nation and a truly American people became central to that agenda,[53] so that popular freedom and resistance to monarchical tyranny[54] spoke to an alternative mythology in which liberty was the central figure of secular religion and divine providence was translated into manifest destiny. The millennial view of America as a nation that would redeem man followed almost seamlessly, merging into what can be called the myth of the republic, a myth that suggested a secular version of redemption.[55] Clearly the millennial myth had become a standard fixture of national identity since the American Revolution, confirming for Americans their faith in the nation as their best hope for what William Hedges calls a "promised thousand-year reign of peace, harmony, freedom, and virtue,"[56] a vision that would serve as a persistent source of America's mythic manifest destiny. Savan Bercovitch describes this aspect of American myth as a dichotomy of optimism and pessimism, utopian and actual experience. The jeremiad theme expressed despair at America's failure to fulfill its revolutionary promise[57] at a time of partisan conflict and division that would strain the Union beginning with its severance from England and lasting to the end of the century. Uncertainty over man's sins and redemption became uncertainty over the fate of the republic.[58] It was a theme that Rush would capitalize on in opposing himself to Cobbett's villainy. Paradise in this view was likely to be lost rather than regained, for nascent Americanism had only tentatively taken hold and was at risk of being squandered. Cobbett stood for the threat to the legacy of liberation.

Even as republicans replaced the pulpit as a forum for politics with their own form of natural law,[59] making republicanism a form of divine sovereignty, the revolution—with its promise of happiness, freedom, and equality—appeared to have God's endorsement as part of His plan. The Achilles heel of such a construction was that, as Robert Ferguson contends, "open-ended ideas of liberty under natural law were hard to control, and [the new rulers] were especially alarmed by the exaggerated sense of rights that followed therefrom."[60] The republican appeal to natural law gave William Cobbett an excuse to appeal to freedoms that his enemies believed exceeded what an orderly society under republican law could sustain. Rush's task in the trial would be to argue Cobbett down from such a perch, using tools fashioned from the rhetoric of patriotism, the voice of the people, the claims of privacy, the welfare of the state, and the needs of public order. His prosecution of Cobbett would capitalize enthusiastically on classical and biblical imagery to reinforce a civil liberties argument harnessed to the troika of personal privacy, republican virtue, and moral authority as they were protected in civil law. The loss of honor exemplified by Cobbett, the declension of manners and public respect, were all part of the same secular jeremiad in which the punishment of the offender and the reconstitution of civility in the all too litigious Philadelphia legal scene would provide for the blessings of liberty that reconstitution of a truly republican paradise demanded.

THE JEREMIAD NARRATIVE

The transformation of the Puritan jeremiad into a secular revolutionary narrative was in another aspect a story of health. Just as the jeremiad fed into the travails of press wars, professional reputation, and political instability, and just as it spoke of everlasting redemption and eternal life, so it spoke to the spiritual and political health of the nation. Not only did fever imagery emanating from the French Revolution and the yellow fever epidemics of the 1790s inform it,[61] but the jeremiad narrative informed conceptions of health which took on a cosmic dimension and required a divine physician whose remedies soared above merely earthy cures. The disease He treated was a second-order natural event in line with biblical pestilences, plagues, and floods—a collective disaster that spoke of the state of man's relation to God rather than his own personal bodily needs. Global political forces were implicated in English and French infestations of the American body politic and the fever of revolutionary excess. Addressing the bodily imbalances of humoral theory, the religious narrative presented a mantra of avoiding sinful excesses like ostentatious display and lustful desire. Moral virtue trumped republican virtue as a sign of health; collective welfare and self-sacrifice trumped individualistic, opportunistic economic behaviors as treatments; and mercy trumped rewards for merit as prognosis. If the virus went into hiding only to return, its recurrent epidemic nature demanded not symptomatic relief or selective remission but addressing the underlying disease which afflicted all equally. No one had immunity—neither the young, the innocent, and the spiritually pure, nor the rich and the powerful. Just as medical rescue was unlikely in pestilence, so would activating God's mercy require an Armageddon.

The language of disease cropped up in eighteenth-century legal, political, and economic discussions with frequency, utilizing such terms as fever, infection, contagion, contamination, pollution, and plague. Old world Europe considered its colonies in America a pathogenic environment, a sick culture that needed curing.[62] By contrast, the new world regarded its lands as a new Eden free of the sins and diseases of corruption identified with the lands from which its citizens had fled, making the advent of the fever more difficult to justify and understand. The new world linked itself to the laws of nature and considered the institutions it developed in line with the natural order. The relationship between health and the political order, as described by Thomas Jefferson, was one in which health was associated with a free and republican government[63] to which Benjamin Rush added that those who embraced republican virtues were blessed with good health.[64] As with the humors of the physical body, the humors of the political body required balance, so that political disorders required a properly republican form of government that gave equal representation to and balanced each of its parts.[65] Even Rush's controversial newspaper notices sharing his views on yellow fever and yellow fever remedies with the public[66] assumed a connection between health and republicanism that would put the power of health in the hands of its citizens to maintain America's republican virtues. Rush's addiction to the invention of new medical theory and practice reflected his republicanism as well, for Rush felt he had discovered an American system of medicine[67] that superseded that of the British and placed all fevers under the dominion of a single fever.[68] Rush's theory held that secular vice and a lack of religious spirit, like disease, pervaded the body politic and that physical disasters were related to federal causes while moral causes were related to republican virtues. His political analysis, in sum, read very much like a medical diagnosis of the political body in which "Antifederal infidelity and Federal hypocrisy, with all the vices that flow from both, pervade every part of the United States. A bitter and unchristian spirit has likewise divided our citizens."[69] Rush had attached medical theory to national destiny. Having achieved a perfect government, the nation must now, he contended, adopt the goal of perfecting a complete medicine, which his method would accomplish.

Rush faced the problem of justifying an epidemic like that which afflicted republican Philadelphia and of squaring belief in a benevolent creator with the evils wrought by epidemic disease. For Rush, both the new land and the men who inhabited it needed to be seasoned to make good on their new life.[70] Relying upon the legal principle of usufruct, Rush argued that improving the land made it healthy, that is to say productive of healthfulness, whereas unimproved land gave rise to miasma, or pestilential vapors.[71] Applying humoral theory, Rush held that excess ought to be offset with a correction to bring the body, political or physical, back into balance.

The religious dimensions of disease ensured that the fever epidemic would find in the religious community an alternative means of telling the story of yellow fever. Just as Americans feared foreign invasions of its body politic (a political pathology) and foreign infiltration of diseases into the health of its communities (a physiological pathology), all in the context of the growing pains of a new nation-state,[72] so did their religious sensibilities lead them to conceive of medicine in religious terms as a critical, if not central, metaphor for eighteenth-century beliefs. The healing offered by religion both overlapped and competed with medicine's way of healing, providing a story with long, deep, traditional roots in the community. Authors of sermons spread ideas, reflected understandings, and created language that capitalized on medical themes as a way of reaching out to a diffuse audience, providing the devout with a way to frame their thinking on other than religious subjects. Illness, like pestilence, famine, and war, thus became one of the divine power's key weapons so that it was God who should be consulted when one was ill and He who was ultimately the healer. Illness was directly related in this scenario to guilt, on man's part, and discipline, on God's, with an implicit understanding that those who relied upon physicians alone for care of the body were to be criticized.

Embedded in sermons from Lutheran, Quaker, Episcopal, Methodist, Universalist, Congregationalist, Reformed Dutch, Scotch Presbyterian, Baptist, and Church of England divines, the yellow fever epidemic became a seedbed of religious interpretations, like Rush's comparison of himself to Jeremiah,[73] that analogized affliction and outcasting and framed illness as punishment for lack of faith.[74] The jeremiad spoke to the judgment that God would reign down upon those who abandoned His law and to the need to repent to be saved in His sight. The prophecy of such judgment was refracted politically to point the way to the building of a nation and to the creation of a people worthy of God, keeping in mind that the new republic was still in its infancy and not yet worthy of being regarded as an instrument of democracy. Relevant questions were thus raised about the captivity of a people who deserted their God and their need for rescue, a circumstance that led in biblical time to the flight from Egypt.[75]

The message of the jeremiad was one of a sick people in need of a cure and of God as a divine physician whose extreme medicine would treat the diseased soul and raise the stricken patient to the heavenly kingdom of God. In this scenario, God was both disease and physician. The cure was to accept God's judgment, to succumb, not to resist. In one sense, man was God's victim, His unempowered dependant, wayward creation, and His favored child all in one. So long as there was evil, man needed God as the only force powerful enough to battle it; at the same time, as an all-powerful being God raised questions about His own omnipotence by His tolerance for evil. In this scenario, sin was the disease agent, God's mosquito, and thereby the real cause that man needed to address. Yet to sin was no more than to say that one lived in the world that God had created. Cleaving to the earth was, consequently, itself a sin for in this way man sucked up the poisons of the world. If to live was to sin, the grave was constructed as a preferred entry to heaven. As he waited for the grave, man was left to wander in his sinful wilderness, embrace devastation as a friendly act of grace, and await His intervention. No action on man's part, whether to flee the epidemic or to remain behind to serve, was consequential. The only way to work out God's plan and thereby forgive man his sins was to follow God's law. God was, in sum, a model of rightness in allowing evil to teach man a lesson about his sins. He represented a model of Justice that joined wrath to mercy, which required tolerance of unfairness, submission to wrathfulness, and enjoyment of undeserved mercy.

THE IMAGE OF FEVER

The disease metaphor most pertinent to the foreign fears and party politics of the eighteenth century analogized French influence and "fever," as reflected in secretary of the Navy George Cabot's contention in 1798 that French principles "are more to be dreaded . . . than a thousand yellow fevers."[76] A republican newspaper that spread French ideas was described by a competitor as "a nuisance more virulent than the Yellow fever."[77] The "fever" of the slave revolt in 1793 Haiti and the French refugees it sent flooding into Philadelphia,[78] together with the suspicion that the French privateer Sans Culotte had carried yellow fever to the city,[79] reinforced links between revolution, abolitionism, the French Terror,[80] and disease that became a magnet for political dissensus. Church of England William Smith's yellow fever sermons, for example, tied the French "fever" to providential judgment through "the wild principles and restless conduct of their partisans here" who, as swords of destruction, inflicted judgments to punish their transgressions.[81] In a similar vein, and as part of a struggle to avoid a second revolution, Rush considered mob violence and public vice pestilences comparable to yellow fever and was concerned with treating them as a danger to the social order of the body politic.[82] To avoid shedding blood like that unleashed in the French reign of terror, experts ought to supervise bloodletting as it was applied to the political body. Bleeding would lessen popular rage and open up "new means of curing moral and political maladies."[83]

Fever, however, was not always to be dreaded, for according to Rush the American Revolution was regarded as a fever of liberty, in this case a fever whose beneficence blew open "all the doors and windows of the temple of nature."[84] He was later to suggest a certain ambivalence on this issue, however, arguing that an "excess of the passion for liberty" was possible and that indeed it did occur after the peace of 1783 when citizens became "inflamed by the successful issue of the war" so that their "opinions and conduct . . . could not be removed by reason nor restrained by government." This condition Rush regarded as a form of insanity which he labeled "*Anarchia.*"[85]

Once fever imagery overflowed its medical context and became implicated in the political debate,[86] fever, contagion, and contamination were conflated to suggest a pathology that was both indigenous and exogenous. Such a mixed metaphor captured the internal imbalances of humoral theory, the external threat of contagions brought from foreign places, and the instability of infections of local origin to portend an even greater threat than any one of them could independently instigate on its own. Fever was thus a dominating, if overdetermined, image that inserted itself in a rash of uses over time,[87] its provenance as easily located in the heavens, in foreign lands, or home-grown as a local illness. America understood itself to be an object of fear to the Europeans who died in great numbers when they encountered the new world while, at the same time, it feared foreign influences that brought new diseases to the new world through colonization and trade.[88] The most dangerous diseases were indeed foreign ones—in both directions—so that portraying disease events as encounters with strangers was as instructive as associating them with groups with which one was in opposition.

Loss of life in the yellow fever epidemic could, in any event, be viewed as a means of controlling disease. It redressed the unhealthful urban growth that Thomas Jefferson,[89] Mathew Carey,[90] and Noah Webster[91] complained of, so fever might, in that sense, be welcomed for its restorative effects. It was indispensable to revitalizing American culture which renewed itself in a redemptive response to the scourge that had afflicted Philadelphia.[92] From Rush's perspective, in sum, the epidemic provided a laboratory of medical theories, much like his practice among the poor when he began doctoring and like the hospitals of the continental army during the American Revolution. But yellow fever was always more than merely a medical laboratory. It had been, as we have seen, situated as an experiment in political, legal, and economic order and as an acid test of moral values and religious belief. The test, for our purposes, would be expressed most fully in the conduct of the *Rush v. Cobbett* trial.

This study will address the *Rush v. Cobbett* trial in three parts: first, by examining Benjamin Rush, then by considering William Cobbett, and, finally, by focusing on the trial itself. Chapter 1, "Benjamin Rush and the Culture of Medicine," reviews the state of eighteenth-century medicine and Rush's role both in its practice and in medical feuds of the yellow fever epidemics. Chapter 2, "Malpractice Law and Benjamin Rush," provides the legal background that framed Rush's performance as physician. It then examines his decision to prosecute Cobbett. Chapter 3, "William Cobbett and the Scurrilous Press," addresses Cobbett's role as a journalist, the state of the press, press satire, and press feuds. It then examines his attacks on Rush and the medical profession during the 1797 yellow fever epidemic. Chapter 4, "Libel Law and William Cobbett," considers libel and sedition law and specific relevant cases, including cases related to Cobbett's experience with the law. It then examines the state of eighteenth-century legal practice, the setting of the trial, and Cobbett's absence from the trial.

Getting to the trial, Chapter 5, "*Sangrado v. the Cloven Foot*," dissects *Rush v. Cobbett* in terms of the presentations of prosecution and defense counsel and the trial narratives they constructed. Cobbett's posttrial analysis of the trial is presented as a complement to the defense case. Chapter 6, "The Trial Concluded," considers Justice Shippen's charge to the jury, the role played by the jury, including the trial verdict, and a critique of the defense team's performance. This chapter concludes with an analysis of trial strategy. The afterword provides the aftermath of the trial as both Cobbett and Rush suffer reputational losses, Cobbett by fleeing to England and Rush in his political eclipse. Examination of Hugh Henry Brackenridge's satire of the Rush-Cobbett feud in his novel *Modern Chivalry* completes the study as a last word on the subject.

NOTES

1. Rowe (1994, 239–40).
2. Dallas (1790), an abbreviated set of trial reports for the Pennsylvania Supreme Court, was one of the earliest collections; Rowe (1994, 203–4). Another early set of reports appeared in Connecticut in 1789; trial reports did not appear with any frequency until after 1800 and did not become common until the first half of the nineteenth century; Cohen (1993, 29); Surrency (1981, 50–58). Appointed to the Pennsylvania Supreme Court at the end of 1799 (Leary, 1965, 14), Hugh Henry Brackenridge clarifies the way in which he regarded such reports: "the sentiments delivered are supposed to be, and frequently are, the notes of the counsel, the judge, or of the reporter himself who catches in court, the argument of the opinion. This, with all the attention and quickness that is possible, cannot be done; for the pen of the most ready writer, will not be able to keep pace . . . with the oral expression; and therefore the substance can only be obtained; and even with regard to this, misconception, or omissions, are unavoidable"; Brackenridge (1814, 1: 88–89).
3. Cohen (1993, 31).
4. Cohen (1993, 14–16, 29).
5. Surrency (1981, 55–56).
6. Clark (1939, 146–47).
7. *Gazette of the United States*, 3 October 1797; *Porcupine's Gazette*, 5 October 1797.
8. Lerner (2000, 213). The Pennsylvania Supreme Court evolved from a court that performed both an appellate and a trial function for both criminal and civil cases to one that acted as an appeals court for errors from the lower courts, thereby separating the trial and review functions of courts clearly in the nineteenth century and establishing itself more clearly as the superior court in the state. In *Rush v. Cobbett*, however, we find the case being tried before a court that had not yet evolved a clear distinction between review and trial functions or between criminal and civil law. When it sat as a trial court (*nisi prius*), the court could only render judgment and try both issues and facts if it was sitting en banc, as it did in *Rush v. Cobbett*; Rowe (1994, 173, 175,184). As Rowe makes clear, before the American Revolution, the number of cases removed to the supreme court for trial was quite small and required the involvement of a cost that exceeded over $100 initially, by 1806 over $500, which was linked to the value of the property in dispute. The same structure continued after the revolution even

after judicial reforms in 1791, still giving criminal and civil cases access to the court as first trier of facts. Indeed, restriction of the court's trial function only began during the first decades of the nineteenth century; civil trials ended for the largest part in 1809 and fully in 1834. Civil cases called before the supreme court in the eighteenth century would be tried in a court that overshadowed other trial courts as a more prestigious body, causing the city great delays and expense as suits increased in the latter part of the century. The choice of cases was apparently "on a strictly nonlegal basis" (178–83).

9. *Philadelphia Gazette and Universal Daily Advertiser*, December 20, 1799. Trial reports were likely stimulated by public interest in increased newspaper coverage of trials. More complete transcripts, like the *Rush v. Cobbett* trial, were rare indeed until the growth of influence of legal counsel and the solidification of a truly adversarial trial system, which we do not find until the end of the eighteenth century, together with the emergence of official court reporters—the first of which was appointed in Massachusetts in 1804; Rowe (1994, 203–4); Cohen (1993, 26–31).

10. *Porcupine's Gazette*, January 1800; Cobbett (1801a, 12: 159).
11. See Dallas (1790) and Dallas (1905); Addison (1800); Yeates (1871).
12. *Porcupine's Gazette*, January 1800; Cobbett (1801a, 12: 159).
13. *Rush-Light* I, February 12, 1800; Cobbett (1801a, 11: 216).
14. *Rush-Light* IV, March 31, 1800; Cobbett (1801a, 11: 354).
15. *Constitutional Diary*, December 14, 1799.
16. *Constitutional Diary*, December 14, 1799.
17. *Philadelphia Gazette*, December 20, 1799.
18. Carpenter (1800, 1).
19. Carpenter (1800, 66).
20. *Rush-Light* I, February 15, 1800; Cobbett (1801a, 11: 216).
21. *Rush-Light* III, March 15, 1800; Cobbett (1801a, 11: 344).
22. Wald (1995, 2).
23. Wald (1995, 13).
24. Madden (2006, 241–72). See also, Fortune and Warner (1999).
25. Terrell (2003, 100–32).
26. Madden (2006, 252).
27. See Madden (2006, 252–53); Latour (1988, 5).
28. Miller (1996, 129–47, see also, Miller (1997, 79–95).
29. Miller (1996, 140).
30. Eisenberg (2007, 552–55).
31. Eisenberg (2007, 552).
32. Kopperman (2004, 572).
33. Terrell (2003, 101).
34. Terrell (2003, 102).
35. Williams (2000, 55).
36. Williams (2000, 67).
37. Onuf (2000, 97).
38. 26 January 1799, letter to Eldridge Gerry; Washington (1854, 4: 271).
39. Onuf (2000, 97).

40. See Onuf (2000, 13, 80, 98–99, 102, 105, 195, 206).
41. April 2, 1798, letter to Mr. Pendleton; Washington (1854, 4: 230).
42. Onuf (2000, 99).
43. Onuf (2000, 102).
44. May 9, 1798, letter to James Lewis, Jr.; Washington (1854, 4: 241).
45. Onuf (2000, 100, 108).
46. September 6, 1819, letter to Judge Spencer Roane: "the revolution of 1800 . . . that was as real a revolution in the principles of our government as that of 1776 was in its form, not effected by the sword, as that, but by the rational and peaceable instrument of reform, the suffrage of the people"; Peterson (1984, 1425); Onuf (2000, 80–81, 105).
47. Onuf (2000, 14, 16).
48. Onuf (2000), 85, 108).
49. Onuf (2000, 99).
50. June 1, 1798, letter to John Taylor; Washington (1854, 4: 247).
51. November 26, 1798, letter to John Taylor; Washington (1854, 4: 259).
52. Onuf (2000, 85, 108).
53. Laracey (2008, 33).
54. Laracey (2008, 34–35).
55. Hedges (1981, 5).
56. Hedges (1981, 5).
57. Hedges (1981, 6). The providential call for reformation that the jeremiad trumpeted forth was for Puritans merely a down payment on a plan for revolution that fulfilled itself in America's prophetic history in 1776. Sacred destiny and political destiny converged in these terms in a quest for an identity and a mission that was distinctively American in a historical sense and that joined laments and threats to hopes and celebration, a particularly American optimistic form of jeremiad. As Bercovitch presents it, this jeremiad became the foundation for the new republic, so that its founders (now the native American revolutionary fathers rather than Puritan migrant founders) became the touchstone for future generations. They would act as a referent point and a model to live up to in achieving an American identity that fulfilled the national prophecy of an American mission. The biblical wilderness became the American wilderness, sacred errand became economic and political progress, the ahistorical millennium became an historical new republic, and biblical fathers became revolutionary founders; Bercovitch (1978, 12). With the emergence of this new model, historical events displaced the importance of theocracy, "transmitting a myth that remained central to the culture long after the [Puritan] theocracy had faded" (17).
58. Bercovitch (1978, 6–7).
59. Ferguson (2004, 54–55).
60. Ferguson (2004, 75).
61. Yellow fever epidemics occurred in Philadelphia beginning in 1793, 1797, 1798, and 1799; see Duffy (1953).
62. See Bewell (1999).
63. Rosen (1952, 35).

64. Rush linked virtue and government in regarding law-giving as a moral faculty and judging as a function of conscience; Terrell (2003, 127); Rush (1815, 1: 263–78); Kornfeld (1984, 197–99).

65. Miller (1997, 84).

66. *Federal Gazette*, September 12, 1793, October 7, 1793; *Philadelphia Gazette*, September 4, 1798.

67. Kopperman (2004, 572).

68. Holmes (1966, 257–58); Kornfeld (1984, 197–99).

69. September 15, 1798, letter to William Marshall; Rush (1951, 2: 807). According to Terrell, Rush saw the relationship of virtue and the physical as a direct and literal one and linked "such physical factors as climate, diet, disease, music, and odors [to] a person's ability to distinguish and choose between good and evil" (2003, 108).

70. Bewell (1999, 40–41).

71. Rush (1815, 1: 267–68); Bewell (1999, 41).

72. See Harris (2004).

73. December 26, 1811, in a letter from Rush to John Adams; Rush (1951, 2: 1116); Rush compared himself to Jeremiah, referring to what he considered his persecution and suffering for telling the truth about medical treatment for yellow fever; Kopperman (2004, 568). Toward the end of the eighteenth century, religious interpretations were less likely to stress direct causation, assigning man's sins as the cause of God's anger; Watson (1991, 144).

74. Ryken (1998, 209–10); see Bloch (1985); Kirschner (2003, 198–229).

75. Ryken (1998, 436).

76. Samuels (1987, 188).

77. *Massachusetts Mercury*, September 25, 1798, in Miller (1951, 92).

78. Pernick (1997, 121).

79. Samuels (1987, 189); Pernick (1997, 124).

80. The French Revolution resulted in a reign of terror in the very same year as the 1793 fever epidemic in Philadelphia, constituting one of the reasons why that epidemic (above others in the young republic that were equally devastating, if not more so) took on a mythic character; Kooperman (2004, 539). The Reign of Terror took almost seventeen thousand lives, many by guillotine, and as many as forty thousand prisoners, many of whom either died or were executed; Doyle (1990, 258); Gough (1998, 77).

81. Smith (1880, 1: 392–93).

82. Miller (1997, 80–84).

83. Rush as quoted in Miller (1997, 89); 25 November 1806, Rush letter to John Adams; Rush (1951, 2: 935). See Williams (2000, 63); Rush (1947, 333).

84. Rush (1791), as quoted in Kornfeld (1984, 190).

85. Rush (1815, 1: 277), as quoted in Rosen (1952, 40).

86. In terms of fever as an indicator of excess freedom, Philip Gould considers that the "danger of unregulated 'freedom'" was an issue at the heart of American identity and that "republican selflessness and liberal self-interest" were in conflict and raised doubts about the limits and nature of that freedom; Gould (2000, 160–61).

87. See Kilpatrick (1990, 254–80). Quakers took "fever" to relate to a curable disease that resulted from poverty and the conditions under which the poor lived.

Their philanthropic and medical treatment was intended to return the poor to the "inner light" within them, their equality before God, and their self-reliance, essentially a religious cure for their condition (257, 262, 266–67).

88. Bewell (1999, 10). One estimate holds that the new world population declined 50 to 95 percent as a result of colonial contact, a mortality rate comparable to that of the Europeans who colonized them.

89. August 2, 1805, Jefferson letter to Volney; Washington (1854, 4: 572); see Chinard (1947, 45–52).

90. See Carey (1794, 10).

91. Webster (1947, 34, 100–103, 105). See, in particular, December 18, 1797, a letter to William Currie.

92. Kornfeld (1984, 198–99).

1

Benjamin Rush and the Culture of Medicine

Benjamin Rush's practice as a physician in Philadelphia began in a medical community described by Simon Finger as "a ramshackle, piecemeal assemblage."[1] He was positioned as one of an emerging coterie of university-educated physicians, more especially in that he held a medical degree from a prestigious European medical school, Edinburgh University. Among other Americans abroad, Rush would find the experience of studying outside the country strengthened his sense of national identity.[2] Added to his foreign medical credential and to his dramatic and intensive battlefield education in medicine, Rush's appointments to practice at Pennsylvania Hospital and to teach at the College of Philadelphia Medical School identified him as a singularly formidable presence and a man who would not suffer fools gladly.

QUACKS AND FACTIONS

Medicine itself was in a highly fluid state, a period referred to as "the golden age of quackery,"[3] and quacks were said to "abound like Locusts in Egypt."[4] The advantage quacks had in the marketplace was tied to their willingness to avoid speculative advice and to provide durable consumables, something that offered the consumer at least an incrementally better chance than probability that it might be efficacious. Satirized by Philip Freneau—a republican editor, journalist-poet, and cultural historian of sorts—a product like Perkins's metallic rods might not have been the last word in medical appliances, but its inventor knew he was competing in a patient-centric universe against wiser designs and wiser heads, each capitalizing on the appearance of science. Not only was *caveat emptor* the new watchword, but medical inventions would have to survive the crucible of consumerism, however ecstatic the public was about their promise:

> *Perkins*! what verse is equal to your praise
> *What hocus*-pocus from sick beds can raise!—
> *Pains in the head, or palsies in the joints*
> Henceforth shall yield to your *Metallic Points*. . . .
>
> Touch'd by your magnet, dead men shall revive,
> Old Bachelors for Humen's blessings strive—
> Maidens, averse to men, be taught to love,
> And wives—long barren—now prolific prove.[5]

Dr. Perkins was not the only culprit to be feared for his "magnetic" appeal. Freneau exposed as well a Dr. Brydone whose device "to guard against the effects of lightning" made the extravagant promise that

> The *beaver* on your lovely scull
> (Secure as salamander's wool)
> Will help repel from your dress'd head
> What strikes us, timid wretches dead.[6]

Elite physicians like Benjamin Rush resisted being associated with quackery as it posed significant risks to their reputation, status, and honor, the very concerns that precipitated Rush's decision to prosecute William Cobbett. Nevertheless, during the epidemic, the rate of failed treatments and resulting deaths and disagreements within the profession over what treatments would work best led to public loss of confidence and to physician feuds that erased many of the distinctions that elite physicians had tried to establish between themselves and practitioners they considered unlearned.[7] If the truth be told, any physician was liable to be called a quack, although the term was most frequently used to describe those willing to cater to gullible consumers in a proto-capitalistic scene characterized by self-promotion, secret nostrums, and advertising[8] that earned itself the name of quack bills.[9] Such early terms as urinarians, urine-casters, urine gazers, and piss prophets were associated with quackery, capturing the practice of smelling, tasting, and viewing the texture of patients' urine, which was common among physicians from ancient times. Charlatans, mountebanks, ignoramuses, and imposters were terms used to suggest the flamboyance of know-nothings and healer-dealers at the fringe of scientific medicine.

While quacks might have proposed outlandish cures, precious little of science was expressed in the practice of those who considered themselves regulars. Indeed, many therapies considered quack treatments were engaged in by both learned and unlearned physicians, including the purging, puking, blistering, and clystering that was common at all levels of healing from folk to natural and rational medicine. Doctors who relied upon abstract reasoning and medical theories nevertheless tried to distinguish themselves from empiric practitioners whose treatments were rooted in their own experience, or who exploited what they learned from observing the human body and from experimental treatments. But then these practices were not restricted to quacks either, as regulars engaged as well in such means of supplementing their medical knowledge.[10] Still, where doctors sold the ineffable—high-sounding advice in Latin jargon—those considered quacks or empirics tended to sell commodities—drugs and secret potions. Where regular medicine was treated as a special province for the elite who maintained a private relationship between a physician and his patient, marketplace medicine of the type considered quackish was open to the public, available everywhere, and permitted self-diagnosing before and self-dosing after the commodity transaction. Indeed, to "quack oneself" meant to self-dose. If quackish practices meant bringing medicine to the level of the marketplace,[11] physicians of all stripes seem engaged in such activities, to the point where medical manuals for self-help care, puff pieces, newspaper advice during epidemics, and defenses of physicians' reputations and practices appeared frequently in the press.[12]

THE CULTURE OF MEDICINE

In the midst of such a disjointed medical scene, the advent of yellow fever acted as a test of the mettle of contemporary medicine. Reappearing after a twenty-eight year absence from the city,[13] the yellow fever epidemic in Philadelphia in 1793 pressured medicine both as a profession and as a science. Until the end of the century, and even beyond, there was little clarity in how or whether medicine would be effectively regulated,[14] other than by voluntary controls and a promise of licensing that, unfortunately, would not take hold until the next century.[15] The American Revolution had clearly delayed the development of medical societies in many places, although it did allow for experimental medicine, established some standards of practice, and provided administrative experience among the physicians who served in the continental army hospitals and camps.[16] The citizens of Philadelphia were nevertheless faced with a city-wide health emergency in which an entire urban population was at risk and with no organized public health services to speak of.[17] Preoccupied with establishing a federal government and writing state constitutions, bureaucrats had little time to deal with public health, so that the devastating reappearance in the nation's capital of the yellow fever left Philadelphia with little more than a port health officer to oversee a quarantine station.[18]

Philadelphia's College of Physicians would step forward with recommendations for stemming the progress of the epidemic, and those individual physicians who remained in the city would offer exemplary service. But divisions among physicians over treatment, lack of control over the proliferation of marketplace medicine, and little scientific understanding of the cause of the disease left medicine at the mercy of happenstance. By mid-September, 1793, George Washington, Thomas Jefferson, and Alexander Hamilton had fled the city as had Governor Thomas Mifflin of Pennsylvania, the state legislature,[19] local officials, and the wealthy and not-so wealthy who had means to move into the countryside. The seat of municipal, state, and federal government in the 1790s, Philadelphia was left bereft of all three and would be forced to rely on volunteer efforts to beat back the epidemic.

Surrounding towns and distant cities refused Philadelphia's products and refugees, essentially cutting the infected city from the rest of the world. The trapped residents were otherwise unable to sustain themselves as businesses ceased operating, jobs became scarce, and foodstuffs were impossible to find.[20] The effects of isolation on the city, as a result of quarantine proclamations by cities as close as Lancaster and as far away as Boston, were intense. Lancaster prevented carriages from running to and from Philadelphia, prohibited the import of Philadelphia goods, and appointed ward leaders to execute its orders.[21] Massachusetts governor John Hancock's proclamation required searches of all persons and their baggage coming from the city and their detention and cleansing "so as effectually to prevent the introduction and spreading of said infectious Disease among the good People of this Commonwealth."[22]

Mayor Mathew Clarkson had remained in the city, but without a bureaucracy to run he could only publish a plea to the citizens of Philadelphia to serve as volunteers on a committee to relieve the overwhelmed overseers of the poor and "to contribute their aid in the present distress."[23] At its first meeting, the committee reported ten members, a number that would expand as specific tasks arose and increased by nineteen new members on September 14, to procure money, and by forty-six new members on October 8, when assistant committees were set up in ten city areas.[24] The core committee took on any job required to support the sick and the dead, organizing a fever hospital, transporting victims to the hospital or cemetery, burning or burying the clothes and bedding of the sick, and hiring doctors, nurses, and bleeders.[25] It procured money for "furnishing suitable accommodation and supplies for the use of the afflicted"[26] from banks and benefactors and appointed parties to disperse funds to poor families at their homes. The committee received applications for relief, kept records of those admitted to the hospital, those it buried, and the orphans they left behind, and provided a home for orphans that eventually required the acquisition of the Loganian Library.[27]

Gifts of shirts and shifts, of bedding and hospital provisions were accepted and distributed; surrounding towns opened subscriptions to aid the committee, sending money, vegetables, sheep and fowls, and sundry articles. One sizeable donation of $5000 was transmitted with a note from the Common Council of New York to the effect that the council was "deeply impressed with the awful judgment of the Almighty on the American Nation, in permitting a pestilential disease to lay waste and disorganize that once populous, well regulated and flourishing sister city, the seat of the Empire."[28] The council hoped that God might stay the course of the disease and "say it is enough."[29] Mayor Clarkson responded by sharing the committee's hope that "the Almighty disposer of all events be graciously pleased to protect your citizens from the dreadful calamity with which we are now visited! whilst we humbly kiss the rod and improve by the dispensation."[30]

William Shippen, Jr., as vice-president of the College of Physicians in 1793 and an old foe of Benjamin Rush's from their days of service in the Continental Army hospitals, wrote up the college's directions to Governor Mifflin for preventing further spread of the epidemic. Alongside prescriptions of a personal nature—to wear clothing suited to the weather, to avoid the sun and evening air and "all fatigue of body and mind"—Shippen advised against "unnecessary intercourse" with the infected and the burning of fires, prescribing instead burning gunpowder and using vinegar and camphor on handkerchiefs in the presence of the illness. His more substantial directions provided for the establishment of a fever hospital for the poor, sanitation of the streets and wharves of the city, and burial of the dead.[31] In addition, he recommended placing marks on infected houses and putting a stop to the incessant tolling of church bells. A larger report filed by the college in 1795 lobbied for the establishment of a committee on the Health Laws to propose legislation to combat the fever. The advantages of such a committee for the medical community, the college noted, were that physicians would more likely judge rightly "when several are concerned" in interpreting the contagion, and from acting in concert will derive "the support of [their] professional Brethren."[32] Governor Mifflin's yellow fever proclamation, which contained additional instructions on containing the sick and the dying, made the committee an official board of health in 1797. The proclamation required that yellow flags be placed on the corners of streets communicating with infected parts of the city and that inspectors be given the power to establish all necessary and beneficial regulations. Any person who should interfere with their ability to enclose infected houses or "to suspend a yellow flag or flags from any house or houses, place or places . . . or take down, destroy, and conceal such flag or flags from public view" was liable to be sent to the State Island Hospital and to face prosecution.[33] Reaction to the proclamation was quick to arrive.

The public cried out for relief from being dragged from one's home and transported to a "stinking and infected hospital" and begged "the Almighty to preserve [citizens] from the clutches of the heroes of the yellow flag."[34] Mifflin's response to the epidemic led to accusations of a republicanism that rivaled only that of the French, who were themselves engaged in a different kind of fever, a revolutionary one.

RUSH'S TREATMENTS

As the College of Physicians' discussions over the Committee on the Health Laws and the medical debate over the source of the fever revealed, Philadelphia was plagued by untested therapeutics of all sorts and the inability of the medical profession to distinguish medicine as a science. Contention among physicians was a necessary consequence of the confusion in medical treatments and the kind of competition that arose in the marketplace of medicine.[35] It reflected a factionalism that was unavoidable so long as the profession was not stabilized by means of regulation, licensing, and consistent training requirements. Beyond such institutional considerations, medical differences, not only among elite, sectarian, and empiric competitors but within the ranks of similarly trained and practicing physicians, characterized the profession as disunified and led to subversion of one another's practices. Doctors disagreed on effectual therapies and underlying principles, and the actual state of medicine was in "an intellectual quagmire"[36] that left physicians open to making mistakes as they performed defensive medicine to protect their reputations and avoided difficult cases whose high risks for success were likely to leave them reputationally challenged. Factions became monitors of individuals, which proved an expensive and inefficient process and stultified growth within the profession.

Conservative treatments were offered by doctors with experience in the fevers of the West Indies, foremost among them Dr. Edward Stevens, notable for his successful treatment of Alexander Hamilton, and Dr. Jean Deveze, responsible for reorganizing the Bush Hill fever hospital. Rush, by contrast, offered an aggressive purging and bleeding regimen, which was widely controverted and attracted much commentary, and yet was adopted by large numbers of physicians who were influenced by his reputation as perhaps the most prominent member of the Philadelphia medical establishment. Laid out in great detail in *An Account of the Bilious Remitting Yellow Fever*,[37] the treatments Rush sponsored were reducible to a handful of principles and applications.[38] He operated, first, from the presumption, shared by many of his contemporaries, that the atmosphere "favoured the accumulation of the contagion of the city."[39] The air was static and warm, what Rush described as a "morbid constitution,"[40] or a miasma (a taint or a virus), in which marsh or vegetable putrefaction was likely to generate an "effluvia that sickened the body and produced fever."[41] He experienced such sickness in his own home, which he regarded as a lazaretto[42] from the heaviness of the air and the fullness of death resident in the bleedings conducted by his pupils in his shop:

> From the want of a sufficient number of bowls to receive their blood, it was sometimes suffered to flow and putrify upon the ground. From all these sources, streams of contagion were constantly poured into my house, and conveyed into my body by the air, and in my aliment. Thus charged with the fuel of death, I was frequently disposed to say with Job, and almost without a figure, to "corruption, thou art my father; and to the worm, thou art my mother and my sister."[43]

Expressed in many ways, from rotting vegetation at the wharfs and in the marshes to the foul air emanating from the homes and bodies of the dead and from the cemeteries, this bad air accounted for the contagion, according to Rush, so that he denied the possibility that the disorder was imported rather than locally generated.[44]

Rush's theory of contamination was of some importance to the economic health of Philadelphia, provoking a medical debate over whether the source of the fever was imported contagion or the result of local conditions of putrefaction. Applying Rush's theory, Noah Webster directly indicted the cities of his times: "Those cities which are built must remain at present the *sources of poison* and the *graves of men*. But provisions should be made by the state to alter them and convert them into shady and healthful towns, by purchasing lots as fast as they become vacant, in sufficient numbers to render the streets open and airy."[45] Commercial interests in the city blamed Rush[46] for fostering the idea that the city was unhealthful. The College of Physicians argued that it found the case for contagion from foreign ships that visited Philadelphia—citing the Arethusa, the Hind, and the Iris—much more persuasive.[47] Individually, physicians were less certain.[48]

Extending the concept of environmental corruption to the human body, Rush contended it was essential to evacuate the abdominal viscera to discharge its contents.[49] In this way, the very material of the disease would be eliminated, that is, the fermenting putrid miasma would be cut off at its source in the body. The rather well-known story Rush told of having discovered in his library an old text given him by Benjamin Franklin just before his death (a story clearly intended to add greater luster to his "discovery")[50] attributed his theory of evacuation to Dr. Mitchell of Virginia who published on the yellow fever epidemic of 1741. Rush was quick to assert that the inspiration led to further experimentation on his part. He explored his new "train of ideas"[51] to find suitable dosages and collected "the first trophies of the new remedy."[52]

Rush's theory was "to abstract excess of stimulus from the system."[53] Purges were his initial method of choice, the more extreme and frequent the better, but he did not rely exclusively upon them, allowing that other means of removal needed to be incorporated. He tried such collateral treatments as a light diet, sweating, cold compresses, foot plasters, blisters, and wrapping,[54] only to settle on bleeding as the best complement to purging. Experimenting with balancing the stages of the disease, the human pulse rate, the degree of fever, and the amount of fluids evacuated, he arrived at a system of aggressive treatment that he felt was essential to implement at early onset of the disease.[55]

Rush's theory of purging was intended to divert the force of the fever by "creating an artificial weak part in the bowels"[56] and thereby to protect the liver and brain from congestion. He discounted evidence from dissections that demonstrated blackening, inflammation, and laceration of the bowels as the result of mercury purges like those he recommended.[57] Rather, he claimed that the same effects occurred when no mercury was administered, convinced that even "a dozen or twenty stools [could be made] in a day . . . without making even a material breach in the constitution."[58] Far from indicating a pathology, the discharge of black matter was, in his mind, a positive sign of delivering disease from the body. He thus encouraged "the beneficial effects of a plentiful spontaneous diarrhea in the beginning of the disorder, by hemorraghies from the bowels."[59] Rush was equally sanguine about the application of purges by inexpert hands, absolving himself "from its having been taken contrary to the printed directions by many people."[60] The fault was not his if an insufficient number of people were available to administer purges or if the inordinate demands on his own time required him to train assistants. His theory, he asserted, would result in the conquest of yellow fever not through "the effects of accident . . . [but] the triumph of a principle."[61]

Rush testified to bleeding in the same terms he had to purging—he was against moderate evacuation and insisted on early application of treatment.[62] The effects of bleeding, he found, raised the pulse, lessened blood pressure, prevented vomiting, made purging easier, and relieved delirium and pain.[63] Rush rejected the notion that he used bleeding indiscriminately, contending that he monitored it and that its application depended upon whether the blood dissolved or proved fizzy, "the state of the pulse . . . the degree of pain" and which day of the disorder it was applied.[64] Where bleeding caused death, he attributed it, much as he had purging, to inappropriate administration of his regimen, that is, to "the quantity of the stimulus abstracted by being disproportionate to the degree of indirect debility."[65] Such debility, he explained, resembled a man struggling under a disproportionate weight which, if gradually reduced, would allow him to gradually accommodate himself, but if relieved suddenly was likely to lead him to stumble and fall.[66]

Rush's preferred practice was frequent, small bleedings, although when pressured he would take a pint to twenty ounces.[67] Children and the old, he argued, needed equally large bleedings, as he indicated in taking thirty ounces in five bleedings from a girl of nine.[68] Rush's cure took an amount of blood from fever victims that, combined with the deleterious effects of heavy doses of mercury or calomel to purge, ipecac to vomit, profuse sweating, blisters, or cupping, and laudanum to subdue the effects of vomiting and purging, was guaranteed to debilitate patients even more than the fever itself. In one letter in 1793, he referred to bleeding when the pulse rate was as low as forty-eight,[69] and in another he spoke of taking "sixty, seventy, and even eighty ounces, and in most cases with the happiest effects."[70] A third letter in 1794 acknowledged taking blood "*twelve* times in *six* days; taking at least 140 ounces of blood—sixty of which he lost in four & twenty hours, by five bleedings,"[71] although he boasted that as a general practice by 1798 he was only taking "ten to twelve ounces of blood two to three times a day."[72] It is not difficult to see why, as Rush's colleague Dr. Griffitts admitted with regret, "the use of the lancet is still so much dreaded by our physicians."[73]

DOCTORS' WARS

Rush's discoveries about the progress, causes, nature, and treatment of what he called the malignant, contagious fever[74] were, he contended, "treated with ridicule and contempt" by physicians and citizens who discredited his findings. As a messenger of tidings that "thus disturbed the repose of the public mind," Rush found himself among a small group of doctors that rendered themselves, as he put it, odious in the eyes of their fellow citizens.[75] Even physicians like Dr. Wistar, who viewed the controversy from a discrete distance and who resisted publicly deciding on any of the remedies being debated, contributed to Rush's discomfort. Their failure to join him, in itself, Rush held, "tended more or less to distract the public mind, and to lessen the confidence of the citizens in the simple and powerful remedies which I had recommended."[76] More troubling, reactions to Rush's bleeding practices led to what he called a "clamour against me . . . to *drum me out of the city*,"[77] to the point that "*Terrorists* said that we bled our patients to death."[78] To "expose this falsehood," he offered a reward of fifty guineas to any who might produce evidence against him.

In self-defense, Rush claimed that his intent was not "to expose the mistakes of those physicians who found as many diseases in our city, as the yellow fever had symptoms."[79] Rather, he wished to vindicate himself. There would prove to be, like monotheism, only one truth rather than many diseases, that is, he would lead science on this question to a unitary theory of disease[80] rather than a paganism that added "to the mortality of mankind, by prescribing for the names of diseases."[81] He left no doubt, at the same time that he would regard disbelief of his view on the subject of yellow fever "as much a mark of deficiency of reason, as it is of reading and observation."[82] In pursuing his account of the fever, Rush was to arrive at a view that would not tolerate the heresy of compromise, which he considered "a criminal compact between physicians."[83] Changing his own practice was out of the question, and negotiation with other doctors was unlikely to change how his brethren practiced medicine. The dilemma was the same, he contended, as that of a Mohametan and a Jew trying to worship the Supreme Being in the same temple.

Rather than accommodate the orthodoxy of those he referred to as regular physicians, Rush played the part of a reformation theologian of plague science. He posited two rationales for his position: the scarcity of physicians in the time of epidemic and the resistance of many physicians "that prevented the universal success of purging and bleeding in our late epidemic."[84] The resolution for Rush was to take the treatment of pestilential fever out of the hands of physicians entirely and place it in the hands of the people.[85] The advertisement of remedies in newspapers, handbills, and posted notices that the profession considered quackish practices were for Rush tools of public education. Placing information in the hands of the people would allow them to engage the fever earlier and provide for greater numbers of caretakers to obviate the public's fear of helplessness. Unlike most of his contemporaries, Rush felt he could safely entrust the people with the cure of pestilential fevers, if only because of his faith in "the simplicity and uniformity of their proximate cause, and of their remedies."[86] Rush rested his case in the principle that God would permit "no evil to exist which does not carry its antidote along with it."[87] He relied as well upon a tradition of fever epidemics in the West Indies in which patients were trusted to replace their own judgment for that of physicians. He did so in spite of having rejected other less controversial aspects of West Indies fever medicine, among them a conservative course of treatment and a belief in contagion rather than contamination as the source of infection. Rush's radical approach placed diet, purging, and bleeding in the hands of women, apothecaries, and clergy as well as poor blacks he had himself trained as assistants. He argued that physicians were not needed to prescribe what mistresses of families routinely prescribe and administer—from air, water, and light to bark and laudanum.

American medicine could hardly have been expected to embrace Rush's devaluation of professional medical treatment nor to embrace his idea that a time must come when access to such remedies as he proposed "shall be considered the most essential articles of the knowledge and rights of man."[88]

In Rush's view, "It is no more necessary that a patient should be ignorant of the medicine he takes to be cured by it, than that the business of government should be conducted with secrecy in order to ensure obedience to just laws. Much less is it necessary that the means of life should be prescribed in a dead language, or dictated with the solemn pomp of a necromancer." In pursuing self-education, Rush placed his own writings above less useful things taught in schools, holding that not only should the citizens of Philadelphia have in their own hands the means of curing themselves but that all the knowledge necessary might be taught to children of twelve in a few hours. Physicians, universities, and medical associations had only confused the scene and contradicted each other in their publications and teaching. His own publications, by contrast, would deliver the people from the fears, pride, and formalities of medicine which were now to be discarded "as the deceptions of witchcraft were, above a century ago."[89] What more republican form of medicine could one propound? People who purged and bled themselves, he insisted, exceeded the success of even those poor blacks he had trained, while the latter's success "was unparalleled by what is called regular practice."[90]

It was no surprise that Rush found himself engaged in a war of doctors in which he felt himself ridiculed. His claim that the most serious source of epidemic distress came from "the dissensions of the physicians about the nature and treatment of the disease"[91] was not about to ameliorate that ridicule nor endear him to those who endorsed more moderate treatments. Nor was he about to sponsor confidence in the message he delivered by admitting that his opinions "are not popular with our citizens"[92] or by appealing to his readers not to reject his view on yellow fever merely "because it is opposed by so great a majority of physicians of Philadelphia."[93]

Rush found some relief in "a daily lessening" of the "diversity of sentiment," until a letter signed by A. K. (whom Rush identified as Dr. Adam Kuhn) appeared.[94] Kuhn described at length a recipe for a fever mixture that sponsored wine, water, and bark along with cold baths, to be administered every four hours. If nausea or diarrhea followed, Kuhn recommended drinking chamomile tea with vitriol, taking laudanum, and administering bark by clyster. Dr. Edward Stevens of the West Indies was prominently acknowledged in Kuhn's letter for his contributions to this cure, an acknowledgment reinforced by an impressive letter[95] published two days later in a number of newspapers by Alexander Hamilton, Secretary of the treasury in Washington's administration, who wrote, he said, from "Motives of humanity" as a witness who testified by way of "discharging a duty" and in the hope of abating "that undue panic which is fast depopulating the city."[96] Hamilton's letter constituted a testimonial to Stevens's cure: "His mode of treating the disorder varies essentially from that which has been generally practiced. And I am persuaded when pursued; it reduces it to one of little more than ordinary hazard. . . . I venture to believe that if adopted and if the courage of the citizens can be roused many lives will be saved and much ill prevented." Rush's remedy now faced clear competition and a pedigree with legs. Crediting Stevens with saving his life, Hamilton had no doubt that, if asked, the doctor would freely impart his ideas to the public to add a knowledge base equal to that already provided by Rush in the public venue. The College of Physicians of Philadelphia followed up with just such a request to Stevens to supply further public information, which he did.[97]

Throughout this exchange, Rush continued to respond in the newspapers and to the College of Physicians by objecting to such well-intentioned communications, expressing his fears for the health of the city, and providing his own experience as testimony against such "a method of treating the present disorder, which if persisted in would probably have aided it in desolating three fourths of our city."[98] To comply with all the requests for assistance, Rush continued to promote his own remedies. He made them available for the public's use at apothecary shops, advertised his cure in the newspapers, and advised the public "by no means to use wine and bark."[99] As the wars continued, Dr. William Currie embraced the Kuhn/Stevens cure,[100] Wistar wrote to refuse to commit, and Rush's acolytes, doctors Porter, Annan, and Mease, rose to his defense. Never one to desert a losing cause, Rush continued to issue defenses of his practice well into October,[101] making certain to note a short retraction by Currie, more of a clarification to be sure, in which Currie tried to calm the roiled waters by acknowledging agreement among physicians that bleeding and purging were themselves requisite and that the debate was rather about the name of the disease than the mode of treatment, a concession to the public mood more than to medical integrity.

In sum, Rush's theory of unitary disease, his insistence on local contamination, his extreme purging and bleeding treatments, his advertisement of remedies, his campaign to replace physicians with home treatment, and his public war of words with other physicians further destabilized the contemporary medical scene at a time of social disruption and medical crisis. His moves were not only bound to have significant repercussions for the profession but would leave the public uncertainly trapped in the midst of warring factions. Having lost confidence in a medical establishment that was tearing itself apart from within, the public was bereft of administrative relief since the city had essentially closed down and was being run as an ad hoc exercise by a volunteer committee.

In the hurly burly world of such medicine, it is not surprising that the public lost confidence in treatments that were as likely to kill as to cure, and that doctors campaigned in a war of words and feuds. Freneau's 1779 poem "The House of Night; Or, Six Hours Lodging with Death" captured the contentiousness that infused the ranks of physicians. Dreaming in a cemetery, the poem's narrator entertained the idea that death was dying and that he was witnessing the end of death's "melancholy reign." The narrator heard "confused murmurs, scarce distinguish'd sounds" in a graveyard from which

> disputes arose
> Of surgery, and remedies for wounds.
>
> Long were their feuds, for they design'd to talk
> Of anchylosis and the shoulder-blade;
> Of femoris, trochanters, and whate'er
> Has been discuss'd by Cheselden and Mead.
> And often each to prove his notion true,
> Brought proofs from Galen or Hippocrates.
> But fancy led me hence and left them so,
> Firm at their points of hardy no and yes.[102]

During the terrible time of the epidemic, caterwauling among physicians especially diminished the cultural authority of medicine as a field in which no one won and all lost so long as physicians continued to feud in public. In the midst of challenges to good and evil, law and order, fear and suffering, the epidemic created a scene in which the physician played a role at the forefront of death and disease as a potential source of balance and calm. But far from being revered, he was tarred by his association with the fever, so that, as "The House of Night" depicted, "the grim physician at the door" was an image of death and reminded readers that "remedies have small avail,/Assist expiring death once more to walk."[103] The doctors of Freneau's "No. XII. To the Philadelphia Doctors" (1797) were "a ghastley crew," "troops of butcher boys" each defending his own whim. "Poor Florio," the patient, cried out "Dear doctors! let me die in peace" and begged "doctors! doctors! do not fight." In his semiconscious state, the patient aptly named his physician "doctor Devil":

> He promises all fees to pay,
> But they go on in angry fray,
> *Poor Florio Frets,—and well he may.*
>
> Each looks at each with angry eyes,
> As if contending for a prize;
> Or rob him, if the sick man dies.
>
> One talks of cure by calomel;
> But his wise brother, Sydrophel,
> Swears 'tis the nearest road to hell.
>
> While *this* the LANCET recommends,
> *Another* for a *blister* sends,
> And warmly each his whim defends.[104]

Freneau delivered a devastating critique of quarreling Philadelphia physicians setting upon each other in career-destroying feuds. The errors of doctoring ranged from unequal training, and sometimes none at all save instinct, to over-reliance on academic texts and preferred schools of thought.[105] Patients were harassed by physicians who chased after them or who flocked around them, each demanding a fee and competing to gain favors. The physician's immediate victims, however, were the already-weakened patients who were more likely to survive their diseases than their physicians. The proliferation of medical theories, treatments, and practitioners—from numskulls (presumably quacks) to a doctress (likely a trusted female of the neighborhood with experience in caretaking), old-style doctors (probably self-trained or apprenticed to a physician) and the university-trained (those who read Dr. Sydenham at the Edinburgh medical school)—left poor Florio in deathly distress fantasizing himself a patient of the devil. Freneau framed the battle between patient and doctor as an archetypal struggle of God and Satan over the souls of the dying in "The Book of Odes" (1797), playing on Hamlet's soliloquy:

> And the angel Michael disputed with the Devil about the "body of Moses."
> *Ancient History.*
> To bleed or not to bleed—that is the question!
> Whether tis better in our beds to suffer
> The slights and snufflings of outrageous doctors,
> Or, by the *Lancet*—quit them.[106]

The epidemic having brought resistance to physicians to a head, Freneau's "No. XI. To the Philadelphia Doctors," a companion piece to "No. XII," critiqued an entire profession caught disputing, wrangling, and cursing within its ranks. The poet invoked the welfare of a whole city ("still to knaves a prey") and called upon the history of medicine itself (from Galen, of ancient times, to Boerhaave, a near contemporary of the poet) to argue his case. Balancing the excesses of doctors who took as much as four-fifths of the blood from the body against the "secret [that] has leak'd out" that simple herbs and teas administered by old women were capable of taming the epidemic, Freneau pictured a city betrayed, first, by its quibbling divines and then by its quarrelsome physicians:

> In ancient days divines, in dismal humour,
> With disputation kept the presses going;
> Wrangled about some wonderous mighty things
> The difference 'twixt' a *shadow* and a *shade*'. . . .
> And you, wise doctors, take the wrangle up,
> Each cursing all who will not drink his cup.
>
> Well! *you* decide, who are in GALEN read—
> Take *Boorhaave's* [*sic*], if you please—whatever system—

(Why are men such that doctors can enlist 'em?)
Whether your methods be the *right* or *wrong*,
And man's existence shorten or prolong,
We feverish fellows, must be—*put to bed*.[107]

Wary of the preferred therapeutic, heroic bloodletting, the poet decried those who would drain the body dry. Where nature herself was left to lead the way with "herbs and teas," health returned and doctors with their bookish learning were made irrelevant.

In the light of public perceptions that fed Freneau's constructions of the medical profession and medical practice in the years of fever, Rush would have found himself professionally vulnerable and personally contentious even if Cobbett had never entered the picture. A difficult, arrogant figure, he was both envied and feared by his peers for his oversized medical reputation and his jealous regard for growing and protecting it. As a professor of medicine, a medical writer, a practicing physician with an appointment at the Pennsylvania Hospital, an innovator in the care and treatment of the mentally ill, Rush had been professionally recognized and affiliated with all the major institutions in Philadelphia—from the first medical school and the first hospital in the new nation to the College of Physicians of Philadelphia and, later, the Academy of Medicine, which he founded. Rush represented his profession in all its complexity and difficulties as no other figure did. To take on Rush was thus as good as to attack the medical profession as it was known in the early republic. A unique figure in the medical profession, he stood front and center in a time of medical crisis and was a mentor to more medical students than any other physician of his times; he acted, in sum, as a lightning rod attracting criticism and praise that shaped a reputation that soon became conflated with that of the profession itself. If Cobbett wanted to ridicule American medicine, Rush was the ideal candidate.

NOTES

1. Finger (2010, 38).
2. Finger (2010, 40).
3. Inglis, as quoted in Williams (1990, 78).
4. William Smith in 1757, as quoted in Williams (1990, 78).
5. Freneau, "Reflections on Dr. Perkins' Metallic Rods," (1986, 565–66). Unless otherwise noted, references to Freneau's poems refer to the Hiltner edition (Freneau 1986). The poem reads in part:

Rickets and rheums shall at your presence fly
Like Satan's self, when holy water's nigh;

No more with drugs our stomachs shall be loaded;
Doctors: behold your system quite exploded!—
By one poor iron rod, and one of brass
Boerhaave himself is prov'd to have been an ass.—

Hereafter sick, all potion, drug, or pill
We'll shun, and trust to your *enchanting* skill:
Even mental ills shall cease at your approach,
Pride, Vanity, and Longings for a coach.
If rightly *paw'd*, some girls, that I might name,
Who, shopping, pilfer without fear or shame,
Shall, when your influence they are made to feel,
Be cured of their propensity to steal—

Time-Piece, 12 April 1797; see Freneau (1815, 1: 84–87).

6. Freneau, "On a Young Lady," (1986, 563). The poem reads in part:

Why should *You* fear the electric fire
Who thus advances, a moving spire,
With Cupid's darts,—so fair and tall,
Not to be kill'd—but kill us all—?

See Freneau (1809, 2: 27).

7. Self-described as regulars (Blake, 1959, 45), elite physicians were viewed by those on the marketplace side of medicine as potential monopolists who colluded with members of other degreed "crafts," such as lawyers and divines, to retain their professional privileges by excluding competition. Those who thrived in the marketplace, by contrast, capitalized on an antiprofessional sentiment in the public, failed attempts to systematically license members of the medical profession, and a growing concern with physical health; see De Ville (1990); Shryock (1967). Sympathy for herbal remedies and familiarity with the common folk made these practitioners easily accepted in the poor areas where they largely practiced. Having to maintain an itinerant trade, they were dependent upon the belief of those they were to count as their clients and had to keep ahead of the curve of their own failed medical experiments. Their strongest tool was their reliance on providing what patients wanted and on patients' willingness to believe their promises; Williams (1990, 81–82). By this description, irregular, unapproved, unlearned physicians operated much as tribal healers, dependant as much upon self-healing and the power of the mind as upon the efficacy of any treatment they had to offer. Genuine and counterfeit, however, were distinctions left to the eyes of the beholder.

8. Prohibitions against quackery were expressed in similar terms in the AMA code in 1846:

> It is derogatory to the dignity of the profession, to resort to public advertisements or private cards or handbills, inviting the attention of individuals affected with particular diseases—publicly offering advice and medicine to the poor gratis, or promising radical cures; or to publish cases and operations in the daily prints or suffer such publications to be made;— to

> invite laymen to be present at operations,—to boast of cures and remedies,—to adduce certificates of skill and success, or to perform any other similar acts. These are the ordinary practices of empirics, and are highly reprehensible in a regular physician.

As quoted in Burns (1969, 118).

9. One such bill, written by a quack disguised as a regular, defended the enhanced value of the marketplace:

> Publishing of Medicines thus shamefully *defamed* by *ignorant* pretenders, must be restored into esteem by the *learned*, which will prove most *advantageous* to the people; and it is their interest to *incourage* skillful experienced *Artists* that they may not *lock* up their *rare* inventions and *fortunate* experiments, confining them within the narrow compass of a *private* practice; but rather that they expose their *Arcanum* to publick use, that all who stand in need may partake thereof . . . the *meanest* of the people may purchase the *best* of Medicines. . . . Those who will not undergo, or cannot bear the *charge* of a course of Physick, may receive great *relief* by a *single* Medicine. . . . Physicians then will be stimulated to *out vye* and *excell* each other in the *rarity* and *excellency* of their Remedies, being to undergo a publick Tryal. . . . These publick great *advantages* as great *reasons* being considered, the *learned* Physician need not be ashamed to publish an *extraordinary* Medicine of his own designment and elaboration (although *ignorant* bold fellows have *abused* the Custom) for if Physicians must *shun* all that they do, then must they *leave* their practice too.

As quoted in Porter (1989, 198).

10. See Porter (1989); Porter (1995, 371–475); Williams (1990, 77–89); Myrsiades (2009, 60–66).

11. If fail they must, quacks at least led to a future of tested science, specialized therapies, and instruments itching to come on stage and try their luck. Medicine would change because commerce would make it respond to the realities of the world and because empirics would set its competitive feet on fire. Buyer and seller would have to arrive together at a way of seeing and legitimizing medicine that would challenge suspect status and that would test failed therapeutics. Medical experimentation would break from reliance on traditional practices based on abstract rational medicine and humoral theory. It would lead to a new professionalization of medicine and a medicalization of society that would to some extent define the second half of the nineteenth century.

12. Quackery shifted the medical world away from being based on status and the physician-patient relationship to being based on an exchange of commodities and services, making medicine more competitive and encouraging innovation. Unlike physicians with university education, "tinkling theory and vacuous verbiage," as medical historian Roy Porter puts it, irregulars who were self-taught or trained by apprenticeship kept nothing back from the public and exposed themselves to competition in the public market, as one advertisement said, from an "overriding sense of public responsibility" and a desire not to leave the common man without recourse to the fullest airing of competing remedies to save him from disease and death. Porter (1989, 193, 198).

13. Yellow fever epidemics occurred in Philadelphia beginning in 1648, then in 1699, 1741, 1747, 1749, 1762, and 1765, and then again in 1793, 1797, 1798, and 1799; see Duffy (1953).

14. Duffy (1953, 24).

15. Duffy (1953, 27).

16. Shryock (1967, 19); Finger (2010).

17. See Powell (1965); Estes and Smith (1997); Duffy (1953); Duffy (1990); Blake (1959); Rosen (1974); Rosenberg (1992); Ranger and Slack (1992).

18. Duffy (1990, 38–39).

19. Duffy (1990, 39).

20. See *Minutes* (1848).

21. September 19, 1793, College of Physicians of Lancaster, Proclamation; see Estes and Smith (1997, frontispiece).

22. September 21, 1793, John Hancock, Governor of Massachusetts, Proclamation; *Early American Imprints.*

23. *Minutes* (1848, 7).

24. *Minutes* (1848, 56–57).

25. Powell (1965, 173–94).

26. *Minutes* (1848, 12–13).

27. *Minutes* (1848, 45–46).

28. *Minutes* (1848, 73).

29. *Minutes* (1848, 74).

30. *Minutes* (1848, 77–78).

31. August 26, 1793; College of Physicians of Philadelphia (1798, 2–3).

32. January 6, 1795; College of Physicians of Philadelphia (1798, 8).

33. August 24, 1797; Cobbett (1801, 7: 41–42).

34. *Porcupine's Gazette*, 26 August 1797.

35. See Myrsiades (2009).

36. Conrad, Neve, Nutton, Porter, and Wear (1995, 379).

37. In his exhaustive examination of the history of the disease, Rush (1794) systematically considered the work of other doctors, sixty-six of whom he named, and writings on plagues and fevers from the eleventh to the eighteenth century in places ranging from Constantinople, Cairo, Syria, Rome, Vienna, Hungary, Bengal, Hispaniola, the East and West Indies to England and each of the United States in individual years from 1665 to 1795. He reviewed the symptoms, causes, and epidemiology of diseases ranging from jail and hospital fever, measles, mumps, pestilence, plague, small pox, scarlatina, tertian fever, lying in fever, influenza, and pleurisy, among others, to differentiate the disease as a specific type he called the bilious remitting yellow fever.

38. Kopperman (2004, 539–74). Kopperman concludes that the weight of evidence in Rush's medical thinking was intuitional, that he relied upon discovering a therapy first and then elaborating a theoretical framework, that is, that he justified his work after the fact rather than tested a theory (550). He apparently was not a fan of postmortems, and he seldom experimented: "Rush's approach was highly rational, much

logical extensions being based on a relatively small mass of precepts, observations, anecdotes, and 'facts'" (552).

39. Rush (1794, 80).

40. Rush (1794, 103).

41. Rush (1794, 80, 110). In a complementary account of "effluvia," Noah Webster framed William Currie's position as one in which "vegetable effluvia from low marshy grounds produce intermitting and remitting fevers, and these fevers are never contagious, but that *human* effluvia produce continued fevers of a nervous or putrid kind, which may be and usually are contagious"; Webster (1947, 19); see Webster (1970).

42. Rush (1794, 247).

43. Rush (1794, 242).

44. Rush 1794, 116).

45. 20 December 1797; Webster (1947, 110).

46. Along with Rush and among others, Jean Deveze, who had practiced in Santo Domingo (Haiti), adopted the contamination theory.

47. College of Physicians of Philadelphia (1798, 26, 28-37); see College of Physicians of Philadelphia (1799).

48. Perhaps the most thorough discussion of differences appeared in a series of publications that began with Rush's defense of the local putrefaction theory in 1793 and led, first, to William Currie's response (1794) in the same year and then to a response by Noah Webster 1797 (1947) in a publication shopped around unsuccessfully by Rush. See Spector (1947, 1–18).

49. Rush (1794, 141).

50. Rush (1794, 140).

51. Rush, (1794, 142).

52. Rush (1794, 144). Kopperman's analysis (2004) of Rush's development of a medical therapy for yellow fever contends that "the method Rush adopted in 1793 marked a radical departure from common practice" in that he went farther than any of his contemporaries ever had (541). He attributed Rush's presumed "cure" to three sources. He notes first a letter to John Rodgers, October 3, 1793, in which Rush claims he "adopted and extended" a bleeding treatment he learned in 1762 from Dr. Redman, with whom Rush had apprenticed. Rush cited as well the report from John Mitchell in 1741 on purging, as well as the work of Thomas Young in the Continental Army on purges. In each case, Rush intensified the cure (542, 554). Rush used emetics as well, but they were not identified with him. The purging was considered conventional, although not in the heavy doses he prescribed, for which he was faulted by many other physicians (544–45). Copious venesection for the fever appears to have been Rush's distinctive contribution, one in which he significantly departed from the practice of others, and one that truly set him aside from other practitioners (546, 554, 564).

53. Rush (1794, 145).

54. Rush (1794, 198–203).

55. According to Madden (2006, 256), Rush held that "a person need know neither the classification of disease nor its root cause but rather the effect on the system in order to know how to treat it." His writing, Madden contends, focuses on his person

in the sense that it was he in whom ideas occurred and that he relied upon his intuition more than theory or empirical evidence. Indeed, Kopperman attributes Rush's heroic bloodletting to Rush's own nature, contending that "the radicalism in the method . . . came from the man himself" (2004, 574).

56. Rush (1794, 172).

57. Rush (1794, 176). Dissections were a regular part of the work of the fever hospital in Bush Hill under the direction of the French physician who goes unnamed in Rush's account—the admirable Jean Deveze, who took the moderate approach of the Stevens school. See Deveze (1794); Lane (1936, 202–26).

58. Rush (1794, 175).

59. Rush (1794, 172).

60. Rush (1794, 178).

61. Rush (1794, 145).

62. Rush (1794, 185–86).

63. Rush (1794, 182–84).

64. Rush (1794, 193).

65. Rush (1794, 194).

66. Rush (1794, 197).

67. Rush (1794, 190).

68. Rush (1794, 190). Kopperman (2004) notes that Rush ignored traditional safeguards in his practice of medicine. First, he came to dismiss "reliance on nature as a guide to therapy" (555), whereby physicians tended to intervene only when nature indicated. Rush, Kopperman asserts, "did not regard nature as being anxious to cure and, if it was possible, able to cure" (556). Rush considered that violence was necessary to cure violent diseases. The second safeguard was to avoid extreme practice and the third was to honor the condition of the patient (557–58). Rush used extreme treatments on all classes of patients.

69. To the College of Physicians; Rush (1951, 2: 661); *Federal Gazette*, September 12, 1793.

70. Letter to Dr. John R. B. Rodgers; Rush (1951, 2: 694); *Federal Gazette*, October 7, 1793.

71. "Extracts of Letter from Dr. Rush and Others, on the Subject of the Yellow Fever," College of Physicians of Philadelphia Library, handwritten manuscript 10a175, 167; September 18, 1794.

72. "To the Citizens of Philadelphia," in Currie (1798, 48), September 3, 1798; *Philadelphia Gazette*, September 4, 1798.

73. Rush (1794, 190).

74. Rush labeled yellow fever a malignant, contagious fever to distinguish it from what he called the commonly recurring remitting fever.

75. *American Daily Advertiser*, August 29, 1793.

76. Rush (1794, 166).

77. Rush (1794, 164); September 19, 1794.

78. Rush (1794, 169); May 5, 1795.

79. Rush (1794, 70).

80. One problem in treating diseases was related to their classification. Yellow fever, for example, was identified by fourteen different names; Kopperman (2004, 560). Rush, as a result, preferred to avoid diagnosing by symptoms and to rely upon the state of a disease, ultimately resorting to a unitarian theory whereby there was only one fever, indeed only one disease, which required one treatment (560–63). Kopperman notes, "that a single treatment might be successful against all disease was generally rejected by contemporary thinkers" (562). In any case, Rush, according to Kopperman, vacillated, favoring the application of "a small number of remedies to treat a wide range of diseases" (563).

81. Rush (1794, 70).

82. Rush (1794, 70).

83. Rush (1794, 246).

84. Rush (1794, 225).

85. Rush (1794, 224).

86. Rush (1794, 225).

87. Rush (1794, 225).

88. Rush (1794, 226–27).

89. Rush (1794, 228).

90. Rush (1794, 223). Clark (2008, 209–50) explores this aspect of Rush's practice as an expression of Rush's "scientific pretensions to craft a genuinely American understanding of the nature of his fellow citizens' diseases and the proper social relations necessary for their cure" (209). Rush, he argues, not only regarded the question as one of "the proper role of medicine in a democracy," (218) but concluded that man's health depended upon the social order of the nation, insofar as "simple, orderly, and pious democracies had few diseases" (227). Rush's reinvention of medicine to empower patients' self-treatment was thus intended to democratize medicine by reducing reliance on physicians (to the point that as few as three physicians would be needed for a city of forty thousand, 237), simplifying medicine, and reducing resistance to treatment. Whereas Rush pursued what he called republican medicine, Clark goes further than perhaps his sources allow in claiming that republicans sought out his therapy and federalists did not, thereby politicizing medicine along party lines.

91. Rush (1794, 91).

92. Rush (1794, 119).

93. Rush (1794, 117).

94. Published on September 11, 1793, the letter was written September 7, 1793; Rush (1794, 147).

95. September 11, 1793; Hamilton's letter is on deposit at the College of Physicians of Philadelphia Library.

96. As quoted in Rush (1794, 152).

97. *Federal Gazette*, September 16, 1793.

98. Rush (1794, 150–51); September 11, 1793.

99. Rush (1794, 161); September 16, 1793.

100. Rush (1794, 162); *Federal Gazette*, September 20, 1793.

101. See *Federal Gazette*, October 11, 1793.

102. Freneau (1986, 57).
103. Freneau (1986, 60).
104. Freneau (1986, 602–3). The rest of the poem reads:

> If *Florio* on his bed complains
> Of feverish pulse, and boiling veins,
> And whims and fancies in his brains,
>
> Then round him flocks a ghastly crew
> Of doctors old and doctors new,
> And doctor Numsculls—not a few.
>
> Hoping that each had learnt his trade,
> He waits with patience for their aid,
> But scarce a word of HELP is said.
>
> Each quotes some book, by way of sham,
> Or reads dull stuff from *Sydenham*;
> Which some approve—and others damn.
>
> At once he hears a barbarous noise
> Like that from troops of butchers' boys,
> That every hope of life destroys. . . .
>
> Listening to all they have to say
> At last the patient swoons away—
> *Poor Florio Frets,—and well he may.*
>
> In Fancy's dreams, he thinks he roams
> In realms, where doctor Devil foams,
> With Syndrophels and *Curry-combs*.
>
> Reviv'd at length—he begs release,
> And whines, 'Pray let your bawlings cease,
> Dear doctors! let me die in peace.
>
> Oh! had I sent for doctress Nan,
> She would have found some better plan
> To get me on my legs again.
>
> She, with her cooling tamarind tea,
> At least would not have murdered me:
> Come! if you love me, do agree—
>
> Good heaven! you cannot all be right;
> You keep me in a wretched plight—
> Ah! doctors! doctors! do not FIGHT.'
>
> Here they begin still louder fray;
> To him 'tis death—to them 'tis play—
> *Poor Florio dies,—and well he may.*

Time-Piece, November 15, 1797; see Freneau (1809, 2: 8–10).

105. For literary views of physicians as a source of cultural perspectives, see Moss and Peterson (2004); Silvette (1967); Paster (1993).

106. *Time*-Piece, November 13, 1797; Freneau (1986, 601).

107. Freneau (1986, 601). The rest of the poem reads:

> And scribbled much of 'way of man with maid.'
> At length, as fades the *crown*
> Their bludgeons they lay down; . . .
>
> Ah, Philadelphians! still to knaves a prey,
> Take your old philosophic way;
> When from the *native spring* you seiz'd your draught,
> Health bloom'd on every face, and all was gay—
> Dejection was remote—and Nature laugh'd.
> A question now, of *mighty weight* is put,
> Whether *to bleed a man is best, or not,*
> When scarce three drops (or not one drop) remains
> In the poor devil's veins!—. . . .
>
> A secret has leak'd out—be cautious, doctors
> (The whole shall be disclos'd *in room with lock'd doors*)
> OLD WOMEN, with their *simple herbs and teas*
> (And asking hardly two-pence for their fees)
> Disarm the dreadful epidemic fever;
> Make it as tame and innocent,
> (Whether home-bred or from West India sent)
> *As continental soldier, turn'd to weaver.*

Time-Piece, November 13, 1797; see Freneau (1815, 1: 146–47).

2

Malpractice Law and Benjamin Rush

Having positioned Rush medically, it remains to view him in the legal context within which a physician would be placed at the end of the eighteenth century. In spite of what could only be considered a climate of permissiveness over, even tolerance for, medical mistakes, Rush would not have been entirely exempt from medical liability. Early American law established both the responsibilities that a physician like Rush was required to assume and the limits of any charges that could legitimately be made against a doctor's practice of his profession, providing the legal context within which the Rush-Cobbett feud took place. Just as the balance of persecution of the press and the excessive privileges taken by the press clearly figured in Rush's choice to prosecute Cobbett, so did extreme medical practices and the perceived need for competent physicians inform Cobbett's press attacks on Rush.

MALPRACTICE LAW

Medical malpractice was implicated as soon as Rush's practices began to be attacked as a danger to the life and health of his patients. Malpractice as a legal construction did not become a truly substantive issue until the early nineteenth century, so that doctors before that time would not, as a rule, have expected patients to sue.[1] What this tells us is not necessarily that patients maintained an inordinate trust in the physician-patient relationship or that the status of the profession was such that suits were inconceivable. Rather, the medical tradition had held as a relatively coherent fabric over time—by one calculation the prevailing tradition lasted from ancient times essentially until the end of the eighteenth century[2]—so that a significant, that is to say meaningful and wholesale change, was emerging and imminent although not to become significant and dominant until the latter half of the nineteenth century. According to Kenneth De Ville, by 1835 medical suits would no longer be rare, the period from 1790 to 1835 having established their potential.[3]

As the body of law that informed malpractice in the young nation, English common law on malpractice was dominated by "assumptions about the nature of the doctor-patient relationship,"[4] many of which were culturally bound or linked to customs and traditions. If neglect, unskillful management, and injury were apparent in medical practice, they were no more so than trust, belief, and loyalty. Medicine was, after all, made up of religious, political, and cultural components, a mix of morality and virtue, community values, partisan loyalties, and legal constraints, as much as it was art, science, or commercial enterprise. At the same time, under common law medical malpractice was based on a claim for damages for a civil wrong, a breach of duty that covered negligence and want of skill. Blackstone's *Commentaries*[5] located medical malpractice as a private wrong, not contract law, and cited harm due to neglect or unskillful treatment without force as the standard for liability. Force did not apply once one voluntarily placed oneself in a physician's care, for there could then be no interference with one's person.[6] De Ville puts it that "the physician's liability and responsibility for his patient emanated not from a commercial contractual relationship agreement but from the affirmative act of entering into the doctor-patient relationship."[7] On the physician's end, false accusations of malpractice could constitute defamation, oral or written, done to one's person or reputation rather than to real or personal property.[8]

In actual cases of malpractice, the most frequent charge was failure to act, that is, the defendant "did not do that he should have done," so that he "defaulted in the discharge of some customary duty incident to a public calling."[9] A party who undertook a duty in effect "warranted his special preparation for it," so that the legal expectation was that "Any person engaged in a common calling was bound to carry on his trade or occupation 'rightly and truly as he ought.'"[10] At the same time, underlying medical principles, medical theories, and bedside practices varied from physician to physician, so that in determining breach of duty, it would be difficult to speak convincingly of an ordinary standard of care.[11] A defendant could, of course, respond that the act was not within the scope of a common calling and that he was thereby not liable for the harm.[12] By extension, not naming oneself a creature of some common calling could obviate one's responsibility, a tactic adopted by practitioners identified as quacks or empirics who fell outside the definition of regular physicians and practiced their own brand of medicine, although many were themselves trained in the same way and to the same standards as more traditional physicians. But whether a physician was considered traditional or a quack, he could not be bound by law any more stringently than any other man whose employment required ordinary skill, a standard for workers no less than for professional men. Here, as a later legal source was to say, an implied contract based on common law would apply: "Every person who offers his services to the public generally, impliedly contracts with the employers that he is in possession of the necessary skill and experience which is possessed ordinarily by those who practice, or profess to understand the same art of science."[13]

Added complications in establishing a standard of ordinary skill arose from an American context in which the lack of physicians and surgeons controlled much of the debate and was frequently referred to as the rationale for an operational definition of negligence. The conditions under which American physicians operated complicated a common definition of medical practice as extreme differences existed that were linked to physician inexperience, geography, competition from untrained practitioners, and differences of medical theory.[14] Under these conditions, the accepted standard was ordinary skill or care and common sense rather than the best standard of care available, the latter a reference to the standard of care available to graduates of medical schools rather than itinerant physicians or practitioners in urban rather than rural areas.[15] Several malpractice cases and medical commentators raised the prospect that surgeons, in particular, would become scarce in rural areas if negligence standards required more than the ordinary care available in the geographical area in which a physician practiced, that is, "the inexperienced and the unlearned attend to the surgery in their way, or it is not attended to at all."[16] Consistent with such an argument, in urban areas, where more medical opportunities obtained and medical education was more widely available, doctors were held to a higher "common practice standard."[17]

Like geography, differences of opinion among physicians interfered with a common, accepted standard of care, so that operationally one's judgment applied, that of both the physician and of the patient. Because the patient was expected to choose a physician of good judgment, even though he was no judge of scientific qualifications, should he fail to do so, "the result is fairly to be attributed to his own mistake, and is not to be visited upon the head of the man who has done his best endeavor in his service."[18] In both preserving patients' right of choice and guaranteeing a sufficient supply of physicians and surgeons, the law was thereby predisposed to support a proliferation of quacks. Differences of opinion among physicians exacerbated this situation, leaving each practitioner to use his own discretion in choosing what he thought would be successful based on his own "best judgment." He was "not responsible for the errors of an enlightened judgment, where good judgments may differ," so long as he had the necessary knowledge and the errors he made were errors any prudent man might have committed.

He would be liable, thereby, only where his errors "could not have arisen except from want of reasonable skill and diligence."[19]

THE PATIENT'S DUTY

Patients bore their own share of responsibility in the world of medical malpractice. The most relevant contribution appeared to have been their initial choice of a physician. The expectation that patients would choose wisely meant it was their duty to prefer traditional physicians and to recognize that freedom of choice left them open to the predatory behavior of quacks. In the absence of licensing and regulation of the medical profession, *caveat emptor* became the prevailing principle in early American physician-patient relationships. In his lectures to students Benjamin Rush, for example, conveniently made it the patient's responsibility should competition and predation on the part of practitioners lead to a bad choice.[20] The issue was less one of confidence in a practitioner, his training and education, or even his specialty, than one of ensuring that patients paid the full cost should they choose to employ or contract with an empiric (that is, a practitioner who relied upon his own experiences).

Because the criteria for physician liability was unclear, until 1800[21] a patient would have to prove, first, "affirmatively a duty of care owed by the defendant and a breach of that duty, resulting in damage."[22] Second, the patient had to prove that he had not himself been delinquent, that is, that he had not been careless and thereby contributed to his own illness. The patient's duty to the doctor thus played a large role in any possible conviction in a malpractice case. Not only were patients responsible to choose a physician of good judgment and to follow the doctor's prescriptions, but should they engage another physician they were liable to the charge that they had thereby deserted their doctor and his treatments.[23] Medical treatment, it could be argued, required a consistency of care that could hardly be guaranteed by multiple hands. Rush himself rarely consulted in other physicians' cases and he rarely called upon other physicians in his own cases: "the patient will suffer by it," he lectured to his students, "for nothing but a strong constitution can save him from being injured or destroyed by the hands of two physicians, who are influenced in their practice by opposing theories in medicine, or who are personally hostile to each other."[24] Like calling in another physician, Rush regarded the act of dismissing one's family physician as a screen for patient noncompliance. He assumed that dismissal occurred "without a just or even imaginary cause, and that too with as little feeling as they dismiss a servant, or dispose of a family horse . . . in order to justify their indelicate and capricious conduct."[25] Rush anticipated here a powerful legal defense in terms of the patient's responsibility for his own injury through contributory negligence.

Rush was careful to cover his own potential future errors by instructing his students that their patients' obedience to the physician's prescriptions should be nothing other than "prompt, strict, and universal," given the likelihood that a "failure in any one of these particulars may be the loss of a link which may render the whole chain of a physician's plan of cure useless or hurtful."[26] As Rush expressed it, placing responsibility once again on the negligent patient, medical science was not to be faulted for being uncertain or imperfect. Rather, the patient's own ignorance was at issue as well as his negligence in not reaching out in time for the assistance of a physician.[27] Even in a period of wide debate over the efficacy of heroic purging and bleeding and widespread acknowledgement of the limitations of the physician's craft, Rush was so far convinced of the superiority of the medical practitioner's judgment over that of his patient that he warned that instances of physician mistakes were "rare, compared with the number of deaths which have occurred from the refusal or neglect of patients to comply with the prescriptions of their physicians."[28]

A patient's recovery from an illness might well occur when a doctor's advice was not followed and such recoveries might be considered physician errors, but for Rush, as for the general public and the courts, patient noncompliance and not physician incompetence or the profession's lack of scientific understanding was the base line in considering physician liability. This presumption was one the patient-plaintiff would have to overcome in any court case, along with the negative burden of demonstrating the physician's lack of ordinary skill and care and the positive burden of proving the patient had not himself contributed to his own injury. In effect, the patient had effectively consented to the injurious or deadly treatment, which presumed a waiver of liability or at the very least shared responsibility. If one assumed that the physician-patient relationship constituted a contract, then not only would both parties have had to agree to the treatment that led to the injury, but the patient had to have accepted some risk by virtue of the agreement. He could only blame himself for having entered into the agreement, so that his ability to gain a verdict that placed strict liability on the part of the physician was largely an impossibility.

In sum, the standard for patient responsibility, as formalized in 1809, was that "one person's being at fault will not dispense with another's using ordinary care . . . a delinquent patient cannot recover irrespective of the fault of the defendant."[29] The burden was on the plaintiff to show he was not guilty of having been careless.[30] In this framework, to be held liable the physician-defendant must, first, be known to have been of a calling whose special duty and preparation bound him to carry out his trade with an ordinary degree of skill and care, as commonly agreed upon.[31] He must as well demonstrably have acted outside the reasonable bounds of such a duty, and he must have directly been the cause of some harm to the patient. At the same time, the patient must not have contributed by his own carelessness to his own injury or possess some underlying condition itself responsible for his injury.[32] Such a standard could only have assisted Rush in his case against Cobbett, for the latter's burden of proof in a buyer-beware culture, together with the unprovable link of care to catastrophe, was sufficient to sink any malpractice attack Cobbett might choose to launch.

MEDICAL AUTHORITY

Beyond contract law and the duty of common care, questions of social, religious, and cultural authority affected the number and success of medical malpractice suits. Religious necessity in accepting misfortune as the work of God inhibited suits as did the prospect of seeing admired members of the community taken to court.[33] By the same token, the moral persuasion of small, cohesive communities prevented a greater use of the courts. It would take the social leveling that occurred with the advent of Jacksonian democracy before the public would begin to object to the kind of deference demanded by the elite.[34] Before physicians would be willing to testify against fellow physicians or to join in legal actions against them,[35] communities would have to lose their power to control individual behavior, individualism would have to assert itself, and medical schools would have to proliferate, all nineteenth-century developments.

In the courts themselves, malpractice cases were almost exclusively won or lost based on the medical evidence. It was thus necessary to distinguish what was right from what was wrong and to determine what the facts were upon which conclusions were drawn.[36] With specialized knowledge like medical knowledge, the court and the jury found themselves reliant upon medical experts to provide guidance on the facts. A great deal relied upon "the intelligence and ability of the witness to combine existing facts, which, when combined, lead the mind . . . to a necessary result, to which the mind must give it its credence."[37] Eighteenth-century medical testimony, unfortunately, relied less upon empirically tested propositions (that is, reliability and verifiability) than upon reasoning, theory, and observation, so that truth and facts were exactly what it could not offer. As a result, medical testimony depended upon opinions, which were often contradicted. The question was whether such opinions were a close enough fit to meet a legal standard: "An opinion is the judgment which the mind forms on any proposition, statement, theory or event, the truth or falsehood of which is supported by a degree of evidence that renders it probable, but does not constitute absolute knowledge, truth or certainty."[38] Less promising, circumstances testified to and facts presumed to have been demonstrated were often so vague, prejudicial, contradicted, or lacking credibility that judges often did better to lay them aside than to utilize them in a charge to a jury. One legal expert summarized the problem from the perspective of the medical professional who might be asked to testify:

> A man, whether learned or not, whether in court or out of court, will talk clearly upon a subject he well understands, whether it is scientific or otherwise; but unless it is clear in his own mind, his account of it will be confused and unsatisfactory. No amount of windy pretension or technical verbosity, will help him out of the ridiculous position into which he has voluntarily and impudently placed himself, by pretending to do what he is wholly incompetent to accomplish. It is this profusion of disagreeable assurance, empty pretension, gassy reputation, wise looks and big words, that so often disgust the court and counsel, and bring disgrace upon those who are really high-minded, learned and candid.[39]

Since much of the prosecution's case depended upon the credibility of medical witnesses and how well they performed their role in a case, it was critical to determine the private nature of medical judgment as it informed a physician's opinion under oath. Private knowledge proved to be a highly individual blend of the physician's own experience and habits of mind. Moreover, professional witnesses were seen as a surrogate jury, since so much relied upon their opinion of the facts, so that a witness "must hear all the evidence that the jury hears; he must connect it; he must reject what does not bear upon the case; in fact, he discharges all the functions of a jury, except as to the credibility of the witnesses."[40] Since opinions were arrived at on the basis of a witness's own experience and in private study, they were not publicly verifiable as other evidence might be. Judges tended to be suspicious of such opinions, especially when controverted by medical opinions provided by opposing counsel's witnesses or when they constituted positions that were little more than that arrived at by "an unlearned man of sense," that is, "the good sense of an unlearned jury."[41] Jealous of the court's prerogatives, a judge could easily conclude the medical witness's displacement of the jury's role was problematic.

With so many difficulties associated with testifying in court, medical witnesses were faced with conflicting responsibilities. Not only did professional groups call on them to support individual colleagues under legal attack wherever possible and to avoid joining such attacks upon them, but physicians were expected to keep an eye on the interest of the profession, the reputation of which would not survive constant controversy or injudicious interference with a colleague's therapy.[42] Even when interrogated under a hypothetical, witnesses were instructed to remain aware of the ethical dilemma in which they might find themselves and choose loyalty to the medical profession over the truth. That the medical witness might not prove equal to the complexities of such a conflicted task was, it was clear, a shared concern, suggesting one reason why courts rarely convicted defendants based upon medical witness testimony.

PHYSICIANS AND THE LAW

The legal snapshot on medical liability that described the conditions under which *Rush v. Cobbett* would have been tried covered the years from the middle of the eighteenth century through the first three decades of the next century. Although malpractice cases did not arise in great numbers in a time frame before or close to the trial, a handful of cases occurred that would be useful for our purposes: a bloodletting case in 1767; an accusation against a Dr. Woodruff in 1779; and a trial of the quack Samuel Thomson in 1809. These cases reflect the patterns of prevailing legal and medical issues as well as public perceptions that contextualized the *Rush v. Cobbett* trial. Although the Rush trial was not one in which Rush was himself prosecuted for malpractice, his rationale for bringing libel charges depended upon Cobbett's having effectively tried him in the press for just such malfeasance. Equally, Cobbett's defense relied to an extent—implicitly or explicitly—upon construing Rush as a malpracticing physician.

Whitworth and Young

A rare case on bloodletting in Boston in 1767[43] provides an early starting point for this discussion. First, we find that the case was tried in the press and that it involved a feud between two doctors in which Dr. Young attacked Dr. Whitworth as an "empirick." The delineation of a physician as an empiric or quack could have occurred in any of several contexts. Lack of training or education as a physician could have led to the appellation, even if the physician had practiced one of several recognized or approved forms of medicine. If he had engaged in an idiosyncratic form of medicine, presumed to develop his own secret form of treatment, or attacked a professional colleague in the press, he would equally have qualified for the designation. The fact that a practitioner advertised his services in a newspaper or handbill was considered a sign certain that he was a quack.[44]

The use of the newspaper venue to "try" one's case before the public was not uncommon. Indeed, doctors' wars, widely carried out in the press, were intended to influence public perceptions, to defend one's reputation within the medical profession, to influence an ongoing trial, or to reverse the public or social effect of a verdict. Public exposure of cases in the press proved embarrassing to elite members of the profession whose efforts to enhance the professional status of medicine depended upon public trust in the reputation and status of physicians. In a 1779 case involving Aaron Craig, a professor of physic, for example, Hezikiah Woodruff claimed Craig had been incited by persons with

> motives of private Interest, to propagate that a certain *John Costner*, late deceased, was carried off from this World by and through the Means and Medicine I prescribed for his Cure. Thus has he, with certain vehement and turbulent Impulses peculiar to himself, endeavored to blast my Character as a Physician as well as a Christian, and thereby render me of as little Service to Society or to Mankind as he himself is.[45]

Woodruff rested his case with the publication of three depositions, sworn on oath, leaving it to the "impartial and discerning Publick; with whom I am perfectly pleased my Shield of Reputation should stand or fall" to judge the matter.

In the 1767 newspaper case, Doctor Whitworth found himself compelled to defend himself in the press against "an ignorant Emperick displaying his malice against me in a News-Paper, only because I was unhappily necessitated to condemn his ill grounded practice."[46] The empiric's female patient presented vomiting blood, constantly coughing, experiencing pain in the stomach and difficulty breathing, and displaying symptoms of emaciation, weakness, a quick pulse, and depressed spirits. Whitworth "mentioned to the family [the patient's] error in not calling assistance earlier, and delivered such a prognostic, as every honest sensible physician would in a like case." Reflecting some knowledge of the legal requirements in such a situation, Whitworth made clear that the patient was herself in error and that he had himself fulfilled his duty to the patient in advising the family of her dire prognosis. He had, he felt, met the common sense standard of ordinary reasonable care. At this point, Whitworth experienced every eighteenth-century physician's greatest fear—that the family would call in another doctor who would treat the patient without taking into account Whitworth's earlier treatment:

> I found a porringer with at least twelve ounces of blood, which I was informed had been taken from my patient by one *Young*. I was offended by the impudence of the fellow who has thus stole in, without ever consulting me, or knowing what I had previously done; and astonished at his stupidity in thus depriving the miserable patient of the little prospect she before had of recovering. I expressed my just resentment, and told the family that it was impossible for the woman to

> bear such a loss of blood, and that the consequence would infallibly be a much speedier dissolution, than would otherwise have happened. I then took my leave with a design to quit the patient.

Whitworth's legal position as a physician who was superseded in treating a patient was nonetheless protected on two counts. First, the burden of responsibility shifted away from him to the new physician, and, second, he was able to withdraw from the case without liability. Although he subsequently reentered the case when the intruder was dismissed, his inability to save the patient's life did not leave him at legal risk, irrespective of medical testimony to the contrary:

> As to the authorities which he has produced in his vindication, I will just premise, that all the authorities on earth can never make that right which is essentially wrong—But justice to those authors . . . what they designed for the good of mankind, has unhappily been misapplied; they never intended to countenance every quack who is just able to read their writings, in promiscuously bleeding the innocent blood of their fellow men.

Calling upon the authors of medical texts, as well as the medical faculty of Boston and general knowledge itself, Whitworth created a common consensus upon which an ordinary standard could be based. It was a standard that would cover him and leave his competitor vulnerable as a mountebank, an outsider who could not claim to participate in "our business" and who would not have understood or embraced "our duty":

> I now appeal to every gentleman of the faculty in this or any other place, for a justification of my censure upon the Mountebank. Every gentleman knows that blood-letting in such a case as the above described, must be attended with the most fatal consequences, as it is directly contrary to every indication of cure. . . . In short, none but a fool or a madman would ever have proposed blood-letting in such a case; and the event was such as might reasonably have been expected.

Whitworth presented himself very much like a lawyer trying a case. Representing himself as an expert witness, his press testimony detailed the state of medical knowledge and what was expected in terms of skill and care. Creating the impression of a legal brief, he appeared to understand those elements of the law that most required his attention and the need to present a narrative within the structure of the trial. In effect, he cross-examined Young and responded in his own defense. Young was presented as having claimed to have warned the family of the seriousness of the patient's affliction, so that a latent condition or the seriousness of the illness could be used in his defense. The patient's constitution or the illness itself was thus represented as having carried her off and not the doctor's treatment or skill or lack of either. Whitworth countered with his own claim that Young had contracted to cure the patient: "As to what he says of having signified to her nurse that her case was desperate and scarce any hope of recovery, I can only say that the person who attended in her chamber, informed me that Young said that altho' her case was very hazardous yet he believed HE could cure."

Beyond all else, Whitworth's determination to try the case in the press put the empiric in the dock in the larger battle fought around medical regulation, commercial competition, and professional licensing. In the immediate case, the battle was fought in an urban area, Boston, where medical schools, medical societies, and apprenticeships with elite European-degreed physicians prevailed and where the standard of care was closer to the extraordinary by comparison. But as part of a more general debate informed by a newspaper account of the trial published for general distribution, the battle reverberated in rural areas where jealousy of urban physicians, an inadequate number of available physicians and surgeons, and poor to no medical training obtained, and where the standard of care was closer to the subordinary, bordering on gross malfeasance.

Situational logic argued that differing standards would have to coexist or there could be no standard at all. But Whitworth claimed limits to such relativity. He accused Young of standing for all that undermined an acceptable practice of medicine. An acceptable practice should be located somewhere between the self-policing of fellow physicians through a medical society and an informal system of approved abilities based on study and training, but absent formal licensing. What was not acceptable, in his view, were the ignorance, fraud, and quackery with which he charged Young:

> It is much to be regretted that a man who has nothing to recommend him, but his unparalleled impudence, should receive the least countenance in this place, where there are persons of approved abilities—but a fellow who descends to the lowest art of ingratiating himself with people, whose constant employment in other business renders it impossible that they should be judges of real merit, will always be able to seduce some of the unwary into his snare—Thus this fellow who is the ridicule of all the truly learned, is the great Apollo of the ignorant; they greedily swallow his jargon, and dub him a man of boundless erudition, only because they cannot find any meaning in what he delivers; they are struck with astonishment at his miraculous fictions, and with a kind of devotion attend with gaping mouths, whilst he informs them of his remarkable dreams . . . thus the ignorant are deluded, and impiously cheated out of their lives . . . it is certain that medicine in the hands of the ignorant, is like brands, arrows and death in the hands of a fool . . . tho' the gentlemen of the faculty may think that it is sufficient to treat such Empericks with contempt; yet I believe upon serious reflection, they will not find it consistent with the principles of benevolence,

> to *suffer* (if they can prevent it) their fellow citizens to be cruelly butchered by the rash hand of a vain boaster; they can have only this consolation, that such ignorant conduct will serve as a foil to set forth with greater luster their own superior abilities.

Samuel Thomson

In an 1809 case, *The Commonwealth v. Samuel Thomson*, the Massachusetts Supreme Court tried the founder of the medical sect called Thomsonianism. In this case, the defendant was called by the patient to treat him. As described in the court decision, Thomson "announced himself as a physician, and professed an ability to cure all fevers, whether *black, gray, green, or yellow*, declaring that the country was much imposed upon by physicians, who were all wrong, if he was right. He possessed several drugs, which he used as medicines, and to which he gave singular names."[47] Administering emetic powders of tobacco, marsh-rosemary, and bark of bayberry bush, a mixture he called "coffee," Thomson puked his patient three times within a half hour on Monday and sweated him all night. He followed with two bouts of emetics on each of the next two days, sweated the patient with vinegar on Thursday and administered emetics five more times on Sunday, at which time the patient went into convulsions. The convulsions continued for two more days before the patient expired on Tuesday. Without producing any witnesses to show that any previous patients had "experienced any fatal effects," the solicitor general claimed the defendant had used a similar medicine on other patients who had died. The one witness the state did call testified he had been relieved by the powders, as a result of which the defendant "was not put on his defense" as "the court were satisfied that the evidence produced on the part of the Commonwealth did not support the indictment."[48]

In a review of malpractice law in 1877, Milo McClelland found this singular case to be the only one in which empiricism was charged as murder—felonious homicide—based on "the administration of nostrums by charlatans."[49] The facts of the case were not contradicted, nor was the witness impeached, so that the case reduced in the Chief Justice's charge to the jury to a single question: "That the deceased lost his life by the unskillful treatment of the prisoner, did not seem to admit of any reasonable doubt; but of this point the jury were to judge. . . . But whether this treatment, by which the deceased lost his life, is or is not a felonious homicide, was the great question before the jury."[50] Conviction required that the murder be committed with malice express or implied, which the charge to the jury did not sustain. Before malice could be reached by the jury, moreover, an intent to do harm had to be present, irrespective of the level of negligence on the defendant's part:

> It has been said that implied malice may be inferred from the rash and presumptuous conduct of the prisoner, in administering such violent medicines. Before implied malice can be inferred, the jury must be satisfied that the prisoner, by this treatment of his patient, was willfully regardless of his social duty, being determined on mischief. But there is no part of the evidence which proves that the prisoner intended by his practice any harm to the diseased. On the contrary, it appears that his intention was to cure him.[51]

The intent and expectation of curing could not, the judge instructed the jury, be overcome by simple ignorance, however deeply it might have run, absent some showing that the defendant had killed before and knew of the injurious effects of the treatment on his patients. It was therefore not a felony "unless he, however ignorant of medical science in general, had so much knowledge, or probable information of the fatal tendency of the prescription, that it may be reasonably presumed by the jury to be the effect of obstinate, willful rashness at the least, and not on an honest intention and expectation to cure."[52] So long as he remained ignorant, the empiric was excused, the law was hamstrung, and the public was vulnerable to his malfeasance. Where ignorance and good intentions were an excuse and a reasonable medical knowledge standard did not apply, the burden was on the patient to choose his physician carefully. The inconceivable became conceivable under cover of honest intent, and murder by nostrum became no murder at all: "On any other ground consistent with his innocence," the court observed, "it is not easy to conceive that . . . he could expect a repetition of these fatal poisons would prove a cathartic, and relieve the patient; or that he could mistake convulsion fits, symptomatic of approaching death, for a hypochondriac affection."[53]

RUSH AND MALPRACTICE

Given the confused state of malpractice law it is not surprising that Benjamin Rush was never sued for malpractice, although the attacks against him by Cobbett in *Porcupine's Gazette* suggested that he could have been. He was, after all, a physician accused of responsibility for wholesale deaths, both directly and indirectly, as a result of his own medical practice, the bleeders he trained and employed to extend his ability to treat patients, and his publication of instructions for cures for yellow fever. It was not, in sum, that Rush was not a candidate for malpractice litigation, either by number of deaths or extent of injury, but that courts were not a likely venue in which to address his presumed malpractice, which might very well explain Cobbett's insistence on attacking him in the press. Given the law on malpractice, a case against Rush would not have had a realistic chance of success. Suits were so infrequent that complaints would have had to outweigh doubts about bringing them to the law at all. Moreover, divine providence justifications for illness and misadventure discouraged patients from pursuing such cases in court. Should a patient bring a case to court, not only would the burden of proof have been on the patient to prove physician error, but the physician's reputation would have predisposed the jury in his favor. Indeed, malpractice trials reported in the early nineteenth century showed that the majority of juries favored defendant-physicians.[54] The potential loss of physicians where they were in short supply not only made communities reluctant to bring in a verdict against doctors but a judgment against an established physician was bound to have an effect on the community in which he was embedded. The physician's responsibility for an injury would, in any case, have been difficult to prove, particularly where doctors disagreed, as they clearly did about the practice of bloodletting and purging, and where expert witnesses were available on both sides of the case. Only gross negligence would register against the physician, and even then an honest intention to cure would offset the charge.

Whether Rush could have been successfully tried in a malpractice case is, of course, a hypothetical question. Once posed, however, the prospect is supported by the fact that he had a large patient base of poor people, the class that would become most closely tied to suing physicians after 1835 when malpractice suits increased significantly.[55] Rush's argument that he did not make a habit of pursuing fees from those who did not pay would have made it less likely his poor patients would have sued him. On the other hand, patient suits were often instigated by other physicians in internecine feuds over medical influence and authority. In such a case, Rush would have proved a prime candidate, having engaged in so many and lasting a number of conflicts with his fellow professionals. As regulars protected those in their immediate professional circle and attacked those outside it, lack of professional solidarity became itself a prime factor leading to malpractice suits. Moreover, the fact that Rush practiced in an urban center meant he should have been liable to a higher standard of medical care, an easier case to prove. Accusations against him of quackery would as well have weighed more heavily against him in such a setting.

Physicians who explicitly promised to cure a patient, as Rush appeared to have done in guaranteeing the efficacy of his yellow fever regimen, left themselves open to suits on the grounds that such a promise constituted an ordinary contract and the failure to cure constituted a breach of promise. Assuming the care of a patient could itself be regarded as an implied contract, although the contract would not have been to cure but merely to treat according to common or prevailing standards of care. Rush, it is true, was later in his career to back away from insistence on his cure, which in itself could have constituted recognition on his part that he had gone too far or evidence that he had not intended a guarantee.

A critical issue for Rush was whether his care represented standard or ordinary care. Differences over treatment among physicians would have helped his case, for he was only required to exercise care that was consistent with his own school of practice. In fact, physicians did disagree over yellow fever treatments, so that a suit related to such a case would have been groundless. No common standard of care had been established and Rush, as a result, would have been regarded as much in the right as any other physician. Witnesses testifying against him from other schools of practice would simply have been balanced by those from within his own camp, with no prevailing standard to tip the balance, so that the uncertainty of medicine would have been Rush's ally. In any case, the testimony of physicians in *Rush v. Cobbett* was largely of a type that would not have helped Rush in a medical malpractice suit. For one thing, Drs. Dewees, Coxe, and Mease were interested witnesses, as they had themselves been libeled by Cobbett as Rushites. Moreover, their testimony related in large part to Rush's reputation as a republican rather than as a physician. Where Rush's medical practice was implicated—in Dewees's claim that Cobbett solicited Rush's services for his family—it was not directly related to the treatment itself, but only to the patient's confidence in calling upon the physician.

Rush's best defense in any potential malpractice suit would have been his prestige as a physician, a line of argument that his legal team in *Rush v. Cobbett* pursued vigorously. The team cast Rush in the role of Hippocrates of Philadelphia and portrayed him as savior to the city's suffering citizens to offset Cobbett's accusations linking Rush to the bloodsucking Sangrado and to the quackish practices of the commercial medical marketplace. At the time he practiced, a physician like Rush could depend on status-based privileges that were respected by the community. A decline in status that would feed malpractice trials after 1835 had not yet undermined public confidence. Rush might have faced some of the competitive medical practices that would later become endemic, but he did not have to deal with the egalitarian social changes that challenged the elite status of the medical profession as a whole in the nineteenth century. Nor did he face technical advances that increased patient expectations or that inspired a later breakdown in the kind of medical explanations that were based on traditional customs and divine providence. Such developments made patients more willing to sue and would, in time, radically alter the medical picture. They were not, however, prevalent in Rush's time.

When Rush practiced, much medical care continued to be delivered through folk medicine, home care, patent medicine, herbal remedies, and handbooks on health care. A patient would, as a result, have had a difficult time determining whom to sue or distinguishing physicians from grocer-apothecaries, barber-surgeons, innkeeper-bleeders, or bonesetters as parties liable to being sued. Indeed, given the state of medical science, physicians shared with other practitioners the herbal and chemical medications, sweating therapies, purging, puking, bleeding, and cupping treatments then available. One might have thought Rush would have been protected by his association with a hospital or his teaching at a medical school. But degrees, appointments, and attending privileges were not tightly linked to more efficacious practice, even where education and professional status distinguished one in a community. In fact, when medical schools began to flourish in the mid-nineteenth century, malpractice suits began to proliferate. Apparently, the production of a surfeit of physicians raised patient expectations and stimulated competitive practices that left many patients disappointed by the treatment they received. In response, physicians under threat were more likely to choose familiar remedies and resist the development of new technologies.[56] Regulars pressed for licensing to seal their command of the medical market, which made the public suspicious of monopolistic practices that flew in the face of prevailing open markets.[57] Under these conditions, malpractice suits became a means of keeping the marketplace open to patient choice and of enlisting juries to protect the public from those who failed to fulfill their duty of care.[58]

Conservative medical practice, like that of Drs. Stevens and Deveze, supported expectations that standard therapies would yield reasonably consistent positive results. Rush's extreme version of heroic bleeding, by contrast, was clearly on the margins of such treatment and was thereby open to cries of malpractice and quackery not only in medical writing but in the press; his treatments were both widely excoriated and passionately defended. In Rush's favor, the eighteenth century was still a period in which the expectation that a physician would do something, or create the appearance of doing something, represented part of the treatment. Rush's dramatic treatments profited greatly from the patient's desire to see, with his own eyes, his physician was indeed practicing his craft. His heroic practices, moreover, had the benefit of being presented as an advance in the technology of healing discovered and applied by Rush himself as an invention specific to treatment of the yellow fever.[59] It was not until the early nineteenth century that therapeutic nihilism arose to privilege the power of healing nature over human interference in response to excessive medical practices in the earlier century.[60]

To his credit, Rush's brush with malpractice occurred in relation to an epidemic disease rather than an injury like a broken leg. A case like *Lowell v. Faxon* (1824)[61] some two and a half decades later fell under a more predictable, almost mechanical standard of care.[62] There, orthopedic injuries reflected active lives, individual responsibility, and the potential for physical well-being and perfection at a time when a physician's failure to meet expectations, to demonstrate technological progress, or to achieve physical health informed an increase in malpractice suits.[63] Rush's earlier practices were excused by residual theories of providential responsibility in which people's collective misfortunes were seen as the acts of an angry Old Testament God. The natural order of second causes was understood to have been created by God and then set off to carry His law into operation. Because God's order was reinforced by the social norms of a nonlegal order and informal venues for resolving disputes were honored by the community, going to court meant stepping outside communal practices and values.[64] This association discouraged assumptions about individual physician responsibility and the malpractice suits attached to such responsibility. Epidemic medicine of the type Rush was accused of practicing thus capitalized on a mind-set that excused physicians like Rush from liability and kept them out of court. In sum, it was well after Rush's time that juries began to favor the patient-plaintiff[65] and popular sentiment turned against physicians. Rush, it appears, was socially insulated from malpractice suits, a consideration that must have affected the choice Cobbett's legal team made in deciding against a malpractice attack on Rush as their primary defense.

RUSH'S DECISION TO PROSECUTE

Having considered the complications of successfully pursuing a case of malpractice against Rush—at least in the courts—it remains to consider what Rush might have hoped for in pursuing his claims against Cobbett. Given Rush's history of feuding behaviors, one possibility is that the trial represented for Rush a legal version of a duel, that is, an end-game strategy emanating from a challenge to his honor. Feuding was very much a part of Rush's nature, a tactic he pursued across his career that ranged from feuds with his medical students and protégées—here one thinks of Nathaniel Chapman and Charles Caldwell[66]—to those with his superiors in the medical department of the continental army, leading to Rush's collusion with John Morgan, director general of the Continental Army hospitals, in abetting the infamous court martial of Morgan's replacement William Shippen, Jr.[67] Territorial disputes among physicians during the war[68] and what Simon Finger refers to as "hierarchical attitudes" within the medical department and among its units became structural influences on Rush's relationships, affecting his social rank and his political connections.[69] During his service in the army and in his medical writing about military medicine, Rush was nothing if not intemperate and a disciplinarian,[70] attitudes that would carry over to peacetime. They would resurface, problematically, in the yellow fever epidemics of 1793 and 1797—where patients were not to be treated like soldiers obliged to obey a superior's commands and other physicians did not regard themselves as commissioned officers under a unified command—and they would lead to his infamous feuds with physicians like William Currie and Adam Kuhn, among others.[71] Having learned what he knew of medical management of epidemic disease from the disorganization and maladministration characteristic of the continental army medical camps and having studied medical politics at the center of a court martial centering on mismanagement of medical resources, Rush's wars with doctors over yellow fever treatments and over the shape of the medical profession, in the College of Philadelphia Medical School and Pennsylvania Hospital, come as no surprise. Rush's professional history thus included a lifelong defense of his reputation in which honor, ambition, medical competition, status conflicts, and organizational pressures defined him as a public figure.

So long as his feuding remained private or involved lower level stakes, Rush could refrain from prosecuting Cobbett. But certain critical factors led him to take a more aggressive course than his lawyers would have liked. Cobbett's attacks, after all, had been made publicly; they were persistent; and Cobbett would neither retract nor refrain from his attacks, even under the threat of a restraining order, the infamous peace bond applied by the Pennsylvania Supreme Court to control press libels.[72] Not only were Cobbett's attacks intense and humiliating for a man in Rush's prominent position,[73] but they became progressively more difficult to ignore. Corollary issues—the state of eighteenth-century law and changes in the legal climate—offered further complications. The young nation was at a point in its development where resistance to making use of courts in private matters dissipated as communities became less homogeneous and as morality became an issue to be dealt with in the court rather than in the church. In terms of conflict resolution, moreover, courts had much to recommend them, given the fatal prospects offered by duels. Having avoided duels across his life, Rush now found himself in a situation where his feud with Cobbett was likely to lead him into just such a cul-de-sac and where Cobbett, whose military history favored dueling (as an extended feud with the newspaperman Mathew Carey amply demonstrated),[74] would have had a decided advantage. Prosecution became, all things considered, a preferable and less deadly option.

Timing was a factor in Rush's decision as well, for the feud occurred at a time when medicine as an institution was beginning to stabilize and factionalism among physicians was decreasing. The public, as a result, was less forgiving of disputes like those of the doctors' wars which undermined confidence in the profession. For the profession to grow, physicians would have to move to a new way of relating to one another, leave behind old social norms, and develop relationships that had greater regularity and predictability. Rush's decision was thus more in line with what the times demanded and the future would come to expect. High stakes gambles such as duels might survive into the new century, but they were not endorsed as a social norm and carried high costs that risked community harmony and cultural order. Once a truly American law established its own rules and procedures and produced a reformed court system—a process already partly in place in the late eighteenth century—the neutrality and anonymity of legal order would prove an attraction that litigants like Rush, seeking more stable relations, would embrace.

One key consideration in Rush's choice to prosecute was the generally contentious political climate which had led to an excessive number of libel suits. Not only were the large number of libel suits against public figures of special concern to the Pennsylvania Supreme Court (and a personal cause of its chief justice Thomas McKean), but they characterized the Philadelphia legal scene as a particularly litigious venue. The frequency of such suits was featured both by the prosecution team and the judge's charge to the jury in the Rush case. Both the prosecution and the defense had to deny at length that their clients were litigious. Rush's team, in particular, raised the issue as a central part of the case and developed it at length. Joseph Hopkinson tried to address the public's concern over how Rush was expected to address such excess and decay. He was sure that Cobbett, who appealed for public protection, regarded Rush's prosecution as persecution of freedom of the press, a contention he considered absurd and perverse. Hopkinson questioned whether Rush could be considered a persecutor merely for applying "to the tribunal of his country for the justification of his character, and the redress of his wrongs."[75] Rush, after all, had done no more than to seek the dignity and truth of a legal remedy rather than the immorality of a duel—the latter being the recourse of those who failed to access the law to resolve their conflicts. In what sense was he guilty of persecution, Hopkinson asked, "when he calls his assassin to open, fair and dignified ground, to the courts of justice of his country, making the great issue between them TRUTH, and consenting to stand or fall, to be justified or disgraced by this infallible arbiter." Should government and the law fail to deliver on their "promised protection of our lives, property and reputation," Hopkinson warned, the prospect of private feuds and vigilantism must necessarily follow: "an immediate, nay, a justifiable resort to private vengeance for private wrongs; an immediate and a necessary introduction of murder and assassination."[76] Ingersol joined him in raising the dreaded specter of dueling as the likely alternative to sufficient confidence in the law, adding that law must never become cover for the guilty, as indeed Cobbett, who had experience in the courts, was said to use the law "for his protections against force and even against libels."[77]

Working out his legal options, Rush had one remaining choice to make and that was whether to pursue a criminal or a civil suit against Cobbett. Legally, he could have pursued a criminal case. The fact that he resisted doing so suggests that he chose the lesser of several evils and one that would win him credit without too much risk. Rush's legal team considered that he had pursued an honorable course, not filing for a criminal indictment—where, except for sedition cases, the defendant was not permitted to justify the truth of his words.[78] He filed, instead, a civil case, "the great issue being truth."[79] Had Rush filed a criminal indictment he would have had the advantage of being a witness, a privilege he would forgo so that, as Rush's legal team represented, "we come fairly into the field with an action which puts the parties upon an equal footing."[80] On Cobbett's side, Edward Tilghman argued that the party who made a charge did so under oath,[81] whereas the accused would have had to answer the complaint by denying it unsworn. The equality of which Jared Ingersol boasted, as a result, still left Cobbett at a disadvantage both because his evidence would have been regarded as less credible and because the prosecution did not yet truly carry the burden of the production and persuasion of proof.[82] Free, fair, equal, and just, it was clear, were relative terms that retained for Rush much of the privilege he sought under the law, while they left Cobbett vulnerable.

It is clear that Rush's decision was complex and conflicted. The prosecution might, for example, have been represented as solely directed at Cobbett, but the original charges included the American John Fenno and his paper *Gazette of the United States*, charges that were dropped, arguably to allow the prosecution to focus on the theme that Cobbett was an alien, but just as likely because an American (and a federalist to boot) might have been harder to convict. Even more importantly, as Rush admitted in his memoir *Travels Through Life*—in which he commented rather extensively on his motives for taking Cobbett to court—Rush was actually responding to a much wider audience of critics whose works Fenno and Cobbett had published in their newspapers. Cobbett's original sin, it appears, might have been no more than to have reprinted a piece in 1797 that had already appeared in Fenno's paper, followed over a six-week period by other pieces by Rush's "enemies."[83] At first, the perceived assault was no more than that Rush was mistaken as the author of a set of directions for the treatment of the fever that had actually been put forward by Dr. Griffitts. The "torrents of abuse" directed against Rush on that account appeared, as Rush put it, "in a paper conducted by one Cobbett, an English alien who then resided in Philadelphia."[84] William Currie identified himself as the author of the worst of the attacks against Rush's "practice and character, and particularly against [Rush's] political principles," although he was only one of a handful of such authors. Rush ranted against all those whose lives he had saved, and one (Currie) whom he had befriended and forgiven, and who had yet written to destroy him. He referred to "All these different attacks"; to "some" attacks put forth "as a just punishment for my political principles"; and to those "many more [who] acquiesced in them" to destroy his influence as "a man who had aimed to destroy the credit of their city" by identifying it as a source of the fever. Rush concluded that "Their design proved successful. They lessened my business, and they abstracted so much of the confidence of my patients as to render my practice extremely difficult and disagreeable among them. To put a stop to their injurious effects upon my business, and the lives of my patients, I commenced civil actions against both the printers."[85]

Consistent with events across his entire professional career,[86] Rush's primary concern was with the growing weight of professional opinion against him. Indeed, following his comments on the charges he presented himself as determined "to oppose the weight of associated numbers to the influence of the College of Physicians"[87] by forming his own association, the Academy of Medicine. Having done so, he immediately related, "Their [his critics] publications in favor of their opinion fell dead from the press." Cobbett, he then noted, was fined for his publications and removed to New York where "he vented his rage in a number of publications of the same complexion," publications "purchased, lent, and read with great avidity"[88] and whose contents were used to insult his children at school and in the streets. Just as he had filed suit against Cobbett to prevent the publication of the words of his enemies, so did he threaten a suit against the bookseller who disseminated Cobbett's attacks to force the withdrawal of the materials. In the words of the memoir, the "virulent invective" of his professional colleagues was the focus of his ire, separate from the actions of the printer, even if communication of the invective in print had become the actual subject of his suit. Rush thus represented his action as an effort to restrain uncollegial assaults by his critics and to do so by preventing their publication and sale.

Lest alleviating the threat to reputation prove too cold and selfish a motive, Rush's prosecution team launched the idea of the necessity of a free man's access to the law, playing on the security of home and family as the very foundation of social order. Hopkinson reframed Rush's prosecution of Cobbett in terms of his responsibility to three duties: "to the laws of his country," "to his fellow citizens," and "to himself and his family." To allow an "abandoned and dangerous offender" to roam free violated Rush's responsibility to his neighbors. Failure to protect his own reputation stained the "honor and purity" of his family, a stain that would then descend "as a shame upon his children" and leave his wife open to "the deep wounds of public reproach."[89] True enough, Rush was deeply concerned for the safety of his impetuous sons who had put themselves in harm's way by coming to his defense. As Rush was to write in his instructions to his friend and agent Brockholst Livingston in considering two additional suits against Cobbett, the courts and the public would not be indifferent to the risk "a grayheaded and inoffensive citizen runs every hour of his life of hearing of murder being connected in one way or other with the names of his sons. . . . Let nothing be done in it unless you are sure the force of law can be effectively employed to silence him [Cobbett], and thereby to restore my sons to calmness and safety."[90]

Livingston cautioned Rush in an exchange of letters after the trial against continuing to pursue Cobbett too aggressively: "All that is required of us is that a person be not harassed with two suits at the same time."[91] He had no difficulty, on the other hand, should Rush wish to "hold the party to bail,"[92] although "In the Supreme Court no bail can be taken in such suits." Rush, however, was not easily to be constrained. He first proposed a criminal suit, then crossed it out and gave Livingston a choice of "criminal or civil as you may think proper."[93] Livingston was clear on the criminal charges:[94] however much Cobbett "deserves every punishment that can legally be inflicted on him," he did not "think that much can be done criminally against him." Nor would the present grand jury be likely to "listen to a complaint against the fellow." Livingston was apparently concerned that Cobbett might file a civil suit against Rush's son John, either for stalking him or for proffering a challenge. Livingston both assuaged Rush—holding it a "disgrace to our police that Cobbett is allowed to stay in the country"—and dissuaded him from taking further action, that is, Livingston held out little hope and did not "think it worthwhile for you to bring another action in your name against him."[95]

Expanding the idea of a father's love to a theme worthy of sentimental drama, Hopkinson waxed eloquent that libel suits might prove to be Rush's "guardian angel,"[96] allowing the husband and the father to redeem himself and rescue his family. How else, Hopkinson pleaded, was he to protect his children?:

> Manlier passions swell, agitate and enflame the breasts of his sons—They burn, they burst with indignation, rage, revenge, drive them headlong to desperate deeds, accumulating woe on woe. With difficulty the prudential advice, the parental command of the father restrain their fury—With difficulty they are prevented from taking immediate vengeance on their cruel oppressor—Be patient my children, said he, I am deeply injured, but the laws of my country offer me justice, and point out the road to redress. It is tardy, but it is certain and ample. Delay may be painful to you, but the duties of a good citizen require it.[97]

Of interest here is the subtitle of Rush's *Travels*, "written for the use of his children," which helps to clarify this aspect of Rush's intent. Rush expressed his "wish that it may not be read out of the circle of the family, and that it may never be published."[98] Creating for his children a history that should provide "entertainment and instruction," a traditional neoclassical prescription, Rush qualified his comments on his enemies and on Cobbett. While others had exulted in his ruin, he claimed, he had refrained from "mentioning the names of my medical enemies" and entertained no desire for revenge. His children ought not to remember the wrongs done to him, but should treat his enemies as friends with whom "We shall soon lie down in the grave together."[99] Whatever happened in the trial, Rush wanted history as it would be read in his family to record his persecution, not at the hands of one alien, but at the hands of his own countrymen and fellow professionals. That he filed suit against Cobbett alone would have to satisfy his need for self-justification, but it was by no means the whole picture.

The nature of the attacks in the press that preceded the Rush case, as well as the debate centered around alien and sedition proceedings that were ongoing as the case was called to trial, raised the stakes for Rush to a heightened level. Given the threats to his reputation, the assaults on his beloved republicanism, the risk to his medical practice, the exposure of his family, and the very real prospect that he might lose his case against Cobbett, one could have easily anticipated the high rhetoric of the trial, disruptions in the courtroom, and the overflowing passion of the spectators upon hearing the verdict. Rush thus ran a considerable risk of self-censure and damage to his reputation by insisting on prosecuting Cobbett. Public opinion might, after all, render its own verdict in terms of perceptions of malpractice.

Ultimately, Rush's lawyers, if not Rush, were reluctant to file the suit, and they advised him against it. Although Ingersol accepted Rush's request to represent him, he wrote that his client, as a man of experience, should not "be surprised of meeting with ingratitude" in spite of the risks he took to his life in ministering to the sick. Suspending "any opinion upon this subject, until I shall have an opportunity to confer with you," Ingersol went on to suggest that the harm Rush feared to his reputation as a result of newspaper libel was not a cause for concern and that resort to the courts was unnecessary "to guard against the imputations of Envy, excited by eminence of character."[100] Hopkinson, by contrast, considered and rejected his colleague's advice in his opening address at the trial, offering that the trust upon which a physician depended to practice his profession suffered from even the slightest threat to a pristine reputation: "It has been strangely suggested by some (for this suit has been a subject of pretty general conversation and concern) that Dr. Rush's character is too well known and established to be injured by the attacks of Cobbett, who is not worth his serious attention, and therefore he should recover no damages in this action. . . . Of a physician this is most emphatically nice. His reputation is a fabric delicate as air, the slightest gust of popular prejudice or caprice dissipates it, even suspicion destroys it; if he is distrusted he is ruined."[101]

Rush himself, it is worth noting, reconsidered the wisdom of going to court later in his life. In 1809, in a dream he recounted to John Adams, he depicted a great crowd milling about in a hall that Rush took to be a mental ward.[102] One man endeavored to turn copper into gold, another was preparing an elixir to "restore man to his original antediluvian longevity." A young man in the corner of the room was fashioning a pair of wings to fly from the Schuylkill River to the Delaware River. Thinking himself surely caught in a madhouse, Rush turned to leave:

> "Stop!" said a little old man who appeared to be the master of the house, "and tell me where are you going." "To the town meeting," said I. "You are at it already," said he. "What! in this receptacle of madmen?" said I. "Yes," said he, "they are an epitome of all public bodies, whether assembled in town meetings, state legislatures, congresses, conventions, or parliaments, and of all the statesmen and philosophers, whether at courts or in a closet, who expect to produce by their labors, *wisdom, justice, order,* and *stability* in human governments."[103]

In sum, Rush's decision to prosecute Cobbett took on a number of aspects. It was both strategic and passionate, professional and personal. It was a question of timing, law, politics, and family dynamics. Rush's professional history, feuding behavior, legal opportunities, and sense of public responsibility all played a role. Given the evidence, it is too simple to say that republican politics dominated his thinking or that his aversion to federalists and the British directed his actions, even if these themes permeated the trial rhetoric of the prosecution team.[104] It is enough that if his professional life and personality had not been so politically marked he might not have prosecuted. But that is not the same as a claim that he made the choice for political reasons. Cobbett's acts might more easily be described as politically motivated. Rush's make a better case for complex causation.

NOTES

1. De Ville (1990, 1–2).
2. See Conrad, Neve, Nutton, Porter, and Wear (1995).
3. De Ville (1990, 1–4); Burns (1969a, 52–54).
4. De Ville (1990, 156–57).

5. Blackstone's *Commentaries* was published in England in 1765 and appeared in its first American edition in 1771–1772; Blackstone (1774).

6. The applicable doctrine, trespass in case (rather than trespass, which requires strict liability and intentional direct injury), reflects negligence, nonfeasance, and the absence of force; Morton J. Horwitz (1977, 89).

7. It was not until the mid-nineteenth century that the law moved away from "*status-based* responsibilities growing out of a physician's role as a public servant to *contract-based* responsibilities emanating from bilateral agreements"; De Ville (1990, 162). What emerged in the nineteenth century was a residual form of contract that resurfaced from eighteenth-century private forms of agreement between two parties. These were supported by community standards and implied obligations that reinforced and extended such agreements. In the mid-nineteenth century, status was under assault, professional identity devalued, and marketplace medicine emerged. These developments led to a momentary flirtation with contract law that reflected the needs of the marketplace and the need for commercial agreement expressing a meeting of minds. A commitment to perform according to that agreement rather than according to membership in a professional group, the relationship of physician and patient, or the physician's duty to provide a common standard of care was a necessary part of such commercial agreements. Patients were at a disadvantage in arrangements where they were not equal bargainers with doctors and could not freely consent to medical treatment with knowledge equal to what the physician had. The drift toward contract was only temporary and was not in any case to lead to absolute liability. Moreover, the failed application of contract law clarified in the end that the medical world differed in significant ways from the commercial world. Flirting with contract law helped medicine resolve its identity crisis and settle into a relationship with patients that left physicians a little less free to claim an elite status and a little more willing to accept their role as public servants (162–63, 185).

8. See De Ville (1990, 156–69).

9. Wex Malone (1986, 18–19).

10. Malone (1986, 20).

11. Even in the case of procedures no longer considered particularly risky—such as amputations, obstetrics, and vaccinations—but which posed the bulk of malpractice cases, ordinary care was challenged. De Ville (1990) notes that attacks against physicians for being experimental may have been intended to create resentment in rural juries against the pretentious "scientific" medicine of urban physicians and to argue for local standards of care as the basis for a judgment. Such attacks, however, disadvantaged those with superior skills and impeded medical innovation. They had the effect of protecting physicians with lesser skills and discouraging charges of malpractice (21). On the other hand, a medical malpractice suit could be used to control untrained practitioners whose treatments were hardly experimental or intended to advance medical science.

12. Malone (1986, 20); Elwell (1860, 22).

13. Elwell (1860, 21–22).

14. Elwell (1860, 19–35).

15. In an 1864 case, *Braunberger v. Cleis*, the judge's charge to the jury made clear that such conditions continued to influence the legal standard of care well into the nineteenth century:

> The law does not imply . . . the highest degree of care and skill attainable or known in the profession. If it did, but few would be competent to practice the medical, surgical, or any other profession. For but few comparatively, possess the requisite natural endowments, the industry, energy and perseverance, the opportunities for study and improvement, and the experience necessary and indispensable for the attainment of the highest degree of professional skill.

Medical and Surgical Reporter (1865, 555–58, 569–73).
See McClelland (1877, 127–45).

16. Elwell (1860, 22). Elwell went on to say, "what man, even of skill and talents, would undertake to practice medicine, if some little want of ordinary skill, or failure of ordinary skill, or failure of ordinary diligence, or even some trifling want of carefulness, might sweep from him the earnings of a long life of drudgery" (27).
17. Elwell (1860, 23).
18. Elwell (1860, 29).
19. Elwell (1860, 29–30).
20. Rush (1811, lecture 14, 318–59).
21. Malone (1986, 21).
22. Malone (1986, 26).
23. Elwell (1860, 29–32).
24. "On the Duties of Patients to their Physicians"; Rush (1811, lecture 14, 326).
25. Rush (1811, lecture 14, 327).
26. Rush (1811, lecture 14, 324).
27. Rush (1811, lecture 14, 321).
28. Rush (1811, lecture 14, 324).
29. Malone (1986, 117).
30. Malone (1986, 130).
31. Elwell (1860, 29–31).
32. Elwell (1860, 20–22, 25, 31).
33. De Ville (1990, 20–21).
34. De Ville (1990, 24).
35. Mohr (1993, 38–39, 111–16). Professional medical codes mitigated against a physician testifying on such matters. "Let it be distinctly understood that those individuals immediately implicated are entitled to the sympathy and assistance of as many of their professional brethren as may be necessary to sustain them. And where it is possible to avoid it, let not a member of the profession be found in the ranks of the prosecution"; The Ohio State Medical Code (1859), Elwell (1860, 9). Elwell himself offered what appears to be conflicting advice: the physician "is not to take into consideration the influence which his testimony may have on the prisoner at the bar" and "It is not proper for him to call in question the testimony of another witness . . . leaving the jury to judge of its credibility" (305). Medical witnesses were thereby

likely to be caught in conflicts that risked their own disgrace, situations in which they resorted to analogies and hypotheticals.

36. Ellwell (1860, 263).
37. Elwell (1860, 265–66).
38. Elwell (1860, 273).
39. Elwell (1860, 303).
40. Elwell (1860, 310).
41. Elwell (1860, 282).
42. Burns (1969b, 28).
43. Whitworth (27 April 1767).
44. As a term, "quack" was defined most fully in state medical society codes that emerged in the early 1800s; see Burns (1969b).
45. Woodruff (1779).
46. *The Boston Gazette and County Journal*, April 27, 1767.
47. McClelland (1877, 385); see Thomson (1843).
48. McClelland (1877, 388).
49. Mc Clelland (1877, 391).
50. Mc Clelland (1877, 389).
51. Mc Clelland (1877, 389).
52. Mc Clelland (1877, 390).
53. Mc Clelland (1877, 390).
54. De Ville (1990, 59).
55. De Ville (1990, 43).
56. De Ville (1990, 154).
57. De Ville (1990, 86).
58. De Ville (1990, 87). Whereas Rush was somewhat insulated legally, he did practice at the cusp of a move from social norms to legal order and at a time when being a regular physician had few advantages over being a quack. Indeed, quacks did not present as an elite, in either power or wealth, so that they appeared as one with the people and not as class enemies. Neither did they put themselves forward as professional experts, sponsor monopolistic practices, or have deep pockets as possible legal targets. They thereby presented to juries as participants in rather than enemies of a free market at a time when free markets were gaining in appeal. When malpractice suits began to proliferate, plaintiffs considered regulars more likely objects of suits partly because they elevated expectations of professional expertise and an agreed-upon standard of care against which they could be measured. Some procedures, like bloodletting, obstetrics, orthopedics had become so standard that they were regarded as mechanical treatments, constituting prime areas for potential malpractice suits (109–10).
59. Proof of malpractice, in any case, required evidence of wrongdoing in terms of the harm done to the patient's body. A fetus or a pregnant woman's death during delivery appeared, for example, self-evidently related to the medical care she received. It certainly presented a clearer presumptive cause of death than a predisposing condition attributed by a physician to the patient herself or attributed by clergy

to predetermination. Similarly, a disfigured or gangrenous limb provided an external sign of harm in the patient's body that could be taken as evidence of malpractice. With heroic treatments for yellow fever, by contrast, an autopsy had to be performed to discover the internal organic damage done by toxic mercury-based calomel and blood and fluid depletion. Living victims had to be taken at their word that they were harmed and could still be rebutted by a medical diagnosis of a condition that preexisted the physician's treatment and that had presumably predisposed the patient to the debility he claimed.

60. See Warner (1986).

61. Lowell (1825).

62. One judge in 1827 represented in a case before him that whereas some areas of medicine were "beset by great difficulties, the employment of a man midwife and surgeon for the most part, is merely mechanical, and therefore held to a higher standard of performance"; as quoted in DeVille (1990, 8–9). Mechanical it might have been, but such procedures were still sufficiently unpredictable that they could not serve as a platform for practice. Certainly, as in *Lowell v. Faxon and Hawks* (1824), the defense could argue that "The work of a physician is all tentative and experimental. . . . New observations and discoveries are continually enlarging the field and changing the instruments of professional power"; DeVille (1990, 16).

63. De Ville (1990, 111–13).

64. See Myrsiades (2009, 17–33).

65. De Ville (1990, 89).

66. See Myrsiades (2009, 77–115).

67. See Myrsiades (2009, 144–77).

68. Se Myrsiades (2009, 116–44).

69. Finger (2010, 48).

70. Finger (2010, 46).

71. That Rush's troubles with Cobbett did not differ significantly from such feuds suggests that Rush collected enemies indiscriminately. He made enemies of loyalists as a signer of the Declaration of Independence, of slaveholders with his antislavery sentiments, of federalists with his fervent republicanism, of other physicians with his support for William Cullen's theory of controversial taxonomy of diseases, John Brown's theory of the unity of diseases, and his own theory of excessive purging and bleeding. Rush was the first to admit that he paid a stiff price for his contentiousness, resulting in infrequent referrals of patients and few invitations to consult with other physicians. More importantly, his challenging behavior would more than once take him to the brink of a duel. In one celebrated instance, his son John challenged a presumed enemy of his father, Dr. Andrew Ross, to a duel and subsequently caned him. Ross challenged the elder Rush to meet him at a known time and place, which prompted Rush to swear a warrant against his challenger.

72. Peace bonds were, according to Rowe (1994), "a sum of money that the accused was required to guarantee in advance, and that would be forfeited if he or she carried out some explicitly forbidden act" (108). The supreme court used its considerable powers of discretion to ensure that even where an individual had been acquitted, he might be placed under a bond to secure future good behavior. Such a practice

was used against both the journalist Cobbett in the Yrujo case and Eleazer Oswald (240–41, 271).

73. Cobbett not only made the thin-skinned Rush a laughing stock among Cobbett's federalist friends who found Rush a convenient and welcome target, but his acts instigated Rush's hotheaded sons who took Rush's cause as their own; see Myrsiades (2009, 108–11).

74. See Carey (1799a; 1799b; 1942).

75. Carpenter (1800, 17).

76. Carpenter (1800, 19).

77. Carpenter (1800, 63).

78. *Rush-Light* IV, March 31, 1800; Cobbett (1801a, 11: 378).

79. Carpenter (1800, 17).

80. Carpenter (1800, 57).

81. Carpenter (1800, 49).

82. Langbein (2003, 8, 258, 261, 266).

83. Rush (1948, 99–105).

84. Rush (1948, 99).

85. Rush (1948, 101).

86. Myrsiades (2009, 77–115).

87. Rush (1948, 103).

88. Rush (1948, 103).

89. Carpenter (1800, 8).

90. March 5, 1800, Rush letter to Brockholst Livingston; Rush (1951, 2: 816). Ingersol's concern that his client's sensitivity to slights led him to rush into unnecessary litigation is repeated in correspondence between Rush and Livingston after the trial in which Rush makes clear he continued to want to see Cobbett confined and fined and asks Livingston to pursue Cobbett with two more suits, one for payment of the trial judgment and a second to silence him; Rush Manuscript, Historical Society of Pennsylvania (March 5, 1800, vol. 29, letter 82).

91. Rush Manuscript, Historical Society of Pennsylvania (December 25, 1799, vol. 29, letter 81).

92. Rush Manuscript, Historical Society of Pennsylvania (March 19, 1800, vol. 29, letter 84).

93. Rush Manuscript, Historical Society of Pennsylvania (March 5, 1800, vol. 29, letter 82).

94. Rush Manuscript, Historical Society of Pennsylvania (March 19, 1800, vol. 29, letter 84).

95. Rush Manuscript, Historical Society of Pennsylvania (March 8, 1800, vol. 29, letter 83).

96. Carpenter (1800, 19).

97. Carpenter (1800, 19).

98. Rush (1948, 23).

99. Rush (1948, 104–5).

100. Letter to Rush; Rush Manuscript, Historical Society of Pennsylvania (October 20, 1797, vol. 29, letter 80); see Clark (1939, 147).

101. Carpenter (1800, 12–13).

102. Rush was well informed about mental illness. He is given credit for establishing mental health care in America, at Pennsylvania Hospital, and wrote prominently about it as a leader in the field.

103. February 20, 1809, letter to John Adams; Rush (1951, 2: 995).

104. Included in a trove of letters from a Moravian woman who lived in Lititz, 1762–1804, written to her family in Wales and to Elizabeth Drinker of Philadelphia, an unpublished letter on deposit at the National Library of Wales sheds additional light on several of the questions raised by the trial. I am indebted for this lead to Scott Paul Gordon of Lehigh University who discovered the letter and was kind enough to share it. The writer acknowledges her friendship with Benjamin Rush, whom she refers to as "a valuable Friend of Mine," whose "Conversation was most Edifying," and who visited her several times upon her last visit to Philadelphia. She proceeds to provide an account of the trial in which Cobbett, as the reader must have heard, fled Pennsylvania because of the lawsuit. Cobbett's libels against Rush before the trial are described as "Pleasentries, which [Cobbett] in a vein of Levity wrote concerning [Rush]," suggesting that his audience took his earlier writings as a form of satire. The writer is clear that "His Sons it is, who have forced their Father to sue Cobbit," and that she believes Rush regretted having sued, as "could he recal what he has done, he would gladly give up half his estate." She offers that she can only pity the fact that so good a man as the doctor "should be brought before the world like a Spectacle!" As for Cobbett, his sin, the writer suggests, was "more for his being such a thorough English Man than for his Crime." Having been fined "a Sum Sufficient to ruin him," a fine that "the most impartial" felt "was too severe," Cobbett "has now dip'd his Pen in Gall, and knows no bounds in Retaliating on doctor Rush the Injury he supposes done him"; "being provoked he publishes the bost [*sic*] bitter Truths (for Cobbit is no Liar) his very Enemies acknowledge that." Apparently she considered that Cobbett's reputation for veracity made his latter writings the worse blow as they did "the Doctor more Injury, than the former Pasquils." The letter in question, dated May 23, 1800, and written by Mary Penry, is Item 1390 in the Penrally Collection, National Library of Wales.

3

William Cobbett and the Scurrilous Press

In 1755 the *Boston Gazette* made the claim that the press's role was "essential to and coeval with all free Governments,"[1] indeed that it was a fourth branch of government in its prerevolutionary role in the movement for freedom. Because the press had built up a backlog of public support that led to its being viewed "as a natural part of a democratic system,"[2] liberty, one could claim, was protected wherever the press was free. The press's support was nevertheless fragile, its role highly controversial, and its relations with the state in the new republic unstable. By the end of the century, Hugh Henry Brackenridge, a newly appointed Pennsylvania Supreme Court justice, would argue that presenting the press as a corrective to government excess was a subterfuge "to throw off the *law* altogether."[3] Editors, he contended, arraigned characters at their own bar in cases of libel, without an appeal to the courts, and thereby made the common law itself "a subject of *defamation.*"[4]

Newspapers only began to flourish with the growth in political parties in the 1790s,[5] so that the partisan press and political partisanship were harnessed together in the last decade of the eighteenth century. The success of the partisan press depended upon its irreverence, its use of ridicule and invective, its disregard of the personal status of those it attacked, and its skill at catering to the common reader. In all these aspects of eighteenth-century journalism, William Cobbett was a master. Mel Laracey contends that by 1800 the role that partisan newspapers played in American political development was critical and that they were "a fundamental part of American political life at the mass communication level,"[6] to the extent that Jefferson's election and the confirmation of that election in 1801 could be attributed to the republican press. Fundamental principles that would contribute to the national identity entered the public discourse through newspapers and became embedded as part of the American consciousness. Newspapers in that sense shaped public opinion in a purposeful way as Americans in the eighteenth century tended to rely upon newspapers to form their ideas, making it all the more problematic when irresponsible partisan journalism took precedence in public debate in the end of the nineties.[7]

The decade of the nineties would begin with the federalists in the ascendancy and end with the republicans ready to recoup power. Public opinion would become the coin of the realm as the century ended with power in the hands of a republicanism that stood for the people's right to call its government to account and with the Constitution, as republicans interpreted it, embracing the political authority of the people and a libertarian press. If, in Madison's words, public opinion was the "real sovereign,"[8] the people were in the position of influencing government and the press was in the position of exposing bad administration, the two together working toward the smooth functioning of democracy and sealing the connection between self-government and the press. With the repeal of the Sedition Act in 1802, and the verdict in *Rush v. Cobbett* just a memory, the First Amendment would be back in business.

At the center of the debate over private reputation, public criticism, and sedition, the partisan press played a critical role. Newspapers like Cobbett's *Porcupine's Gazette* provided the forum through which political ideas could be explored and conflicting alternatives negotiated. They did so in a way that could be said to have accelerated the development of a distinctive sense of Americanism, just as Jay's Treaty and the XYZ Affair defined the struggle for American nationality in the second half of the nineties.[9] It was not going to be enough to link the French Revolution to the American as a way of creating a transnational revolutionary identity into which Americanism could be fit. Nor would it be sufficient to frame colonial Anglo-Americanism as a continuing identity that linked America to an English identity. In fact the virulence of the debate over these nonconverging alternatives was to push advocates toward an American identity that was beholden to neither, a legacy politically indebted to strategizing that emphasized patriotism to defuse Francophile appeals.[10] The federalist embrace of a "national character that viewed American interests as fundamentally separate from European affairs" would appeal not only to federalists but to republicans who found it the better course to distance themselves from the French Reign of Terror.[11] With the radicalization of the French Revolution and France's declaration of war against England in 1793, Americans were torn between French and English appeals and threats which the new nation had to navigate.[12] British and French interference with American shipping unsettled the government while the French undermined the promise of the American

Revolution by flaunting the excesses of its own upheaval. Thus, from 1795 to 1798, an American identity was beginning to crystalize even as partisan newspaper attacks escalated and the Alien and Sedition Acts became law, raising the destabilizing prospect of a war with France and eventuating in the striking defeat of the Federalist Party in the 1800 elections.

Even as republicanism was busily impressing itself as the next political wave, federalists were so much in charge of the government in 1798 that, with the passage of the Alien and Sedition Acts, it became clear that a republican journalist was at risk of being accused of sedition merely if he registered objections to federal government policies or elected political figures. Indeed, passage of the acts appeared at one point to predict war against France, equating pro-French dissent with sedition.[13] Such an accusation was only made easier once the republicans switched from a federal to a state level of political activity, in effect conceding the success of such attacks. In Philadelphia, Francophobic attitudes were reinforced by such public events as a riot in early May as well as the immense crowds that greeted John Marshall's return from France, which signaled a diplomatic failure to reach agreement with the French.[14] As *Rush v. Cobbett* made clear, the Alien and Sedition Acts rankled Rush's republican counsel who made much of turning the accusation of sedition and the characterization of alien against the federalist Cobbett at a time when the possible overturn of the federalists in a national election made such turnabout very much fair play. The prosecution tactic was not entirely without risk. The election of a republican president was, after all, only a contentious possibility in a political scene in which civil war was threatened by some if a republican won and the dissolution of the union was posed in seriously threatening terms—comparable in its sense of political threat only to Lincoln's election in 1860.[15]

COBBETT AND THE PRESS

In the midst of the press wars and political uncertainties of the nineties, Cobbett's popularity as a member of the partisan press was such that it was not possible to ignore him without paying a heavy price. Enthusiastic assessments of Cobbett's status as the most widely read journalist of his times might not prove surprising coming from Cobbett biographers, but we find impressive confirmation of figures on his subscription base from historians. Cobbett's *Porcupine's Gazette* reached some three thousand readers at a time when the most important republican newspapers (Freneau's *National Gazette* at the beginning of the 1790s and Benjamin Franklin Bache's *General Advertiser* and, later, *Aurora*, in the late 1790s) peaked at 1,700.[16] At a time when the republican Fisher Ames was to contend that government itself was no match for the influence of newspapers (which "will first overawe and then usurp it"),[17] even those whom Cobbett attacked, like Joseph Priestly and James Callender, had to acknowledge his indisputable priority over other journalists.[18] Cobbett profited, of course, from the fact that in 1795 three-quarters of existing newspapers were sympathetic to the federalists and that among federalist editors he had no competition to speak of, not even the estimable Fenno of the *Gazette of the United States*.[19]

As a federalist, Cobbett profited from the influence the British faction was able to exert by using the church, courts, and entertainment as well as taverns and coffee houses to create public opinion, what one commentator referred to as the "Pulpit, the Press, the Bar and the Theatre,"[20] catching public opinion in the many places that it congregated. But when they tried to use the courts to emasculate the republican press, the federalists were not as lucky as they were elsewhere. Juries were initially reluctant to indict or convict, and the party suffered from accusations that the federalists did not honor the constitution's speech and press rights. Where the party had a nascent winning argument—its endorsement of neutrality amid pressures to join with the French or the English in their war with each other; its replacement of Anglophile and Francophile sentiments with themes of native American patriotism; and with its emphasis on stability rather than protest and revolution—Cobbett failed to follow the party's lead. When the party split over seeking an alliance with Britain in 1797 and creating a large standing army (which played into republican hands), Cobbett predictably stood with the English rather than taking an American perspective. In 1799, after the XYZ Affair and before the convening of his libel trial at the end of that year, reports appeared of his arrest for sedition for criticizing Adams's dispatch of a new diplomatic envoy to France.[21] During the debate over the Sedition Act of 1798, Cobbett, it seemed, had been so concerned that it might be applied to him if it passed that he "consulted a lawyer about its application in his case."[22] The irony was that Cobbett supported prosecution for seditious libel only so long as he was on the same side as Adams's administration.[23] The threat of deportation might in any case have been just that, a threat, but Adams had the ability to deport any alien he considered dangerous without trial under the Alien Act of 1798. The threat to Cobbett was even more persuasive once one considers that Cobbett was attacked for stirring up the public to civil war in 1798 by suggesting republicans were threatening secession.[24]

When it came to the Rush prosecution, Cobbett again felt that he was at the wrong end of privilege, in this case professional rather than political. The federalist editor John Fenno argued that the press was itself being "trampled under foot by groundless prosecutions" in what he called, referring to charges filed by Rush against him and Cobbett, an attempt to establish "a libertine medical tribunal." Because physicians used the press themselves to influence the public by attacking editors, a court trial was in one way a welcome relief which Cobbett's fellow federalist had "no doubt will complete the downfall of quackery and empiricism."[25] Fenno's complaint that doctors were themselves guilty of libel against and persecution of members of the press was taken up by Cobbett in his criticism of Dr. Coxe, one of the witnesses for Rush in the trial. Had Cobbett as a member of the press made statements like Coxe's, Cobbett claimed, he would have been "charged with the heinous charge of *degrading private character.*"[26] J. W. F., an anonymous contributor to the *Porcupine Gazette*,[27] felt as well that doctors should not be free to speak what in a journalist's mouth would have been a libel. A victim himself of a medical professional's ire, he directed his commentary to Dr. Caldwell in celebrating a peace bond served against the "assassin" who had "lately aimed a stab at my reputation" but who had now been deterred "solely through the fear of incurring the punishment of a contempt of court." Even doctors expressed their fears that their own tribe had gone too far. One doctor caught up in the doctors' wars[28] indicted the profession's "absurd publications" which had reduced medicine not only to "supporting a very dangerous practice," bleeding, but to endangering the profession itself: "In the list of misfortunes brought upon the city of Philadelphia by the prevailing epidemic, must be included the degradation of its medical character. Prior to the appearance of this formidable disease, the physicians of Philadelphia were esteemed the most eminent on the continent of America; they have since sunk from that state of exaltation to a condition bordering on contempt."[29] Another published notice took the controversy one step further, recommending the indictment not of editors but of members of the medical profession. The author announced himself prepared to give private satisfaction to "the gentleman alluded to" in his notice, who would, he was certain, remain undeterred "by continuing these murderous courses [of bleeding], by anything but a presentment from the Grand Jury."[30]

PORCUPINE AND STYLE

The construction of Cobbett as a danger to the republic was supported as much by his own self-presentation as by how the republican press or the medical establishment construed him. Indeed, the perception that he was evil incarnate was clearly helped along by the fact that he presented himself as without remorse, unregenerate, skillful, and arrogantly sure of his rightness, to the point that the figure that emerged from behind his language was that of a stock type of the stage villain.[31] Cobbett created crises as if they were made for him. A protean force in this regard, his ambiguous nature led to quick and subtle shifts of political position. His shifts were as much to be admired as abhorred for all that his opponents could neither anticipate nor easily defend against them. For this reason, he represented a threat for which there was no cure short of expelling him from Philadelphia, which Rush's team effectively accomplished by means of a punitive fine that put him out of business.

Cobbett was the traitor within, an enemy secreted in the bosom of the nation, working his poison directly into the national bloodstream. He was seen variously as a lightning rod for federalist discontent, then for monarchical restoration, and finally for idiosyncratic villainy. With the federalists at risk of being cast from power by the electorate, Britain discounted by diplomacy with France, and Cobbett accused of libel verging on sedition, treason had a new face and its name was Porcupine. The way was open for an outsized verdict against the journalist both in the jury box and among those of the reading public. The judgment was definitive even among Americans who still felt some allegiance and loyalty to Britain since the memory of treason as it applied to the crown was a poor contender against American nationalism and republican honor and virtue.[32] Cobbett made the choice an easy one by his vitriolic performance in the press. Rejection of Cobbett provided another opportunity to define patriotism and nationalism oppositionally, making him the model of bad manners, antirepublican virtue, and poor citizenship. A verdict against Cobbett was a verdict that demystified the monster. It made sense as an expression of republican sensibility and was justified as well by a providential endorsement expelling the snake from the new Eden; in expelling Cobbett, America proved it was worthy. Religion came in handily where the yellow fever epidemic could be inserted, with its religious fiction of apocalypse, millennialism, and jeremiad. In this disaster, Cobbett was easily cast as the Satan who must be banished, Rush as the martyred Christ, and public welfare the prize that would be redeemed.

Cobbett's reinforcement of the hyperbolic characterization expressed in the republican press and in the prosecution's case in *Rush v. Cobbett* was clearly linked to his prowess as a writer. Scott Howell makes the point that Cobbett's strength lay in his ability to remain close to his subject, to provide unique responses, and to offer specific, particular versions of events. Unconcerned with inconsistency, Cobbett focused on exciting the sensibilities and reaching for the visceral. His writing was extemporaneous and hardly "intellectually neat and tidy."[33] He refused to adhere to arcane rules of grammar and found them an elitist instrument that marginalized vulgar voices. His powerful writing spoke for those without the skill to express themselves effectively, largely commoners without influence.[34] Cobbett thus developed a populist rhetoric that proved a form of "intellectual vernacular,"[35] prose that had a muscular quality and appealed to a wide band of readers who were unimpressed with classical knowledge or forms and who relished a less educated American approach to things. His writing as a result was often referred to as biting, full of ridicule, wit, and invective, shocking and direct. In his own times, he was routinely accused of black-guardism and "billingsgate"[36] language to indicate the depths to which he would descend in attacking his enemies. There was no question that he intended to proselytize rather than to pursue a pristine form of ideological politics and that he was willing to do so as much by satire, sophistry, and personal attack as by addressing an issue.

Karen List makes the point that Cobbett had developed his own journalistic style, one that was unabashedly partial and blunt and that would read as his readers might have spoken. "His language," she claims, "was simple and incisive, his prose strong and clear."[37] Spirited and energetic, his prose has been qualified as "democratic," that is, colloquial and with a ring to it of common sense and practical logic.[38] As Leonora Nattrass puts it, his language was a good fit for his intent, which was to be read as "transgressive and politically enabling," a style, she contends, that might explain his success with the audience he addressed.[39] But Cobbett's style did not end with purely populist, partisan wrangling, for his whole approach to content suggested a broader fit with a species of millennial writing that bemoaned the degeneracy of his times.[40] Given the prevalence of apocalyptic sermonizing in America and its jeremiadic proclivities, both in terms of divine prophecy and political vision, this aspect of his styles was an easy fit with American tastes. Cobbett's nostalgia for America's prerevolutionary colonial condition and for the days of Britain's Magna Carta, that is, for "some mythical prior state of social harmony," has been described as a search for a time before the "political Fall."[41] It was a time before disruptive "republican" progress, before destabilizing democratic experiments, French influence, and international revolution. Cobbett's conservative way back to one's forefathers was clearly not the way back that the republicans imagined. On the other hand, it shared in common with the republican view a sense of decline from a golden age, of a better time before men ceased living up to the great deeds of their progenitors. What Cobbett did not anticipate, however, was how that sense of declension would be spun by the prosecution against him in *Rush v. Cobbett*. Nor did he anticipate how elite rhetoric tied to classical and biblical forms and allusions would rise up to assign him the role not of a transgressive and politically enabling force for colloquial speech but of a regressive and oppressive alien voice that would reverse the course of the American Revolution and cast down the Puritans' beloved image of America's shining city on the hill.

In *Rush v. Cobbett*, Cobbett's lawyer Edward Tilghman had set the defense standard for his client's satirical writings. Cobbett, he asserted, practiced the art of ridicule, a standard that "is surely the test of truth,"[42] to which Rush's counsel Jared Ingersol responded that ridicule was itself a form of untruth and that Cobbett's artful ingenuities were no more than to render truth a *ridicule*."[43] Setting a prosecution standard, Ingersol associated ridicule with the arch-deism of Shaftesbury, for whom ridicule represented a subterfuge for attacking Christianity "driven from the field of *Reason* and *Argument*."[44] Heaven's gospel, Ingersol argued, is itself made ridiculous "by distorting its sense, and by partial representations." The prosecution even posed its own test to reveal untruth: if the sheep is exposed for the wolf; "if the veil is seen through" and the "'cloven foot' discovered."[45] Motivated by intent to make sport of and thereby to diminish a man's reputation, the prosecution's case argued, ridicule met the standard of malice set by Blackstone.[46] Should they be represented as "*Stuff, Nonsense and Ribaldry*,"[47] the prosecution considered that malicious publications like Cobbett's were then in truth ingenious efforts of the "most severe, atrocious and indecent personal abuse"[48] and thereby more dangerous than open attacks. Lest Cobbett's "equivocal ambiguous stile" and insinuation merely cast suspicion and appear innocuous, the prosecution was prepared in the alternative to argue that the "assassination malevolence"[49] of which Hopkinson spoke and the meanness and "*cool deliberate malice*"[50] spoken of even by defense counsel were even more to be feared.

TRIAL BY PRESS SATIRE

Cobbett's satiric accusations against Rush were thus taken as a true trial by press, a way of pillorying a public figure by ridiculing him in a court of public opinion that was every bit as humiliating as conviction in a court of law. Satires might have served as messages warning members of the community that some threat was imminent, but to respond by filing a suit was as good as to recognize oneself in the satirist's depiction[51] and to acknowledge that some found one in need of correction, exposure, or comment. Responding not only gave substance to attacks but implied fear and suggested possible guilt. It raised questions of whether one might not have actually violated some community norm or value such that some witness raised a complaint, positing the colloquial possibility that smoke indicated fire. Printing his satires might thus have risked a libel suit for Cobbett, but it was no more a risk than the risk Rush ran if he took Cobbett to court. For Rush to succeed, he would need a judge who identified with potential targets of press abuses and a jury that represented readers who were themselves offended by the satires.

Satire had itself over the course of the eighteenth century become a prevalent way of addressing abuses by political figures. The successful verdict for the publisher Peter Zenger in his trial in 1735 had stimulated the public appetite for political satires of public officials and made it less likely that a politician would prosecute libel.[52] It made juries more open to satire as a way of correcting public officials and left public figures who proceeded to prosecute the press vulnerable to juries operating as public surrogates in trying the trial that "tried" the trial by press. Alison Olson regards the process as one in which press humor, a mixture of satire and journalism, was performed by the defense before the jury as a public audience.[53] As in *Rush v. Cobbett*, little evidence exists of how juries arrived at their decisions or the roles they believed themselves to be playing. But it is clear that in many ways press satire focused the jury's, as well as the public's, attention on certain values, that it targeted a public figure for violating those values, and that it demonstrated the possibility of using humor to expose and correct public figures. Moreover, it flourished since before the Revolution,[54] commonly operated under the color of a trial by press, and was expected to perform the role of a balance to government excess. It did so under the pretense that the press performed the positive role of giving a voice to the people who themselves acted as a jury for the press.

PORCUPINE'S PRINTS

Cobbett's self-presentation was transmitted not only through the verbal print medium but in visual print culture which fleshed out even more fully his already high profile. Two prints in particular proved of special interest: a caricature of Peter Porcupine from 1796 by M. L. E. Moreau de Saint Mery and a print from 1798 on a congressional feud, again including the figure "Porcupine." Moreau, a Philadelphia printer, printed the first caricature in the midst of a pamphlet war in 1796.[55] Cobbett described the scene in a letter to his father: "half a dozen *Doctors* or the devil knows what" and ten times more printers came "bustling, running and flying about in all directions to announce my fame to the impatient public."[56] It was a scene he relished as the attention he received was bound to enhance his already burgeoning reputation.[57] His competitors attacked Cobbett with claims that he had just escaped hanging in England and imprisonment in France when he arrived in America[58] and accused him of being an agent in the pay of the British government, which was meant to explain his pro-British position on political issues. The irony of Cobbett's situation was apparently lost on his enemies for far from being reflexively pro-British, he had been a critic of English government while in England; although he had gone to France as a friend of its antimonarchical politics, he became a rabid Francophobe once in that country. Entering America as a republican, and having petitioned Thomas Jefferson for a job, he was, similarly, to position himself as an English monarchist and to become a pariah in the eyes of French-leaning American democrats. If anything, Cobbett had to be taken on his own terms as American federalists were to discover to their chagrin. They would, in the end, try to provoke President Adams into using newly passed Alien and Sedition Acts, designed to restrain republicans, to chase their old federalist ally Cobbett out of the country. It would take the republicans in a subsequent legal effort—the *Rush v. Cobbett* trial—to make good on the federalist threat.

As for the caricature by Moreau, Cobbett provides, with just a hint of tongue in cheek, perhaps the best interpretation of its intent:

> This is a caricature, in which I am represented as urged on to write by my old master King George (under the form of a crowned lion), who, of course, comes accompanied by the devil. The *Jay*, with the treaty in his beak, is mounted on the lion's back, though, by the by, it has ever been said, by the democrats, that the lion rode the *Jay*. His Satanic Majesty holds me out a bag of money, as an encouragement to destroy the idol, liberty, to which he points. The American Eagle is represented as drooping his wings in consequence of my hostility, and America herself on the same account, weeps over the bust of Franklin. This is almost the only part of the print of which I find fault; for, if by America the people of America be [sic] to be understood, I believe most of those who have read my essays will do me the justice to say, that I have endeavoured to make America laugh instead of weep.—As to myself, I am the hero of the piece, I am brought forward to the front of the stage, where the artist makes me trample upon *Randolph's Defence*, the *Rights of Man*, Old *Common Sense*, *Madison, Gallatin*, *Swanick*, and *Peter Pindar*. How this blundering fellow came to place *Pindar* among the rest I cannot imagine. It discovers a total ignorance of that author's writings and of my opinion concerning them.[59]

As the source of the print, Moreau was presented by Cobbett as a degraded exhibitor of "poor miserable catch-penny pictures," a man "cursed with the scribbling itch, without knowing how to scratch himself with a good grace."[60] Cobbett pictured Moreau as one who, knocking down Bastilles, aspired to legislate for the universe and scorned to yield to monarchs. Inconceivably lowering himself to wage "a puny *underhand* war" with one of King George's poor foot soldiers, Moreau had done no more than to perform a cartoon trick for the "Goddess of *French* Liberty."[61] Moreau responded in his notes on an American journey, exposing a clear distaste for Cobbett's style of writing, his politics, and his ability to change his stripes. Despite his wit, Cobbett was reduced to a wrongheaded, if genuine, fanatic in Moreau's book, a man who utterly scorned Americans and was, above all others, "violently attached to his native country."[62]

The caricature deserves an extended reading, if for no other reason than to capture the spirited nature of Cobbett's interactions with his peers, but even more so for its ability to offer a window into the irreverence with which American politics was treated by the press, an attitude much complained about by the prosecution team in *Rush v. Cobbett*. The caricature provides a sepia-tinted portrait of the porcupine whose legend, leaving little to the imagination, confirms Moreau's view of Cobbett: "See Porcupine in Colours just Portray'd,/Veil'd in darkness, acts the assassin's part,/And triumphs much to stab you to the heart." The porcupine fully extends his quills as he spews forth slips of paper bearing the names of those he attacks (the republicans Gallatin, Swanick, and Madison, among others), alongside statements that "These have too much merit" and "I Hate this country & will sow the seeds of discord in it." The porcupine is goaded on by the triad of the royal lion ("Go on dear Peter, my friend & I will reward you," a reference to accusations that Cobbett was in the pay of the English government), the jay that rides him ("Treaty of amity and Commerce 1795," referring to the federalist Jay's Treaty with England during the latter's hostilities with France), and their satanic acolyte ("More scandal, let us destroy this Idol liberty," which together with the devil's offer of a bag of gold supports the English king's presumed offer of a bribe). The distraught female figure of liberty, to which the devil points, paired with a drooping eagle clutching a pole topped by a French-style cap, prostrates herself over a pedestal-mounted image of Benjamin Franklin, American emissary to France from 1776 to 1785. Draped around the base are scraps reading, "1500 Ame'n seamen Impres'd by british," "No navy!!," "600 ships adjudicated," "Lost neutrality," and "Treaty with France 1778." Indicating the counter position, to that posited by the opposed figures of the lion and company, the scraps point to British impressment of seamen and seizure of ships, arguments against a standing navy, and an alignment with the French which deprived America of neutrality in the hostilities between England and France. The figure of the porcupine thus appears to be posed in a mediating position between French and British factions, suggesting one federalist view that expressed patriotic American rather than Francophilic sentiments. At the same time, it is clear that the sentiments pouring forth from the porcupine's own mouth are less artful and more clearly hostile. Indeed, buried beneath a striped flag at the feet of the lion are the darkened features of the Magna Carta and two other treaties, collateral damage that does not speak well for likely conciliation. Moreau presents us, in sum, with the kind of confusion, indeed chaos, with which many credited Cobbett in his writings.

Cobbett's remarks about the caricature raise some interesting questions. The jay, for example, rides the lion, as Cobbett pointed out, rather than the lion riding the jay. Politically, discussion around Jay's Treaty had it that Britain was calling the shots in that negotiation and that America had signed a bad treaty. In that sense, the "jay" could not be said to have ridden the lion, although visually it might have proved implausible to represent the lion in the dominant position. Equally, Cobbett's contention that the devil acted the role of a "Satanic Majesty" gives the devil more than his due for the devil's role as a sidekick to the lion-King is more on the order of a prime minister than a majesty. The reference to liberty as an idol takes us back to Cobbett's attacks on America's infatuation with international revolution, the result of American liberation from its status as a British colony and republican support for the French Revolution. Cobbett vociferously objected to the American contention that it had not merely freed itself from Britain but that it was a freer country than the motherland. His position was always that democracy represented the tyranny of mob-ocracy and that monarchy offered more protected freedoms, in particular a freer press.

The tears America sheds in the caricature over Franklin's bust reflects what Cobbett felt was a dangerous attachment on the part of the American public for the memory of Franklin. Cobbett had no good thoughts for Franklin, a sentiment that partially explained his ongoing feud with the *Aurora*, the press of the latter's grandson Benjamin Franklin Bache. Even so, he considered that America would laugh rather than weep at Cobbett's words, relying upon the widely held opinion that his success in America was the result of his satiric humor. Cobbett was unafraid to rely upon his readers, who, he was certain, would do him justice in admitting his words touched them, though at the very basest level of "billingsgate" humor. That he found fault with this one aspect of the caricature is no more than to say that Cobbett presented himself publicly as savoring his role of attack dog and that he openly exposed himself to the contempt of those he injured. Centered in the skirmish, Cobbett took it that he was, as he said, "the hero of the piece," rather than merely a target, and thereby a man willing to take on all comers.

Leonora Nattrass, in her study of the politics of Cobbett's style, speaks of Moreau's caricature as a reaction to Cobbett's ability to entertain his readers at the expense of his enemies. His use of ludicrous insults and tongue-in-cheek extravagance to libel his enemies in the tradition of Jonathan Swift, to whom he felt himself indebted,[63] suggested, she contends, that "however damaging and extreme his invective, the function of his comic attacks is not to reveal truths." Nor was he writing merely to collude with his readers or build a relationship. He was, rather, using humor to challenge and subvert, "to seduce readers into *traitorous* laughter, treacherously at the expense of their own beliefs."[64] Cobbett's style explained in this regard not only the virulence of the responses he elicited from his enemies but the recklessness with which he proceeded in provoking public opinion, disorienting his political allies, and libeling public figures who posed a danger to political values he had fixed upon. All of these features of Cobbett's performance in the political arena would come home to roost in the *Rush v. Cobbett* trial.

While Cobbett was waiting for the Rush trial to be called, a second print of interest was published illustrating Cobbett's continuing attacks on republicans and republicanism. In the print in question, Porcupine promises to pursue the republican congressman from Vermont, Matthew Lyon. Several prints in 1798 caricatured the feud between Lyon and congressman Roger Griswold of Connecticut which ended on the floor of Congress with Griswold cudgeling Lyon with a cane and Lyon responding with a pair of tongs. One such print is titled "Cudgeling as by Late Act of Congress."[65] In another, titled "Congressional Pugilists," the battle takes place in front of a framed image of two dogs facing off, which is itself titled "Royal Sport," a reference to the popular view of Congress as an elitist institution. A piece of doggerel is attached at the bottom of the print, which reads: "He who in a trice struck Lyon twice/Upon his head, enrag'd Sir/Who seiz'd the tongs to ease his Wrongs/And Griswold thus engag'd Sir."[66]

As far as Cobbett was concerned, it was always open season on republicans, but Lyon proved a particularly inviting target, if only because he came out "spitting." As it turned out, Lyon had been cashiered as a lieutenant in General Gates's army following a cowardly retreat of his detachment in battle. He was trailed, as a result, by a questionable war record as well as a deadly rumor that the general had forced him to wear a wooden sword when he was drummed out of camp.[67] Lyon's extreme Jeffersonian republicanism as both a journalist and then a congressman led Griswold to taunt him about the wooden sword incident, which Lyon met by spitting in his face. Accounts of a proposed duel, which Griswold side-stepped, and a subsequent trial, in which Lyons was convicted of sedition[68] for an item he had published, kept the feud alive in the press throughout the year.

In the print in which Porcupine is featured, a clear distinction is made between the federalist Griswold—suited up in gentleman's dress and waving a handkerchief—and the republican Lyon—featured as a figure of a lion showing his claws, "girded with *a wooden sword*,"[69] and trampling upon a scroll labeled "A Ve. . . . t Politness." Porcupine sits at Griswold's feet, his quills in full flower, crying out "My quills shall pierce & my press shall black" in response to Griswold's "What a beastly action." The reactive federalist depends upon the surrogacy of his pet to respond to the beast, whereas the beast stands alone ripe for battle, a popular image of the difference between the two party positions. The republican press gave Lyon the edge in the bout, with the Connecticut paper *Bee* arguing that "Federalist barking against 'the Lyon' was echoed by '*curs*' . . . but the king of beasts laughed 'their vain attempts to scorn'."[70] *Carey's United States Recorder* in Philadelphia imagined the federalists crouching "like Spaniels" before the British lion even as they cried out to punish the "American Lyon."[71]

Cobbett took it as his mission to correct the republican press's version of events, particularly that of Bache's *Aurora*, by providing a "more correct statement of the fact."[72] Parodying the pseudorefinement of the congressional committee assigned to enforce the behavioral rules of the legislative body, Cobbett expressed the public's anxiety over "whether it was tobacco-juice, or natural saliva, that the Honourable Matthew Lyon, Esq. squirted into the face of his brother Legislator."[73] In the following month's edition of *Porcupine's Gazette*, he addressed the "Lyon in Congress" in terms of his choice of venue, concerned that "no man of any description was ever before known to *spit in another's face*, except in some dirty grog-shop or blackguard brothel."[74] Using such language as the "violent attack and gross indecency," the "filthy conduct of this spitting hero" and "*the man of spittle*," Cobbett proposed to memorialize "the whole business as notorious as the courage of Alexander, or the cruelty of Nero" by republishing the record every fortnight so long as he published, whether it be fifty years or more.[75] Cobbett continued to remind the public that Lyon "while the House was in actual session, *spit* the nauseous slime from his jaws into the face of ROGER GRISWOLD" and that in justifying himself, he did 'utter these word: 'kicked in the *arse*,' meaning the posteriors or hinder parts."[76] Refusing to let go of the gift that kept on giving,[77] Cobbett went into detail in subsequent issues about the dueling congressmen's comic-heroic engagement with "thick hickory stick" and tongs and the "shower of blows, such as never fell on the devoted hide of Don Quixote or his incontinent steed Rozinante."[78] With such matters he passed his time until the trial would be called.

PRESS FEUDS

Cobbett's effect on his American hosts was as clearly fed by his feuds with other journalists as it was by engaging with people like Moreau and Lyons and with powerful public figures like Rush, McKean, Edmund Genet, Joseph Priestly, and John Adams. The flurry of attacks that flew among journalists involved such figures as the republicans Philip Freneau, Mathew Carey, and Eleazer Oswald as well as the federalists Cobbett and Fenno. Carey, for example, published a poem, *The Plagi-Scurriliad* (1786), dedicated satirically to "our right-truly, well-beloved and long-adopted son," Oswald, that illustrated the kind of mutual recriminations exchanged among members of the press, in this case between fellow republicans. The poem—set in the Court of Pandemonium in which "their majesties, DETRACTION, SCURRILITY, and DULLNESS"[79] reigned—advised Oswald to make certain he never told the truth when a lie would serve as well and that he regard all things fair in seeking his fortunes in war.[80] Should anyone protest by asserting his innocence,

> 'Gainst such poltroons—such dastardly fellows,
> Who're only fit to grace the gallows,
> Swear fiercely you will crack his pate,
> And must have vengeance soon or late.[81]

With this advice, Carey launched the libelous Oswald into battle. Should his lies be found out, Carey advised, Oswald could always fall back on a challenge to a duel or continuous warfare, leaving him no worse off than before; should he win, he delayed the day he would be exposed.

Joining the fray, Philip Freneau construed Oswald as an irresistible force of nature that would ultimately blow itself out, but not before he gave pause to anyone bold enough to challenge his slurs. Freneau recommended ignoring Oswald's barbs and resting on one's reputation, for the world knew the knave for what he was and the afterworld was poised to damn him:

> Should Oswald's scribblers call you all that's base,
> Abuse your stature and blaspheme your face,
> Make you the worst and vilest of your kind,
> With not one spark of reason in your mind,
> Who would to Oswald's rancorous page reply,
> So fam'd for scandal, and so prone to lies?[82]

Under the constant threat of being charged with libel, Carey would complain that publishers were charged with libel as often by those who made such charges from wickedness as by those whose motive was "to keep beggary and starvation from the door."[83] Unrepentant publishers were, on the other hand, careful to keep open a back door of self-justifying counterattacks so that they might creep out from under "the penalties of the law against libelers."[84] A publisher had several options. The most instinctive was to meet slander with slander or redress an attack by means of the cudgel, with the option of hiring help to administer an assault. Carey expressed his own fear that he might be marked out in this way by some "such lurking assassins as [his competitor] might employ, or as might employ him."[85] In his feud with Cobbett, Carey was in fact threatened with assault for a libel Cobbett feared he might publish. For his part, Cobbett was depicted wincing "at the *lex talionis*," the tooth for a tooth retaliation of a truly free press.[86] Anxious to avoid a duel—a likely outcome as Carey's feud with Oswald demonstrated and Cobbett's reputation threatened—Carey claimed "a decent regard for the laws of the state"[87] in refusing Cobbett's challenge. Carey felt he had been libeled by "the Grub-street Gazette" (referring to London's Grubb Street journalists)[88] and that he had proper grounds for a court action. Cobbett's intention, he was firmly convinced, was clearly to blacken his fame and injure him in his business.[89] Carey's duty was thus "to bring the question fully and fairly before a court of justice"[90] in a suit for damages. Only the inefficiency of the law and his lack of confidence in the law held him back: "Poor satisfaction to be derived from dancing attendance in courts, to have perhaps a few hundred dollars decreed, after an expence of time worth probably double the amount!"[91]

Determined to try his case in the press, Carey published his correspondence with Cobbett in a pamphlet called *Plum Pudding*. Cobbett reciprocated with a literal gift of "plum pudding," plates of venison and jelly which his servant carried to Carey's print shop. Carey responded by dispatching a six-foot Irishman to Cobbett's store with directions to drop the plates in the middle of the floor and "to be ready to defend himself in the event of aggression."[92] At this point, Robert Goodloe Harper, Cobbett's lawyer, attended Carey with three members of Congress in tow. Carey reported the scene:

> "I understand you have been giving it to Cobbett," to which Carey answered, "I have treated him in his own style. I have no idea of fighting a man with a small sword, who has a wheelbarrow full of brickbats to knock my brains out. I have given him brickbat for brickbat." After some further conversation, "give me," says he, "a copy; for I like to read *all these blackguard things*." Irritated by this rudeness, I said, "then, sir, you must like to read your own speeches, for by—*they are among the most blackguard things that have appeared in this country*." He bit his lip, changed colour, and appeared undetermined whether or not to knock me down, which he could readily have done. At length, he walked off quietly, with tarnished laurels.[93]

In his *Autobiography*, Carey referred to his feud with Cobbett as having its origins in "[s]ome sorry scribblers, who did not dare to attack him themselves, [and] strove to embroil us together."[94] Jostled toward a duel, as he said, like Jolter and Pallet in Smollett's *Peregrine Pickle*, Carey saw himself and Cobbett as "both consummate cowards, [who] to prevent them from running away . . . [were] pushed towards each other."[95] Carey admitted he was fully aware of the power of Porcupine's pen, of "the great influence [Cobbett] had on public opinion—and the danger of his injuring me in my business and in my standing in society."[96] Moreover, he felt justified in refusing to engage his better-positioned opponent in physical combat, citing in a letter to Cobbett "the inequality arising from a disparity of strength and size, and from my lameness. . . . Arms have been your trade for years. I have never drawn but two triggers in my life. Here, therefore, the inequality returns, though not in so great a degree."[97] In his effort to resist dueling, Carey resorted to a code of honor defense by means of which a gentleman may not duel with a posted coward, that is, a man who, like Cobbett, had previously declined a duel. Carey argued that challenging a man who "when he was called to account for his villainy hen-heartedly took refuge under the strong arm of the law, and swore his life against the challenger, would sink me almost to a level with yourself."[98]

Carey chose, rather, to publish a satiric poem, *The Procupiniad*,[99] the title of which slyly referenced Cobbett's *Porcupine's Gazette*. It was only his second foray into the world of scurrilous poetry. The first, the *Plagi-Scurrliad*, had appeared some thirteen years earlier and ended in a duel in which Oswald shot Carey in the thigh. The possibility of a serious outcome was apparent here as well, for, as Carey noted, "it is not improbable his friends may oblige me to call once more on them for assistance."[100] Directed against Cobbett's otherwise unstoppable pen, going public with *The Porcupiniad* constituted a trial by press, public exposure, and punishment in an effort to isolate Cobbett as an outsider and as a threat to a nation that had only newly liberated itself from foreign tyranny:

> From Britain's isle our hero came,
> In quest of fortune, pow'r, and fame;
> Was hither by the premier sent,
> To dictate to our government—
> Our state affairs to regulate,
> And Britain's cause to advocate:
> Columbia's sons to fill with ire—
> Our public councils to inspire
> Old mother country's wrongs to feel;
> In her defence to sharp the steel,
> And make to heav'n the last appeal:
> Our forces muster against France,
> And in the cause of kings advance:
> To fight the battles of the Lord,
> To propagate his holy word,
> And spread the gospel with the sword: . . .
>
> Nor even Satan's horrid self,
> Did e'er breathe more infernal rage,
> Than he has shown, through ev'ry page
> Of his vile writings. A fierce flood
> Will pour abroad, of human blood,
> In civil war, if this curst knave
> Our morals longer can deprave.[101]

Cobbett had by this time been charged by Rush with libel and was awaiting prosecution in the trial, which would not be held until nine months after the poem was published. Carey might well have intended to influence the proceedings by alerting the public to the threat of a fearmongering agent of the English king. Indeed, Carey published a witness's deposition[102] that accused Cobbett of damning Americans in their struggles with the British. Cobbett had presumably used the words "no curse bad enough can happen to them, for their infamous declaration of independence; but I hope soon to see the two countries united again." The witness then added that Cobbett had "damned this deponent for an English rebel."[103] Anticipating the alien-sedition argument that Rush's lawyers were to raise against Cobbett in the trial, Carey's feud with Cobbett reflected the temper of the times and informed the pool of communal knowledge from which the jury would feed as it rendered its swift verdict only two hours after deliberation. Public print exchanges like those that occurred among journalists were intended to influence public opinion as well as any likely case that might follow, including the prosecution presented against Cobbett. That Cobbett was engaged in press wars with fellow journalists, attacked private reputations, and made subversive remarks about the new republic had indeed constituted a persuasive line of argument against the English journalist's reputation. His contentious personal history as a man who provoked private vengeance and thereby breached the public peace constituted a second line. The third, and possibly most damaging, line was his posture as a figure of the alien, an English fifth columnist intent on reversing the American Revolution. These three themes would inform the Rush legal team's attack on Cobbett and would prove resonant with its American jury, a local jury of citizens taking responsibility for its neighbors and asserting the welfare of its neighborhood.

COBBETT'S ATTACKS ON RUSH

Confluent with Cobbett's press feuds, the newspaper attacks on Benjamin Rush that instigated the civil action against Cobbett reflected a controversy that had embroiled the entire medical community in doctors' wars that compromised both medical authority and the confidence of the public in the medical profession. The attacks occurred in the midst of a yellow fever epidemic in 1797 that afflicted the city just as John Adams began his presidency (1797–1801), taking over the reins of power from George Washington. The city was still reeling from the devastating epidemic of 1793, just four years earlier, when George Washington's administration fled the capital city and left it to the management of a volunteer citizens' committee and a handful of physicians—among the latter the redoubtable Rush—who cared for the sick and supported a fever hospital at Andrew Hamilton's commandeered Bush Hill mansion. Rush had in 1793 aggressively promulgated a presumed fever cure that divided physicians over its extremism and its efficacy, a cure that would resurface in 1797 with equally divisive effects. Nurses, carters, and gravediggers hired from the black community by the citizens committee and trained by Rush to bleed and purge the sick were accused of exploiting the sick even as physicians were accused of quackery, casting doubt on those managing the disaster. Such attitudes transferred to the epidemic in 1797, once again with Rush at the forefront of medical management of the fever.

In his attacks, Cobbett was especially harsh on what he considered profiteering by physicians during the epidemic, citing Rush's associate Dr. Michael Leib, to whom he referred as a "new-born son of Esculapius," the Greek patron of physicians. His comments focused on what was considered a particularly cogent sign of abuse, the use of a horse and chair. Leib, a representative in the state legislature, had been provided with a horse and chair by the Board of Health[104] to allow him to tend to his patients. As Rush had argued in 1793, such transportation was critical to the welfare of doctors: "It would be an act of great humanity to the city to provide all the physicians and bleeders with horses and chairs, as it will be impossible for them long to escape the disease while they are so much predisposed to it by constant fatigue."[105] The public nevertheless protested that when such privileges "are not to be got for certificates," it was an ill wind that "raised Doctor Leib from the dirt into a one horse chair."[106] Carriages became targets of protest from the inhabitants of Germantown who, objecting to the favoritism Leib received, treated him like doctor death:

> a horrid *grinning* monster,
> With steed raw bon'd and lash tremendous;
> Driving his chariot wheels o'er smiling Peace
> And rosy Health. And spreading all around
> Terror, anguish, and despair.[107]

Rush himself, for all that many called him the "father of medicine, the great philanthropist," as the journalist John Fenno complained, was not only one of those bleeders who drove their young apprentices "about the city in their chariots, shedding blood wherever they go," but had upgraded his "Equipage of Death" to a two-horse version as he, too, thrived on the yellow fever:

> When hungry *Death* was scarce of food,
> It drove a shabby horse and chair;
> But now he's gorg'd with *human blood*,
> He rattles in a chaise and pair.[108]

In "A Hard Case," Cobbett partnered physicians he believed flourished during the time of fever with undertakers of the dead, who had themselves been criticized for overcharging desperate patrons. Indeed, an ad in Andrew Brown's *Philadelphia Gazette* for cabinets for the dead explicitly linked the two through Rush: "Mr. Brown's customer is said to be in partnership with *Dr. Rush*; or, at least, the joiner is said to have entered into a contract with the Doctor; according to which, the latter is to receive twenty dollars for every one of his patients for whom the former furnishes a coffin."[109] Bleeders, Cobbett argued, were the worst offenders and the death industry's most industrious suppliers:

> Once a bleeder, to death dealing practice imur'd,
> As he always *kil'd* twenty for one that he cur'd.
> To a grave digger said, passing through the churchyard;
> "So, friend, I perceive you're at work very hard."
> "Hard indeed," says old Delve, "here I toil ev'ry day,
> And can scarcely get suction to moisten my clay:
> Nay, double work rarely subsistence procures,
> Tho' while going my own, I am *finishing yours.*"[110]

Cobbett sealed the connection of bleeding and death in citing the words of Boileau to a physician, a Dr. Perrault, to the effect that

> You say, then, you blood-sucking elf,
> That you've been our physician all round!
> I swear that you ne'er bled myself,
> And the proof is—*I'm yet above ground.*[111]

The cumulative imagery of carriages, bleeding, and death suggested a picture of Rush riding about in privilege with his acolytes amidst the carts, hearses, and litters that clogged the streets bearing the sick and dying. An anonymous author associated such doctors with the quackery of the vulgar rich who advertised their remedies and sold curative powders,[112] while Cobbett linked them to the French since the carriages that enabled them "to drive themselves into practice were painted in the French style."[113]

Sangrado the Bleeder

Cobbett's most resounding blow in the dispute with Rush was his association of the physician with Sangrado, an infamous fictional bleeder in Alain Rene Le Sage's work *The Adventures of Gil Blas of Santillane* (1735), a work that first appeared in English in Tobias Smollett's popular translation in 1749. Cobbett's use of the term Sangrado to skewer Rush did not occur in a vacuum. The term had a history in English sources from at least 1742 when Henry Fielding referred to Sangrado in *Joseph Andrews* as a doctor who "used his patients as a vintner doth his wine-vessels, by letting out their blood, and filling them up with water."[114] Le Sage's English translator, Smollett, had his title character in *Peregrine Pickle* (1751) treated by a "disciple of Sangrado" who "scarce left a drop of blood in my body."[115]

In 1756, Joseph Warton, in an essay on Pope, referred to Le Sage's creation as a figure "who have indeed been the object of almost every satirist,"[116] an indication of how widely spread knowledge of the bleeder-quack had become over the twenty-one years since Le Sage's work first appeared in Spain. In 1777, James Beattie satirized Sangrado in an essay designed to separate truth and skepticism. Beattie contended that the connection that linked truth to skepticism was as simpleminded as Sangrado concluding that good health causes distemper since being healthy is a necessary condition of being disorderly.[117] The Sangrado figure had become a perverse figure who turned the world on its head to assert the ludicrous.

Sangrado's whimsical perversity was once again in evidence in an anonymous song in 1783. Here, calling a doctor celebrated because he "is not on the plan of Sangrado" was no more than to say "His nostrums are sure, not the product of whim."[118] We find references again in a pantomime in 1788[119] and a sermon by Joseph Dennie in 1796.[120] The common perception of Sangrado was that of a quack who drained the body of all its blood only to follow with an infusion in which "every vein must be inflated [with warm water] like a bladder."[121] Patients not only did not get better,[122] but they were left prostrate, that is, either maimed or wounded;[123] their only hope of survival lay in finding a different physician.[124] Such outcomes were the necessary result of treatment by the Spanish bleeder who, as a physician, based his extreme treatments on the notion of a single cure for all diseases. Indeed, William Heald's summary notion of Sangrado in 1789 was that of a "grand catholicon" who fit all diseases to one plan.[125]

In Le Sage's terms, Sangrado was the source of so many deaths that his apprentice, Gil Blas, remarked, "in no less than six weeks we made more widows and orphans than the siege of Troy. By the number of burials, one would have thought that the plague was in Valladolid."[126] Cobbett's use of the term "Sangrado" conjured up just such an image of the quack bleeder, as he conflated Rush's practices with those of his fictional counterpart. Cobbett first ascribed the name Sangrado to Rush during the epidemic of 1797 in "A Puff Equal to Dr. Rush's," which became an exhibit at his libel trial. A "puff," it deserves noting, was regarded in the eighteenth century as a self-aggrandizing advertisement that rendered a physician liable to the title of "quack."[127] Rush had provided what was really no more than a printed notice of instructions for the public to follow in treating yellow fever, responding to requests for advice he had been unable to answer and allowing that "*his mercurial purges* . . . may now be had with suitable directions at most of the apothecaries."[128] Cobbett compared Rush's presumed cure to a quackish remedy, Spilsbury's Antiscorbutic Drops, advertised, he represented, as a cure known for more than twenty-five years as far as remote parts of the world. Cobbett added a note for Rush in brackets: "*[There's for you, Master Sangrado! Beat that if you can.—As to the IMPURITIES OF THE BLOOD, I am sure, you have a more effectual remedy than brother SPILSBURY].*"[129] Pairing Rush's public service notice with an advertisement for a patent medicine was, for Cobbett, a gambit meant to open the physician to a charge of quackery.[130]

In a subsequent issue of *Procupine's Gazette*, Cobbett again took up Le Sage's *Adventures* charging, "Who can read the following extract from *Gil Blas* without being tempted to imagine that the author forsaw the person and practice of Rush."[131] The extract featured a baggy fellow with a grave air who called for a bleeder and offered, *"It is a gross error to suppose that blood is necessary to the conservation of life."* Cobbett went on to provide a "medical scrap" from the novel to amuse Rush and one of his students, Dr. Caldwell:

> *what a quantity of innocent blood was spilt!* But I do not know how it happened; *all our sick died* [just like Dr. Caldwell's '*three unfortunate characters*']. . . . "Sir," said I one evening to *Dr. Sangrado*, "I take heaven to witness, that I follow your method with the utmost exactness; yet, nevertheless, *every one of my patients leaves me in the lurch.* It looks as if they took a pleasure in dying, thereby to bring our practice into discredit." . . . "Why truly, child," answered he, "I have reason to make pretty much the same observation. *It is not often that my patients get out of my hands alive*; and if I were not so sure as I am of the principles on which I proceed, I should really think my remedies most destructive. . . . *I have published a book in which I have extolled the practice of bleeding*, and would thou have me go and deny my own work?"—"Oh! No," said I, "God forbid! That would *ruin your reputation*. Perish rather the nobility, clergy, and populace, to the last man."[132]

After the fact of the trial and in his own defense in *Rush-Light*,[133] Cobbett added a storyline in which "the wild and novel practice" of bleeding five to six times a day in combination with severe purges sparked "very warm discussion" among physicians.[134] At the head of the bleeders was Dr. Rush, indeed he was the originator, Cobbett opined, "unless we believe that such a man as *Doctor Sangrado* really existed." Rush, moreover, was isolated by his position on bleeding, Cobbett exaggerated, "for in the works of no other medical writer could Rush find a sanction to his practice, and it is well known, that every eminent physician in Philadelphia, Kuhn, Wistar, Stevens, Hodge, Monges, Currie, etc. etc. totally disapproved of it." Setting aside the medical witnesses that Rush had described as having volunteered to testify at the trial (doctors James Mease, William Dewees, and John Redman Coxe) and a rather large group of less aggressive bleeders, Cobbett took a reductionist view of the doctors' wars and the variety of positions on the issue of fever therapies to imply that, with the exception of Rush's own professional "posse," the medical profession had come down against such practices.

Raising questions of terminology, Cobbett went on to address the plaintiff's claim that in calling Rush a *Sangrado* he intended "to call him a *quack.*"[135] He relied upon the prosecution's borrowed definition that a quack was "*a boastful pretender to physick; one who proclaims his own medical abilities and nostrums in public places*"[136] and, in a flurry of paralogic worthy of a sophist, contended that since Sangrado did not proclaim in the marketplace, even if Rush did, Sangrado was no quack. If he was no quack, calling Rush a Sangrado was not to call him a quack, which made this no slander. Cobbett was thus no slanderer, the oral counterpart to libel, even by the terms of the prosecution's own game.

A true rhetorician, Cobbett took on the challenge of demonstrating that his use of the term "Sangrado" was justified by both Rush's counsel (Jared Ingersol) and his own (Robert Goodloe Harper), both of whom, Cobbett claimed, had been heard to say that Sangrado was indeed a quack "damned to everlasting fame."[137] As the defendant, he claimed he would "in no case, seek for safety under the leeward side of the law. Whether the word Sangrado be slanderous or not, he will allow you to assess damages against him for the application of it, if he cannot prove to you that that application was *just.*"[138] The truth of a slander, after all, constituted a standard of proof in common law that could be argued in one's defense. What he must do, he announced in his version of the test, "is to prove that the great man, whom he has designated by the name of another, bears such a resemblance to that other as the tenour of his words does evidently imply." Such sleight of hand would consider whether the "American Sangrado" resembled his fictional model in his "*person,*" "*general character,*" or his "*medical opinions, practice, and fame.*" His task thus entailed comparing excerpts from the novel and from Rush's own writings to weigh the fantastic Sangrado against the idiosyncratic Rush.

Cobbett cited first Sangrado's statement that "a patient *cannot be blooded too much!*" and matched it to Rush's "You should bleed your patients *almost to death, at least to fainting.*"[139] Where Sangrado trained a footboy to bleed, Rush had claimed that the procedure "might be taught to *a boy or girl of twelve years old*, in a few hours. I taught it in less time to several persons (the two *negroes* for instance) during the prevalence of our late epidemic. We teach a hundred things in our schools less useful."[140] That Sangrado was called "the Hippocrates of Spain"[141] and Rush "the Hippocrates of Pennsylvania" and that the former, as Le Sage depicted him, proved sober, rational, and singular in his thinking,[142] clinched the case that Sangrado was the very likeness of Rush. Still, for Cobbett the truest point of comparison was the arrogance of the Spaniard, his certainty with regard to rational medical knowledge, and his lack of concern for clinical experience and scientific proof.[143] As a cultural statement of popular perceptions of the state of medical knowledge at the outset of the epidemic, the construction of Sangrado the bleeder-quack in *The Adventures* was, in sum, more than merely a text from which legal arguments could be crafted. Having inspired a generation of writers, Sangrado served as a stalking horse who provided a culturally resonant assault on bleeders and was thereby central to the case Cobbett made to his readers in *Rush-Light*.

Fully cognizant of the Spanish bleeder's cultural clout, the famed republican journalist Philip Freneau, like Cobbett, framed the epidemic in terms of a culture of bloodletting, medical confusion, and doctors' wars, and frequently referred to the Sangrado figure. In "The Procession to Sylvania," "Slender's Journey," "Vexations and Disasters," and "The Village Merchant,"[144] for example, Freneau cited the quack's wild ideas and bold flights and traced his peregrinations to new unguarded cities where he might ply his trade. But none of his poems were as pointed as "Dr. Sangrado's flight," a variation on "Orlando's Flight" (1793) in which instead of a citizen fleeing Philadelphia to escape the ravages of the fever and the high costs of physicians, the public was offered the physician himself fleeing his practice and leaving citizens to their own defenses: "Took horse—clapp'd spurs—and off he flew,/*Leaving his* sick *to fret and scold*;/Some soldiers, thus, to honour lost,/In day of battle quit their post."[145]

As critical as he might have been of physicians, Freneau was no fan of Cobbett's and was hardly joining the fray as an ally. Rather, he directed his caustic wit to capitalize on Cobbett's claim that "lancet and calomel" rather than the epidemic had "slaughtered thousands," and he advised the blackguard Peter Porcupine[146] to join the fallen hosts and subscribe to Doctor Rush's system to preserve Philadelphia from "the future exercise of canes," adverting to the feuds, beatings, and duels resorted to by physicians and journalists of the period. Freneau's words anticipated John Rush's failed attempt to avenge Cobbett's newspaper attacks on his father Benjamin, which only reinforced Cobbett's determination to destroy the elder Rush's medical practice. Freneau, meanwhile, had a surer cure, death, which, he counseled, resolved both the physician's excess and the journalist's attacks:

> "While with the loss *of blood and spirits some faint*,
> Others are seen to rise, triumphant,
> O'er *slaughter'd* thousands sent to Pluto's shores,
> Were Stygian water in dull torrent roars—

> What hosts, what myriads fell
> By *lancet* and *calomel*—
> All gone, in Philadelphia's epidemic,
> And sent the substance of mankind to mimic!"
> So said that Man divine,
> Bold *Peter Porcupine*. . . .
> Now, Peter! Take advice from Doctor Rush;
> And—convert to the *system* you would crush;
> Pray, let him draw your *blackguard* blood;
> [and calomel might, also, do some good.]
> *Four thousand drops* exhausted from your veins
> Will save the future *exercise of canes:*
> And, tell him to be speedy with his lancet,
> For 'tis a truth; and many dare advance it,
> That howe'er in life *well fed*,
> No Doctor bleeds a man—when dead.[147]

The republican Freneau was not about to reinforce Cobbett's federalist attack against Rush. He would prefer, figuratively, to see Cobbett dead or, more realistically, to see him flee the city pursued by the prevailing fever of republicanism that attended the *Rush v. Cobbett* trial.

The Vintner's Tales

Insinuating himself into the doctors' wars in which Rush was a featured participant, Cobbett's third line of attack appeared in *Porcupine's Gazette*[148] in the form of a serial tale of bloodletting involving a tavern keeper and a hostler that, like the Sangrado analogue, was fated to become a prosecution exhibit in *Rush v. Cobbett*. To relieve his insomnia, the simple tavern keeper had read "the soporific essays with which our scribbling physicians and their hopeful pupils have so generously favoured the public."[149] His slumber, he asserted in the first of the three satires, has "given wonderful relief to my distressed imagination." Attracted by the opportunity offered by the yellow fever epidemic and persuaded by the relevant experience and resources he had garnered in his tavern trade, he was determined to join the medical fraternity: "As by these dissertations I find the whole materia medica is beautifully reduced to the very simple system of copious blood-letting and comfortable evacuations, I have determined to desert a trade thus ruined by the fever, and commence a business which has that fever for its support."[150] His qualifications for prescribing medications, he averred, flowed from his experience in furnishing "copious draughts [and] . . . mixing compounds" as a barman, even as his success at bloodletting humans would be no less than that of drawing blood from horses. He and his cohorts had at hand the cordials to revive those who fainted from the procedure and the carriages to drive themselves into practice under "the appellation of Vintner Physicians."

The tavern keeper's proposal to turn bleeder carried the appearance, even as a satire, of as much rationality as any other offer to serve in the epidemic and was in step in its simplicity with what the marketplace was inclined to bear. Medicine had become a business with no pretense. Reductionist thinking had simplified its practice, and disease had become a question of supply and demand with considerable room for consumer choice. Providence had provided for a convenient increase in demand in the bleeding trade, and the present deficit of bleeders (the result of physician flight, a high death toll, and public debate over bleeding) offered the tavern keeper an immediate opening into the field. The epidemic, a rod of God which man had invited by his profligacy, turned bad fortune into an opportunity that the tavern keeper, among others, was prepared to exploit.

In the second piece in the series, the tavern keeper set up the essentials of a bleeder's practice. First, he held a meeting of his brethren (as Rush and other physicians liked to call their fellow professionals) who determined to form a college to take their diplomas, a reference to Rush's creation of the Academy of Medicine and to the unregulated training and licensing of physicians that fostered such associations. Dr. Coxe, a student of Rush and a witness for the prosecution at the trial, was invited to "favour us with a prefatory oration in praise of the noble science of blood-letting."[151] The brethren then addressed "a serious expostulation to the public on their prejudice against the new practice," imitating Rush's own appeals to the public. They decided not to announce the taverns in which compounds could be had, as indeed Rush had not, "as we believed each of our brethren was well qualified in that respect. The superior merit of some, who sell stale porter, dead cider, etc. will be soon discovered by their respective patients."[152] Leaving such matters to consumers, as indeed Rush had himself recommended, opened them to abuse, a form of *caveat emptor* that afflicted Rush's own theory of popular self-treatment.

That tavern keepers kept carriages addressed the earlier complaint that horses and carriages "are not to be got for certificates" and effectively reminded Cobbett's readers of bleeders like Dr. Leib whose access to a carriage suggested that he had found some good in the disease.[153] Sensing an affinity with the physician's trade, the tavern keeper prepared his horse and carriage and painted on its side the sign of a French hostler. The hosteler's "merits and *sang froid* in the use of the lancet," Cobbett wrote, "are, I believe, unrivalled; for I believe he was an *eleve* of Robespierre's," whereby Cobbett linked bleeding, republicanism, and the excesses of the French Revolution to suggest the political associations of such a practice. The excesses cited were not only those of French "blood-letting" but those of the tavern keeper's lower-class hired nurses who would "never desert their patients, as I have engaged to supply them constantly with excellent gin and have also promised them the pillage of such of my patients as may be determined to die."[154] Here Cobbett recalls Rush's training of poor black assistants in the 1793 epidemic to bleed his patients and subsequent accusations by Cobbett's nemesis Mathew Carey that such assistants had charged excessive fees, deserted patients, and plundered property.[155]

The tavern keeper's own hostler reprised the state of quackery in the free-for-all epidemic marketplace by deserting his master to found his own practice: "Would you believe it, Mr. P. [referring to Cobbett's pseudonym "Porcupine"]—, that the rascal [the hostler], after reading my essay in your paper, purchased *Dr. Rush on the Yellow Fever,* and has been studying ever since, to my great loss and mortification. And now the wise illiterate thinks he can commence business for himself. But let him remember that *Ne sutor ultra crepidam—The cobler must not go beyond his last.*"[156] The hostler, imitating Rush, entertained the medical community with his own Latin-inflected essay, having become infected with "*cacoethes scribendi,*" an "incurable itch to write." Neither his lack of credentials, the lack of regulation, nor the threat of being sued constituted obstacles, based on the example he had before him of his copractitioners and his conviction that, as a conscientious man practicing a quiet profession, he was protected, echoing Freneau's line, by the fact "that *dead men never tell tales*." Given the poisonous effects of his liquors and the brutality of his bleeding, he would be covered by the privilege conveyed to physicians of burying their mistakes. Directly naming Rush ("Dr. Rush, the great patron of the art" of bleeding")[157] in this piece allowed the prosecution in the trial to call it into evidence.

In the third of the series of satires, the hostler responded to the tavern keeper, currying favor with an unnamed philanthropic genius meant to stand for Rush: "A devil, nay, the prince of devils, he must be, who dares to ridicule that godlike philanthropist, that saviour of men, whose omniscient genius discovered this remedy, and whose godlike benevolence industriously, incessantly labours to propagate it for the good of mankind." Here, the hostler borrowed the contentious language of the doctors' wars to accost those who opposed the practice of bleeding. The problem, as he saw it, lay with those who denied its efficacy: "I wish the Tavern-keeper, Medicus Spectator, and all the enemies of the lancet, no other punishment than a severe attack of the yellow fever, and their liberty to use the lancet or not, which would either reform, or free the world of all stupid quacks, and give free scope to the *sword*, the *shield,* the instrument of health."[158] The satire reduced science to an illiterate's insistence on his own anecdotal experience and an out-of-hand rejection of the experience of others. Recalling Rush's own posturing on the issue of medical knowledge, he insisted that "those only recover who are bled freely, which is sufficient to determine me in favour of blood-letting." Cobbett's satire in the vintner's tales proved, in sum, dead-on, having created a prose parody that, if not on the level of Le Sage's *Adventures*, was not only among the most astute of the time of yellow fever but a classic end of the century take on American medical culture.

NOTES

1. Smith (1988, 7).
2. Smith (1988, viii).
3. Brackenridge (1814, 286).
4. Brackenridge (1814, 287).
5. Smith (1988, 158).
6. Laracey (2008, 7).
7. Laracey (2008, 8, 10–11).
8. As quoted in Smith (2008, 71).
9. Hale (2003, 128–29). Matthew Hale makes the point that in the period from 1793 through 1798 an intense contest erupted over American national identity, exacerbated by the Anglo-American Jay's Treaty and capped by the exposure of the French XYZ Affair. The contest was one over pro- and anti-French sentiments and the threat to American sovereignty that was provoked by a perceived identification of French and American interests (128, 167, 169).
10. Hale (2003, 134, 151).
11. Hale (2003, 154, 156).
12. Sharp (1993, 69, 163-64); Gustafson (2000, 234).
13. Sharp (1993, 179, 184).
14. Sharp (1993, 175).
15. Sharp (1993, 226).
16. Stewart (1993, 17, 610, 614).
17. Stewart (1993, 640).
18. In 1797, Callender, for example, referred to Cobbett as "the most popular writer now in America"; List (1983, 24, 26).
19. Scherr (2003, 8).
20. Stewart (1969, 258).
21. Stewart (1969, 387); List (1983, 19).
22. *Carey's United States Recorder*, 19 May 1798, 21 June 1798; Stewart (1993, 465, 809 n53).
23. List (1983, 30).
24. Stewart (1993, 350).
25. *Porcupine's Gazette*, October 5, 1797.
26. October 28, 1797; Cobbett (1801a, 7: 274).
27. October 19, 1797; Cobbett (1801a, 7: 250).

28. October 24, 1797; Cobbett (1801a, 7: 258-63).
29. October 24, 1797; Cobbett (1801a, 7: 258).
30. *Porcupine's Gazette*, October 7, 1797.
31. As a stage villain, Cobbett would come off as the very antithesis of the stage Yankee who emerged in 1787 in America's first successful professional play, Royall Tyler's *The Contrast*. A figure of honest industry, native integrity, and common sense, natural and clever, the Yankee was not cunning in the way of a Shylock, a character with which Americans were familiar in performance as early as 1752 and a characterization that fit Cobbett like a glove. The caricature of the would-be English Lord in the same play reflected America's distaste for English attitudes and English society, a characterization that placed Cobbett on the distaff side of American values; Moody (1966, 31, 148).
32. Ferguson (2004, 141).
33. Howell (2001, 10).
34. Howell (2001, 12); see Smith (1984).
35. Smith (1984, 41).
36. "Billingsgate" was a term used to refer to abusive low-class language, taking its name from a gate of London where there was a fish market.
37. List (1983, 8).
38. Nattrass (1995, 5–7).
39. Nattrass (1995, 4, 9, 60–61).
40. Wilson (1994, 18); Nattrass (1995, 21).
41. Nattrass (1995, 21).
42. Carpenter (1800, 51).
43. Carpenter (1800, 59).
44. Carpenter (1800, 58–59).
45. Carpenter (1800, 62).
46. Blackstone (1774, 3: 125).
47. Carpenter (1800, 58).
48. Carpenter (1800, 57).
49. Carpenter (1800, 9).
50. Carpenter (1800, 51).
51. Olson (2000, 229).
52. Olson (2000, 224).
53. Olson (2000, 224).
54. Olson (2000, 224–26). Satire flourished in the Anglo-American world, according to Olson, in the first quarter of the eighteenth century and was exemplified in England by such satirists as Addison, Gay, Pope, and Swift, establishing for our purposes the context out of which Cobbett—who greatly admired the English satirists, particularly Swift—produced his attacks on Rush (226).
55. Cobbett (1801b, 2:54–56); Green, (1983, 150); Clark (1939, 68-70); Nattress (1995, 50).
56. As quoted in Green (1983, 151).
57. Cobbett answered his critics at length and in detail in Cobbett (1797).
58. Green (1983, 151).

59. Cobbett (1801b, 2: 54–55).
60. Cobbett (1801b, 2: 56–57).
61. Cobbett (1801b, 2: 57).
62. Moreau de St. Mery (1947, 211).
63. Nattrass (1995, 50–51).
64. Nattrass (1995, 50).
65. Etching by C. P. Eldwood, 1798.
66. The print identifies the event as taking place in Congress Hall in Philadelphia, February 15,1798.
67. Stewart (1969, 567).
68. *Lyon's Case* No. 8, 646, 1798 U.S. Circuit Court of Vermont, October 1798.
69. *Porcupine's Gazette*, February 1798, Cobbett (1801a, 8: 72).
70. *Bee*, March 14, 1798, in Stewart (1969, 569).
71. *Carey's United States Recorder*, February 15, 1798, February 19, 1798, February 22, 1798, February 27, 1798.
72. *Porcupine's Gazette*, January 1798, Cobbett (1801a, 8: 68).
73. Cobbett (1801a, 8: 69).
74. *Porcupine's Gazette*, February 1798, Cobbett (1801a, 8: 72.)
75. *Porcupine's Gazette*, February 1798, Cobbett (1801a, 8: 77, 87-88).
76. *Porcupine's Gazette*, February 1798, Cobbett (1801a, 8: 89).
77. Cobbett went to the trouble of devoting an entire issue of *Porcupine's Gazette* to the sedition trial in October 1798.
78. *Porcupine's Gazette*, February 1798, Cobbett (1801a, 8: 91).
79. Carey (1786, 24). Carey termed his work a "hudibrastic" pamphlet (modeled after *Hudibras,* by Samuel Butler). He published it after he had an altercation with Oswald that ended in a duel. It included three pieces: "Gulliverus of the Hero," by the pseudonymous Scriblerus; "The Plagi-Scurriliad"; and a mock "Epitaph" for Oswald.
80. Carey (1786, 36–37).
81. Carey (1786, 41).
82. Freneau (1986, 167).
83. Carey (1799a, 19).
84. Carey (1799a, 14).
85. Carey (1799a, 18).
86. Carey (1799a, 47).
87. Carey (1799a, 16).
88. Cobbett was referred to as a "garrett-scribbler" from Grubb Street in a letter penned by the pseudonymous Paul Hedgehog (the pseudonym of Carey's brother James) to Bache's newspaper *The Aurora*; see Cobbett (1797, v).
89. Philip Freneau facetiously proposed a tax on the press, "Proposing a Taxation upon News-Papers," to offset the reputational costs of such assaults as Carey suffered, which reads in part:

> Subjects were never good that were too wise:
> In every hamlet, every trifling town.
> Some sly, designing fellow sits him down,

On spacious folio prints his weekly mess,
And spreads around the poison of his Press.
Hence, to the WORLD the streams of scandal flow,
Disclosing secrets, that it should not know,
Hence courtiers strut with libels on their backs;
And shall not news be humbled by a tax!

Freneau (1795, 377).

90. Carey (1799a, 18).

91. Carey (1799a, 15).

92. Carey (1942, 34).

93. Carey (1942, 34).

94. Carey (1942, 30).

95. Carey (1942, 30).

96. Carey (1942, 30).

97. 1796 letter to Cobbett; Carey (1942, 32).

98. 1798 letter to Cobbett; Carey (1942, 33). In a flourish, Carey declaimed that were he not so unequal in strength he would drag him from "the inmost recesses of your dungeon-like labyrinth . . . sow-skinning you, till Argus himself should not be able to perceive a hair's breadth upon your carcase but sore upon sore; so that, were you and Lazarus candidates for the commiseration of the public, you would carry off the palm" (33). Carey (1799b) cited self-defense and put the matter forward for public criticism. He considered himself "very wantonly and unjustly attacked" by Cobbett and anxious to avoid "a controversy with such a man, void of candour, honour, and truth" (iii). The attacks having continued for two years and four months, Carey tried to navigate between, on the one hand, halting the poisonous public attacks and, on the other hand, forestalling a duel:

> I once more declare my unwillingness to be driven to extremities with you. What is past, I am willing to try to forget. But never dare to disgrace my name by introducing it into your filthy paper. If you do, you shall sorely repent it. You will too late regret the temerity that urged you to an engagement in which you have nothing to gain—but much to lose.
>
> I have laboured hard to avoid a contest with you. This is my final effort. If it proves in vain, on your detested head be the consequences. (iv)

99. Carey (1799b) is the second time that, as Carey says, he had reconnected with the Muses, for which he blames Cobbett's having "led me to visit the ladies again, and renew our acquaintance" (vi). Carey's brother James had earlier, in 1797, written a mock-heroic poem on Cobbett as well which he ascribed to Henry Hedgehog; Carey (1797); Clark (1939, 94, 104, 191); see List (1983).

100. Carey (1799b, vi).

101. Carey (1799b, 10–13).

102. Sworn by Jacob Sevoss before a justice of the peace on July 3, 1798; Carey (1799b, ii).

103. Carey (1799b, ii); see Carey (1799a, 2).

104. *Porcupine's Gazette*, September 18, 1797.

105. 16 September 1793; Rush (1794, 162).

106. *Porcupine's Gazette*, September 23, 1797.

107. *Procupine's Gazette*, September 23, 1797; Cobbett (1801a, 7: 185).

108. *Porcupine's Gazette*, October 5, 1797. In *Rush-Light* II, February 28, 1800; Cobbett (1801a, 11: 274); Cobbett refers to one report in which a viewer describes Rush's carriage as like "*the chariot of death, driven by the devil.*" Cobbett himself described Rush's carriage in the following terms: "A queer looking hutch, big enough to hold only one man. It has glass doors and windows, it is drawn by one horse, and has an elevated box, from which a negro fellow lashes his poor four-legged fellow citizens" (note, 274). The prevalence of the carriage as a sign of Rush's prominence is well captured by a cartoon that appeared following the verdict in *Rush v. Cobbett*: "Just after the 5000 dollar decision, the Rushites published a triumphal caricature, representing Rush with the above equipage [a chariot], driving over a Porcupine, and squeezing out of its throat great quantities of *blood* and dollars" (note 274).

109. *Porcupine's Gazette*, October 6, 1797. The journalist Mathew Carey drew much the same conclusion: "Several classes of people were highly benefited by the public distress. Coffin-makers had full employment, and in general high prices for their work" (1794, 74).

110. *Porcupine's Gazette*, October 26, 1797.

111. *Rush-Light* III, March 15, 1800; Cobbett (1801a, 11: 336).

112. *Porcupine's Gazette*, October 12, 1797.

113. *Porcupine's Gazette*, September 18, 1797 and September 26, 1797.

114. Fielding (1793, 2: 4).

115. Smollett (1794).

116. Warton (1756, 216).

117. Beattie (1777, 126).

118. "The Infallible Doctor, a New Song. Sung in the Character of a Merry Andrew" (1783, 23–24).

119. Bates [1788].

120. Dennie (1796).

121. Dennie (1796, 70).

122. Smollett (1794, 148).

123. Belnap (1796, 208).

124. Smollett (1794, 148).

125. Heald (1789, ix).

126. Le Sage (1749, 72).

127. *Rush-Light* III, March 15, 1800; Cobbett (1801a, 11: 310).

128. *Federal Gazette*, September 12, 1793; see Rush (1951, 1: 660-61); *Rush-Light* III, March 15, 1800; Cobbett (1801a, 11: 311). Advertisements were placed by chemists and druggists as well for "Dr. Rush's *celebrated* mercurial purging and sweating powders for preventing and curing the prevailing *putrid fever,*" to sell "Doctor Rush's Mercurial Sweating Powder for the Yellow Fever, with printed directions for taking the same, prepared and sold by permission"; *Porcupine's Gazette*, October 7, 1797; see Rush (1951 1: 661 note 1).

129. *Porcupine's Gazette*, September 28, 1797.

130. The puff to which Cobbett referred was one of several that Rush had published or would publish, none of which would have profited Rush who routinely provided medications for his patients out of his own pocket. Apothecaries did, however, publish their own advertisements for "Doctor Rush's Mercurial Sweating Powders" (*Federal Gazette*, September 12, 1793) and Rush did indicate that the medicines he recommended could he had "with suitable instructions" at several apothecary shops, which he named; *Philadelphia Gazette*, September 4, 1798.

131. *Procupine's Gazette*, October 17, 1797.

132. *Porcupine's Gazette*, October 21, 1797.

133. *Rush-Light* III, March 15, 1800; Cobbett (1801a, 12: 307–43); *Rush-Light* IV, March 31, 1800; Cobbett (1801a, 12: 370–83).

134. *Porcupine's Gazette*, January 13, 1800; Cobbett (1801a, 12: 140).

135. *Rush-Light* III, March 15, 1800; Cobbett (1801a, 11: 313–14).

136. From Addison, *Rush-Light* III, March 15, 1800; Cobbett (1801a, 11: 310).

137. *Rush-Light* III, March 15, 1800; Cobbett (1801a, 11: 313).

138. *Rush-Light* III, March 15, 1800; Cobbett (1801a, 11: 314).

139. *Rush-Light* III, March 15, 1800; Cobbett (1801a, 11: 316).

140. *Rush-Light* III, March 15, 1800; Cobbett (1801a, 11: 316–17).

141. *Rush-Light* III, March 15, 1800; Cobbett (1801a, 11: 318).

142. Le Sage, 1749 (n.d., 55).

143. As Sangrado exclaimed in Le Sage's novel, "this opinion may seem strange to such raw physicians as Cuchillo; but . . . if such as he were capable of reasoning philosophically, instead of decrying my method, they would become my most zealous partisans"; Le Sage, 1749 (n.d., 65). The physician simply named his own practice a "system" and pursued it by trial and error, irrespective of its devastating consequences:

> the physician came in, and looked very foolishly, notwithstanding his long practice of dispatching patients. Nevertheless, far from imputing the canon's death to his watery draughts and evacuations, he observed as he went out with an air of indifference, that the patient had not lost blood enough, nor drank a sufficient quantity of warm water (58).

The patient, for his part, simply accepted his fate as foreordained, refusing in the end all treatment and absolving the physician of all blame for his ills: "I see plainly that I must die, in spite of the virtues of water: and though there is scarce a drop of blood left in my body, I don't find myself a whit the better; which is a plain proof, that the most expert physician in the world cannot prolong our days, when their fatal period is arrived" (56). Collateral parties fell in line as well, for the system extended throughout the network of relations that served sickness and death: "The notary . . . asked what physician attended the canon: I answered Doctor Sangrado. At that name, seizing his hat and cloak in a hurry, 'Zooks,' cried he, 'let us make haste; for the doctor is so expeditious, that he seldom gives his patients time to send for notaries: that man has choused me out of a great many jobs'" (57). The outcome for the physician was no less than an increase in status, practice, and income. For his part, the patient was rewarded with a place in the doctor's book of patients, a register, as it turns out, of the dead:

> I was invested with the charge of this book, which might have been with great justice styled a register of the dead; for almost all the people whose names it contained gave up the ghost. I inserted in it (to use the expression) the names of those people who were to set out for the other world, as the clerk of a stage-coach office registers those who take places. The pen was seldom out of my hand, because there was not at that time a physician in Valladoid of more credit than Doctor Sangrado, who had acquired great reputation with the public, by a pomp of words, a solemn air, and some luck cures which had done him more honour than he deserved. (59)

144. Freneau (1795, 13–15, 322, 343, 347).
145. Freneau (1795, 448).
146. Peter Porcupine was a name that Cobbett frequently used to describe himself; see, for example, Cobbett (1797).
147. "To Peter Porcupine," *Time-Piece* October 25, 1797; see for comparison, Cobbett's "A Hard Case," *Porcupine's Gazette*, October 26, 1797.
148. *Porcupine's Gazette*, September 18, 1797; September 26, 1797; September 27, 1797.
149. *Porcupine's Gazette*, September 18, 1797; Cobbett (1801a, 7: 164).
150. *Porcupine's Gazette*, September 18, 1795; Cobbett (1801a, 7: 164–65).
151. *Porcupine's Gazette*, September 18, 1797; Cobbett (1801a, 7: 196).
152. *Porcupine's Gazette*, September 26, 1797; Cobbett (1801a, 7: 196).
153. *Porcupine's Gazette*, September 23, 1797.
154. *Porcupine's Gazette*, September 26, 1797; Cobbett (1801a, 7: 196).
155. See Carey (1794); Jones and Allen (1993); Bacon (2001).
156. *Porcupine's Gazette*, September 26, 1797; Cobbett (1801a, 7: 195).
157. Carpenter (1800, 5).
158. *Porcupine's Gazette*, September 27, 1797; Cobbett (1801a, 7: 202).

4

Libel Law and William Cobbett

As a journalist, Cobbett exemplified the plight of the partisan journalists in his profession from John Peter Zenger in 1735 to Eleazer Oswald in the 1780s and the Sedition Act targets William Duane, Benjamin Franklin Bache, James Thomson Callender, and Thomas Cooper. In many ways, the press had succumbed to the same "contagion of liberty" that had arisen from the American Revolution, a contagion that demanded freedoms for the press that would prove unsustainable. The fever of freedom that raged around the press would destabilize not only the public support the press sought but the consensus the republic so critically needed to survive as a new nation; it was a fever that fanned party politics, breaches of the peace, and foreign influence and that inflamed abuses of power and destruction of reputation. Supporters of a free press contended that a man would survive attacks on his reputation, but that suppression of the press would lead to the loss of general liberty.[1] Proponents of individual privacy and social order, on the contrary, held that without determined enforcement by the legal system, press freedom linked to party politics and personal libels would lead to almost unthinkable risks to public peace. Resolving the conflict between liberty of the press and libel relied upon libel law as it developed from common law to the 1735 *Zenger* case,[2] the Pennsylvania Constitutions of 1776 and 1790, the Bill of Rights in 1791, and later the Alien and Sedition Acts in 1798.

LIBEL LAW

The debate over libel law centered in America on limits of free speech and a free press so that civil libel could control assaults on private reputation to protect privacy and seditious libel could be used in public life to absolve the state and its officials from scurrilous scrutiny of its actions and conduct.[3] This debate was critical to establishing order and peace in political discourse, the lives of public men, and the affairs of government in a nation newly established and threatened in its very legitimacy, so that a good public opinion of the government became essential to maintaining the state. At the same time that involvement of the people in its own governance was critical to the operation of democracy, protection of those elite who served as public officials became necessary to maintain their ability to govern. Suppression of political speech was on a collision course with the critical role the press played in allowing a marketplace of ideas to inform the public and to address government corruption, conflicting as well with the affection the press had engendered by the role it had played in the revolution in supporting the independence movement. The threat of assaults on personal reputation, of inciting the public to riot, and of disruptive partisan political parties on the one hand and the important role the press played in protecting free speech, providing a free flow of information, and exposing chicanery on the other became the touchstones of American libel law.

The judges of the infamous English Star Chamber in the seventeenth century provide the floor for our discussion, for they essentially exercised complete discretion in proscribing all attacks on public officials and the state. The very fact of publishing a comment was sufficient to find guilt, irrespective of malice or the truth of the comment.[4] Defendants in America were better protected under civil procedures in English common law libel, essentially adopted in the states as a carryover from colonial law, than under criminal prosecution. In civil law they could introduce a justification of truth in their defense—indeed, they were required to do so—or offer a justification by virtue of a "privileged occasion" where the comments were made.[5] In effect, "the truth could be no libel,"[6] as both truth and privilege were considered absolute justifications if successful.

In criminal prosecutions, as William Blackstone's *Commentaries* made clear, however, "the tendency which all libels have to create animosities, and to disturb the public peace, is the sole consideration of the law,"[7] so that "the dissemination, or making public, of bad sentiments, destructive of the ends of society, is the crime which society corrects."[8] Here, the truth of a libel made it an even greater threat under what was to become the traditional rule that "the greater the truth, the greater the libel."[9] As for the privileges of the press, Blackstone held that indeed a free press was essential to a free society "but this consists in laying no *previous* constraints upon publication."[10] Moreover, the press was only strengthened if, having abused its responsibility to use publication wisely, it was then censured. The press could thereby not "be abused to any bad purpose, without incurring a suitable punishment . . . to censure the licentiousness, is to maintain the liberty of the press,"[11] which was to become the mechanism whereby press liberty was to be distinguished from license.[12] By the 1790s an English common law interpretation of criminal libel gave the courts, in John Randolph's words, "unlimited license to punish"[13] and left the press facing little protection of its freedom.[14] In sum, what Blackstone added to libel law was that freedom of the press entailed no prior restraint on publication and that criticism of the government or public officials was criminally liable, that is, that the liberty of the press was not unlimited.[15]

The Zenger trial in 1735, essentially conducted under Blackstonian law, contributed several principles of its own to the American libel law debate, although judges largely disallowed them. These principles would have permitted the use of the truth as a defense in criminal libel trials and would have given the jury the right to decide both the law and the facts of a case. More significant was the influence of Cato on republican thought in the debate. A free people, this line of reasoning held, required that corrupt officials be exposed, so that the truth was never libelous. Government control of speech and press was dangerous, whereas a free press would not only allow errant government to correct its errors but would give vent to popular feeling to prevent rather than incite riot, improving the people's judgment in the process.[16] This influence counterposed itself to the British view of seditious libel, which recalled English suppression, and encouraged juries to assert the common man's view of the law by nullifying the law if necessary.

Two other sites for American libel law—state constitutional law and the Alien and Sedition Acts—provide more immediate sources for libel trials leading up to the *Rush v. Cobbett* trial, as well as for the trial itself. The Pennsylvania constitution of 1776, for example, was relied upon by Eleazer Oswald in two libels trials, 1782 and 1788, as well as Cobbett's indictment in the Yrujo case, while the constitution of 1790 informed the Rush trial. In 1776, the Declaration of Rights, section XII of the Pennsylvania Constitution provided "That the people have a right to freedom of speech, and of writing, and publishing their sentiments; therefore the freedom of the press ought not to be restrained." In 1790, Pennsylvania shifted course somewhat, influenced by press controversies of the 1780s. Article IX, section 7 read,

> That the printing-presses shall be free to every person who undertakes to examine the proceedings of the legislature, or any branch of government, and no law shall ever be made to restrain the rights thereof . . . every citizen may freely speak, write, and print on ony subject, being responsible for the abuse of that liberty. In prosecutions for the publication of papers investigating the official conduct of officers or men in a public capacity, or where the matter published is

> proper for public information, the truth thereof may be given in evidence; and in all indictments for libels, the jury shall have a right to determine the law and the facts, under the direction of the court, as in other cases.

Here, the Zengerian principles were imported into the state constitution to allow truth as a criminal libel defense—although with the deletion in the constitution of a phrase, "in justification," which would have offered the defendant a "complete defense"—and to enhance the jury's role with regard to determining the law as well as the facts. The constitutional debate over the issue of public conduct, moreover, led to the addition of the term "official," which gave less protection to the press.[17] Reinforcing the Pennsylvania Constitution, the First Amendment of the federal constitution, ratified in 1791, promised that "Congress shall make no law . . . abridging the freedom of speech or of the press."[18]

Following passage of the 1790 constitution, a decade of debate eventuated in the passage in 1798 of the Sedition Act, adding statutory law to the mix. This body of law effectively set the stage for the Rush trial as it reflected the tenor of the times and codified the body of law that would inform the republican prosecution in *Rush v. Cobbett*, a civil rather than a criminal case tried in state rather than federal court. The Sedition Act represented a return to Blackstonian strictures aimed at any person who shall write, publish, or assist "knowingly and willingly" in writing or publishing "any false, scandalous and malicious writing or writings" against the government, Congress, or the president "with intent to defame . . . or to bring them . . . into contempt or disrepute; or to excite against them . . . the hatred of the good people of the United States, or to stir up sedition within the United States."[19] Public peace was the central concern of the act, which presumed a limited right to discuss public persons. Like the Pennsylvania Constitution of 1790, however, and unlike Blackstone, the act included the two Zengerian principles of a truth defense and an enhanced role for the jury even as intent and malice became critical aspects of the proscribed conduct. According to the act's chief architect, Robert Goodloe Harper (Cobbett's lead attorney in the Rush trial), conviction could only follow from a publication that was false, malicious, and printed with criminal intent.[20] The libertarian free marketplace of ideas—the notion that truth would trump falsehood if they were allowed to compete, the true flushing out the false from the battleground of ideas—was nevertheless nowhere in evidence. Indeed, to require the prosecution of falsehood left every speech act at risk, as truth often appeared untrue and the people were often convinced by deception.[21] What was taken for truth was often received orthodoxy, while what was actually true was in fact elusive. Moreover, truth was treated in the act as a question of fact, when the kind of truths that were being bargained over were more aptly described as thoughts, ideas, interpretations, and opinions and thus unlikely to be demonstrable by means of evidence.

LIBEL CASES

If we look at several selected cases involving the press, libel law, and seditious libel—Zenger, Oswald in 1783 and 1788, Callender in 1800, Cooper in 1800, and Cobbett's encounters with the Pennsylvania Supreme Court and Chief Justice McKean in 1797, 1798, and 1800—the trajectory as well as the legal context that informed *Rush v. Cobbet* in 1799 becomes clear. In the Zenger case, the *New York Weekly Journal*,[22] credited with being the first American party newspaper, was attacked for a press libel that tended "to create differences among men, ill blood among the people, and oftentimes great bloodshed between the party libeling and the party libeled,"[23] what would become a common breach of the peace argument right up through the end of the century. Arguing the Zenger case—a libel against Governor William Cosby of New York—Andrew Hamilton claimed for Zenger the privilege of publishing the truth and hoped that "in so doing he has committed no crime,"[24] knowing full well that counsel was throwing up a line of argument for which there was then little basis in the law. What Hamilton relied upon, as it turned out, was a community values view of the jury in which he appealed to the jury to try the case as neighbors: "The law supposes you to be summoned *out of the neighborhood where the fact is alleged to be committed*; and the reason of your being taken out of the neighborhood is *because you are supposed to have the best knowledge of the fact that is to be tried.*"[25] Hamilton reminded the members of the jury that they, like the defendant, had an interest in the trial, not a self-interest but one that, as Chief Justice De Lancey's charge to the jury reluctantly admitted, spoke to the understood need that "governments must have the good opinion of the people or it cannot subsist." The chief justice lamented that Hamilton, upon this premise, had gone to great lengths to incite the jury to disregard the judge's instructions.[26] Hamilton appealed to their sense of honesty, law, and justice in which, he argued, "lies our own safety." To the judge, he quoted "an old and wise caution *that when our neighbor's house is on fire, we ought to take care of our own.*"[27] Indeed, Hamilton was not above raising the specter of Brutus's ghost to warn jurors that by excusing the influence of authority, they were "assisting Caesar to forge those very chains which one day he will make you yourselves wear."[28]

Reports of trials in the press were themselves regarded as a form of trial by one's neighbors. Indeed, press involvement, in one form or another, became an almost unavoidable element of jury trials under the theory of a jury of one's neighbors. The role of press interference in a trial as a means of publicly appealing to one's neighbors, and thereby potentially influencing jurors, was greeted with skepticism in the judiciary not only because of the invalidity of such trials by press but because of their effect as a court of last resort on the legitimacy of the court.

Eleazer Oswald

Like the themes of jury independence, trial by press, and party-inspired libels, the themes of public order, breach of the peace, and peace bonds permeated libel trials. In a case in 1783 involving Oswald, McKean had argued that "if redress could not be obtained from the laws of the commonwealth, every man would consider himself the guardian of his own reputation, and the laws of nature would take place; and in such a case, we should hear of assaults and batteries, cutting off ears, challenges, assassinations and murders without end."[29] Both the independence of juries and the authority of the judge to conduct the business of the court were issues in this case raising concerns like those of Judge DeLancey in the Zenger case about controlling counsel and the jury. McKean had Oswald brought before him in this case for publishing a piece, "A Friend of the Army," in which he said Oswald had libeled both the chief justice and the court in an indictment proceeding against a Colonel Proctor. As he was to charge the jury in a second case against Oswald in 1788, McKean's complaint was that Oswald "asserts that his judges are influenced by passion and prejudice—willingly seeks to corrupt the source, and to dishonor the administration of justice."[30] McKean ordered a surety to force Oswald into future good behavior which Oswald promptly violated by reprinting the offending piece and publishing a second piece, "A Hint to Grand Juries," advising the grand jury to consider implications for the liberties of all in delivering a verdict in his case.[31] The members of the jury defied McKean's charge, were returned to reconsider, and were ultimately dismissed as they refused to deliver a true bill against Oswald.

Publishing his own comments anonymously under the pseudonym Jusperitus,[32] the chief justice took the position that slanderous words were not held sacred by the Pennsylvania Constitution when expressed through the press and that, given the inflammatory influence newspapers had come to have, the writer should be punished. A party to the case, Thomas Proctor—whose judicial treatment by McKean had prompted Oswald's inflammatory attack—without knowing it was the chief justice of whom he was speaking, asked the public to judge the motives of those who speak "under anonymous signatures (the common refuge of assassins and robbers of virtue and recognition)."[33] Oswald and McKean, as well as supreme court Justice Bryan who joined in the war of words under the pseudonym Adrian, debated the validity of a jury that appeared to call and examine its own witnesses out of court in defiance of the chief justice's directions. A third judge, Francis Hopkinson—McKean's alienated brother-in-law—went to print himself to complain that "if the justice's will had passed for law, all the gentlemen of the grand jury must have been the basest vassals to the judges."[34]

In the case against Oswald in 1788, the printer's defense pointed out, and McKean conceded, that the law gave "to every citizen a right of investigating the conduct of those who are entrusted with the public business; and they effectively preclude any attempt to fetter the press by the institution of a *licenser*."[35] McKean nevertheless contested the proposition that the right to examine the government could permit bias and intimidation, referring to the attacks made against judges who must try such cases. Oswald's defense of the press in a trial exhibit in the case,[36] by contrast, argued that the press expressed not dissension but love of liberty. Constraint of the press was thus a "doctrine incompatible with law and liberty, and at once destructive of the privileges of a free country in the communication of our thoughts, [that] has not hitherto gained any footing in *Pennsylvania*: and the vile measures formerly taken to lay me by the heels on this subject only brought down obloquy upon the conductors themselves." He could only hope that the same love of liberty pervaded his fellow citizens, who would "not allow the freedom of the press to be violated upon any refined pretence, which oppressive ingenuity or courtly study can invent."[37] Oswald was, in any case, wrong on the law as the English common law doctrine of libel was largely recognized as part of Pennsylvania law that had repeatedly been upheld.[38] As McKean put it, "The law upon the subject is of immemorial antiquity."[39] Once again Oswald discussed the pending case in his newspaper and was again charged with contempt. The question, McKean posited, resolved itself into "whether you shall bend to the law, or the law shall bend to you, it is our duty to determine that the former shall be the case."[40]

Oswald's troubles with McKean have been represented as "The first successful legal assault on a partisan press since the Revolution."[41] In sum, his cases illustrate a favored tactic—the use of peace bonds as a form of prior restraint to ensure good behavior without the necessity of securing an indictment or a conviction,[42] a practice that would continue in force through the sedition trials and that, in 1806, became the subject of then-governor McKean's failed appeal to the Pennsylvania legislature to formally authorize good behavior bonds.[43] McKean showed himself in the Oswald case to be a judge who was comfortable with a neo-Blackstonian approach to libel law in which peace bonds augmented the law. Even so, he was willing to consider malicious intent and good motives to distinguish statements meant to enhance the public good from those meant merely to defame.[44] As he was to remark in the Yrujo case against Cobbett, McKean was willing to consider truth as well, but only for criticisms of official conduct, and that such criticisms "must not only be true, but 'candid' and 'decent' also."[45] Irrespective of his ameliorating gestures, McKean's support of legal restraints on the press demonstrated that federalists were not alone in favoring libel prosecutions, a preference that would become more apparent among republicans after Jefferson's ascent to the presidency.[46]

Sedition Cases

The state of the law as it applied to Cobbett from 1797 to 1800 was part and parcel of the court's experience with the Alien and Sedition Acts. Here, it is helpful to consider two cases tried under those acts in the federal circuit court—those of James Thomson Callender and Thomas Cooper—both from 1800 with Justice Samuel Chase presiding. The Cooper defense, on charges of defaming President Adams, argued that official power should not be unlimited and that it cannot be enforced by attacking the press.[47] Moreover, if the country itself was divided on both the power of government and restrictions on the press, half the country at any given time would be critical of official power and thereby open to prosecution. A free people, the defense asserted, deserved open discussion and the same freedom that George Washington and John Adams enjoyed in their presidencies—to disagree with policy and to express themselves freely in matters of public importance.[48] How, indeed, Cooper asked, would a free people make a free choice without open and free discussion?[49]

Rawle for the prosecution argued in opposition that "the defendant shall not be found guilty of publishing defamatory writings, unless they be false, nor altho' they may be false, shall be considered as guilty under the law, unless the intent of the publication appear to be malicious,"[50] offering in effect a truth defense qualified by malicious intent. Justice Chase was less inviting in his charge to the jury, in which he opened not only by prejudging the defendant's case as well as the defendant himself, calling him a "Traverser": "When men are found rash enough to commit an offense such as the Traverser is charged with, it becomes the duty of the government to take care that they should not pass with impunity."[51] Cooper had, in Chase's words, intended to defy the government, to censure and to find the president "unworthy the confidence of the people"[52] and thereby incite the hatred of the people, as cited in the Sedition Act, against him. In sum, Chase charged the jury to consider the case as a double bind: if Cooper has written truly, we must all hate the president; therefore, his attacks are either not true or, if true, they breach public confidence in those who must rule. In either case, his acts are punishable.[53] Irrespective of the dilemma Chase had posed for the jury, he required that the "Traverser" defend himself by proving, to the marrow, that every charge he made was true,[54] alleviating the prosecution's burden to prove them false.

As for the Callender case, Justice Chase's charge to the jury was no less partisan, having, as one witness testified, expressed his desire to see Callender convicted even before the trial began.[55] Callender, like Cooper, was charged with libeling President Adams, which was as much in Chase's view as to assault the sovereign people themselves and lead to the destruction of government.[56] The words of the indictment cited Callender's "cowardly insolence" and characterized him as a "hoary-headed incendiary,"[57] whereas Callender's counsel, Mr. Hay, considered his client's words were no more than "a question of opinion only" and thereby open to discussion by men of different opinions. Thus, there could be no question of proving or disproving his assertions, so that "the privilege of giving the truth in evidence was a nullity."[58] Referring to Callender, as he did to Cooper, as "the Traverser," Chase's response was passionate: "The Traverser charges him [Adams] with being a murderer and a thief, a despot and a tyrant! Will you . . . excuse yourself by saying it is mere opinion—or, that you heard so?"[59] Clearly, the Sedition Act's proscription against language that would bring a person "into contempt or disrepute" was at issue here.

The prosecutor, Mr. Nelson, was quick to ask that not only the good of the country but the rights of the individual needed protecting. Citing the politics of the case, he argued that it was not necessary in preferring one man for the presidency that another must be maliciously and falsely slandered.[60] Finally, the defense asked the jury to disregard an act of Congress, the Sedition Act, as it contravened the constitution; rather, the jury ought, "according to the dictates of conscience and the laws of the country,"[61] to refuse to convict. Chase, predictably, denied the jury such a nullification verdict in his charge, contending that no petit jury can usurp the federal jurisdiction by exercising a presumed right to declare a law's unconstitutionality.[62]

Cobbett and the Law

From the time the charges were filed in *Rush v. Cobbett* until its final disposition, Cobbett was involved in a dozen legal actions. They included in the Yrujo case a failed application to remove the case to the federal circuit court, indictments at both the federal and state levels that were returned ignoramus, and conviction and an appeal for violation of a peace bond.[63] In the Rush case, they included a failed application to remove the case to the federal circuit court, a conviction for libel, an appeal for a new trial, an action by Rush to recover the fine, and a petition by Cobbett to avoid payment.[64] Moreover, unlike Rush, who was never sued for professional malpractice, Cobbett's legal troubles all had to do with the pursuit of his profession and were related to fellow journalists as well as political figures, from Mathew Carey to the Spanish Minister Yrujo, Justice McKean, and President Adams.

The history of press prosecutions exemplified by the Zenger and Oswald libel cases, taken together with the Cooper and Callender sedition cases, suggests that judges like DeLancey, Chase, and McKean were intent on reigning in the press and had few compunctions about ensuring they could do so. Like his pseudonymous use of the press to influence public opinion in the 1783 Oswald trial, McKean played more than one role in his pursuit of Cobbett. Not only did he file the charges himself in 1797 to take Cobbett before the grand jury for libeling the Spanish minister to the United States, Don Carlos Martinez de Yrujo—soon to become McKean's son-in-law—but McKean went to the extreme of stepping down from the bench to testify against Cobbett in that case and then returning to charge the jury. He reminded the jury in his charge that Philadelphia was rife with undisciplined publishers and that libel had become a national crime, revealing to them that he had himself bound over Cobbett and calling on them to do their part in turn.[65] The grand jury failed to heed his advice and (as in the Oswald case) returned a bill of ignoramus, dismissing the charges against Cobbett and thereby preventing his being taken before a petit, or trial, jury. McKean was not, however, to be deterred from taking action and, accordingly, held Cobbett in contempt, as he had done with Oswald, for violating a peace bond pledging good behavior during the course of the grand jury hearings.

Cobbett replied to the recognizance case in *Respublica v. Cobbett* (1798) contending that "he was an alien, a subject of the king of Great Britain"[66] and that this was a suit against an alien by a state. Since the Judicial Act gave the federal circuit court authority over civil cases involving aliens, he was entitled to have his suit removed to that court. Nothing barred federal jurisdiction since the case was to recover a debt, "though in the name of the commonwealth," as opposed to a criminal case involving a breach of the law. The commonwealth responded that removing to a federal court "would prostrate the authority of the individual states" and that the suit, though not called a criminal case was, in fact, "a suit of a criminal nature."[67] Presiding over the case in the Pennsylvania Supreme Court, Chief Justice McKean's decision affirmed the state's jurisdiction on the grounds that the Judicial Act "did not extend to actions brought against aliens by a state" and that the recognizance, albeit a civil suit, that is, a contract suit, "was taken to prevent criminal action by the defendant [and] . . . for no other purpose."[68]

Chief Justice McKean, speaking for the supreme court, refused Cobbett's application to federal court, as Cobbett reported, "without the least hesitation, without consulting his associates, and without giving any reason whatever for his decision."[69] Cobbett's own counsel had strongly resisted his application as prejudicial to his case. He, nevertheless,

> resolved on removing the cause, notwithstanding the repeated remonstrances of my lawyers, who made use of every argument that could be thought of, to persuade me to abandon my intention. They were fully of opinion, that there was no danger in the Supreme Court of Pennsylvania, and that declaring myself in open court, a subject of the King of Great Britain, would be tantamount to a declaration that monarchy was preferable to republicanism, and would of course not only be very offensive to the Court before whom such declaration was made, but would inevitably tend to render me odious in the eyes of the people of America.[70]

His lawyer at the time, Mr. Thomas, a man in whom Cobbett had little confidence and whom he believed had been bribed,[71] rose to speak in a trembling voice to present the petition. Cobbett described the scene:

> For some time he did not make himself heard. There was a great talking all round the bar; Levi, the lawyer, was reading a long formal paper to the Judges, and the Judges were laughing over the chit-chat of the day. Amidst the noisy mirth that surrounded him, there stood poor Thomas, with his papers in his hands, like a culprit at school, just as the boys are breaking up. . . . The moment the sound of the word *Cobbett* struck the ear of M'Kean, he turned towards the bar, and having learnt the subject of the petition, began to storm like a madman. A dead silence ensued. The little scrubby lawyers . . . crouched down for fear, just like a brood of poultry, when the kite is prepared to pounce in amongst them; whilst hapless Thomas, who stood up piping like a straggled chicken, seemed already to feel the talons of the judicial bird of prey. . . . M'Kean did, indeed, grin most horribly, and I could very distinctly hear, "*insolent scoundrel!*"—"*damned aristocrat!*"—"*damned Englishman!*" etc. etc. from the mouths of the sovereign people.[72]

Cobbett compared the legal argument in the hearing in March 1798 to a Punch and Judy show ("Pulchinello and the Devil")[73] throughout which the members of the court never stopped talking. They apparently found the case less entertaining than their own conversation. When their conversation ended, "M'Kean, turning his head towards Hopkinson, bawled out: '*Ha'nt you most done?*' This put an end to the *law argument*, in a moment. No showman, with the help of a wire, ever produced more ready or more implicit obedience; and kite[74] M'Kean now hastened to put an end to the farce, by declaring . . . *that the petition of William Cobbett should not be granted.*"[75]

In *Respublica v. Cobbett* (1800), the court found against Cobbett on the Yrujo recognizance, this time with Chief Justice Shippen, McKean's acolyte, presiding and McKean himself a newly elected governor of the state. The court determined, public protest to the contrary, "the guilt of a party may be determined in a suit *scrie facias*[76] without a previous conviction."[77] Arguing a tautology, Shippen held that libels destroyed "public and private happiness" which resulted in breaches of the peace; in turn, breaches of the peace led to the need to keep the peace. For the court's part, he concluded, libels thereby "merit every discouragement to which they may be legally subjected,"[78] including prior restraints on the press in the form of peace bonds. On this issue, however, the public was not in the court's corner. The supreme court's insistence on using a peace bond approach to silence Cobbett meant that the accused had in advance of breaking the law to guarantee a surety that could be forfeited, ensuring that the defendant would not commit a particular prohibited act. It was a strategy used on the smallest provocation to require a defendant to assume a weighty financial burden and a constraint on his freedom, even if he was acquitted of the original charges in a case. A party need not be charged nor need he be given an opportunity to defend himself before the imposition of the peace bond, aspects of the process that recalled the excesses of English rule in the colonies and broke with common law's proscription against prior restraint.

Here, Cobbett would have had the sympathy of his critics, even if their politics prevented them from supporting him openly on the issue. The fact that prior restraint was not explicitly resorted to in the Rush case—in spite of what appears to have been Rush's original intent by suggesting nothing be spoken on his behalf in the press—suggests that the supreme court had indeed exceeded the limits of the public's patience in pursuing Cobbett.[79] Irrespective of the public's sentiments, Shippen continued McKean's enmity for the press in his conduct of the 1799 *Rush v. Cobbett* trial and in the 1800 Yrujo recognizance case *Respublica v. Cobbett*. The Pennsylvania Supreme Court under Justice Shippen's leadership would continue to be criticized, as the historian of the court G. S. Rowe would put it, for being "too quick to facilitate libel suits and too quick to encourage those who would use the court against their political enemies."[80]

Cobbett's *The Republican Judge or the American Liberty of the Press* (1798) is a useful resource for teasing out Cobbett's issues with the American judiciary and the press, as well as the key political themes upon which Cobbett relied over his career in Philadelphia. The year 1798 is, in particular, a useful time to sample his sentiments, as just one year earlier the charges were filed in *Rush v. Cobbett* and one year later the case would actually go to trial. Moreover, *The Republican Judge* was written, as its subtitle (*American*

Liberty of the Press, as Exhibited, Explained, and Exposed, in the Base and Partial Prosecution of William Cobbett) tells us, in an effort to explicate Cobbett's judicial problems with the Supreme Court of Pennsylvania as the Rush case's trial court. It was the very work whose publication led McKean to pursue Cobbett for violating a recognizance for good behavior in the Yrujo case. The title figure in the work was, of course, then-chief justice and soon-to-be governor McKean, and the case directly addressed in the work was the 1797 Yrujo case. That the grand jury refused to issue an indictment in a case in which the chief justice had become so personally involved, and so judicially over-invested—as prosecutor, witness, and judge—gave Cobbett all the ammunition he needed to claim persecution by and corruption of republican government in Pennsylvania. As he revealed in a letter dated April 10, 1798, that prefaced the work and was addressed to "Englishmen," a set of controlling contentions had dominated his thinking: that the French were engaged in a terroristic revolution; that France was bound on destroying American government; that republican government in America was enamored of the French; and that America believed not only that it exhibited "the happy effects of a finished revolution" but that Britain would be happy if it too was "revolutionized *into a republic*."[81] The sole object of the work, Cobbett clarified, was to guard his neighbors against an evil, which was a duty he would embrace even "were I a native American."[82]

The Francophobic frame within which Cobbett couched his thoughts was in fact referenced in McKean's charge to the jury in the Yrujo case, where the judge made clear that journalists in Philadelphia used "vulgar and opprobrious language, not only against the French nation and their allies, but the very men in power with whom the ministers of our country are sent to negociate."[83] He complained of the tendency of these papers to "frustrate a reconciliation . . . and provoke a war *between the sister republics* . . . nay, to subvert all *Republican* governments whatsoever." The reference to President Adams's attempt to negotiate with the French in the aftermath of Jay's Treaty with England in order to sidestep the possibility of a war with France suggested that the pretense of a libel trial masked, in the Yrujo case as in *Rush v. Cobbett*, a desire to conduct a sedition trial against an editor with pro-British sentiments. It would, as a result, come as no surprise to those who followed the *Rush v. Cobbett* trial that Cobbett would be prosecuted as much for his attacks on republicans and for his status as an alien as for his presumed libel of Benjamin Rush.

In the Yrujo case, Cobbett attacked the Spanish minister for his vitriolic criticism of England at a time when Spain was under the heel of France and its king sat on his throne at the pleasure of the French. The Bill of Indictment held that Cobbett had maliciously defamed both the King of Spain and his minister, that he had thus disturbed the peace existing between the United States and Spain,[84] and that he had thereby offended the "peace and dignity" of Pennsylvania.[85] True enough, Cobbett had published a piece in *Porcupine's Gazette* referring to the Spanish King as "the supple tool" of nefarious French politics and to his minister as "governed, like a dependant . . . by the direction of the French agents in America."[86] The French themselves were accused of spreading the "poison of their principles among the mob" and having corrupted "rebels and parricides" with money.[87] Yrujo was thus to be regarded as "half Don and half Sans-Culotte," according to a second piece that Cobbett published in his newspaper.[88] Cobbett's argument was that if such words were libels then any book may be construed a libel,[89] and that he had, in any case, only printed, not written, the words in question.

What Cobbett principally objected to in *The Republican Judge*, however, was McKean's charge to the jury. Here, he claimed, the judge rushed past such "trifling offences" as treason and murder to arrive "at the more solid and substantial sin of LIBELLING."[90] McKean's argument was the familiar one that the journalist had breached the public peace and stirred up "families and friends to acts of revenge, and perhaps of bloodshed,"[91] the fear of which justified the most severe laws. The coolness and deliberation of their authors and the long life and wide propagation of the libels themselves constituted for McKean the dangers that libels posed.[92] The "moral turpitude" libels implied took away a man's reputation which, "more dear than life itself," leads to bad blood, revenge, and breaches of the peace.

Even so, McKean presented himself as making a fine distinction between preventing the press from publishing a piece and holding it responsible for abuses once it is published. In spite of the prohibition that his use of a peace bond implied, he contended that free will was allowed and only abuse of that free will was to be punished.[93] Equally, the use of the courts to register complaints rather than advertise them in the press was promoted so that citizens would have a means of redress through the law which alone offered fairness and justice. There should thus be no need to accuse through the press, particularly in Philadelphia where for years past such scurrility had raged that "libeling has become a national crime [which] distinguishes us not only from all the states around us, but from the whole civilized world."[94] McKean's greatest fear was that men like Cobbett would provoke the nation into war and make it impossible for officials to negotiate with foreign powers.

Admitting his own interference in the case in binding over Cobbett to ensure future good behavior, McKean appealed to the jury to do its part by returning a true bill. In Cobbett's words, McKean's charge was unlike that of a judge and more like the "impassioned pleadings of an advocate,"[95] a personal rather than a judicial apeal that employed all his persuasive powers to bring the law down on Cobbett. As for himself, Cobbett argued, he never slandered any one "if the promulgation of useful truths be not slander."[96] Rather, his mission had been a just one: "To undeceive the misguided, by tearing the mask from . . . artful and ferocious villains,"[97] more particularly from the very men in public life whom the judge felt honor-bound to protect. For Cobbett, public figures were "*more open* to the censure of the press";[98] for McKean public figures ought to be immune from criticism.

In practice, and certainly as such distinctions affected *Rush v. Cobbett*, public and private reputations and acts,[99] federal and private actions were not easily distinguished. The Cobbett defense in the Rush case, for example, held that Rush might have been a private figure but that he performed a public role and was thereby a public figure whose actions were open to discussion. The Rush prosecution held that Rush was indeed a private figure but that attacking him raised issues of breach of the peace that threatened the social order and thereby had public implications. Cobbett's reaction to McKean's view of libel law, in sum, was that it violated the spirit of the state constitution. If publications "must not only be *decent*, *candid*, and *true*, but, besides all this, they must 'have an eye solely to the *public good*'," and if "Not only the *facts* are to be established, and the *manner* and *stile* approved by the court, but even the *motives* . . . may be construed into a ground for punishing him,"[100] then the republican claim that truth could be no libel was a fraud.[101]

As a back story to *Rush v. Cobbett*, it is useful to note that, as with the Yrujo case, we see the republican judicial apparatus shifting its treatment of libel. On the cusp of McKean's governership and Jefferson's presidency, the republican response to federalist prosecution of seditious libel was to move cases from the federal to the state venue, from criminal to civil cases, and from a focus on political expression to personal reputation, both public and private.[102] Such a tack meant that the republican prosecution of Cobbett could be framed not only as a question of defending reputation rather than attacking the press,[103] but as a way of serving the public good by ensuring that the best men would remain in public life. In procedural terms, it meant that the loss in the 1797 Yrujo case, a criminal prosecution, would be matched with Rush's filing of a civil case against Cobbett in the same year and in the same state court. Not only were Cobbett's petitions to remove both his cases to a federal court denied, but Rush's triumph in his case two years later would avenge Yrujo's loss and justify the Rush case as a republican response to federalist sedition trials.[104]

CHANGES IN LEGAL PRACTICE

What we find reflected in the libel and sedition cases we have considered are several developments in legal proceedings that describe the conditions that applied to the *Rush v. Cobbett* case. As William E. Nelson makes clear, the movement in American law changed from enforcing the prerevolutionary "morals and religion of the people" to protecting their postrevolutionary "property and physical security."[105] From 1760 to 1774, the colonies had focused on offenses against morality; by the end of the century, the nation focused on economic and political crimes. The country's survival was at stake, not its spiritual health. The sins of concern were no longer those against God but those against one's fellow citizens, their property, their livelihoods,[106] and their country. Questions of rebellion and authority were the foremost orders of business in the new nation, that is, issues of order and power, not religion and morality. In its developing state across the eighteenth century, American law moved from its earlier push against the envelope of English occupation to an unsettled state of party politicking over power relations in its own government. The threats of economic instability, mob rule, and riot would require a stable legal system and a new role for the courts that would deal less with suits between citizens and more with prosecutions by the government and resolution of the role of government in the lives of its citizens.[107] Over the course of the eighteenth century, American law thus transformed the way it understood its role as an agent of social change and social policy in the republic.

Eighteenth century law was very much under the sway of what Nelson considers an "unquestioning acceptance of British precedent,"[108] which, for better or worse, defendants would have to live with. More to their benefit, however, was the established inscrutability of juries, including the jury's relative independence from the influence that judges exerted through their charges and through the practice of returning juries to reconsider verdicts the judge found unpalatable.[109] Entering the eighteenth century, as Stephan Landsman offers,

> Counsel seldom participated, few, if any, rules of evidence constrained enquiry, judges routinely examined witnesses and defendants in the most vigorous, and at times ruthless, manner, only prosecution witnesses were allowed to swear testimonial oaths and thereby enhance the credibility of their statements, jurors were free to utilize private knowledge gained outside the confines of the courtroom, judges frequently introduced their political views into proceedings, and there was virtually no appellate procedure.[110]

Early in the century, the accused did not in essence enjoy the right to remain silent in court. Defendants who chose not to testify would go unheard as counsel could not speak for them. By contrast, if they chose to testify, they had to do so without the right to testify under oath, which diminished the presumed veracity of their testimony from the juror's point of view. Neither was there a presumption of innocence, as the accused bore the responsibility to demonstrate he was not guilty.

As late as *Republica v. Oswald* (1788), the accused was placed in the position of acting for himself in spite of the presence of counsel, although by now defendants had the right to speak under oath. The residual "accused speaks" model still influenced prosecutors like Mr. Lewis in the Oswald case who represented favorably the necessity for the accused to speak in his own defense, asserting that Oswald was not, as some complained, compelled to convict himself by his testimony but might be able

> by his own oath to purge and acquit himself, in spite of all the testimony, which can possibly be produced against him. . . . The court employ no compulsion in this respect. He may either answer, or not, as he pleases: if he does answer, his single oath, in his own favour, will countervail the oaths of a thousand witnesses, and if he does not answer, his silence corroborates the evidence which has been offered of the contempt, and the judgment of this court must necessarily follow.[111]

Attempting to capitalize on a climate in which the accused when silent was suspect, Alexander Dallas, William Duane's preference for counsel in his 1800 sedition case, had in fact recommended to the defendant that he adopt an "accused speaks" strategy on the grounds that extenuation was best presented to advantage by the accused rather than counsel.[112] Some defendants still felt they had no choice but to represent themselves (the accused in *U.S. v. Cooper*, 1800, for example)[113] because they considered their counsel manacled or gagged in court or because they wished they had spoken in their own behalf (as Cobbett wished he had in *Rush v. Cobbett*).

A disconcerting jockeying over authority in the courtroom had resulted from the failure to delineate the roles of the judge, counsel, and the jury. Coming off a period in which judges had a great deal of authority in the court, both in the conduct of the trial and in their charges to the jury, the judge could no longer assume the functions of witness, prosecutor, and to some extent jury, nor could they easily replace counsel who challenged them. With full development of an adversarial system, the judge ceased interrogating witnesses and was expected to assume authority over question of the law and charge the jury with clear instructions on judging based upon the facts of the case.[114] Judges lost influence over juries as counsel gained in importance and were left to apply rules of evidence to offset counsel's new authority from unduly influencing jury verdicts on behalf of their clients.[115] With the advent of meaningful representation by counsel as the century progressed, the accused enjoyed the opportunity to be represented by a trained voice and the plaintiff in a criminal trial to be represented by a public prosecutor.[116]

With the diminishing influence of judges, rules of evidence developed that gave defense counsel the ability to challenge witnesses and proof, insist upon corroboration of testimony, challenge confessions, and protect the accused from self-incrimination, while the burden of proof would shift to the prosecution. Probable cause, exclusion of evidence, and credibility tests would emerge as standards of proof became established. Counsel could open a case and address closing arguments to the jury rather than merely examine or cross-examine witnesses, and judges ceased acting as interrogators.[117] Most importantly, the form of the modern trial process would solidify, creating some order in the court, providing a structure for presenting a case and fixing due process as a norm.

THE VENUE: THE PENNSYLVANIA SUPREME COURT

Beyond the developments in libel law, the history of prior libel and subsequent sedition cases, and changes that the legal process was undergoing, *Rush v. Cobbett* would also have to deal with the history, traditions, and power of the Pennsylvania Supreme Court. The mystique of the site chosen for the *Rush v. Cobbett* trial ensured a contest that would reverberate with Jefferson's message for the resurrection of republicanism. The Pennsylvania Supreme Court was ensconced in the west wing of the Pennsylvania State House,[118] later to be known as Independence Hall, just across the hallway from the eastern meeting hall, known as Independence Chamber for the obvious reason that it was there that the Second Continental Congress delivered the Declaration of Independence. Frank Etting in 1891 referred to the signing of that document as "the Magna Charta, the memorable act which sanctified the whole building—the already expected 'Runnymede of America'."[119] Having begun its metaphoric transformation as a workshop for liberty, a breakout from England, and an establishment of an independent state,[120] the building was subsequently to be known as the site of the ratification of the Bill of Rights in 1791, George Washington's inauguration in 1793 and his Farewell Address in 1797, as well as John Adams's inauguration in 1797.[121] Jefferson's words were thus completely aligned with the sentiment expressed by the building itself: the connection between 1776 and the 1790s was unavoidable and resonant with political possibilities. *Rush v. Cobbett* was, as a result, to be tried in a chamber that was symmetrically situated to balance Independence Chamber. For the ten years (1790–1800) that Philadelphia served as capital of the United States, it was sandwiched between the U.S. Supreme Court in the east building (Philadelphia City Hall) and the U.S. Congress in the west building (Congress Hall).

The historical significance of the site could not have escaped its occupants during the time of the trial and surely added to the fervor with which the litigation was invested. Sealing the link that joined 1776 and 1798, *Rush v. Cobbett* enhanced its position as a meaningful event in republican politics by virtue of the very architecture that housed it, allowing it to take its heat from the themes forged by Jeffersonian republicanism in the crucible of the Alien-Sedition Act years and to add its own spark to the flame that would carry Jefferson to the White House in 1800. A founding signer of the very declaration that separated the colonies from their parent, as indeed was Chief Justice McKean himself, Rush was, as his counsel contended, a shining beacon for Philadelphia, the court audience, and the jury. It was no coincidence that the performance space in which the trial played out resonated with the prosecution's chosen theme. The jury in its verdict would find it difficult to avoid mirroring the culturally significant themes Rush's counsel would feature: America as a chosen land; Americans as a chosen people; the testing and redemption of such a people; and the promise of republicanism as a hope for the future of America and its cultural exceptionalism.

With all the resonance offered by the supreme court as a site for the Rush trial, Rush's application to the court was a calculated move. Of the civil cases heard in that space, only select ones were chosen. George Washington, for example, filed with the court in 1786 to hear a property case. As court historian G. S. Rowe explains, Washington's lawyers did so "on the assumption that the Supreme Court would be more sympathetic to him and his case and . . . interpret the law in Washington's favor. Their assumptions were well founded."[122] Rush's standing in the city would ensure that his case would be one of those likely to be heard.

The choice of the supreme court as a first trier of fact for a civil case was made "on a strictly nonlegal basis"[123] and carried with it the cache of having a more prestigious body try one's case, a strategically useful consideration from Rush's perspective in trying to resurrect his reputation. Under the *nisi prius* system prevailing in the court, judges could oversee trials as well as appeals.[124] As well, they could try both civil and criminal cases, the conduct of which did not differ in general.[125] That this court handled criminal cases might well account in the Rush case for Shippen's charge to the jury with regard to damages—that it could award both exemplary and compensatory damages,[126] that is, as Cobbett complained, both civil and criminal damages. Moreover, sedition as a criminal case was the special province of the supreme court, so that it is not surprising that the political influence of seditious libel cases reverberated across the spectrum of civil and criminal cases the court oversaw.[127]

Once the court accepted his case, Rush could capitalize on his association with at least two of the court's prior members. His younger brother, Jacob Rush, had after all been appointed by McKean to serve on the court for seven years, from 1784 to 1791.[128] McKean himself had benefited politically from Benjamin Rush's support in 1788 in the fight for ratification of the federal constitution, a fight in which McKean was heavily invested. Rush's good opinion of McKean is evidenced in a letter he wrote claiming that the ratification was "carried by a great law officer [McKean] to denote the elevation of the government of law and justice above everything else."[129] The ratification came in the same month that the publisher Eleazer Oswald filed an impeachment proceeding with the Pennsylvania Assembly against McKean and two members of his court—Jacob Rush and William Atlee—to remove them from the bench.[130] Oswald considered that Benjamin Rush had instigated the 1788 supreme court case against him to stymie his opposition to the federal constitution,[131] which together with Rush's support of McKean would have endeared Rush to the court, putting him on the right side of the press controversy and aligning him politically with the chief justice, who essentially was the court over his twenty-two-year tenure (1777–1799). In a final twist, the court that sat for *Rush v. Cobbett* (Edward Shippen, Jasper Yeates, and Thomas Smith—who themselves survived an impeachment battle in 1804 over the use of a peace bond)[132] was likely to be sympathetic to Rush's case. Clearly monolithic in its makeup,[133] the court was made up of conservative republicans who shared the same political philosophy and maintained connections typical of the state's elite, wealthy class. Shippen in particular found good reason to be sympathetic, for at the time of the Rush trial McKean was in the process of replacing himself as chief justice on the court and Shippen was in contention.[134] McKean had been urged to appoint Benjamin Chew, a former chief justice, and at least three other candidates were presented: Jasper Yeates, Moses Levy, and James Ross. Shippen's performance in *Rush v. Cobbett*, in effect avenging McKean for Cobbett's attacks on the chief justice, may well have tipped the balance in Shippen's favor.

In the run-up to *Rush v. Cobbett*, the Pennsylvania Supreme Court had to deal with problems of its own that could potentially affect the conduct of the trial. Critically, the court had to define state jurisdiction and defend it against encroachment by the federal courts, particularly in light of federal excise taxation and land claims[135] and their potential threat to respect for state law and public order.[136] The tension in the supreme court's struggle to assert itself as a state court was palpable. The federal court's concern for the rights of out-of-state and foreign citizens (with its implications for national identity and foreign policy) and the state's concern for its citizens' rights (with its implications for regional security and the welfare of the local citizenry) were mirrored in Cobbett's application to try the case in a federal court and Rush's decision to take it to the Pennsylvania Supreme Court. The inconsistency of disqualifying Cobbett from a federal trial in the Yrujo case on the grounds that the action was essentially a criminal matter and then reversing itself to disqualify him in the Rush case because the case was a civil one went largely unnoted by the court.[137]

In addition to its struggle for state's rights, the court needed to assert itself as a viable and independent institution separate from the legislature and with the authority to validate the constitutionality of the laws passed by the legislature.[138] It had, as well, to justify its self-presentation as an elite institution, which ran counter to republican ideas in the eyes of the public,[139] and its reliance upon English common law and legal practices. A big part of the court's dilemma as it related to *Rush v. Cobbett* was the reputation the court had engendered under Chief Justice McKean, particularly on the issue of libel law. The more power the court aggregated to itself[140] in its criminal and civil as well as its original and equity jurisdictions, the more critical the court's harshness against publishers of libel became, which set the tone for the court from the 1780s through the 1790s.[141] As Rowe expresses the court's dilemma, "By 1799 a substantial number of Pennsylvanians held the position that the high court stood as a barrier to legitimate democratic and egalitarian aspirations."[142] This was a conception of its function that the court would have to dispel if it was to exercise itself as a powerful institution defending the public interest under newly elected Governor McKean's republican administration in 1800.[143]

The court's application of common law on libel was tied to its assumption of the functions of an equity court. As an equity court, the Pennsylvania Supreme Court's reliance upon principles of fairness and natural law allowed it to go beyond positive law to redress what it considered failures of justice,[144] clearly a problem for the court in the 1790s.[145] Equity translated in some cases into an exercise that preferred the court's idea of justice, political favoritism, or personal agendas to established precedent and legislative authority.[146] It expressed itself in a form of discretion that voided laws and presented as judicial activism,[147] redefining rights not only for those involved in libel cases but for minors, blacks, women, the poor, and former Tories as well as in cases of property and inheritance rights.[148] By the end of McKean's chief justiceship, the court was guilty of an activism that produced widespread resistance,[149] even as judicial discretion was hard to see and difficult to track in malleable situations and in the hands of elite and aggressive judges.

Rush v. Cobbett was thus tried before a court that was caught in a transitional period and that found itself under assault. At the same time, the court was a powerful institution pulled in different directions. Accused, on the one hand, of abusing its powers and of failing to express republican values, the court, on the other hand, performed the role of teaching about the law both as a lesson and as a form of theater. The justices' opinions on the great cases of their time were intended to educate on citizenship and to inform on legal and political philosophy. Its judicial reputation would have significant reach through the collection of law reports of supreme court cases, such that its rulings, as Rowe claims, "redefined the lives of people throughout the state in important regards."[150] If republican values were short shrifted by the court, if its activism was resisted, and if the court was attacked for its elitism and reliance on English legal practices, *Rush v. Cobbett* offered a route to accessing the public and making a course correction that would mediate the court's relationship with the citizenry and its attacks on the press. Indeed, the verdict might itself have represented the best response the court could make to the frequent, vociferous attacks upon its legitimacy. The case was, after all, a high profile case that aroused public feelings under conditions where the high court was regarded with ambivalence, if not resentment, and where McKean's own charges against Cobbett and the latter's unrelenting attacks on the chief justice motivated the high court. The Rush case was a good match for the court's jurisprudence, since the very issues that defined the court after the revolution—libel, a free press, English common law, the proper use of the law, federal and state jurisdiction, republican values, and political philosophy—were the very issues raised in the Rush case.

Still, the legitimacy of the court was at stake in the late 1790s in the same way that the revolution itself seemed at risk. As an institution reflecting the struggle over the meaning of independence that pitted federalists against republicans, the court had to address laws, customs, and values under changed social, political, and economic conditions, just as it had to balance individual and collective interests and deal with the egos and private agendas that had notably characterized the court under Chief Justice McKean.[151] An involved citizenry and contested political questions demanded much from a court that had yet to develop the character of a lasting institution.[152] Facing the replacement of the chief justice after his extensive tenure and anticipating significant reforms should Jefferson win the election, the court was caught in an interstitial period where much was demanded in terms of the definition and use of its power. *Rush v. Cobbett* thus came at a critical time in the history of the court. As a high profile case, it would be tried in the midst of serious personal, ideological, and institutional pressures on the court that could not help but affect it. Indeed, one could argue that the court's sensitivity to the need to resolve its questioned authority and to pressures exerted toward popular sovereignty[153] might have tempted it to split the difference in the Rush case by applying common law libel (which favors government, public men, and public order) in a way that privileged a local hero, privacy of the individual, and republicanism (state law) over federalism (federal law) and that preferred republican (native Americanism) over federalist ideology (as a stand-in for the English).

FLEEING THE TRIAL

With the court that was to try *Rush v. Cobbett* enmeshed in a legitimacy crisis, and with the plaintiff entangled in a decisional web, it was Cobbett's turn to struggle with the case's prospects. Whereas Rush could be construed as having taken great risks to access the law, Cobbett's departure for New York on the eve of the trial left him open to charges that he had taken the coward's way out. Cobbett left for New York on December 9, four days before the case was tried,[154] and was convinced that after more than two years of court delays the case might never be called. His departure, he later argued, encouraged "the American Sangrado to push the cause to trial."[155] Cobbett's absence from the trial foreclosed the prospect of his meaningfully assisting counsel in his defense. Whatever his rationale for being absent, the old "accused speaks" model would play a dispositive role in the trial.[156] Silence would prove incriminating and the burden of proof would, in effect, revert to the defendant; the accused's right not to incriminate himself would be balanced against the expectation that he would defend himself.[157] One of Cobbett's own lawyers, William Rawle, obliquely noted his empty seat, reminding the jury that "Our client is absent, he has rested his case with you to give your decision upon his rights of publication."[158] Contrasted to Rush's physical presence in the courtroom as a citizen of the city and the nation, a favorite son and a distinguished professional, Cobbett's failure to appear made him look every bit the contemptuous alien, the Englishman, the foreigner, to which the prosecution had gone to great lengths to portray him.

Biographers have offered several explanations for Cobbett's flight from Philadelphia. Writing on the trial, Winthrop Neilson and Frances Neilson call Cobbett's flight a "supreme gesture of contempt."[159] Carl A. L. Binger, a Rush biographer, suggests that Cobbett's attack on President Adams over going to war with France and a threat by Adams to use the Alien and Sedition Acts of 1798 to deport the journalist[160] provided a motive for Cobbett's sudden departure for New York.[161] The biographer and editor of Cobbett's letters, G. D. H. Cole, argues that Cobbett had relocated to New York certain his property would be seized if he stayed in Philadelphia until the case was settled.[162] Mary Elizabeth Clark, a Cobbett biographer as well, conjectures that Cobbett had no real reason to remain behind, as his lawyers did not seem to think it was necessary and any fine from the trial seemed likely to be minimal.[163] She considers that his absence was inadvertent, that Cobbett had lingered on in the city well after his property had already been disposed of, and that he only left when, after more than two years of delay, it seemed the trial would be put off yet again.[164]

Cobbett posited his preferred theory for the trial going forward: his absence from Philadelphia. The evidence for such a claim, however, is conflicting. On the day he left Philadelphia, he sent a letter to Edward Tilghman expressing his confidence in his defense and providing directions in case the trial went against him.[165] In a letter dated five days after the trial began and ten days after Cobbett left for New York, he did not suggest that the trial was hastily put on when it became apparent he would be out of town or that his absence was inadvertent.[166] It was not until three months after the trial, in the fourth issue of *Rush-Light*, which he identified the circumstance most favorable to Rush's chance for success in the trial and the best reason "to push the cause on to trial: which was, *my absence from Philadelphia.*"[167] As he claimed,

> I remained in the neighbourhood of the city (where I was seen every day), in order to be present at the trial, if it should come on. On the 7th of December there was no prospect of the cause being brought to trial; on the 8th, therefore, I came off for New-York, where my affairs required my presence. On the 11th my correspondent wrote me that the cause was put off to another court; but the *very next day*, it was all at once resolved to bring it to trial immediately. This sudden change was produced by an advertisement of mine, signifying *my arrival at New-York, and my resolution to drop the publication of Porcupine's Gazette.*[168]

Eleven days after the trial, he proffered to his friend Edward Thornton that he would "briefly state my reasons for quitting Philadelphia" in his farewell issue of *Porcupine's Gazette* on January 13, 1800.[169] In that issue, he provided the following, with a glancing reference to the thief Macheath of John Gay's *The Beggar's Opera* : "Remembering, as you must, my solemn promise to quit Pennsylvania, in case my old democratic Judge, MACK KEAN, should be elected Governor . . . there are, I trust, very few of you, who will be surprised to find that I am no longer in that degraded and degrading State."[170] Cobbett reminded his readers again in *Rush-Light* that he had promised to leave Pennsylvania if McKean became governor.[171] Apparently Cobbett did not weigh very heavily the prospect that McKean's election might benefit him rather than promote his departure. If the chief justice had not been elected governor of the state the September before the trial, it is likely he would have presided over the case when it was called in December. One could argue that it might have been in Cobbett's favor to have the case heard by another judge. Even if McKean's election to governor had been an incentive to remain in Philadelphia for the trial, Cobbett's feelings about McKean make his remove to New York less unintelligible. His hopes for the kind of trial in which he could prevail on his own terms were minimal at best. Leaving for New York would, at the very least, put him beyond the reach of Pennsylvania law and his old nemesis.

Cobbett could have avoided going to trial at all, according to George Spater, another Cobbett biographer, but he was incapable of standing down sufficiently to allow for such a possibility. Citing a rather full calendar of political events during the two years spent waiting for the trial to be called, Spater points out that the trial might never have gone forward had Cobbett not persisted in stirring the pot.[172] His publication of *The Republican Judge* certainly stoked the political fires, as did Cobbett's active opposition to McKean's candidacy for governor in 1799. The public, meanwhile, was preoccupied with the XYZ Affair, the passage of the Alien and Sedition Acts in the summer of the same year, the threat of an anticipated war with France, and preparations for the presidential campaign of 1800. Thus, while the trial might have been avoided, once Cobbett insisted on drawing attention to himself those very events that had eclipsed it would come back to haunt him. Not only did they infiltrate the trial but they came to dominate the construction of Cobbett as an alien, a federalist, and an Englishman, the very constructions that Rush and his defense team would find so profitable to exploit.[173]

The prosecution's story of Cobbett's flight pictured a man who wished the city of Philadelphia ill, weakening it in its hour of need. The prosecution associated Cobbett with cowardly and unpatriotic miscreants who had fled during the yellow fever epidemic, and it represented Cobbett in highly suggestive imagery of pollution and contamination that identified him with the fever itself and its evils. The sermons of the recent epidemic still rang in the ears of the good citizens of the jury. Many divines had suggested that those who fled should be forgiven and others had suggested that the fugitives did not trust in the Lord, that they chose to show "sinful temerity" and that they lacked faith in good works and God's forgiveness. For Cobbett, flight was thus framed to arouse strong feelings no matter which choice he made, so that merely raising the issue had the potential to split the jury and cast doubt on the defendant.

That Cobbett imperfectly fit the picture of an absconder was of little concern to Rush's counsel and was unlikely to register with the jury. Whereas during the epidemic in the year of the trial he did leave the city, unlike Rush,[174] during the fever of 1797 Cobbett had in fact stayed in the city while many others fled. Still, republicans like Philip Freneau gave neither Cobbett nor his fellow federalist journalist John Fenno credit for remaining behind when the fever raged in 1797. Freneau saw them instead as invasive snakes coiled in the bosom of the city:

> From Penn's famous city what hosts have departed,
> The streets and the houses are nearly deserted,
> But still there remain
> Two Vipers, that's plain,

Who soon, it is thought, yellow flag will display;
Old Porcupine preaching,
And Fenno beseeching
Some dung-cart to wheel him away.

Philadelphians, we're sorry you suffer by fevers,
Or suffer such scullions to be your deceivers;
Will. Pitt's noisy whelp
With his red foxy scalp
Whom the kennels of London spew'd out in a fright,
Has scullk'd over here
To snuffle and sneer,
Like a puppy to snap, or a bull dog to bite.

If cut from the gallows, or kick'd from the post,
Such fellows as these are of England the boast
But Columbia's disgrace!
Begone from that place
That was dignified once by a Franklin and Penn,
But infested by you
And your damnable crew
Will soon be deserted by all honest men.[175]

Freneau featured Cobbett's noisy preaching and his viperous nature, citing him rather for staying to deceive than for stealing away from suffering. The connection with a "damnable crew," those "cut from the gallows," and sneering curs implicitly linked him to scavengers who roamed the city to plunder homes and coffins. Cobbett became one with the infestation and soon, it was hoped, would fly the yellow flag that identified the presence of the yellow fever, to be dragged off in death, as Fenno had been, by a dung-cart. Freneau took up the notion raised in some sermons that those who remained under such conditions were not honest men, but men who risked the lives of others by fostering the festering fever and spreading it to others. When a city was "deserted by all honest men," those who remained must, by default, be villains. Such press commentary helped the prosecution during the trial and reinforced its ability to raise the issue of Cobbett's absence, as well as his presence, in the city.

NOTES

1. Katz (1963, 11–12).
2. Katz (1963, 12).
3. Rosenberg (1986, 12).
4. Rosenberg (1986, 4).
5. Rosenberg (1986, 6).

6. Rosenberg (1986, 78).
7. Blackstone (1774, 4: 151).
8. Blackstone (1774, 4: 152).
9. Rosenberg (1986, 87, 150).
10. Blackstone (1774, 4: 151–52).
11. Blackstone (1774, 4: 153).
12. Rosenberg (1986, 90).
13. As quoted in Hall (1989, 315).
14. Hall (1989, 84–85).
15. Rosenberg (1986, 54, 69).
16. Rosenberg (1986, 49, 89).
17. Rosenberg (1986, 65).
18. First Amendment, United States Constitution.
19. Sedition Act, 1798, Section 3.
20. Rosenberg (1986, 87).
21. Smith (1988, 32).
22. Katz (1963, 8).
23. Alexander (1963, 58).
24. Alexander (1963, 62).
25. Alexander (1963, 75).
26. Alexander (1963, 101).
27. Alexander (1963, 98).
28. Alexander (1963, 96-97).
29. *Pennsylvania Packet*, January 21, 1783.
30. *Respublica v. Oswald* (1788, 325–26).
31. Rowe (1994, 170).
32. Rowe (1994, 171); Shapiro (1991, 89).
33. *Pennsylvania Packet*, February 1, 1783.
34. *Pennsylvania Packet*, January 25, 1783. See Hopkinson's poem written in response to the Oswald case, "A DESCANT ON ADRIAN"S Assertion, that a grand jury is nothing more than a *legal machine* subject to the direction and control of the court" (1792, 1: 228–38); Myrsiades (2008, 167–72).
35. *Respublica v. Oswald* (1788); Dallas (1790, 325).
36. Cited in *Respublica v. Oswald* (1788); Dallas (1790, 319–20).
37. *Respublica v. Oswald* (1788), Dallas (1790, 320).
38. Rowe (1978, 254); Rowe (1994, 196).
39. *Respublica v. Oswald* (1788); Dallas (1790, 329).
40. *Respublica v. Oswald* (1788); Dallas (1790, 329).
41. Rosenberg (1986, 63).
42. Peace bonds were, according to G. S. Rowe, "a sum of money that the accused was required to guarantee in advance, and that would be forfeited if he or she carried out some explicitly forbidden act" (1994, 108). The supreme court used its considerable powers of discretion to ensure that even where an individual had been acquitted, he might still be placed under a bond to secure future good behavior. Such a practice was notably used against Eleazer Oswald and Cobbett.

43. Rosenberg (1986, 107).
44. Rosenberg (1986, 63, 65).
45. Cobbett (1798b, 81).
46. Rosenberg (1986, 77).
47. *U.S. v. Cooper* (Cooper, 1800, 19).
48. *U.S. v. Cooper* (Cooper, 1800, 24, 28).
49. *U.S. v. Cooper* (Cooper, 1800, 21).
50. *U.S. v. Cooper* (Cooper, 1800, 36).
51. *U.S. v. Cooper* (Cooper, 1800, 42).
52. *U.S. v. Cooper* (Cooper, 1800, 44).
53. *U.S. v. Cooper* (Cooper, 1800, 46).
54. *U.S. v. Cooper* (Cooper, 1800, 49).
55. Ellis (1971, 78, 98–99).
56. Miller (1951, 218-19).
57. *U.S. v. Callender* (1800, 4).
58. *U.S. v. Callender* (1800, 17–18).
59. *U.S. v. Callender* (1800, 23–24).
60. *U.S. v. Callender* (1800, 55).
61. *U.S. v. Callender* (1800, 71).
62. *U.S. v. Callender* (1800, 84–85).

63. The Yrujo case was filed as a federal criminal action on August 8, 1797 and was granted a court date, according to Cobbett, for Federal District Court the following April; Cobbett (1798b, 22); Clark (1939, 115) refers to an October date, citing Cobbett in the *Gazette*. Yrujo withdrew the case and filed a bill of indictment with the state on November 27, with charges having been made by Chief Justice McKean on August 18; Cobbett (1798b 24, 26); Clark (1939, 115–16). The bill of indictment was returned ignoramus by the grand jury on December 7. Not only had Rush filed civil charges against Cobbett in October of the same year but the dismissal of the indictment was followed by a filing for Cobbett's violation of a recognizance in Yrujo, which was scheduled for December 1797 but never actually tried until December 13, 1800 when the verdict went against Cobbett. The persistence of actions against Cobbett suggests the kind of determination that was arrayed against Cobbett in Pennsylvania. With appeals and petitions, the Yrujo recognizance case went through a variety of permutations and was not completely resolved until 1819 when Cobbett finally dropped all efforts to contest it, arguing that such peace bonds were no more than a prior restraint upon publishers and therefore illegal; Clark (1939, 116–22); Cobbett's longhand petition to the Pennsylvania House of Representatives is on deposit at the Historical Society of Pennsylvania.

64. Cases related to Yrujo and that targeted Cobbett occurred in 1797, 1798 (two cases), 1800, 1817, and 1819; in addition Davis and North, who put up the bond for Cobbett in the original case, faced cases of their own for payment of the bond in 1801, 1804, and 1805. Cases related to the Rush trial occurred in 1798, 1799, 1800 (two cases), and 1801. Cobbett faced charges in federal and state courts, as well as a mayor's court; he petitioned to the state legislature; he was accused in both civil and criminal

cases; and his cases ranged from libel, forfeiture of a peace bond (recognizance), application for removal to a federal court, recovery of a fine, and application for a new trial.

65. Rowe (1994, 229, 239).

66. *Respublica v. Cobbett* (1798); Dallas (1905, 3: 476).

67. *Respublica v. Cobbett* (1798); Dallas (1905, 3: 468–69).

68. *Respublica v. Cobbett* (1798); Dallas (1905, 3: 474).

69. *Rush-Light* IV, 31 March 1800; Cobbett (1801a, 11: 362). The biographer of Rush's lawyer Joseph Hopkinson reports that the reason for the dismissal of the petition was that the amount of damages could not, as with property, be calculated as more than $500 before the case was actually tried and that therefore the case did not qualify as required under federal law; Konkle (1981, 60). Konkle has the case tried in March before the U.S. Circuit Court, whereas Cobbett's petition indicates the Pennsylvania Supreme Court had been applied to for disposition of the petition; *Rush-Light* IV, March 31, 1800; Cobbett (1801a, 11: 360); Clark (1939, 148).

70. *Rush-Light* IV, March 31, 1800; Cobbett (1801a, 11: 358).

71. *Rush-Light* IV, March 31, 1800; Cobbett (1801a, 11: 358, 367).

72. *Rush-Light* IV, March 31, 1800; Cobbett (1801a, 11: 360–361).

73. *Rush-Light* IV, March 31, 1800; Cobbett (1801a, 11: 362).

74. A kite is a large hawk-like bird of prey.

75. *Rush-Light* IV, March 31, 1800; Cobbett (1801a, 11: 362).

76. *Scrie facias*: requiring the defense to show cause why an action should not be annulled or a judgment not enacted; Garner (1999, 1347).

77. *Respublica v. Cobbett* (1800); Yeates (1871, 3: 93).

78. *Respublica v. Cobbett* (1800); Yeates (1871, 3: 101).

79. Rowe (1994, 252).

80. Rowe (1994, 259).

81. Cobbett (1798b, iv).

82. Cobbett (1798b, v).

83. Cobbett (1798b, 45).

84. Cobbett (1798b, 26–27).

85. Cobbett (1798b, 30).

86. Cobbett (1798b, 32); *Porcupine's Gazette*, July 17, 1797.

87. Cobbett (1798b, 34).

88. Cobbett (1798b, 36); *Porcupine's Gazette*, July 24, 1797.

89. Cobbett (1798b, 37).

90. Cobbett (1798b, 41).

91. Cobbett (1798b, 42).

92. Cobbett (1798b, 43).

93. Cobbett (1798b, 44).

94. Cobbett (1798b, 45).

95. Cobbett (1798b, 47).

96. Cobbett (1798b, 48).

97. Cobbett (1798b, 49).

98. Cobbett (1798b, 56).

99. As Jeffrey A. Smith contends, "It was thus often unclear whether the case was one of seditious libel or personal libel" (1988, 165).

100. Cobbett (1798b, 81).

101. Rosenberg (1986, 78).

102. Rosenberg (1986, 93-94, 96).

103. Rosenberg (1986, 108).

104. The republican position opposing the Sedition Act while Pennsylvania republicans prosecuted Cobbett led Robert Goodloe Harper (Cobbett's counsel and the architect of the Sedition Act) in 1801 to claim rank partisanship in the trial. He complained that federalists needed the protection of the law: "I wish to interpose this law between the freedoms of discussion and the overbearing sway of that tyrannical spirit, by which a certain political party in this country, is activated." 10 *Annals of Congress* 940 (180); Rosenberg (1986, 94, 103).

105. Nelson (1967, 450).

106. Nelson (1967, 462).

107. Nelson (1967, 472–73); Nelson (1975, 175–76).

108. Nelson (1967, 469); see Nelson (1975).

109. See Myrsiades (2008).

110. Landsman (1990, 497).

111. *Republica v. Oswald* (1788); Dallas (1790, 328).

112. Smith (1953b, 146–47).

113. Smith (1953b, 146.)

114. Nelson (1967); Nelson (1975).

115. Lerner (2000, 203, 208, 220).

116. Shapiro (1991, 180).

117. Nelson (1967, 450, 462, 469, 472–73); Nelson (1975, 175–76).

118. Rowe (1994) certifies the location, indicating that "dockets confirm the Philadelphia meetings of the Supreme Court on the first floor of the west wing of the State House" (102).

119. Etting (1891, 94).

120. Mires (2002, 20).

121. Webster (1976, 79).

122. Rowe (1994, 190).

123. Surrency (1976, 183).

124. Lerner (2000, 213).

125. The standard of proof in civil cases like *Rush v. Cobbett* would have been less rigorous than that in criminal cases, and judges would have exerted more influence over juries; Langbein (2003, 7–9, 37–38). In trials, judges like Justice Shippen reserved the right to comment on the evidence in their charge to the jury, under the presumption that jurors were less educated and experienced than judges in sifting the evidence; Lerner (2000, 211).

126. *Rush-Light* IV, 31 March 1800; Cobbett (1801a, 11: 380).

127. Langbein (2003, 331).

128. Jacob Rush was later commissioned with tenure for life president of the Third Circuit, seated in Reading (August 17, 1791). When Philadelphia was made a sepa-

rate district in 1806, he was appointed its president. Unlike his brother, Justice Rush was a strict federalist with a strong penchant for maintaining social order; Richards (1915, 66).

129. July 9, 1788, letter to Elias Boudinot; Rush (1951, 1: 473).

130. Rowe (1994, 194–97).

131. Rosenberg (1986, 62).

132. Rowe (1994, 165–73).

133. Rowe (1994, 202).

134. Rowe (1994, 232, 276).

135. Resolution of land claims between settlers and warrantees who had filed holdings as land speculators or out-of-state purchasers were to test the ability of the court further in adjudicating between local claimants (who preferred state courts) and large landowners (who preferred federal courts); Rowe (1994, 227).

136. Rowe (1994, 104, 116, 219–25).

137. Rowe (1994, 231).

138. Rowe (1994, 119, 199).

139. Rowe (1994, 196, 233, 241–42).

140. Rowe (1994, 77, 179, 194, 201).

141. Rowe (1994, 206).

142. Rowe (1994, 242).

143. Rowe (1994, 244–46.)

144. Rowe (1994, 217).

145. Rowe (1994, 233–52).

146. Rowe (1994, 206–8).

147. Rowe (1994, 216).

148. Rowe (1994, 208–16).

149. Rowe (1994, 216–18).

150. Rowe (1994, 205).

151. Rowe (1994, 250–53).

152. Rowe (1994, 199, 233).

153. Rowe (1994, 244–45).

154. Clark (1939, 153).

155. *Rush-Light* IV, 31 March 1800; Cobbett (1801a,11: 366).

156. Because being represented by defense counsel was a relatively recent phenomenon in a criminal trial—counsel did not appear regularly until the 1780s—the jury still relied to a great extent on the version of events provided by the accused: "there was no clear division of the trial into prosecution and defence cases. Consequently, the jury was not instructed to focus on whether the prosecution had met its production burden. The accused was expected to give his version of the event, and the failure to do so was understood to virtually ensure conviction"; Anand (2005, 427). If the accused was innocent, he was expected to be able to demonstrate his innocence to the jury "by the quality and character of his reply to the prosecutor's evidence" (427–28). See Langbein (2003, 48–66).

157. Langbein (2003, 280, 284).

158. Carpenter (1800, 29).

159. Neilson and Neilson (1958, 9).

160. Binger (1966, 244).

161. See Spater (1982, note 65, 267); Cobbett (1801a, 12: 155).

162. Cole (1937, xl); *Rush-Light* IV, 31 March 1800; Cobbett (1801a, 11: 367, 380–81, 383).

163. Clark (1939, 153).

164. Clark (1939, 168-69).

165. December 9, 1799, letter to Edward Tilghman; see Clark (1939, 153).

166. December 18, 1799, letter to Edward Tilghman; Historical Society of Pennsylvania, Phi 2129.

167. *Rush-Light* IV, March 31, 1800; Cobbett (1801a, 11: 366).

168. *Rush-Light* IV, March 31, 1800; Cobbett (1801a, 11: 367).

169. December 25, 1799, letter to Edward Thornton; Cobbett (1937, 24).

170. *Porcupine's Gazette*, January 13, 1800; Cobbett (1801a, 12: 137).

171. *Rush-Light* IV, March 31, 1800; Cobbett (1801a, 11: 366–67).

172. Spater (1982, 102).

173. The oppositional perspective that cast Cobbett in an alien's role to estrange him was both conscious and persistent. We find it hammered home not only in the prosecution's repeated imagery of pollution, infection, and monstrous deformity but in its labeling of him as a foreigner, an Englishman, and an immigrant. In his draft of a letter to Brockholst Livingston (Rush Manuscript, Historical Society of Pennsylvania, vol. 29, letter 82, March 5, 1800), Rush, in a reference to Cobbett, struck the word "him" and substituted "alien," as if reminding himself to stay loyal to the prosecution strategy when the posttrial period took the continuing feud to a new stage. The tactic was illustrated again when he changed "insults" to "outrages" when speaking of Cobbett's actions. By the same token, he struck his initial negative terminology in discussing the deeds of his sons, changing "assault" to "insult" and substituting favorable terms such as "feelings" for "intemperate," "interview" for "fight," and "obtain" for "attack."

174. Konkle (1981, 61).

175. *Time Piece*, September 13, 1797.

Pennsylvania Supreme Court, in Independence Hall, Philadelphia. The courtroom was built on a plan drawn by Andrew Hamilton and was completed in the 1740s. Photograph by Kostas Myrsiades.

Caricature Against Cobbett.

Legend: "See Porcupine in Colours just Portray'd,/Urged by Old Nick to drive his dirty trade,/Veil'd in darkness, acts the assassin's part,/And triumphs much to stab you to the heart"; The Historical Society of Pennsylvania (HSP). M. L. E. Moreau, 1796.

The balloons read:
"Independence Declared 4 July 1776."
"Spplication 5,500000 Drs."
"Appropriation."
"1500 Ame'n seamen Impres'd by british."
"No navy!!"
"Treaty with France 1778."
"600 Ships adjudicated. Lost neutrality."
The porcupine:
"Rights of Man. Common Sense. Volney. Swannick. Randolph's defence. Gallatin. Madison. Peter Pindar."
"I Hate this country & will sow the seeds of discord in it. These have too much merit."
The lion:
"Go on dear Peter, my friend & I will reward you."
"Treaty of... Treaty of Commerce with France."
" Magna Charter."
The devil:
"More scandal, let us destroy this Idol liberty."
The jay:
"Treaty of Amity & Commerce 1795."

G. Washington in his last illness attended by Doc.rs Craik and Brown; "Americans behold & shed a grateful tear/For a man who has gained your freedom most dear/And now is departing unto the realms above/Where he may ever rest in lasting peace & love"; [1800]. Collection of the New York Historical Society.

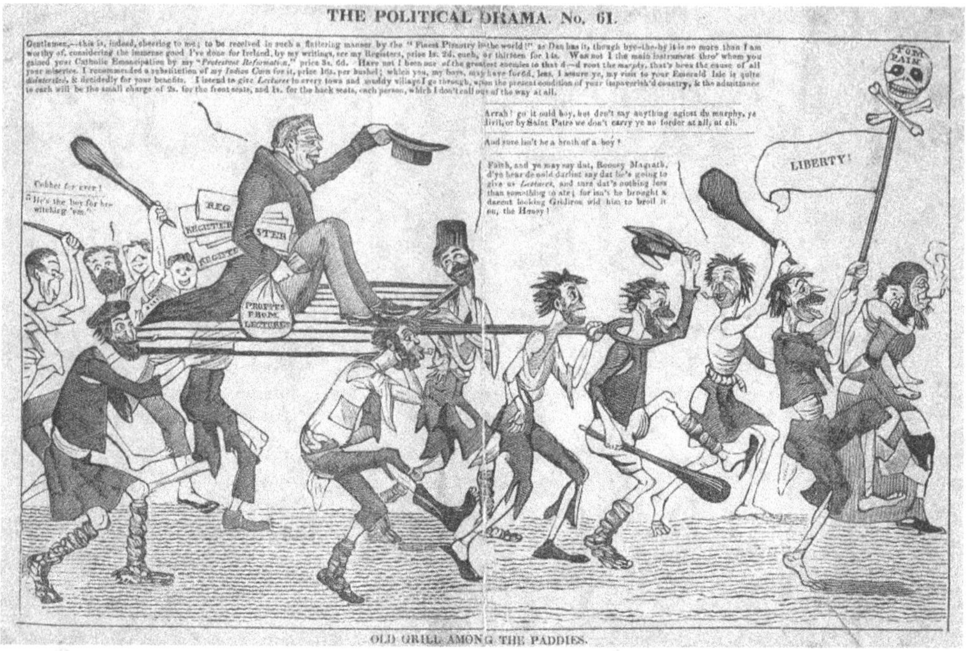

The Political Drama No. 61; Old Grill among the Paddies; [1832]. British Cartoon Prints Collection, Library of Congress. The text reads:

"Cobbett for ever!"

"He's the boy for bewitching 'em."

"Register."

"Profits from Lectures."

"Arrah! Go it ould boy, but don't say anything against de Murphy, ye devil, or by Saint Patre we don't carry ye no furder at all, at all."

"And sure isn't he a broth of a boy!"

"Faith, and ye may say dat, Roomey Magrath, d'ye hear de ould darlint say dat he's going to give us Lectures, *and sure dat's nothing less than something to ate; for isn't he brought a dacent looking Gridiron wid him to broil it on, the Honey!"*

"LIBERTY!"

"TOM PAIN."

*"Gentlemen—this is, indeed, cheering to me; to be received in such a flattering manner by the 'Finest Pisnntry in the world!' as Dan has it, though bye-the-by it is no more than I am worthy of, considering the immense good I've done for Ireland, by my writings, see my Registers, price 1s. 2d. each, or thirteen for 14s. Was I not the main instrument thro' whom you gained your Catholic Emancipation by my '*Protestant Reformation,*' prices 3s. 6d. Have not I been one of the greatest enemies to that d----d ront the* murphy, *that's been the cause of all your miseries. I recommend a substitution of my* Indian Corn *for it, price 16s. per bushel; which you, my boys, may have for 6d. less. I assure ye, my visit to your Emerald Isle is quite* disinterested, *& decidedly for your benefits. I intend to give* Lectures *in every town and muddy village I go through, upon the present condition of your impoverish'd country, & the admittance to each will be the small charge of 2s. for the front seats, and 1s. for the back seats, each person, which I don't call out of the way at all."*

What a Beastly Action; 1798. The event is a quarrel between Matthew Lyon and Roger Griswold in which they resorted to their fists in the House of Representatives. Congressman Lyon (depicted as a lion) was a republican and an Irish-American whom Cobbett attacked in his press. Courtesy of the Trustees of the Boston Public Library. The text/balloons read:

"My quills shall pierce & my press shall black."
"What a Beastly action."
"A Ve....t POLITNESS."

Doctor Sangrado Curing John Bull of Repletion—a hint from Gil Blas—with the Kind Offices of Young Clysterpipe & Little Boney; James Gilray; 1803. Library of Congress. The text/balloons read:

> *"Courage."*
> *"Courage."*
> *"Warm Water."*
> *"Warm Water."*
> *"Reservoir for the Clysterpipe family."*
> *"Courage Johnny!"*
> *"Courage John Bull-Courage!!!"*

Lawyers in term: Designed by Necessity, Executed by Rapacity; 1786. Print shows a defendant pulled from either side by lawyers for the defendant and the plaintiff. British Cartoon Prints Collection, Library of Congress. The text/balloons read:

"Others believe no voice t'an Organ
So sweet as Lawyer's in his Bar-gown;
Until with subtle Cobweb-cheats,
Th'are catch'd in knotted Law, like Nets,
In which, when once they are imbrogled,
The more they stir, the more they're tangled,
And while their Purses can dispute,
There's no End of th'immortal Suit. Hudibras."

"Get along to [Q]uot—you're quite done over-ar'nt you-"

"Oh! The glorious uncertainty of the Law."

"Yes, you have brought the cause to an Issue, and I am to pay all this merely to send the man to prison-this is recovery with a vengeance!"

"[Twobelly] against . . . Attorney's Bill."

"Part of Defendant."

"As if a Defendant were dissected/To see how by Law he is affected."

"Plaintiff's Case."

The Company of Undertakers, whose motto is "Et Plurima Mortis Imago." W. Hogarth; 1736. A group of 12 Quack-Heads examining the contents of a urinal, overseen by 3 figures: Dr. "Spot" Ward, Mrs. Mapp (known as crazy Sally), and Chevalier Taylor, a well-known quack. National Library of Medicine. The text of the print reads as follows:

"Beareth [Sable], an Urinal proper, between 12 Quack-Heads of the [second] and 12 Cane Heads. One consultant. One Chief and [Nebulae], Ermine, One Compleat Doctor issuant, [checkie] sustaining in his Right Hand a Baton of the Second. On his [Darker] and sinister side two Demi-Doctors, issuant of the second, and two Cane Heads issuant of the third; the first having One Eye [conchant] toward the [Darker] side of the Escocheon; the Second Faced [per pale] proper and [Gula, Guardent]. With this Motto 'Et Plurima Mortis Imago'."

A case of infectious fever (from "81 South Street 4 doors from Callowhill Street" Philadelphia) before the New York Board of Health. University of Pennsylvania Archives. The balloons read:

"It all arises from septic . . . generated by azote, it must be neutralized by lime or some ether of the alkalids."

"Ma for man cher docteur you ave raison! Beggar I tink de vite vash is von grand remede ontre de black vomit! Ha? Mais oui il faut apply him exterieurement dat is on de out side of de body ha!"

"Don't you think a little skull cap would be of service."

"A little foolscap you mean."

"Indeed Maybe it's only de toast and today dat he is drink."

"[Do not tell me] . . . outlandish . . . of toast and toady. I say it's the black vomit."

"Drunk drunk oh lord."

"He complains of great giddiness and weakness, being unable to stand, sickness of stomach, difficulty of . . ., the eyes very red, tongue thick and fuzzy, with disagreeable breath, and secretions; highly malignant and inflammatory see how red his nose is!!!"

"A vastly pestiferous delirium."

"A feverish pulse doctor."

"Have him put on board a boat at NOON and send him down to the quarantine ground you understand."

The Reward of Cruelty by William Hogarth, 1751

Hogarth treated the life and death of the fictional thief Tom Nero in a set of four prints, of which the fourth, The Reward of Cruelty, presented the dissection of the executed thief's body. Delivering the bodies of convicted criminals to be anatomized by surgeons was encapsulated in the Murder Act of 1752 as punishment for murder. National Library of Medicine. The text of the print reads as follows:

Behold the Villain's dire disgrace!
Not Death itself can end.
He finde no peaceful Burial-Place,
His breathless Corse, no friend.
Torn from the root, that wicked Tongue,
Which daily swore and curst!
Those Eyeballs, from their Sockets wrung,
That glow'd with lawless Lust!
His Heart, expos'd to prying Eyes,
To Pity has no Claims;
But, dreadful! From his Bones shall rise,
His Monument of Shame.

The Times: A Political Portrait

Anonymous, 1795. Collection of the New York Historical Society. The text reads,

Triumph Government: perish all its enemies.—Traitors be warned: justice though slow is sure.

George Washington is trying to move forward but is impeded by James Madison, underfoot, and Albert Gallatin, at the wheel, who is himself held back by Thomas Jefferson. (Caption: "Stop de wheels de gouvernement") The caption on the flag reads "Volunteers." In the background, the American eagle flies overhead as men are landing from ships. The caption reads "The cannibals are landing," a reference to Cobbett's The Cannibal's Progress.

5

Sangrado v. The Cloven Foot: The Trial

R*ush* v. *Cobbett* was called for trial on December 13, 1799, before the Pennsylvania Supreme Court, with Justice Edward Shippen leading a three-judge panel that included himself, Jasper Yeates, and Thomas Smith. Six lawyers alternately argued the two sides of the case. Plaintiff's counsel opened (Joseph Hopkinson) and closed (Jared Ingersol); the defense argued in the second position (William Rawle) and the third position (Robert Goodloe Harper); the plaintiff (Moses Levy) returned as the fourth speaker and the defense (Edward Tilghman) as the fifth speaker in order. This mixed order of presentation reflected an earlier form of court proceeding, the altercation trial,[1] in which the efforts of the judge, the victim, and the accused were poorly separated, indeed overlapped. As John H. Langbein puts it, the altercation trial was a form of spontaneous bickering—reminiscent, for our purposes, of the chaos in the supreme court that Cobbett reported in the Yrujo case—"a formless or wandering quality that resembles ordinary discourse, a conversation of sorts, lacking [a] crisp division into prosecution and defense cases."[2] Vestiges of an altercation trial were joined to the "combat effect" of a developing adversarial system which dominated the proceedings. Rivalry among counsel to gain the ear of the jury and partisanship in both the prosecution and defense cases thus competed to distort the facts and undermine witnesses to win an argument.[3] In such a scenario, even if some considered that the altercation format focused more fully on the truth of an accusation than the newer adversarial system, a truth defense based on the facts of the case would have been difficult to mount and even more difficult to argue successfully, and the jury's mettle would have been tested in trying to separate defense and prosecution arguments.

The trial opened a full two years and two months after charges were filed, a delay that Cobbett attributed to McKean's continuing interference in the case and his desire to stack the jury. Cobbett contended that "the base and corrupt Judge contrived the means of postponing the cause seven times . . . till, at last, he found one [jury] from which he was sure of a verdict."[4] Another construction would put Rush's counsel at the center of the delay, for the plaintiff had some hope of using a struck jury to ensure a favorable hearing.[5] It was in the interest of Rush's team to cooperate in the delays in the hope that postponing the trial would have the added benefit of keeping Cobbett on good behavior, a hope that was soon dashed as Cobbett continued to publish attacks against Rush and McKean. It was not altogether clear that a struck jury might not have helped Cobbett too. Indeed, in retrospect in March 1800 he suggested that "The necessary steps were also taken to insure a special jury, who, it was thought by my lawyers and my friends, would be a sufficient protection against the intrigues of the plaintiff and the tyranny of the Court."[6] Each court term that arrived, and each time Cobbett thought he had a jury he could live with, he was nevertheless disappointed to find the trial delayed again. In a form of Russian roulette, court terms passed one after another without the trial being called.[7] The conditions for the trial to go forward, according to Cobbett, only clicked into place when a jury favorable to Rush was empanelled:

> At last, on the 13th December 1799, it was resolved to bring it to issue. The moment I saw the *jury list*, "Ah!" said I, to a friend that happened to be with me, "the action of Rush is to be tried this time." We looked over the list again and again, and after the most mature consideration, we could find but seven men out of the forty-eight, whom we thought fit to be trusted on the trial; but as I had the power of rejecting no more than twelve, there were left, of course, twenty-nine whom I disapproved of, to the seven whom I approved of; and as every one of these seven was struck off by Rush, there remained not a single man on the jury in whose integrity I had the slightest confidence.[8]

Once the trial began and Rush's lead attorney, Joseph Hopkinson (a fiery young lawyer and nephew of McKean who was trying only his second big case)[9] offered his passionate opening, it became immediately clear that a struck jury was not Cobbett's only problem. Hopkinson became the referent for each of the other five pleaders as he was excused, referenced, countered, or endorsed by each of them in turn. He inspired a rowdy reception among the court watchers that many felt influenced the resounding verdict against Cobbett as his high rhetoric buried questions of fact and law in themes that catered to popular prejudice and home-town preferences.[10]

Hopkinson's opening for the prosecution waived his responsibility to stick to the common, in his terms "usual," protocol of an "ordinary" slander trial, and authorized him to establish his own frame of argument.[11] He began his appeal to the jury with the following lines: "It is my duty to open this cause to you on the part of the plaintiff, Dr. Rush. In discharging this duty I shall beg leave to extend it somewhat beyond its usual limits in ordinary cases. I shall not be content with merely reading the declaration to you, and stating the points of evidence by which it will be maintained; but shall also take the liberty of opening to you the views and dispositions with which this action has been brought, and some of the leading principles on which it will be supported."[12] Hopkinson's contention that this was no "ordinary" trial had the effect of excusing the prosecution from having to make its case by means of the charges and the evidence that would support those charges.

In many ways, Hopkinson had made a strategically astute choice, for the trial was to become a tale of competing stories aimed at persuading the jury of a higher truth than that told by the facts themselves. Moreover, Hopkinson's exceptionalism was a good indication of the low regard in which libel suits were held as socially disruptive forms of conflict. Rush's case would not, according to his counsel, qualify among those types of suits designed "to gratify unsocial, litigious or revengeful dispositions,"[13] cases that he contended originated in passion and ended in repentance. Hopkinson elevated the trial to a level of danger that threatened not only the plaintiff and society, but the moral order itself, demeaning ordinary cases of slander that congested the dockets of the courts and distinguishing them from the case presently before the jury:

> it seldom happens, that the kind of slander which the law so seriously contemplates, occurs—The offence is so enormous, so destitute of palliation or defence, so unworthy, so low and detestable, the penalty so exemplary, that few men are found regardless enough of social order and decency, or sufficiently outrageous and audacious to commit it. But when such a case does occur, it rises in terrible pre-eminence above the multitude of actions for defamation which throng the dockets and disgrace the remedy.[14]

Hopkinson's focus on the exceptional nature of the Rush trial clearly resonated with Judge Shippen, whose charge to the jury shadowed the prosecutor's line, expressing his irritation that "offences of this kind have for some time past too much abounded in our city" and, like Hopkinson, urged the jury that "it seems high time to restrain them."[15]

Commenting on Hopkinson's performance, Cobbett described the role played by "the zealous Hopkinson" as "rare sport."[16] Indeed, Cobbett expressed surprise that his adversary's depiction of Rush as one who

> "*in the service of his country . . . has added a fresh and blooming laurel to the head of American genius. . . .* did not delight their eyes as well as their ears, by *showing them some of the sprigs* of the fresh and blooming laurel. So industrious

> an advocate ought, methinks, to have recollected their instantaneous effect which Mark Antony produced on the sovereign people of Rome by the judicious display of a piece of blotted parchment; and though poor Pennsylvania bears none but *bastard* laurel, the "*nice-feeling*" Hopkinson might easily have come into court with a bunch of THAT *under his arm.* It might not, indeed, have been very *fresh* or very *blooming*: but, I dare, say, the group would have ogled it with singular delight.[17]

In Cobbett's construction, the trial was very much a tale told of the death of a tyrant. Hopkinson mirrored Mark Antony's resurrection of the great Caesar (Rush) cut down at his height, this "ambitious" man whose words might once "have stood against the world"[18] but whose blood now flows through wounds Brutus (Cobbett) had made. Brutus's civic sacrifice, by this reading, had been transformed into a self-interested act of rebellion and the courtroom crowd had been roused to a fever pitch over this attack by a presumptively "honorable man."

The Roman references and dramatic effects associated with Hopkinson's performance did not come as a surprise to his colleagues on Rush's legal team. The storyline he laid down, and that Levy and Ingersol developed, was intended to electrify and thereby distract the jury, so that it would fail to notice, as defense counsel Tilghman was to say, that the argument was "foreign to the question at present."[19] Levy, for the prosecution, seemed to have agreed even as he embraced Hopkinson's line of attack on the off-chance it would infect the jury as much as it incited the defense:

> Gentlemen, the principles of law laid down by my colleague, in his opening address were just, and consistent with the English books of law. If, for a moment, his zeal carried him into a state of effervescence, for which he is blamed by our opponents, it is what the most moderate man, who is warmly attached to reputation and character, who has read what was inserted against the plaintiff, can scarcely refrain from showing. Who could refrain a warmth of expression at seeing a worthy, valuable citizen so lavishly abused without provocation.[20]

THE POLITICAL STORY

As opposed to the prosecution's construction of the case, Cobbett's defense would depend upon facts, evidence, a truth defense, and a view of the law of libel that, in other times, in another venue, and with a different jury, he had every right to expect might have prevailed. That it did not prevail was the result of a case presented against him that had all the marks of a political tract and a morality play. The tract constituted an ever-present shadow story of party politics that linked Cobbett to an alien status, association with a party newspaper (federalist), and loyalty to a foreign nation (England).[21] Hopkinson introduced the story by arguing that the tinge of politics was so endemic and furious "that every action of a man's life, from the most important to the most obscure and trifling is traced to party motives and party principles—His attachments and his enmities—his connections in business or otherwise, nay almost the color of the clothes he wears, and the species of diet he feeds on, are ascribed to his party and political principles—This is an unhappy state of things."[22] Highlighting the differences between English and American libel law, Hopkinson contrasted Cobbett's "*true situation* in this country" to "my country" and "our government" and seeded his speech with references to the good reputation of "a citizen of Pennsylvania."[23] Levy provided a converging line of attack that openly declared Cobbett an alien. He reminded the jury that Cobbett "has sworn himself an Alien," holding that "he is not the citizen of a republic" and that he intends to return "to his own country," so that "he has not the same interests at heart with citizens."[24] Indeed, Levy suggested, Cobbett's own country might receive some benefit from the distress of the city, which might have pleased Cobbett: "To him it was not an object whether Philadelphia was desolated or not."[25]

In a variation by Ingersol, the story became one of Cobbett patiently waiting for the city to become a patient itself, "stretched on his bed of sickness; physicians themselves at a loss how to relieve that distress."[26] Cobbett's attacks would have undermined the confidence patients must have in their physicians. By extension, Cobbett, Ingersol proffered, had settled on Rush as the means of bringing republicanism itself to its knees. Having delivered a "republican" eulogium on the occasion of the death of a prominent republican, Dr. Rittenhouse, and being preeminent in his party, Rush represented in this construction a target of opportunity. Indeed, Rush's bleeding practices would have meant little had Rush the republican not been identified with their use. Bleeding was the route to undermining his character without having to make a frontal assault on Rush's politics.

The focus was thereby placed on the malice of a foreign journalist who, in a time of national crisis, self-servingly cried "foul" when a legitimate limit was placed on his liberty. Far from wishing to cure the crisis-creating disease, he interfered with the one man most identified with rescuing the city. If his intention lay in "giving an alarm to the citizens of this country against foreign influence," Ingersol noted, his effect was, rather, "to destroy [influence] when it came from one foreign country [France] and place it on another [England]."[27] In a flourish of patriotism, Ingersol thus rallied the gentlemen of the jury to proclaim themselves with him as republicans in the largest sense; not as members of a republican party but in a broader allegiance against a foreign slur on the American reputation for republican government:

> I trust we are all Republicans—Is there a man who hears me that does not feel and [*sic*] indignation in his breast that an *alien* should abuse him because he is a republican! The citizen of the United States who is not a republican, is a traitor. I am by choice a republican;—I am so by oath: The constitution of the United States is a republican form of government, and a republican form of government is guaranteed to each State.[28]

To be held in the crosshairs of party politics was no small thing. Hopkinson reminded the jury that they, too, were vulnerable to its threats and must hold fast to their courage to preempt any possible move by Cobbett. Doubtless, Hopkinson claimed, he "prepares some attack, which his insufferable arrogance informs him will be formidable and destructive to lawyers, courts, and jury, that shall dare *to do him justice*":

> I will answer that you will not be driven from your duty or your oaths, by a fear of being placed on his *black list*. He has, indeed, the unquenchable and vindictive spirit of an inquisitor, but wanting all power, it is harmless and contemptible—The ridiculous vanity of this man, and his ignorance of his *true situation* in this country and of the *kind of value or use* that has been put upon him, has lead him into an opinion that his voice is the voice of fate, either with regard to public measures and character, or to private reputation. This however is an error which it lies with the public to correct; and they will find their interest and their honor, deeply concerned in doing it speedily and effectually.[29]

Not above fearmongering, the prosecution identified Cobbett as the true-threat to the nation,[30] for some as yet unspecified, anticipated act of terrorism. Rallying the jury members to discard limiting rules and legal niceties, Hopkinson's populist appeal framed events as a declaration of independence from a primordial villainy like that of a former English tyrant from under whose heels they had only recently emerged. Narrativizing the implied threat Cobbett posed, Hopkinson's warning established for the jury a sense of immediacy and self-interest in preserving its own political welfare, even as it provoked disdain and confusion within the defense team. Playing on the unstable condition of a nation only newly liberated and still struggling with issues of unity and the pressures of foreign influences, the plaintiff's story was an originary tale of a nation just born, unstable and still struggling with issues of unity and identity. It was a foundational tale of separation anxiety, the political child severing from its birth parents, England and France, that put squarely before the jury the danger that Cobbett, thrown up on America's shores and seeking refuge from his own troubles in England, posed.

At the time Hopkinson attacked Cobbett's press practices, he was well aware that many had gone too far in attacking the American press, particularly that press sympathetic to republicanism and thereby natural allies of the republican Rush. The irony of prosecuting a federalist editor like Cobbett for libel at the same time that republican editors were being targeted by the Alien and Sedition Acts cannot have escaped Rush's counsel. As an author of the Acts, defense counsel Harper had elsewhere charged that opposition to them was "evidence of 'the deadly hatred of certain people'" toward the United States itself.[31] Casting republicans in a treasonable role in their efforts to leave the country "prostrate at the feet of its . . . foes," Harper would have been well aware of the effectiveness of such an attack and was in a knowledgeable position to defuse its use against a federalist. At the very least, the politics of the situation meant that Rush's team would have to walk a fine line in its arguments attacking press freedom. Hopkinson made the case that press prosecutions might be construed by the defense as a "refuge of tyranny," a reaction to fear of "approaching extreme depravity and licentiousness among a people," but he held that such an evil could only be addressed by punishing an offender, "not by shielding him under the Liberty of the Press."[32] The prosecution thus addressed the perceived fear that by exceeding the bounds of press freedom, press libels would lead to a degeneration of religion and morals that would destabilize the government. As "a phenomenon even in the courts of defamation," Hopkinson offered, Cobbett had come to stand for a pack of libelers, a country full of slanderers.[33] Appropriating an old federalist argument, Hopkinson thus challenged the friends of the press: "These high toned and pretended sons of Liberty, who bawl incessantly about the Rights of the Press, while they blacken it with their detestable crimes; who tell you it is sacred, while they are plunging it in disgrace . . . pretending to be its friends, they are its most deadly foes."[34]

Hopkinson, Levy, and Ingersol each expounded on the privileges and limits of the press, Hopkinson more so than the others. Acknowledging, as the defense had not, that the liberty of the press had caused more ink to be spilt than most other subjects of political interest, and that no other had "excited more anxiety among the people of every free country," he admitted there was no "unity of sentiment" on the subject. Rather, a heated debate had been engaged "to fix its legal or its reasonable bound; to say, 'thus far shalt thou go and no farther'";[35] to say, here is liberty and there libel.[36] To prostitute the power of an institution intended for the public good and to waste it on private malice went well beyond what the prosecution held was a tolerable purpose. To put such power in the hands of those who, like Cobbett, would wield it like a weapon did not describe the intention of those who instituted and preserved the press. In any case, as Hopkinson contended, whatever the content of a publication no one had a right to despoil a neighbor's character; the press had no right to assault a man in his private capacity nor to bring misery upon his family. The debate, Hopkinson held, could only be over how far the press could go to discuss "public men in their public capacities, and public measures in their public tendency."[37] Writing after the trial, Cobbett countered that Rush's character was very much part of the doctor's system of practice. In fact, it was his very character that fed his rash experiments, extreme treatments, and an overweening pride that pressured his contemporaries to adopt his remedies. Cobbett insisted that the private was indeed in this sense public.[38]

If privacy was an impacted issue, a truth defense was technically available to Cobbett's legal team; even the Alien and Sedition Acts of 1798 allowed the truth of a libel not merely in mitigation of a libel but as a true defense. As the prosecution acknowledged, the defendant in a civil action like this might bring forward the truth in justification or in extenuation of the act, "giving it a mild aspect."[39] Cobbett's team nevertheless failed to embrace such a defense in any significant way, possibly because Rush's standing in the city suggested that developing support for such a story arc might fail. Instead, the defense posited that whereas one might believe Cobbett's words to be untrue (Harper, for one, was willing to concede their untruthfulness), they were not either slanderous or malicious. In Harper's words, "I am well convinced that it [Cobbett's piece] was not only unbecoming language, but I believe it to be very untrue, but is it a slander?"[40] Rawle, at least, was clear on the issue of malicious intent: "no malicious design, a temper and disposition absolutely necessary to the conviction of the defendant—no malicious design did exist."[41] Tilghman sealed the deal by adding that extenuation should be allowed if libel be found, but that such a finding would require that Cobbett's words be "written with a particular *intent* of a *criminal* nature,"[42] and that such intent, in the words of the prosecution "*deep, antecedent, concomitant,* and *subsequent,*"[43] must be proved, establishing a particularly high bar for the prosecution to overcome. The prosecution in any case was prepared for such a defense. Levy put it that an attack that used "vulgarity, defamation, and scurrility"[44] or one that expressed "a previous intention of attack,"[45] even in the service of pursuing the truth or serving a high purpose, had little chance of defeating a libel charge.

Once Hopkinson laid the foundation for the argument that a man's private reputation rested outside the range of permissible public commentary, Ingersol provided the common law justification, quoting Blackstone on categories of wrongs respecting the rights of persons to the effect that "You shall not, by a libel, or by a writing, set a man in a ridiculous light . . . and thereby diminish his reputation,"[46] and thus his livelihood. With the limits of liberty of the press set, Levy laid out the elements of libel, which included an attack made in writing "with cool deliberate malice"[47] and with an intent that had "a direct tendency to ruin, or material injury."[48] Not only was the burden on the defendant to show he acted without malice, but the fact that the attack might have been intended as mere ridicule was no defense, Levy added, for the defendant might still have had "malice at heart when he used these words."[49] The intent to excite laughter was insufficient to justify the libel.[50] In sum, as the prosecution presented the case, libel constituted writing a man down to assassinate his character which, being his property, represented a loss that demanded recompense. Awarding or disallowing recompense for this diminishment of Rush's reputational capital—the basis for trust in his profession—was the weapon the law had devised to correct vice and reward virtue.

Levy argued that reputation was the sign of character and character was the grounds upon which property was based. In any argument for equity under the law, character thereby deserved the same protections as property if virtue was not to be denied:

> Gentlemen, reputation is sacred: an injury done to honor can scarcely be redressed. How can youth acquire prosperity or affluence, or age respectability, if that character, which is the foundation of success in every possession, may be attacked with impunity? If upon property there is protection, but there is no protection for character, justice is but partially administered, and it is time now, if for the first time, for an American court of justice to show the world that character is property, and a property most sacred.[51]

The issue, in sum, was whether the protection of property covered a man's character and, then, whether it extended to one's reputation. For Hopkinson it was a simple question. He spoke not of property in a material or physical sense but of property as a fungible form of capital within whose bounds was incorporated "the security in which a citizen of Pennsylvania holds his good name."[52] His focus was not on "any dispute about property"[53] but on character, the protection of which was fundamental to confidence in the nation's system of justice. The invaluable and sacred right to reputation,[54] he concluded, must not become "the undefended victim of assassinating violence."[55]

Rawle's opening for the defense would try to reframe the property argument as a contest of competing property rights: reputation and peace. In this version, the right that all men have in a community to "the happiness, safety and peace of that community" outweighed individual rights. The balance between individual and collective rights had to be properly struck, the private placed in the context of public concerns. Hopkinson would seize upon this frame as his second line of offense in making the prosecution's libel case. Resonating with Blackstonian law and building on the groundwork that McKean had laid in the Yrujo case, Hopkinson spoke in terms of the harassing effect of libel on the courts and the law in the extreme number of actions for defamation that were reaching the courts of justice, a theme that Justice Shippen's charge to the jury would mirror. While Ingersol argued social theory, contending that a law that allows a man no remedy rends the bonds of society asunder and leaves man in a state of nature with his private vengeance,[56] Hopkinson spoke to the pragmatics of the individual as part of the collective, citing the "bleeding victim of his malice [and] . . . the insulted justice of the country."[57] Cobbett had, equally, offended God, for no one, Hopkinson argued, had a right from God to injure another without "just retribution."[58]

In recasting the issue of collective responsibility, it became apparent that Cobbett was on shaky grounds. The prosecution, after all, had invested itself heavily in characterizing him as a figure who threatened the common welfare of the people, their happiness, their safety in society, their justice, and their government. Reprising Jefferson's analogy of 1798 and the revolution of 1776,[59] the political aspect of Cobbett's actions implied that Americans must refight the revolution against the English. Cobbett was thus framed not as a singular publisher of the immediate libels in question, nor were his actions seen as merely part of a pattern of libels that described his career. Rather, Cobbett's acts resonated with political efforts of a group intent on turning back the clock and returning America to its prerevolutionary dependency.

Using imagery that he would elsewhere apply to Rush as citizen-in-chief of a shining city on the hill, Hopkinson represented that the "*true liberty of the press*" was itself "a lofty citadel" that should reward the worthy while they stand in awe, a theme bound to remind the jury of the role played by the press in fostering America's own revolution. Hopkinson argued that true lovers of liberty would preserve its beauty and elegance, its shining walls, and "let not its foundations be sapped by treacherous guardians, till its high walls totter and fall."[60] Confounding religion, morals, law, government, and the press, he risked the slippery slope of rhetorical misrule to locate the cause of social anarchy itself in the lap of libels propagated by the press's failure to rise to its true heights:

> Ask me, what are the evidences of the decay of religion and morals among a people, of the approaching disregard of every social law and duty, of the entire prostration of truth, honor and honesty, of the tottering state of government, of the bursting of the social contract and of the consequent scenes of blood-shed, revolutions and warring chaos, and I will tell you, it is a boundless multiplication of licentious libels, a public encouragement of malicious defamation, and unpunished ravage upon reputation.[61]

Coming round full circle, Ingersol's close for the prosecution, and for the trial itself, argued that the jury should close Cobbett down as the main source of such slander, the licentious press from whose abuse "neither the government nor individuals have escaped." It lay with the jury "to protect character and government, which if you neglect, like the droppings of rain on a stone, it will wear it imperceptibly away: though the progress be slow, the effect is certain."[62]

Floundering in the face of such sweeping assaults, Rawle for the defense took a pedestrian path. He countered that the Pennsylvania Constitution[63] allowed Cobbett to exercise the rights given to him by state law permitting free investigation of matters of public interest[64] and by the federal constitution protecting liberty of the press. Cobbett's defense argued that its client, far from having a malicious intent or being guilty of untruth, published from a sense of duty with a view to sound a public alarm, a position that ought to extenuate the offense. Cobbett expanded the protective umbrella in his self-defense after the trial by arguing that his words intended to point "at Doctor Benjamin Rush for the express purpose of destroying his practice, so far as that practice corresponded with the well-known and justly abhorred System of depletion."[65] His attack on the system and the business was intended as a public duty, so that he ought not to be liable for damages at all.

Focusing on Rush's system was not, however, to provide Cobbett with the mantle of defender of the public in the prosecution's eyes. If Rush's system was so dangerous, it contended, Cobbett was responsible to benefit the public by doing more than arguing his own ignorance of medicine. He must prove a positive alternative that corrected, reformed, or amended Rush's system. Rawle responded by arguing "a very essential ground of our defense":[66] that Cobbett prevented the danger as much as was in his power as a good Samaritan, but without presuming to masquerade as a physician. Rather, the place of the journalist was to engage as a member of a free press on subjects of public discussion. Others were free to declare their opinions about a public question, including doctors whose opposition was potentially much more serious, and Cobbett, Harper argued, had said no more, after all, than "most respectable medical men said."[67] On the one hand, if his commentary was merely personal and not against the system, Tilghman added, Cobbett's charges would be addressed within the controversy itself. On the other hand, at a time of great public alarm, where treatment was no less than poison and death and so much apprehension abounded, how could the debate be other than about the system? The test, if Cobbett was wrong, was that he would be exposed; if right, he would do good. This last line of defense argument added a marketplace theory of patients' rights to its list of justifications. Suggesting a freedom of information defense, Rawle claimed that those upon whom doctors experimented as medical subjects should have as much freedom to choose as their doctors, a freedom dependant upon being informed.[68] Since there was disagreement over how to counter the disease, should the decision not be left to those affected and should they not have the freedom and the information to choose? As to the target of Cobbett's attacks, who, the defense asked, was a more fit object than the man who held the power of a patient's life and death in his hands, the man who was the first in his profession in America, the man who inculcated the very principles that others followed.

THE STORY OF CHARACTER

If *Rush v. Cobbett* was implicated by the prosecution in a political story that read like a national tragedy, that story was matched by Hopkinson to a morality tale that consisted of a personal struggle of cathartic proportions. The prosecution told a three-pronged tale; a father and husband who defended his family honor; a patriot and republican who defended his country's security; and a self-sacrificing physician who played the role of savior of the city. Cobbett was counterposed as an interloper, foreigner, violator of family honor, and a figure of satanic impulses. Initially, it appeared that Rush's reputation was so well established in Philadelphia that it ran little risk of being blemished by Cobbett's attacks. At least that was the position the prosecution took in defusing the notion that "the purity of the object attacked is to justify or lessen the crime of the assailant."[69] Hopkinson presented examples of the virtuous daughter, the morally upright, and even God Himself as against the profligate prostitute, the swindler, and the thief to make his point:

> Is the virtue of the injured, to be the defence of the injurer? Should it not rather be the protection of the just? Have you a daughter of spotless virtue and discretion? Is it then no offence to proclaim her a prostitute? Are you unquestionably upright and honest? Is it therefore no offence to publish you a swindler and a thief, while the real prostitute and the convicted thief would be entitled to exemplary damages?—Why, gentlemen, doctrines of this sort are so absurd, so repugnant to every sentiment of justice and propriety, that the honest heart shrinks from them as from its bane? Let us see to what they would lead us. To slander a man is simply no offence; to vilify a man pre-eminently wise and useful, is something better than merely an offence; and to blaspheme the all pure and perfect God must be highly meritorious.[70]

William Rawle and the defense team lamely responded that "If the system and practice of Dr. Rush has been so useful, so infallible, as you have been made to suppose . . . it is natural to suppose that the feeble efforts of Mr.

Cobbett could not destroy his celebrity, or injure that system, and therefore it could be but little or no offence for him to express his opinion."[71] Cobbett, by this argument, was not in Rush's league and thereby posed no credible threat. Harper added that the defense could not win on the issue of either the plaintiff's or the defendant's character: "The question in this case is not whether the plaintiff is a physician of eminence, a man of worth, a peaceable citizen, a good father, or a tender husband,—was this the point to be discussed, we must shrink from the opposition, and allow the claim to be in his favor, nor is it whether our client has offended against decorum, and every principle of civility and good manners,—or it would be equally difficult to make out a defence."[72] Harper rode the thin edge of the razor when he offered to concede, on the narrow grounds of separating Rush's medical practice from his person, that if Cobbett was found by the evidence to have overstepped and attempted to bring the physician himself into disrepute, the case was lost. He constructed the very slippery slope the prosecution would need to convict: "if I go beyond his opinions and abuse his person; if I go beyond his person and traduce his character, then indeed the pretence that I meant only to traduce his opinions, would not avail me in a court of justice."[73]

Unlike his cocounsel Harper, Cobbett's intimate friend Tilghman was quick to deny Rush the upper ground on the issue of personal attacks.[74] Rush's reputation for feuding with his colleagues in the profession had preceded him,[75] after all, leaving Tilghman the opening he needed to reproach Rush for making severe public pronouncements. Tilghman referred to an open letter in the *Federal Gazette* from Rush to Dr. John Rodgers,[76] read into evidence, to remind the jury that Rush himself was "extremely severe" and that he was led to "great lengths in his attacks":

> It is disagreeable to me to make any observations on the letter which I was impelled by my duty to read at the commencement of my defence. You will collect from that letter [which publicly advertises a cure for yellow fever in 1793] a few ideas which I think may prove that the Doctor has not only been intemperately, but uncommonly severe upon every one who had the misfortune to differ from him in practice. He has said, "As well might there be two suns or two moons, as to suppose that two sorts of fever prevailed in that year," although so many different symptoms made their appearance. His treatment of the Health Laws is equally severe, he does not only speak against the physicians, but against the Legislature itself . . . upon the whole he declares the laws very destructive.[77]

As Rawle said in Cobbett's defense, no man was more public than he who held life and death in his hands and no one more open not only to "public disapprobation, but, public contempt" than a physician who was "unskillful, avaricious, indolent."[78] The doctors' wars, he offered, caught up not merely William Cobbett but the medical community itself:

> So unaccountable and various were the attacks, and so difficult and various the modes of treatment, that it was considered a justifiable subject of public discussion. To some of these publications I might appeal, and shew you how strong, how acrimonious was the language, used even between the members of that learned profession. The subject continued thus, for a long time a subject of public controversy, and much warmth was used.[79]

Since the two competing medical associations of the city, the Academy of Medicine (with which Rush was associated) and the College of Physicians of Philadelphia (from which Rush had separated himself and which took a more moderated approach), held opposing views in treating the disease, Cobbett, too, Rawle insisted, should be free to express his opinion on both the principle and the practice of bleeding. Dr. Rush, after all, was a focus of controversy, a public figure performing a critical public role, so that "Mr. Cobbett was unquestionably exercising his constitutional right to do at that time, what others did, examine Rush's public transactions, in which he thought he was on the side of humanity."[80]

Picturing a crisis the jury had itself lived through just two years earlier—indeed, recollecting the famous epidemic in Philadelphia of 1793—Tilghman called up agitated, public physicians who were "much divided and even parties [that] were formed to support the different systems."[81] Thus, when the fever broke out again in 1797, so did the doctors' quarrels, the numerous publications, and the differences between the learned institutions. Who, he asked, was to say that Cobbett spread more fear than the doctors themselves?: "Whose opposition to Dr. Rush was most serious, that of Cobbett, or that of the Doctors? As you are not sure it was by Cobbett, but must have good ground for believing the other more *potent*, there can be no doubt where his disappointment originated."[82] Tilghman portrayed Rush as a man isolated in his certainty of a treatment that he introduced in 1793 and that was then new, entirely unheard of, and thereby a practice that alarmed the public as much as the fever itself.[83] In Tilghman's tale, Cobbett was thus no more than a foot-soldier: "the physicians were the main battle, and great was the shock, but Cobbett was a mere skirmisher."[84] The public itself was caught in a medical crisis in which Cobbett was positioned as only one among many who regarded the practice in question to be poisonous and deadly. Even if alone, Cobbett's ridicule of so dangerous a system would not only have been proper but justified,[85] Tilghman appealed, playing off of Rawle's construction of a defense of others, or good Samaritan, defense: "If it is justifiable to show that words used with a sincere and liberal intention, in order to prevent mischief, is harmless, is not that man justifiable, who seeing a dangerous system likely to predominate, who prevents, as much as lies in his power, that system being put into action? This I consider as a very essential ground of our defence."[86] Like the argument used to diffuse the attack on Cobbett for sounding the alarm against the French, the defense's argument that good citizen Cobbett was only preventing mischief in the medical community was meant to claim that he, no less, than Rush, had the welfare of his neighbors at heart.

Hopkinson had, however, inoculated the prosecution against such a defense argument by elevating the case above an "ordinary" trial to capture the extreme nature of the threat that Cobbett posed in the midst of the yellow fever epidemic. He had raised the level of the personal story from a struggle between two mere mortals to a battle of good and evil that invoked satanic motives and angelic acts of humanity,[87] archetypal themes of honor and saving grace under the assault of dark forces, and primordial evil against life giving sources of good. Levy argued that in Cobbett's version of the truth "the 'cloven foot' is plainly observable."[88] In Ingersol's close for the prosecution, Cobbett's cloven hoof once more "plainly appears,"[89] establishing Cobbett's motive for his attacks. Cobbett, Ingersol reminded the jury, admitted he would not have bothered himself about the bleeding treatments had it not been Rush who had supported them. "Malice," said Ingersol, "adopts an equivocal ambiguous stile"; it attempts to elude the law "by artful and ingenious constructions."[90] The jury shall be the judge and can see through these expressions, he added, for "if the 'clove foot' is discovered, if the veil is seen through, if the disguise is discovered, the law strips the sheep's clothing from the wolf, and exposes him to indignation in his own natural deformity." For its part, the defense team's objection to wrapping Cobbett in the devil's mantle registered lukewarm; they deflected the attack with qualifications questioning whether "his discussions of public questions show the *cloven-foot*" or "whatever his motive, whatever *cloven-foot* he might have concealed."[91]

To privilege Rush in the minds of the jury and to bring clarity to the ambiguities of Cobbett's subterfuges, Ingersol took the prosecution's imagery of the satanic alien[92] and counterposed it to imagery of physician Rush as savior, creating a clear sense of oppositionality:

> Wearing himself out in the duties of his profession, the Plaintiff, like a saving *Angel*, arrested the arms of Death, exposing himself, when it was difficult which most to admire, the profundity of his professional skill, or the vigor and benevolence of his mind, that bore him up against the dread of infectious scenes, which the stoutest Hero could not have approached without trembling. While thus employed, the foul attack is made; he is announced to the world as a "Quack—Empyric—Potent Quack." and "Grand Empyric," and the confidence of his Patients is withdrawn; he is represented as either by design or ignorance

> destroying "thousands and tens of thousands" of his fellow citizens. He is represented by this printer, as the exterminating Angel, going through the streets and heaping bodies on each other, and practicing little arts and tricks to support his reputation, which would disgrace even a mountebank.[93]

For its part, the defense offered, in Rawle's words, that the plaintiff was improperly construed as "superior to men in general—nay any man—he is an angel from God, clothed with every virtue—with every qualification, while Mr. Cobbett is nothing but a daemon from the infernal regions."[94] Indeed, Hopkinson had pictured Rush under siege and positioned Cobbett assaulting "the sacred fortress of reputation" and braving "the vengeance denounced against him by God and man," a foe that must be struck down by a dreadful swift justice.[95] Balancing a view of Cobbett the outsider invidiously polluting the political center of the nation, Philadelphia, Ingersol had counterposed the native Rush who provided heroic lifesaving care for the ill to other citizens (physicians, officials, ministers, lawyers, and journalists) who had fled the city, deserting their posts. Obscuring the fact that Cobbett had himself remained in Philadelphia during the 1797 epidemic, Ingersol capitalized on Cobbett's absence from the trial. The protagonist, a distinguished local light, after all, sat in plain view in the plaintiff's chair, while the antagonist's chair remained empty; the defendant, the libeling stranger, had left the city.

Rush's tale was thus the heroic tale of the citizen-physician rescuing public health in a time of national crisis, the physician-savior, the angel arresting death.[96] The ramparts of the shining city were best guarded by a figure of heroic proportions, a figure identified by Hopkinson with the ancient Greek Hippocrates. Rush, like his illustrious predecessor, unfazed, braved destruction to perform the good works that would bring health to the nation and rescue it from the throes of disease:

> When pestilence and death, walking hand in hand, swept away the people of Athens with the besom of destruction, the immortal Hippocrates threw himself undaunted into the midst of the danger, and endured the extremes of fatigue and distress to assist and deliver his perishing fellow citizens. How like this was the conduct of Dr. Rush in the memorable and dreadful year of 1793. He then stood foremost and almost alone to encounter and arrest the ravages of death.[97]

Whereas Rush's conduct accorded with that of Hippocrates, the rewards enjoyed by the Athenian were not those Rush enjoyed in Philadelphia. Tottering "into the infected chambers of the sick," having himself "languished on the bed of sickness," Rush deserved better from his fellow citizens:

> It was for the poor and helpless too that he thus exposed himself to destruction. The rich had generally fled—How like is this to the conduct of Hypocrates—I wish I could add how like is Philadelphia to Athens. Athens heaped honors and wealth on her Physician and his posterity; but contumely and defamation have been the reward of ours.[98]

As counsel reminded the jury, Rush the citizen-patriot remained separated from his family and exposed to death and disease to perform his duties while Cobbett, like a hunter to the fox, brought his "intended victim to the ground." If each age martyred its own saints, Rush, Hopkinson was convinced, proved no exception: "This, gentlemen, is what scribblers call, *writing a man down*, and it is a most abominable species of assassination."[99]

Conflating Rush with the selfless Hippocrates and situating him in the shining city, "On this high and dignified ground,"[100] was no less than to recall for the jury what the few churches that remained open routinely proselytized in yellow fever sermons: news of a healing God, a divine physician, a good shepherd who rescued the lost and gave succor to the diseased and suffering. If God was a rescuer in a time of plague, a redeemer with a providential plan, prosecution allusions to the "ravages of death" and the "angel from God" profited Rush. Once again, the prosecution's pretense that this was more than an ordinary trial expressed itself , this time by way of a rhetoric whose metaphoric power ran the range from the atavistic to the apocryphal, rising from the depths of the primordial to the heights of the heavenly. Using imagery reminiscent of the slime, noxious odors, and rot associated with the yellow fever epidemic, Hopkinson depicted Cobbett as a "vile source of falshood [*sic*] and pollution, [who] vomited forth the blackest venom of slander." Issue of the nation, Rush remained unmoved by such vile attacks: "He did not even wipe away by contradiction the filth with which he was covered; determined that the hands of his country alone shall either cleanse him from these foul aspersions, or sink him deeper in disgrace."[101] In Ingersol's final words summarizing the prosecution's case, the imagery of pollution and slander was transposed into the greatest threats an honest man had to fear:

> *Man need not dread a worse foe—it stabs with a word—It is the PESTILENCE working in darkness, spreading CONTAGION far and wide, which the most cautious traveler cannot avoid.—COURAGE cannot defend against its insidious attacks—It is the heart searching DAGGER of the dark ASSASSIN.—It is the poisoned arrow whose wound is incurable.—It is the mortal sting of the deadly ADDER:—nor GOVERNMENT nor OFFICER nor INDIVIDUAL can resist its fatal effects without the aid of LAW.—MURDER is its employment; INNOCENCE and MERIT its prey, and RUIN its SPORT.*[102]

The prosecution compounded the imagery of pollution and assassination with imagery of infestation and turbulence. Slander was pictured as a

> headlong torrent that rushes over the land—like a mighty water rolling from the mountain's top, it spreads and strengthens as it goes—the palace and the cottage are involved in its common ruin—nothing is so high that it cannot reach it, or so mean that it will not descend to it—let not the great promise themselves security in the unblemished dignity of their characters, nor the humble expect safety in their obscurity—like death it comes to every man's door. What is there so pure, or what so sacred that it has escaped this cormorant of defamation. From the highest magistrate to the meanest vagabond nothing has been secure; all men and all nations have been called with an equal tone of authority to the bar of this reproach, and every law, liberty and institution has undergone his *modest* animadversions.[103]

Cobbett was characterized by the perverse image of a torrent that exerted "tyrannical jurisdiction over everything public or private." He was tied to an "arrogant vanity . . . as disgusting as his crimes are detestable."[104] Hopkinson warned that "the wholesome waters of Liberty" not be confused with "the poisoned torrent of Licentiousness" that flowed from Cobbett's press.[105] The Rush case should be exempted from the great roar of press freedom which did not protect against private slander, the heart of this case. On this, "No question has arose," Hopkinson was certain; all men agreed.

Negating the prosecution story, Rawle's very first words directed to the jury an extended objection to Hopkinson's characterization that Cobbett was among those "noxious animals [who] are thrown up . . . from the very dregs and slime of the community, who in more happy times, would have lived and rotted in obscurity":[106]

> I stand up, Gentlemen of the Jury, much more impressed with difficulty on account of the extraordinary and unusual manner with which the gentleman who preceded me has thought proper to open his cause, than of any danger in which my client stands from the accusations on which this prosecution is grounded. . . .
>
> Gentlemen, if you believe the declarations of my opponent, you must be brought to believe William Cobbett to be the most *insignificant* and *worthless reptile in creation*, and that under the shape of a man, he has stalked about *a very monster*—that for him, no justice ought to be had—that he is to be expunged from all ranks of society, that he is to remain an eternal mark for hatred, and courts of Justice are never to consider him as even the object of mercy!—Mercy, that which we all claim, that which we think we are all entitled to, seems not to be his due! Gentlemen, even your opinions and your passions too have been assaulted, and called forth in a manner, which to me, has hitherto been perfectly unknown. This human monster—this most unheard of being—every thing that

> is entitled to the terms of *vile* and *base*, has been represented as the destroyer of the public peace and happiness; as the disturber of the harmony of society.[107]

Harper reinforced Rawle's critique of Hopkinson's abusive language. He called it unbecoming a well-bred man and noted that it was just such a style of speech that Hopkinson's own client had exemplified in filing his case against Cobbett. Tilghman, in the Cobbett team's most stinging rebuke to Hopkinson, vowed that the language directed against Cobbett was itself "utterly destructive of all character and reputation" and not at all what he had expected from a gentleman he respected. "Gentlemen," he appealed to the jury, "you are not to pay regard to the contemptuous light in which the defendant is held by the plaintiff's council: you are not to measure your verdict by their resentment." The prosecutor's extravagant rhetoric had several times labeled Cobbett an assassin, to which Tilghman, with some justice, rejoined, "May we not suppose, after all this that Mr. Cobbett is a man more sinned against than sinning?"[108]

Ambivalent about casting Rush as a threat to the public, the defense had left itself open to a strategy that presented him as an innocent victim. Instead of, minimally, offsetting the libel charges against Cobbett or, on a larger scale, defending by attacking the libel victim, the defense concluded that an attack on Rush seemed counterindicated. Directly accusing Rush of malpractice would not, as a result, become a central part of the defense story, even if the failure to make it so would plague Cobbett's defense throughout the trial. In his own right in *Porcupine's Gazette* and *Rush-Light*, Cobbett had, on the contrary, indicted Rush for sponsoring heroic bleeding from 1793 to 1798 in the yellow fever epidemics in Philadelphia. *Rush v. Cobbett*, as a result, while ostensibly a libel trial about the press freedoms taken by Cobbett, was by implication a public airing of a malpractice attack. The court trial, that is to say, was in Cobbett's mind coterminous with his trial by press of Rush. In this sense, it ought to have offered Cobbett yet another opportunity to call Rush, even if as a plaintiff, before the public to judge his medical practices.

The prosecution was thus free to exploit a strategy in which the beleaguered Rush functioned as a stand-in for the divine physician Himself, taking on the suffering of the people. Standing in their stead, the jury could now be asked, quid pro quo, to take on Rush's suffering as their own, to suppose themselves libeled and to call to judgment the libeler. The trial would play out as a libation poured at the feet of a sacrificed hero:

> Picture to yourselves, if you can, how you would feel, if precisely situated as is the defendant! of what avail would it be to you to be told that it was only *ridicule*? Suppose an infamous picture was put before your door—suppose a pair of horns, describing the conduct of your wife, and that repeatedly, would

> you be satisfied at being told it was "*a test of truth*" and that "*ridicule could do you no injury?*"—Suppose it was a label put, that you were guilty of this or that species of swindling, or worse, suppose this to be inserted in the newspapers—suppose that instead of low, indecent, and ruffian-like vulgarity, you were attacked with a keen satire,—would it be to your benefit that you were cut with a *sharp* knife?[109]

Once the jury was hailed by the story to relive the assault from within Rush's experience, Levy seemed certain they would identify with him:

> Does not the defendant . . . ascribe to [the plaintiff] the murder of his fellow creatures, by the use of bleeding and mercury? Can there be a more severe attack upon a medical man . . . ? What kind of man must he be, who follows a particular system with callous heart and murderous hands, when he sees direful effects attending that system? Who would follow such a system of slaughter . . . but the most abandoned and unfeeling wretch; and who would employ the man that should so embrue his hands in blood?. . . Gentlemen, I ask if this does not set the plaintiff [as] a fit object for the detestation of the world?[110]

In his closing for the defense, Ingersol modeled for jury members the way to take on Rush's suffering as their own, inciting them to experience firsthand his financial losses, his inability to support his family, his age and lost reputation: "My character—my professional and moral character attacked with the venom and art of a daemon—my daily bread about to be taken from me—the subsistence for my family in danger of being lost to me—a head covered with grey hairs—fortune gone in paper money."[111] Rush's story was intended to become the jury's story, the assault on him an assault on it. Generating a consensus within the target audience, his story would drive home a verdict against the party identified as the assailant, based on little more than a false sense of the jury's having been vicariously victimized by Cobbett and of Rush having performed the role of their savior.

In sum, the trial narratives that dominated *Rush v. Cobbett*, the political story and the story of character, depended upon antitheses as useful fodder to figure Rush as the kind of hero the public needed to resolve contradictions and to figure Cobbett as an antihero who ambiguified public experiences to create anxiety in times of uncertainty. Such constructions enabled the prosecution to raise deeply troubling historical themes by means of which jurors might marginalize Cobbett and cast him into moral and political exile. The prosecution's case came to depend upon a configuration in which the defendant matched the subject of the Alien and Sedition Acts. The republican continuing revolution would identify and control traitors old and new, and Cobbett was regarded as both: he stood for the present rebellion that disturbed the new republic's stability by undermining its efforts at diplomacy and casting doubts on its leaders; and he recalled the old corrupt order that labeled true revolutionaries traitors in order to reverse the revolution and restore colonial power. In the complex political terrain of negotiations like those of Jay's Treaty and the XYZ Affair, Cobbett was seen as a threat to republicanism not in the narrow sense of a political party but in the larger sense of a form of government. As a figure "unfriendly to our government, a man ignorant of his true *situation* in this country and of the *kind of value or use* that has been put upon him,"[112] he had become a dangerous weapon in the hands of a foreign power. If he could be characterized as a man who owed no allegiance to the republic and whose contributions to public discourse were distortions of the truth, then the implication was that Cobbett was a man who had benefitted from the nation's laws without respecting them.[113] Redefined as "republican," citizenship excluded Cobbett. An alien, he was vulnerable, as Tilghman pointed out, to being punished merely to "prove how good the government is."[114] According to Ingersol, he was a man without respect for truth or justice for whom the fever of 1797 offered a perfect opportunity to deliver a death warrant to republicanism in the guise of the premier city of the new republic, Philadelphia, and a premier republican, Benjamin Rush. The affliction and lamentation of the fever, together with the success and promise of republicanism could have worked out as a perfect model of the hope of the civic jeremiad had Cobbett not inserted himself into the equation. Man had not the power of creation to form human nature, Ingersol argued, but he had an instrument of his own creation, his law, to oversee the good order of society.[115] Breach of this order weighed the social balance in favor of affliction, whereas the jury's assignment of damages to deter and punish such breaches promoted progress in favor of the promised stability of the republic and its continuing revolution. This was the "high and dignified ground"[116] of which Hopkinson spoke, the confident justice that certified the security of the inviolable right a citizen of Pennsylvania possessed, the valued and sacred right to his own worth and honor. In Cobbett's assault upon a man's reputation lay the apocalypse that tottered high walls; in Rush's republicanism lay the millennium that preserved the "exquisite beauty [and] elegant proportions"[117] of the city of liberty. As an instrument of God's, nature's, and man's laws, the jury must, with the prosecution, strike the balance that attached to each injury a just retribution. In this way only would providence be fulfilled; only then would lamentation be joined to hope. The alternative—too terrible to be considered—was to permit private vengeance, murder, and assassination—man's local version of apocalypse—to interfere with providence working out its plan in a land blessed by God and occupied by His chosen people.

THE SECULAR JEREMIAD

The teleology of an American secular jeremiad accounted to a large extent for the dichotomies we see expressed in the prosecution's case in *Rush v. Cobbett*. Its condemnation of the profane, of false Americans, and its expression of faith in a native destiny point to a strategy that explains themes of crisis and partisanship, by means of which Hopkinson structured his argument, and themes of consensus and resolution, by means of which he appealed to the jury. His speech ranged perilously close to a cacophony of apocalypse, declension, and pollution in an attempt to revive a heroic dream and to call for national salvation. Recalling the American jeremiad's emphasis on the optimism of hope and promise rather than punishment, he exploited the frontier between the civilized order of America and atavistic threats of devolving to a primitive state of private revenge, feuds, and mob actions. Here, the frontier served as a "figural outpost,"[118] a threshold for the redemption of the land from darkness that, as Sacvan Bercovitch describes it, is less a dividing line than a vehicle of the jeremiad "to create anxiety, to denounce backsliders, to reinforce social values, and (summarily) to define the American consensus."[119]

Hopkinson figured Cobbett as a force of declension that disallowed the resolution that jeremiadic rhetoric provided and that would leave Americans in the condition of ungrateful colonials rather than proud patriots, in a world of sacred scapegoats rather than one of manifest destiny. If Cobbett's reverse revolution intended to roll back America's gains in the American Revolution, it was the duty of America's continuing revolution to exorcise this rebellion against a divinely providential and legitimate order that was the antithesis of the corrupt and illegitimate English rule in America from which Americans had liberated themselves. Cobbett did indeed argue that Americans were children ungrateful to their colonial father, the king. If ingratitude to God was the sin most spoken of in the sermons, then in Cobbett's inversion of the secular American jeremiad, the mythic heroes who fathered the revolution had breached their filial obligation by ingratitude to the English king, their secular "father." Thus, to become fathers themselves, these giants raised the specter of disobedience to the law of the father, which—if they became replacement parents—left them without a foundation upon which to demand filial obedience themselves.

The tale according to Cobbett thus made children of the founding fathers, traitors of American revolutionaries, and decline of America's progress. Expressing contempt of Rush—figured as a father himself, in the mold of George Washington, in the prosecution's case—was threatening to the myth of progress and the fulfillment of an American civic millennium. Cobbett's presentation of Rush in the press had made the American rather than the Englishman a force for declension, which thwarted the scenario by means of which Rush would fulfill the American jeremiad and prevented a reading of rescue, redemption, and reward. Factored into the development of a political party system, Cobbett's version of the secular, or perhaps at this point more appropriately the political, jeremiad encouraged a split in filial loyalties that left Americans with a fractured American identity and conflicted party loyalties.[120] In the darkness of the American jeremiad, after all, the English represented the plague from which the chosen must escape and the Englishman the demon to be ritually exorcised, not Rush. Thus, Hopkinson in the trial had to reset local perceptions of the Rush-Cobbett feud so that, operating at an archetypal level, Rush's personal fate would converge with that of the jurors who stood collectively, first, for the public and, second, for America itself. Comparably, such themes as liberty, equality, order, and unity would serve as parts of God's plan for America in a civic millennium.

The larger providential drama of broad universal forces with which Rush's case was infused subsumed Cobbett's narrower sense of politics and limited immediate rights argument. In the prosecution's book, by assaulting the fortress of reputation to "prostrate it in the dust,"[121] Cobbett braved the vengeance of God. Punished by speedy justice, his fate would serve as an awful, infamous lesson to those tempted by depravity, for no man should have the right to injure without retribution or to triumph by arrogance and malice. This prospect, however, was just what the country had allowed. Cobbett, a "cormorant of destruction," had—like the God of vengeance—called all those from the highest to the meanest to the "bar of his reproach." His tyrannical jurisdiction extended, in Hopkinson's words, across "all men and all nations": "like death it comes to every man's door."[122] Cast in this light, Cobbett presented as a fallen angel whose power challenged that of the great divinity. Like the Tower of Babel, his work could not be suffered to stand.

Antipodally, Rush had honored God by rescuing from contempt His chosen people, a people as "different from all the people on the face of the earth."[123] As a physician celebrated by the old world itself, Rush had proved America more than the equal of every part of Europe. He had revitalized it, forged a new covenant for a city to which he brought relief and the approbation of God. Should Hopkinson's audience prove ungrateful for such gifts, the city might again "become at once silent as a wilderness . . . the habitation of death and disease."[124] The lamentations of the wretched and the terrors of the soul would return; the temples of God would be sealed; and the night would once again become heinous—these were the deserts of those who forgot such citizenship, who forgot one "devoted to the most godlike duties he owes to his country." Hopkinson juxtaposed vilification of this "pre-eminently wise and useful man"[125] to the blasphemy against "the all pure and perfect God" in revisiting the promise of providential grace gifted to a city visited by damnable horrors and yet deservedly exceptional in God's eyes. Hopkinson had bifurcated the visage of the Old Testament God of vengeance and grace: He who visited disaster upon the city—Cobbett—and He who shed grace—Rush. In a jeremiadic variant, he extended the Old Testament model of vengeance and lamentation to a threat against the liberties won in America's revolution. Here, a chosen people had won the right to oversee governance of the land from a great height, a lofty citadel from which they rewarded the virtuous and crushed oppression. Their high outlook, intended for the public good, was what Hopkinson pictured as sacred walls of high privilege that had been won and ought not to be lost. This new generation of Americans—the public represented by the jury—was called to arms as guardians of a great legacy it must preserve "from ruin and contempt." It must bring down "wretched imposters," "pretended friends," serpents in the garden like Cobbett who would sap its strength. Better to lose a piece of such liberty (the licentiousness of the press) than the entire edifice (the citadel of press freedom). In this storying of the trial, Hopkinson embraced the transformation of the biblical jeremiad into a civic jeremiad in which a suffering chosen people in an exceptional land won the republic from a despot's hands and must now preserve its gains in a new millennium in which ingratitude to the revolutionary fathers had become the *bête noire* that replaced forgetfulness of a loving God.[126]A signer of the Declaration of Independence, the prosecution reminded its audience, Rush was one of those who "have *done too much, suffered too much, and succeeded too well* in our glorious struggle, ever to be denied by his own or forgiven"[127] by his enemies.

The secular jeremiad arrived at an arguably divine plan carried out through progressive means by human actors toward a more glorious society,[128] the very basis of the prosecution strategy in the Rush trial: Rush as the embodiment of a semidivine figure who carried the truth to a world in need of relief.[129] Rush's transcendence as savior, immortal Hippocrates, divine physician metamorphosed into the public's transcendence to a higher moral order and a better social world where the promise provided by prophecy would be embraced and the people made whole. In this reading, the American jeremiad was as patriotic as it was spiritual and Rush was figured as leading the way to the millennium. Indeed, millennial thought had already inspired movements in such areas as medical reform and abolitionism that promised a better world even as they challenged existing institutions and values to grow a new framework for national culture and identity.[130] In the meantime, each setback, like the attacks on Rush, could be viewed as an assault on this new civic religion, this myth for the future. Attacks supported the sense of threat that served as the alter face to the hope of millennialism, the face of "pestilence and death, walking hand in hand . . . with the besom of destruction,"[131] in Hopkinson's words. Like Rush, before he could stand foremost "to encounter and arrest the ravages of death," each American was vulnerable to declension before he reached his divine destiny in this chosen world. From the highest to the meanest, "all men and all nations have been called."[132] Each son would be charged with fulfilling the dreams of his father to continue the revolution that would lead to the new America. Each attack on the father made the faltering steps of the son more likely to lead to further declension, just as Hopkinson warned in picturing the turbulence of slander "like a mighty water rolling from the mountain's tops." The plan for achieving an authentic American city of God was meant to arouse in sons the spirit of their revolutionary fathers.[133] Cobbett's disruptions of the lives of Rush's sons, diverting them to violent acts, was a sign of further declension, a sign of apocalypse, not of a city on the hill. The provocations that led them to defend their father's reputation were stratagems of a devilish figure intent upon deflecting the continuing revolution onto sidetracks that would stall the promise of the national dream.

In sum, in the prosecution tale of secular jeremiad, the most important characteristics were the threat of evil and a call to action to defeat evil and midwife the birthing of a true nation. The threat was the snake, pollution, turbulence, that is, Cobbett's relegation of American politics and governance to declension. The hope on the most immediate level was the shining hill of true freedom of the press and the protection of reputational rights; in its most extended sense it was the fulfillment of the American Revolution. Declension meant reversing the revolution and reestablishing the colonial experience by undermining basic liberties and breaching public peace and order. The plague of press freedom and the infiltration of a foreign virus constituted the excesses described as man's sin that, more than God's wrath, spread the fever of anarchy and undermined the special status promised to the American people. The shared belief that would lead the jury back to a communal identity as Americans meant living up to the vision for the nation and its progeny that constituted the prophecy to arrest decline and assert the hope of the mission handed over to them by their progenitors. The jury was to complete the mission begun by Rush and his fellow declarers of independence: to make hope a reality and to revive the revolution in its own generation and for its own progeny. A liberation theology for its times, the Rush team offered the secular jeremiad new life for a civic millennium much along the lines of Rush's own extreme treatments for disease, which in providential terms God Himself emulated. Like God, Rush was an ambiguous figure, at once the disease and the physician. In either role, the choice in the prosecution's case came down to letting the will of this secular god be done or facing the vengeance of the fallen Cobbett.

THE CONTRIBUTION OF SERMONS

The scenario from which the prosecution operated was widely disseminated in yellow fever sermons delivered by those divines who remained behind in Philadelphia to succor the suffering.[134] Here, plagues were theologically significant as long as medicine had no convincing explanation for disease. Given that the best efforts humans could bring to such devastation was so unconvincing, the Lord clearly remained a Lord of Lords and the laws of God prevailed over those of man. His word prevailed over the rhetoric of public safety and health so that divine rationales and the providential plan might prevail.[135] Any consideration that the plague might not be God's work, but that of the devil, made God even more necessary, for who greater than an opposing divine force could match Satan's power. Death, disease, and plague, should one credit them to Satan, were acolytes that drove one to trust all the more in God as a resource with angelic weaponry that could compete with and prevail over them in battle. God's justice, after all, was not to be challenged by secular rationales or to be made auxiliary to the presumed efficacy of secular practices. Either God would make the way, create the space, provide the path, or none would be available. Either His providence would provide or no provision would be made. Good shepherd or not, God was as likely to herd his flock over a cliff, lemming-style, as to simply pasture them, with no justification or excuse.[136]

The mixed blessings of Rush's character as the jury would have encountered them in the course of the trial were thereby accountable in terms of the extremism of a deity isolated in His power and absolute in His sense of the rightness of His way. The greater the threat Cobbett presented as a satanic force in the prosecution's case, the more Philadelphia had need of Rush and the clearer it became that the rejection of his enemy was necessary to reestablish order in a feverish world. As Elhanan Winchester, founder of the Universalist Church, modeled the tale, "The angel of death visited our prosperous, pleasant, healthy, but careless city, and for several months threatened to reduce it to a scene of desolation."[137] Rush, by virtue of this telling, would have played the role of the avenger, a good pilot like "Christ for their captain, God's word for their compass, his glory for their pole-star, prayer for their cable, a good hope for their anchor."[138] Congregationalist Samuel Spring prepared his flock well to receive the prosecution's message of the infectious disease spread by foreign influence—in this instance, the French—a "disorganizing poison" more fatal than "a thousand plagues" that had escaped "most sovereign remedies [and] been very imperious to the Federal Government."[139] Reformed Dutch William Linn, by contrast, identified "the pestilence of party"[140] as a form of infectious politics and the yellow fever as the means by which the war against England might now be betrayed to that enemy. A number of republican clerics would have agreed with him, sermonizing, like Scotch Presbyterian John Mitchel Mason, to the effect that both the war against England and the yellow fever were attributable to "the rod of his anger."[141]

The seeds of distress at party politics (aimed at Justice Shippen) and of the social disorder at the hands of the feuding politics of the plaintiff and the defendant (meant to appeal to the jury) were thereby planted in the discourse of the very practical and immediate sermons the public would have been exposed to in churches across a broad spectrum of denominations. Preaching in Christ Church, William Smith tenderized the sentiments of his audience, indeed of potential jurors, in his warnings to them not to suck up the poisons of the earth, desert the company of angels, and grovel with beasts.[142] Winchester would have his faithful beware the apocalypse which, "mounted on his pale horse, seemed to ride triumphant . . . between the city and the tomb."[143] The jury dare not, by this reading, deny the hand held out in the midst of chaos and forget the adorable one, the prince of peace who, in the Quaker Joshua Cresson's words, would set them upon the rock "against which the gates of hell shall never be able to prevail."[144]

The dichotomous depiction of Rush and Cobbett segued easily into the popular religion of the world of yellow fever sermons, if only by inserting the two litigants into the already available archetypes posited by the very spiritual leaders to whom the people fled for explanations of the disaster that had befallen them. As in Henry Wright's public prayer in Bristol, Rhode Island, sermons asked their audiences to regard "the late awful calamity" as a "new and complicated war," to attend to the rod of God and consider its meaning.[145] If yellow fever was imported into the city, German Lutheran J. Henry Helmuth would advise, it was not enough to endure it; the public—like their representatives in the jury—had to consider how it implicated them and how it worked through human institutions.[146] Rush was a primary candidate for just such ruminations, and the jury's empathy for his plight offered as welcome an opportunity as Helmuth might have wanted. Thaddeus Brown would have extended that self-examination to considering how man embraced the plague, since the more that famine and war revealed, "the more immediate agency and direction of the most high."[147] Like Brown, Presbyterian Ashbel Green would have the faithful regard those who remained to serve in the fever-ridden city as against those who fled.[148] Alike in that both were victims of the fever, those who fled risked being construed, as Brown put it, as hiding from the Lord. Thus, "if any rejoice for fleeing and being safe, let them rejoice with fear and trembling."[149] Cobbett, for his part, would have been well warned to stay in Philadelphia for the trial, even as he had done for the fever, if he wanted to share with Rush the credit for having cared for the people's welfare. As Samuel Stearns might have warned Cobbett, submission was no less than a sign of contrition, a mitigating factor that would have stood the journalist in better stead with the jury:

> Serve your Lord, and in him trust;
> That when your days on earth shall cease,
> Ye may be seated with the just,
> In boundless realms of joy and peace.[150]

Brown attributed to those who remained "a mercy from God" who influenced their hearts to stay at their post, holding them blessed that they did so and considering them witnesses of God's mercy in attending those who were lost.[151] Making much the same argument, the anonymous author of the elegy "Fever"[152] expressed the gratitude felt by the citizens of the city toward those who stayed behind, whether doctors or volunteers.[153] Recognizing that God knew who truly served, the elegy tried at the same time to resolve the differences that had arisen among the clergy:

> Some greatly stood—some greatly fell,
> To them the Muse her homage pays
> They knew their duty, acted well,
> And in the Churches is their praise. . . .[154]

COBBETT'S SELF-DEFENSE

Cobbett was bitter about his depiction in the trial narrative and the resulting trial verdict. Sorely disappointed by the defense his legal team had mounted, he was determined to replay the trial in the court of public opinion, this time as his own counsel and by means of a trial by press conducted in his final issue of *Porcupine's Gazette* and over five issues of a new publication, *Rush-Light*, which he published in 1800 in New York. Cobbett's seeming advantage going into the trial had evaporated. Undermined by the rhetorical flourish of the republican Hopkinson's eloquence, his legal team had not presented an effective defense arguing the truth of his attacks, the facts of the case, or the evidence of his publication, a cause for particular concern if one considers that under common law, as Blackstone indicated, most trials were a question of the facts.[155] Cobbett was determined to present his own case and was convinced that he would have won had his counsel embraced the defense that he put forth.

Cobbett addressed three bodies of evidence: the words he used, the testimony of the witnesses, and his press attacks against Rush. On the issue of the words, Cobbett confidently announced that they were indeed and in fact directed at Rush expressly to destroy a practice that Cobbett detested,[156] persisting with the pretense that he only intended to undermine Rush's practice and not his person. Cobbett refused to dodge the prosecution, as his counsel had, by saying that he did not say what he had said or that he had not meant to say it. Instead, he explicitly relied upon a common law interpretation of libel whereby "The words used are to be taken in their ordinary meaning and common acceptance, such as the hearers would most probably impute to them."[157] Thus, Cobbett held that under common law words must be understood not in their worst or best sense but as they are understood by those who read or heard them.[158] In this sense, a common reader would not take it that Cobbett had accused Rush of "criminal killing," for his patients must actually be proved dead and death was not proved by the prosecution.[159] Not only did Cobbett claim to have used the term figuratively, but he asserted that the word "kill," even in its literal sense, was too general. To be a libel, the term must literally be used to mean kill criminally[160] and the killer must have intent to kill and not to cure, as Rush intended.[161] Drawing an analogy to a comparable case, Cobbett argued that the doctors who had unsuccessfully treated George Washington—who died on the day of the trial verdict—made his "*death* speedy and inevitable" by excessive bleeding which "left him no strength to struggle." This statement, by a Dr. Bricknell, did not constitute a charge that Washington's doctors killed him and was not thereby libelous. But, then, neither should such "truth" be muzzled.[162]

Cobbett's second line of argument went to the nature of the evidence of the three physicians Rush called as witnesses: Drs. William Dewees, John Redman Coxe, and James Mease. Cobbett again applied a common law reading, in this instance based on Blackstone's commentary that all witnesses "are to be received and examined, except as are *infamous*, or such as are *interested* in the event of the cause."[163] As common law was applied under Pennsylvania law, the certainty of such interest must be "in the verdict, or the event of the particular suit" and must be proved.[164] Once interest is proved, the witness is declared incompetent to the extent of excluding his testimony. Cobbett proceeded to demonstrate the interest of each of the three witnesses, all of whom testified to Cobbett's prejudice against Rush as a political figure and to his intention to do Rush a personal injury by defaming him. Mease had testified that he heard Cobbett say of Rush, "Damn him, he had better withdraw his cause [suit] . . . or I will persecute him while living and his memory after his death";[165] Dewees related that Cobbett had espoused his antipathy to a republican address Rush had delivered, saying "Damn him, I will attack him for it";[166] and Coxe offered that Cobbett had confided in him "that he did not believe he should ever have said so much on bleeding or mercurials, if Dr. Rush had not been the author of it."[167] In each instance, Cobbett claimed that the witness was himself a bleeder and an acolyte of Rush and that he would have been implicated in the case by virtue of Cobbett's attack on Rush's "partisans." Cobbett had identified them as "the Rushites [who] have slain their tens of thousands"[168] with that Samson of treatments, the mercury purge. Their association with Rush made them all virtually joint plaintiffs in the case.[169] Moreover, each had a private grudge against Cobbett, so that their malice was, as well, private and personal. Cobbett claimed, for example, that he had refused to print an attack on Governor Mifflin of Pennsylvania that had been provided to him by Mease[170] and that he had refused to lampoon a list of physicians provided by Coxe.[171] Dewees's father had been subjected to attacks by Cobbett for corruption in his role of city jailer.[172]

Cobbett could have faulted all three physicians on the issue of hearsay, that is, "the mere declarations of other persons,"[173] since he not only denied their characterization of his conversations with them but considered their testimony "too vague and unsubstantial, to afford any reasonable presumption, as to the truth of the recited fact."[174] Moreover, the evidence Mease and Coxe provided occurred after Rush had filed his suit, so that they were untimely as testimony to Cobbett's motivation for his publications.[175] Coxe so clearly remembered the date of his conversation with Cobbett, and his speech was so full of leading questions, that his conduct qualified as entrapment, as, indeed, did Mease's conduct since he had plied Cobbett with wine on the occasion of the comment to which he testified.[176] Similarly, Cobbett caught Dewees in a significant exaggeration, if not outright misrepresentation, about medical services he claimed to have provided to Cobbett and his family, leading to Cobbett's claim that Dewees's testimony on that point not only threw doubt on the rest of his testimony[177] but represented a breach of confidentiality in Dewees's professional conduct as a physician.[178] The witnesses, in sum, were, by Cobbett's analysis, so discredited that their testimony would have been excluded as evidence had his counsel only confronted them in cross-examination on those points. Certainly, as Blackstone held, confronting adverse witnesses would have provided an "opportunity of obtaining a clear discovery,"[179] an opportunity Cobbett felt himself denied by his trial team. If nothing else, the credibility of the witnesses would have been placed at issue, raising doubt about "the *general character* of the witness for truth, and whether from that general character, he is worthy of credit upon his oath."[180] As far as Cobbett was concerned, the witnesses were themselves guilty of "something very like perjury"[181] as they had given "evidence as manifestly tends to *produce a belief of what is not true*."

Cobbett's defense team, indeed Cobbett in his own defense, might not have presented witnesses of its own but surely the prospects Cobbett demonstrated for dispatching the evidence provided by Rush's witnesses would have eliminated the element of malicious intent from the charges. It would certainly have enhanced the prospects for a truth defense and thereby considerably reduced the possibility of a guilty verdict. If, indeed, malice was not involved and his words were true, Cobbett asserted, then he had done "no more than fulfill his duty in publishing them"[182] and the jury should not be able to find against him. Citing the highest authority he could muster, Cobbett reminded the jury that He who said "Thou shalt not bear false witness" would not be fooled by the "mental reservations"[183] of the witnesses, for whom a higher tribunal awaited, as it did for the jurors themselves.

Cobbett went on to address the evidence of his press attacks against Rush that had been put before the jury. In the trial transcript, charges were leveled against his response to a medical "puff";[184] an extract from and commentary on a letter from Dr. Tilton to Dr. Rush;[185] a satire about a tavern keeper;[186] publication of a piece by A. B. on Rush and Tilton;[187] commentary on publication of another puff from Brown's newspaper;[188] and a third puff.[189] The three "puffs" addressed different aspects of Rush's self-advertisement of his remedy for yellow fever. The first attack on a puff involved Rush's publication for public use of a cure for the fever. Cobbett's commentary opened with the couplet "The times are ominous indeed,/When quack to quack cries purge and bleed."[190] Citing the pervasive use of newspapers "to puff off his [Rush's] preposterous practice," Cobbett called the "poison of their prescriptions . . . the raven's croak to those of the sickly flock." A second exhibit compared a Rush advertisement to Spilsbury's Antiscorbutic Drops, a quack's cure for a variety of disorders from scurvy, gout, and rheumatism to ulcers. Like Rush, Spilsbury had presented his cure as a universal remedy more extraordinary "than any other invented."[191]

The third puff had a somewhat difference provenance. Cobbett charged that it was part of a letter campaign whereby physicians supported each other's work. Cobbett asked rhetorically what object such networked correspondence might "have in view, in these indirect addresses to the public, but that of extolling their own practice, advancing their own fame, and increasing their own profits?"[192] Answering his own question, he concluded that the only rationale for such men to write to each other in this way was to puff themselves like quacks. In this version of the practice, Cobbett represented, Rush had sent a letter to be published out of town, which was then routed back to a Philadelphia paper: “All this bustle of letters and addresses, and prescriptions, in the name of Dr. Rush, is intended to make the duped world believe, that he is the Oracle at Philadelphia, and that all the other physicians are mere glister-pipe Dicks[193] under him—It is a cheap mode of acquiring fame, which he learned from the crafty old hypocrite, Franklin.”[194] The two Tilton exhibits related to the practice of puffing by networking correspondence as well. In an extract from one letter, for example, Tilton recommended Rush’s bleeding and purging regimens in their aggressive forms and even referred to the yellow fever as “*your* [Rush’s] *fever*.”[195] Cobbett’s commentary identified Tilton as “the trumpet, the underling, the mere barber-surgeon of the master-bleeder”[196] and positioned him as one of the Rushites who slew tens of thousands with mercury purges.

The final exhibit was one of the three prose satires[197] featuring a tavern keeper and his hostler turned bleeders that we discussed earlier. The satire in question (the second in the series)[198] provided a picture of a cure gone riot. Having read of Rush’s cure in the newspapers and having purchased Rush’s book on yellow fever, the two men had turned physician themselves and competed for patients. Their limited knowledge of vulgar Latin provided the cachet they needed to appear professional, including several sham maxims in vulgar Latin to guide their practice. Identified with the French, a prerequisite for a republican physician of the Rush school, these bleeders possessed a carriage newly painted with the sign of a French hostler and a cold-bloodedness traceable to the Reign of Terror in their use of the lancet. Having truly grasped the nature of their new practice, they were prepared to pillage their patients, to lay the blame for failed cures on their patients, and to embrace the rationale that the dead make poor witnesses, themes that had been associated with the Rushites in one form or another in the press. The bleeders and their brethren endorsed the idea of a college of fellow bleeders and initiated an appeal to the public regarding its prejudice against bleeding, on behalf of Rush himself.

In asserting the truth of his publications against Rush, Cobbett addressed the four complaints against him in the charges:[199] Rush’s vain boasts, Rush’s quackery, Rush compared to Sangrado, and Rush killing his patients. The prosecution described the last charge as an accusation that Rush was guilty of “killing people with deadly weapons,” that is, “of killing people with his physic.”[200] Cobbett’s common law response privileged neither the best nor the worst sense of the words read, by means of which the prosecutor’s burden had not been met, since the prosecution had not, after all, produced the bodies. In defense of the truthfulness of his charge that Rush made vain boasts, Cobbett allowed that the best evidence of boasting was Rush’s own published claim that his new remedies had rendered yellow fever no more dangerous than measles, influenza, or the common cold and that "*he had been made the instrument in the hands of a kind Providence of curing MORE than ninety-nine patients out of a hundred.*"[201]

As for accusing Rush of being a quack, Cobbett cited the published advertisements that extolled his cure, compared Rush's ads to quack ads like those of Spilsbury (arguing that the quackery of such ads was in fact inferior to those of Rush),[202] and reminded the public again that Rush had assured his public that the disorder was no longer dangerous. That Rush boasted of his cures in such public venues as newspapers, handbills, posted notices in shops, on walls, houses, and pumps[203] left no doubt that he was a quintessential quack, since public advertisement was the very definition of quackish practice.[204] Cobbett cited the extremity of Rush's language in announcing "the almost universal success with which it has pleased God to bless the remedies of strong mercurial purges and bleeding in this disorder"[205] and concluded that Rush's claims were all the more outlandish as they appeared at a time when the numbers in mortality bills were rising from 23 to 119 a month. Rush accompanied his claims with advice that no one who failed to follow his practices should be trusted, an assertion that Cobbett found, under these conditions, indefensible.[206]

On the charge of having associated Rush with Sangrado,[207] Cobbett reminded his readers that Le Sage had parodied the very physician, Botallus, whose bleeding practices Rush had defended.[208] He went on to draw comparisons between Sangrado and Rush in terms of their person, general character, and "medical opinions, practice, and fame."[209] In doing so, he made sure to note the singularity of their opinions, their frequent and large bleedings, their training of apprentice bleeders, their promotion in print of bleeding, and their affinity to Hippocrates.[210]

The final part of Cobbett's self-defense addressed his close to the jury. Here, Cobbett appealed to jury members to act according to their consciences, and he spoke to the motive that informed the prosecution's case. He argued that had he been an American and a republican, rather than an Englishman and a royalist,[211] he would not have been prosecuted. Fenno, the American editor, had after all been charged with libel at the same time as Cobbett only to see the charges against him dropped. Rush's witness Coxe, Cobbett claimed, had written libelous words about Cobbett, yet Coxe had never been charged.[212] Neither had Dr. Bricknell's accusation that George Washington died at the hands of his doctors been treated as a libel. Had Cobbett written such libels, he claimed, he would certainly have been charged.

In spite of his conviction that he had spoken nothing but the truth in his own publications, Cobbett made it a point of honor that he had not authorized his legal team to use a freedom of press defense in the trial.[213] He must, in this sense, refuse American law in his defense, insisting, rather, upon the application of English common law. He provoked the jury by proclaiming that the English had a freer press than the Americans[214] in any case and that Americans had less liberty than Englishmen,[215] provoking the very discrimination he, at the same time, complained of. Nor was American justice, he pointedly declared, to be admired, as his treatment in the Yrujo and Rush cases exemplified.[216] He had attacked republicans, he advised his readers, to warn England not to repeat the American republic's mistake in trying to complete the unfinished French Revolution.[217]

The Rush trial would indeed be tried under the cloud of a rumor[218] that Cobbett was a British agent, a rumor that dogged Cobbett from the time he became prosperous as a journalist in America. The *Aurora*, a republican newspaper, had published a piece by a Paul Hedgehog in which Cobbett, identified as a "*garrett scribbler*" from Grubb Street,[219] was accused of having been forced to leave England and of having to flee from France during its revolution to the United States. In America, he was supposed to have been introduced to a British foreign agent "by the name of *traitor*" who enlisted him in the cause of the king. The evidence of a sudden improvement in his circumstances and his overflowing gall against the French led the author to conclude that "*secret service-money* had been liberally employed."[220]

Cobbett's foreign status was not the last of his worries, whether he insisted on it or others used it against him as a bludgeon. In relation to the Rush trial, the press and the courts proved to all purposes opposed forces before the public. So long as the feud remained alive in the press, Rush was the silent target of unrelenting assault, with the press figured centrally and the discourse open to a universe of participants and observers. To his advantage, Cobbett relied upon using the press to spread news, publicize conflicts, and coalition with allies. Rush's strong suit, by contrast, lay in using the court to control the conflict, preventing news of an assault on his reputation from being widely spread, and playing within a strict set of insider rules. For Cobbett, a foreign figure, to have been acquitted, the social norms of feuds, a free press, and the open marketplace of ideas that privileged freedom of speech would have had to prevail. Rather than be silenced, the voice of the press infiltrated the court through continuing press attacks by the defendant in which Cobbett could play out his own version of lawfulness and order, providing himself in the press the effective voice he felt he was denied in court, a site where the press was shackled and where the prosecution was itself able to speak slander with impunity. Cobbett had to face as well the culture of the court, an ineffable set of customs and conventions, of morality and politics, which served as a reconstituted legal text in the jury verdict. Here a cultural vision of the law trumped not only legal fairness, justice, order, and legitimacy, but allegiance to legal doctrine, standards, and tests as well. It raised the prospect that law was not rule-based but malleable, not determinative but negotiable. Judicial institutions might structure the law and professionals might perform the law, but ultimately they would both play supporting roles in constructing the law.

NOTES

1. The altercation trial was a loose format in which judge and jury questioned and called witnesses and commented on the trial and the prosecution and defense cases were not clearly separated; Anand (2005, 427). The question in an altercation trial was largely one of "what really happened, and did the accused really do it," whereas the adversarial trial focused on "whether defence counsel had succeeded in raising sufficient doubt about the strength of the prosecution case" (428). The adversarial trial did not take hold until late in the eighteenth century. The formless nature of the altercation trial is reflected in *Rush v. Cobbett* by the mixed order of prosecution and defense counsel, as well as by the free form of address to the jury throughout the trial. Participating in an adversarial trial, the defense in *Rush v.* Cobbett failed to capitalize on undermining the prosecution's case, distracting the prosecution, or posing an alternative theory of the crime. See Langbein (2003,10–66).

2. Langbein (2003, 259).

3. See Langbein (2003, 1, 313, 332, 339); Landsman (1990, 487). In the seventeenth and early eighteenth centuries, judges served as advocates for the accused and victims were expected to gather evidence and witnesses and to pursue private prosecution of cases at their own time and expense. In the absence of a professional police force, it was left to justices of the peace or thief catchers in England to deliver the accused to court for a fee, and the accused were expected to consent to trial and to testify on their own behalf; Landsman (502–3); Anand (2005, 407–32).

4. *Rush-Light* IV, March 31, 1800; Cobbett (1801a, 11: 365); see Spater (1982, 269, note 51).

5. Cobbett (1937, xxi).

6. *Rush-Light* IV, March 31, 1800; Cobbett (1801a, 11: 365).

7. *Rush-Light* IV, March 31, 1800 Cobbett (1801a, 11: 365); the sessions referred to were September 1798, December 1798, March 1799, September 1799.

8. *Rush-Light* IV, March 31, 1800; Cobbett (1801a, 11: 365–66).

9. See Konkle (1981, 85–94). Hopkinson acted for the defense in the famous Fries Rebellion, in which Rawle, as District Attorney, and Ingersol acted for the prosecution.

10. Serving as Rush's counsel both before and after the trial, Brockholst Livingston wrote several revealing letters to Rush that suggest the verdict reached in Philadelphia might have been unlikely had the trial occurred either in federal court (as Cobbett would have preferred) or in New York (to which Cobbett removed shortly before the trial began). See Rush Manuscript, Historical Society of Pennsylvania, vol. 29, letters 85 (June 4, 1800) and 87 (May 30, 1801).

11. Carpenter (1800, 8).
12. Carpenter (1800, 8).
13. Carpenter (1800, 8).
14. Carpenter (1800, 9).
15. Carpenter (1800, 2). Shippen went on to advise the jury "To suppress so great an evil" and spoke of "stopping the growing progress of this daring crime."
16. *Rush-Light* I, February 15, 1800; Cobbett (1801a, 11: 239).
17. *Rush-Light* I, February 15, 1800, Cobbett (1801a, 11: 239–40).
18. William Shakespeare, *Julius Caesar*, 3.2, line 119.
19. Carpenter (1800, 49).
20. Carpenter (1800, 38).
21. Cobbett's own counsel Tilghman represented Cobbett in a way that seemed to acknowledge that, as an Englishman during the events surrounding the controversy over Jay's Treaty in 1796, Cobbett was a suspicious figure whose very presence in Philadelphia could be construed as a danger to democracy.
22. Carpenter (1800, 10).
23. Carpenter (1800, 10). Hopkinson's appeal to the jury is reminiscent of the argument he used as prosecutor in the alien and sedition trial of republican journalist William Duane in the same year. In the Duane case he took on aliens with a directness absent in *Rush v. Cobbett* as he advised nonnatives to go back where they came from: "aliens have no right whatever to petition, or to interfere in any respect with the government of this country—as the right of voting in elections is confined to citizens, the right of petitioning is also—if aliens do not like the laws of this country, God knows there are ways and wishes enough for them to go back again"; Smith (1953b, 127).
24. Carpenter (1800, 40–41).
25. Carpenter (1800, 42).
26. Carpenter (1800, 65).
27. Carpenter (1800, 67).
28. Carpenter (1800, 64).
29. Carpenter (1800, 10).
30. Mathew Carey in a 35-page pamphlet *The Porcupiniad* (1799b) also isolated Cobbett as a threat to a nation that had only newly liberated itself from the foreign tyranny of Cobbett's homeland:

> From Britain's isle our hero came,
> In quest of fortune, pow'r, and fame;
> Was hither by the premier sent,
> To dictate to our government—
> Our state affairs to regulate,
> And Britain's cause to advocate:
> Columbia's sons to fill with ire—
> Our public councils to inspire
> Old mother country's wrongs to feel;
> In her defence to sharp the steel,
> And make to heav'n the last appeal:
> Our forces muster against France,

And in the cause of kings advance:
To fight the battles of the Lord,
To propagate his holy word,
And spread the gospel with the sword. . . .

Nor even Satan's horrid self,
Did e'er breathe more infernal rage,
Than he has shown, through ev'ry page
Of his vile writings. A fierce flood
Will pour abroad, of human blood,
In civil war, if this curst knave
Our morals longer can deprave. (10–13)

Cobbett had already at this time been charged by Benjamin Rush and was awaiting prosecution for libel (the trial was held in December 1799, nine months after the poem was published but well after the initial charges were filed in October 1797), so that Carey's publication appeared designed to influence the trial by arousing the public against a fearmongering agent of the English king.

31. Sharp (1993, 178).
32. Carpenter (1800, 16).
33. Carpenter (1800, 14).
34. Carpenter (1800, 16).
35. Carpenter (1800, 15).
36. Libel was the legally controlling term, although throughout the trial it alternated with the term "slander," the two being used interchangeably. They were not, in fact, interchangeable. Slander described spoken defamation and libel described written defamation.
37. Carpenter (1800, 15).
38. *Rush-Light* III, 15 March 1800; Cobbett (1801a, 11: 308).
39. Carpenter (1800, 38).
40. Carpenter (1800, 32).
41. Carpenter (1800, 29).
42. Carpenter (1800, 49).
43. Carpenter (1800, 52).
44. Carpenter (1800, 41).
45. Carpenter (1800, 42).
46. Blackstone (1774, 3: 125); Carpenter (1800, 59).
47. Carpenter (1800, 47).
48. Carpenter (1800, 39).
49. Carpenter (1800, 44).
50. Carpenter (1800, 42–43).
51. Carpenter (1800, 45).
52. Carpenter (1800, 8).
53. Carpenter (1800, 9).
54. Carpenter (1800, 8).
55. Carpenter (1800, 9).
56. Carpenter (1800, 63).

57. Carpenter (1800, 19).
58. Carpenter (1800, 20).
59. Carpenter (1800, 20).
60. Carpenter (1800, 16).
61. Carpenter (1800, 17).
62. Carpenter (1800, 66).
63. Section 3, article 9.
64. Carpenter (1800, 25).
65. *Rush-Light* III, March 15, 1800; Cobbett (1801a, 11: 308).
66. Carpenter (1800, 28).
67. Carpenter (1800, 31).
68. Carpenter (1800, 28).
69. Carpenter (1800, 13).
70. Carpenter (1800, 13).
71. Carpenter (1800, 30).
72. Carpenter (1800, 30).
73. Carpenter (1800, 31).
74. *Rush v. Cobbett* takes place not only in the midst of but coextensive with a long history of physician feuds in which Rush was involved, not least of which was that over the treatment of yellow fever. See Myrsiades (2009, 77–115).
75. Cobbett had a reputation for feuding as well; Carey (1942); Carey (1799a); Carey (1799b).
76. *Federal Gazette*, October 7, 1793. The letter was to Dr. John Richardson Bayard Rodgers and was written four days earlier on October 3, 1793; see Rush (1951, 2: 694–99). Although he fairly represents the content of the letter, Tilghman misquotes the original, which reads: "It would not have been more absurd to have asserted that we have two suns and two moons shining upon our globe" (697). L. H. Butterfield, editor of Rush's letters, refers to this letter as "the best available epitome of his [Rush's] theory and practice in the epidemic" (2: 699, note 1). The letter, according to Rush's October 3, 1793 letter to his wife Julia (2: 701), was written to Rodgers and published by Rush himself in the *Federal Gazette* to address the "large and frequent demands from county practitioners for information."
77. Carpenter (1800, 55). Although the letter also contained Rush's acknowledgement that he had bled patients with heart rates as low as fifty of as much as eighty ounces of blood a day, combined with daily mercury purges, Tilghman failed to call this extreme treatment to the jury's attention or to indict Rush for medical malfeasance.
78. Carpenter (1800, 26). Tilghman and Rawle might have hinted at Rush's extreme treatments but they essentially suppressed this storyline, reluctant to call the issue of potential malpractice to the jury's attention, possibly for fear of either losing on this line of argument, alienating the jury, or clouding the focus on other potentially less objectional lines they chose instead to feature.
79. Carpenter (1800, 26).
80. Carpenter (1800, 27).
81. Carpenter (1800, 50).
82. Carpenter (1800, 51).

83. Carpenter (1800, 50).
84. Carpenter (1800, 52).
85. Carpenter (1800, 53).
86. Carpenter (1800, 28).
87. Hopkinson proceeded to oppose Rush and Cobbett, the one as the peaceful friend of humanity and the other as an enemy of humanity, a distinguished representative of the city against a malignant journalist, the social against the antisocial. On one side of the opposed parties stood a man identified as the very negation of the other; one, by implication, unlike the other in his "fondness for controversy"; one outside the "barbarous" and one within. Rawle objected to such opposed characterizations. What appealed to Rawle as justifiable in Cobbett resonated with the prosecution as unprincipled and malicious. What he considered mere "scurrility," "momentary sensations" and "the impulse of passion—beyond the bounds of strict decency and propriety" became for the prosecution treachery and vengeance.
88. Carpenter (1800, 41).
89. Carpenter (1800, 60).
90. Carpenter (1800, 62).
91. Carpenter (1800, 48).
92. Cobbett fed the prosecution's attacks on him as an alien by his insistence on filing to have the case removed from a state to a federal court, where he could capitalize on his rights as an alien under federal law; May 30, 1801 from Brockholst Livingston, Rush Manuscript, Historical Society of Pennsylvania, vol. 29, letter 87; Rush (1951, 2: 816–17).
93. Carpenter (1800, 56).
94. Carpenter (1800, 24).
95. Carpenter (1800, 9).
96. Carpenter (1800, 56).
97. Carpenter (1800, 11).
98. Carpenter (1800, 12).
99. Carpenter (1800, 13). Hopkinson made certain to refer to "assassination" four times, twice more than opposing counsel Tilghman caught him at (9, 13, 17, 19).
100. Carpenter (1800, 8).
101. Carpenter (1800, 11).
102. Carpenter (1800, 68).
103. Carpenter (1800, 14).
104. Carpenter (1800, 14).
105. Carpenter (1800, 15).
106. Carpenter (1800, 10).
107. Carpenter (1800, 23–24).
108. Carpenter (1800, 48).
109. Carpenter (1800, 39).
110. Carpenter (1800, 43).
111. Carpenter (1800, 63).
112. Carpenter (1800, 10).
113. Carpenter (1800, 48).

114. Carpenter (1800, 54).
115. Carpenter (1800, 57–58, 64–67).
116. Carpenter (1800, 8).
117. Carpenter (1800, 16).
118. Bercovitch (1978, 163).
119. Bercovitch (1978, 164).
120. Bercovitch (1978, 67).
121. Carpenter (1800, 9).
122. Carpenter (1800, 14).
123. Carpenter (1800, 11).
124. Carpenter (1800, 12).
125. Carpenter (1800, 13).
126. Carpenter (1800, 17). Millennial thinking like that in the yellow fever sermons reserved as its end game the achievement of heavenly perfection on earth and what Ruth Bloch refers to as the culmination of history in "the glorious triumph of God's people across the world"; Bloch (1985, xi). Such utopianism infected the revolutionary moment, for all its rationality and pragmatism. Indeed, the development of revolutionary consciousness was both informed by and constituted another step toward the millennium (xii–xiii). Delivering the new nation implied the fulfillment of the millennium, the ultimate meaning of the revolution, so that those who best served the revolution were also those who were in some sense most millennialist (xiv–xv) and those who most fully embraced the rise of a capitalist economy. In *Rush v. Cobbett* the themes of progress and of shining visions interfaced as well to express the mutuality of political and religious themes, that is, to blur boundaries between Enlightenment secular utopianism, republicanism, and the millennium without associating them too intimately (xvi, 130).
127. Carpenter (1800, 64).
128. Bloch (1985, 131).
129. Bloch (1985, 192).
130. Bloch (1985, 231); Howard-Pitney (1990, 8).
131. Carpenter (1800, 11).
132. Carpenter (1800, 14).
133. Bercovitch (1978, 71–72).
134. The sermons on which this study rely include those delivered on yellow fever epidemics from 1793 to 1799 by the following figures: Thaddeus Brown, Joshua Cresson, Ashbel Green, J. Henry Helmuth, William Linn, William Marshall, John Mitchell Mason, William Smith, Samuel Spring, Samuel Stearns, Elhanan Winchester, and Henry Wright, among other materials. See Holifield (2003); Watson (1991); Bloch (1985). Certainly as we speak of community identity, sermons were to have a disproportionate effect on values, practices, and constructions that defined the way people were to live their lives. Compared to theology, doctrines spread through sermons tended not only to reach more people but to create a more active rather than contemplative sense of religion. Through sermons, congregants gained a smattering of religious knowledge and embraced ownership of it, resisting the prospect that an elite was in possession of biblical interpretation, moral precepts, or religious experi-

ence. Considering how sermons functioned and the value they were given, it should come as no surprise that they were infused with an ethics, practicality, and popular appeal that set audiences free to seek natural rather than received religious explanations for events. People felt that common sense, personal revelations, and nature provided the human mind with the evidence it needed for the workings of God as well as proof of His existence. They could read the Bible and popular religious tracts for themselves and looked to the natural order to confirm the usefulness of natural science. They required that religion have a practicality that would lead to ethical decisions and a good life and that would serve as a guide to a loving God. Morality's practical flavor was well served by sermons, given their moral insights and their backing in biblical tales. What could be reasonably preached and what could be reasonably arrived at in people's own minds tended to be endorsed as a form of natural religion much like the natural law that formed the underlying authority of common law.

135. Ryken (1998, 474–75). Biblical law is represented in the sermons in such a way that people could order their lives around it, rather than as an abstract set of ethical prescriptions. Law was not a burden but a gift, and one obeyed because one loved God, a form of gratitude for His goodness. There is thus a relational basis to biblical law in the form of a covenant between parties, a covenant that bears benefits to its adherents and costs to those who break it. If, by this argument, law is loved and represents an opportunity, then squandering that opportunity is a betrayal of the loved one. At some point, and clearly by the time of the yellow fever epidemic, the law became all about negative consequences and about exile because the covenant had been broken. But hope remained and the restorative language of the sermons put the emphasis on a future of return to the law. The law thus had two aspects, indeed one could argue it was rendered ambivalent, depending on its Old or its New Testament face, as it was both about being blessed and about being punished. As a staff, it offered hope; as a rod, it offered bondage (492).

136. Ryken (1998, 681–83).

137. Winchester (1795, 21).

138. Winchester (1795, 4).

139. Spring (1798,17, 18).

140. Linn (1795, 29).

141. Mason (1793, 9, 10, 12). The rod of God is an image of terror used to express God's authority. Ryken (1998, 734).

142. Smith (1880, 387).

143. Winchester (1795, 21). The imagery of an apocalypse was meant to carry listeners out of the everyday into another world where God's order would prevail, a form of adventure tale that suggested events would get worse before they got better and that, like science fiction, indicated that catastrophe must clear the way for a better day; Ryken (1998, 35). In this sense the yellow fever epidemic was a revelation and a promise if one would only persevere. Whereas the yellow fever epidemic seemed largely a question of a local prophecy of doom and a call to repent, there were elements of an apocalyptic end of the world scenario, as described in the sermons, certainly in the hopelessness and the catastrophic judgment that characterized the epidemic, as well as in the appeal to God's sovereignty (36). What appeared less

frequently in the sermons, however, was a vision of the future at the end of history and life, other than the picture they gave of a heavenly home waiting for those taken by the fever. The monstrous strangeness, vivid color, numerology, and visions associated with apocalypse were largely missing, at least in their extreme forms (35–38).

144. Cresson (1803, 19).

145. Wright (1794, 23).

146. Helmuth (1794, 10).

147. 2 Samuel xxxiv; Brown (1798, 9–10).

148. Green ([1799], 7–8). Rush, who remained in the city to his sorrow and his credit excused Green's absence from the city: "I have done him ample justice whenever I have heard his conduct blamed for leaving the city, and have openly declared that I advised him not to come to town at the time he proposed it"; October 30, 1793, letter to Julia Rush; Rush (1951, 2: 733). At the same time, other clerics were not to receive so wholehearted an endorsement from Rush: "Dr. Ewing and Dr. Magaw receive no quarter from the public. The latter I have lately heard was indisposed in the country. I hope this is true. He is a good man and I think would not have left his flock, had his health permitted him to remain with them."

149. Brown (1798, 20–21).

150. Stearns (1794, 9–11).

151. Brown (1798, 23–24). As a German Lutheran, Helmuth—like the Catholic Bishop Blackwell, who also stayed behind to serve in the city—had one of the poorest congregations. His congregation was made up of people who had not the means to flee the city and who, as a result, suffered disproportionately from epidemic fever. The Lutheran graveyard was full to overflowing with the bodies of those who died of fever, leading those who fled to charge that Lutherans must have been most sinful since so many were struck down by the fever. They neglected to account for the Lutherans having kept their church open and having opened their cemetery to all in the city who required burial services and whose own clergy had fled. See Helmuth's defense of his church's practices in keeping open for worship and in the great numbers of burials in the Lutheran churchyard (1794, 43–51).

152. Citizen (1799).

153. See *Minutes* (1848); Powell (1965, 173–94).

154. Citizen (1799, 19–20).

155. Langbein (2003) calculates a rate of 100 to 1. As Langbein says, "Find the facts and the law is usually easy" (1).

156. *Rush-Light* III, March 15, 1800; Cobbett (1801a, 11: 308).

157. Reed (1831, 3: 521); see Blackstone (1774, 3: 124).

158. *Rush-Light* III, March 15, 1800; Cobbett (1801a, 11: 320).

159. *Rush-Light* III, March 15, 1800; Cobbett (1801a, 11: 322).

160. *Rush-Light* III, March 15, 1800; Cobbett (1801a, 11: 323).

161. *Rush-Light* III, March 15, 1800; Cobbett (1801a, 11: 324).

162. *Rush-Light* III, March 15, 1800; Cobbett (1801a, 11: 325).

163. Blackstone (Dublin, (1794, 3: 369).

164. Reed (1831, 3: 364).

165. Carpenter (1800, 21).

166. Carpenter (1800, 21).
167. Carpenter (1800, 22).
168. Carpenter (1800, 4).
169. *Rush-Light* III, March 15, 1800; Cobbett (1801a, 11: 326).
170. *Rush-Light* III, March 15, 1800; Cobbett (1801a, 11: 327).
171. *Rush-Light* III, March 15, 1800; Cobbett (1801a, 11: 329).
172. *Rush-Light* III, March 15, 1800; Cobbett (1801a, 11: 331).
173. Reed (1831, 3: 368–69).
174. Reed(1831, 3: 368–69).
175. *Rush-Light* III, March 15, 1800; Cobbett (1801a, 11: 327, 329).
176. *Rush-Light* III, March 15, 1800; Cobbett (1801a, 11: 327).
177. *Rush-Light* III, March 15, 1800; Cobbett (1801a, 11: 337).
178. *Rush-Light* III, March 15, 1800; Cobbett (1801a, 11: 340 note).
179. Blackstone (1794, 3: 373).
180. Reed (1831, 3: 367).
181. *Rush-Light* III, 15 March 1800; Cobbett (1801a, 11: 342).
182. *Rush-Light* III, 15 March 1800; Cobbett (1801a, 11: 309).
183. *Rush-Light* III, March 15, 1800; Cobbett (1801a, 11: 342).
184. *Porcupine's Gazette*, September 19, 1797.
185. Sent with a date of September 12, printed in *Porcupine's Gazette*, September 19, 1797.
186. *Porcupine's Gazette*, September 25, 1797.
187. *Porcupine's Gazette*, September 26, 1797.
188. Carpenter (1800, 6–7); from *Philadelphia Gazette*.
189. *Porcupine's Gazette*, September 29, 1797.
190. Carpenter (1800, 3).
191. Carpenter (1800, 7).
192. *Rush-Light* III, March 15, 1800; Cobbett (1801a, 11: 142).
193. The term "glister-pipes" (also rendered as "clysters" or "clystars") refers to instruments that looked like supersized hypodermic needles and were used to purge patients rectally to empty the bowels.
194. Carpenter (1800, 6–7).
195. Carpenter (1800, 3).
196. Carpenter (1800, 4).
197. *Porcupine's Gazette*, September 18, 1797, September 26, 1797, and September 27, 1797.
198. *Porcupine's Gazette*, September 26, 1797.
199. *Rush-Light* III, March 15, 1800; Cobbett (1801a, 11: 307–25).
200. *Rush-Light* III, March 15, 1800; Cobbett (1801a, 11: 319).
201. *Rush-Light* III, March 15, 1800; Cobbett (1801a, 11: 310).
202. *Rush-Light* III, March 15, 1800; Cobbett (1801a, 11: 312).
203. *Rush-Light* III, March 15, 1800; Cobbett (1801a, 11: 313).
204. *Rush-Light* III, March 15, 1800; Cobbett (1801a, 11: 310, 313).
205. *Rush-Light* III, March 15, 1800; Cobbett (1801a, 11: 310).
206. *Rush-Light* III, March 15, 1800; Cobbett (1801a, 11: 310).

207. *Rush-Light* III, March 15, 1800; Cobbett (1801a, 11: 313-19).

208. *Rush-Light* III, March 15, 1800; Cobbett (1801a, 11: 318).

209. *Rush-Light* III, March 15, 1800; Cobbett (1801a, 11: 314).

210. Cobbett compares quotes from Le Sage's *Adventures of Gil Blas* (1749) to Rush's own writings to make his case; *Rush-Light* III, March 15, 1800; Cobbett (1801a, 11: 315–17.)

211. *Rush-Light* III, March 15, 1800; Cobbett (1801a, 11: 343).

212. See on Coxe, *Porcupine's Gazette*, October 28, 1797; Cobbett (1801a, 7: 273–76). On Rush prosecuting selectively, see Cobbett's note on Currie, *Rush-Light* III, February 28, 1800; Cobbett (1801a, 11: 271–72).

213. *Rush-Light* III, March 15, 1800; Cobbett (1801a, 11: 341).

214. Cobbett (1798a, 7–8, 51, 77, 92, 95).

215. Cobbett (1798a, v).

216. The Pennsylvania Supreme Court denied Cobbett a federal trial in *Rush v. Cobbett*, which he claimed as his right as an alien, just as Yrujo had withdrawn his suit against Cobbett from the federal court, both under the theory that Cobbett would find a less friendly reception in the Pennsylvania State Supreme Court. Neither was Cobbett to enjoy in either case the privilege of a jury *de medietatae linguae*, whereby a jury for one who is alien born "shall be one half denizens, and the other aliens . . . for the more impartial trial"; Reed (1831, 332).

217. Cobbett (1798a, iv).

218. Cobbett (1797, v).

219. Cobbett (1797, v).

220. Cobbett (1797, vi). Cobbett accused republican journalist Mathew Carey of lending credibility to the charge by asserting "that I must be paid by Britain, because my gazette and censor were so cheap." See *Porcupine's Gazette*, May 5, 1797, as referred to by Carey (1799a, 14).

6

The Trial Concluded

The actual verdict on Cobbett came down, in the end, to the jury. Tilghman for the defense, followed by Ingersol for the prosecution, would present final arguments to the jury capping the narratives each side had presented. A defense foray earlier in the trial had advised the jury that it must "possess no prejudices no opinions—no prepossessions" and that it must hold the two men "on equal grounds." In vain, Rawle had pleaded that "it not be forgotten that William Cobbett ought to have every merit he deserves, and every privilege to which he is entitled—let him have every censure he deserves, and yet, I repeat, both stand upon equal ground before you. Cobbett puts himself upon the issue, and you are to decide according to the evidence, and thus only."[1] Tilghman's closing argument thus began by taking up the theme that equal standing before the law applied to aliens as well as to citizens:

> you should come with minds in the language of the law "like blank paper," and receive such impressions only as law and evidence must make. William Cobbett, my client, though an alien, is entitled to all the advantages which law and justice can bestow; and if he can satisfy you that damages ought not to be recovered from an *American* standing in his place, no damages are to be given against him.[2]

However well meant, Tilghman's closing address to the jury was a pedantic reading of the litany of issues before the court, each issue addressed in its turn. Cobbett had been treated with contempt as litigious, noxious, and cloven-footed, Tilghman offered, even as he acknowledged that he himself "should have deemed it very improper to have used such coarse expressions as Cobbett had used."[3] Still, Cobbett's work was never written out of malice nor with criminal intent. Rather, if Cobbett had judged Rush as too republican—whether one might "dislike [Rush's sentiments] as much as Cobbett [or] perhaps not think it *too republican*"—[4] Cobbett had a right to attack on the grounds of Rush's politics, just as he had a right to write against Rush's medical system, if not his person. On the issue of Cobbett's ridicule, it was "surely the test of truth"[5] and not murder by malice. Nor was Cobbett alone in his harshness, for Rush had himself "not only been intemperately, but uncommonly severe upon every one who had the misfortune to differ with him in practice," even to speak "against the Legislature itself."[6] In this regard, if Cobbett was to be condemned, Rush ought not to be given great damages, for he, too, had expressed himself publicly in attacks against doctors. Indeed, those doctors with whom Rush had quarreled presented a greater threat to Rush than Cobbett had, so that no one could say what presumed harm occurred to his practice or from whom. How, indeed, might one prove a negative, that is, a lack of business? In sum, Tilghman's laundry list concluded, all the charges reduced to one wrong: that Cobbett was, in fairness, liable for contempt. He did publish "from the moment the suit commenced,"[7] when he ought not to, for "the law says the parties ought both to be silent, because everything ought to come before a Jury, who should not have their passions raised, or be prepossessed in favor of either party." Even then, Tilghman appealed, the jury ought not to ruin the man.

Ingersol's admonition to the jury countered that the power of the law must punish in a way that was determinative and that would act as a deterrent. He warned the jury not to engage in wishful thinking or to be naïve in holding too high an opinion of any man:

> Gentlemen, you must take human nature as you find it, and we should not better it had we the power of formation: of [*sic*] the law does not give satisfaction for injuries, it is a sentiment written on the heart of man that *he will obtain it*, and no law will then stop his resentment. Of what avail, it will be argued, was it for me to restrain the impetuosity of my temper and a [*sic*] await the course pointed out by the laws of my country: In vain do I respect them unless damages are given sufficient to stop the progress of a gross offence.—You will have no more complaints of this sort, but they will be obtained in another, and most fatal way, if the law is not sufficiently strong to curb it.[8]

The prosecution's remedy lay in the jury acting the role of a *deus ex machina*, rescuing the injured and returning the court to a natural law and universal understanding that would defeat wickedness, outrage, and malignancy. Sounding a cry in the same tone used by the divines in their yellow fever sermons, Ingersol called on God, nature, and the heavens for justice at the highest tribunal. His direct appeal to the jury to reap the whirlwind amounted to a battle cry authored by virtue itself: "Virtue, bleeding at every pore, calls for justice on her despoiler, and the anxious heart of every honest man pants with impatience to meet in you, THE DEFENDERS OF VIRTUE, AND THE SCOURGERS OF VICE."[9] Under this mandate, the jury was entrusted with retribution against those who injured and vindication of those injured; on their decision hung the character of the country and the respectability of the government in honoring and protecting its citizens and their families. Hopkinson's voice had already called upon the jury to exceed legal doctrine and accept the burden of religious and secular law, of nature and society in justifying Rush's risk in accessing the courts. At the most domestic level, Hopkinson had earlier summoned the jury to act for Rush and his sons, to preserve the laws of nature that provide for the father's legacy to his sons of reputation and economic well-being. He had already urged comprehensiveness in finishing the work Rush had set out to do as citizen, physician, moral guardian, and private prosecutor, work that would cull the ranks of the wicked, and raise up the afflicted. On the national level, the prosecution asked the jury in sum to render a verdict that would complete the nation building only begun by the war against England, to act *parens patriae* on behalf of republicanism to save the nation. The stakes the prosecution case presented could not have been higher.

Justice Shippen delivered his charge to the jury on the second day of the trial, December 14, representing the three sitting justices who heard the case: himself, justices Jasper Yeates and Thomas Smith.[10] Shippen was careful to distinguish the American jury from the English jury, noting early in his charge that "in this state, by the special directions of our constitution, the jury possess the power of judging both of the law and fact under the direction of the court."[11] His charge, however, heavily weighted the court's direction, superseding the jury on the facts, directing them on the law, and narrowing their role to determining damages. His terms of choice stressed the strong sense of public conflict and ridicule that characterized the alien and sedition debate. Cobbett was thereby framed as a dangerous alien whose offence, Shippen noted, could as easily have been tried in the Pennsylvania Supreme Court by indictment as a criminal offence as by civil action. His representation of Cobbett's publications as "certainly libelous"[12] and as admittedly false—so that they could not be justified by a truth defense—left little to the jury's imagination in its disposition of the facts. On the question of malicious intent, Shippen took the position that since malice depended upon personal intent, it rested with the defendant to prove his innocence, a burden Cobbett had not, in his view, successfully borne.

Shippen went on to embrace the prosecution's concerns about what he considered the most serious—and presumably the most republican—issues: the public peace, health, and "lives of our fellow citizens."[13] Whereas the case, on its face, might have been presented as a dispute over free speech or liberty of the press, as Shippen put the question it was essentially one of a threat to private reputation and a breach of the peace. The case thereby challenged a citizen's access to the courts and risked recourse to "duels, Murders, and perhaps to Assassinations."[14] By means of such a frame, Shippen instructed the jury that its "principal subject of consideration" should be the issue of damages. It was free to inflict punishment capable of curing a social disease that "for some time past too much abounded in our city." It was high time "To suppress so great an evil," a task for which, he instructed them, they possessed a power whose exercise would have to be "outrageously disproportionate" and shocking to the conscience before any court would intervene.[15]

With such a set of instructions, the jury took only two hours to convict Cobbett and assign an unprecedented fine of $5,000. Spectators in the gallery and in the environs of the court house broke out into loud cheers, an attitude shared by the press, as Cobbett made sure to note.[16] Embittered by the jury verdict against him, Cobbett had his lawyer, Edward Tilghman, file immediately for a new trial on the grounds of excessive damages. The Pennsylvania Supreme Court unanimously rejected his application. Moreover, Cobbett still faced a possible $2000 fine for violating a "previous restraint," a recognizance in the Yrujo case.[17]

Tilghman advised his client to flee from the writ which demanded payment of a fine that Cobbett had described as greater than all the fines assessed in all such cases put together. Cobbett's excited response in a letter to Tilghman on December 18 represented that "North tells me that you say they will come here and seize my body. Blessed be God, the villains cannot seize my soul. Let them come. Imprisonment in such a cause has no horrors for me. If I should be put to death, I should only share the fate of Roberts and Carlisle."[18] Like Rush's decision to take his case to trial, Cobbett presented himself as far too wedded to his honor as an Englishman and a gentleman to allow his honor to suffer the smallest slight. Told that he could avoid the recognizance fine by leaving the country before a judgment was rendered, he again took a principled stand, this time in a letter to his friend Edward Thornton: "I wish to meet and to repel the upmost of their malice; I cannot bear the idea of running away."[19] Cobbett felt he had no recourse but to put off paying the fine and to mount his self defense in *Rush-Light*. Rush was in the position of having to apply for a sheriff's sale of Cobbett's movable property, file for a trial on the judgment, and explore the possibility of a new suit to keep Cobbett from writing about the trial. For all his protestations, Cobbett did in fact take leave of New York for England when he heard that the case for the Yrujo recognizance, "Old McKean versus Peter Porcupine," as he put it, would be "brought on" in June 1800.[20] Cobbett sailed for England in June. The doctor and the journalist continued their standoff over the Rush fine until the amount agreed upon was finally remitted in October of the next year by means of a negotiation and two guarantors, Benjamin Davies and Richard North.[21]

THE JUDGE AND THE JURY

The most malleable aspect of the *Rush v. Cobbett* trial was the jury and the role it played in determining the verdict. Here, Cobbett held a view that was distinctly different from that of the prosecution. Hopkinson had framed the jury's position in the trial as self-interested to the extent that they ought, like Rush and like Hopkinson himself, to anticipate an attack from Cobbett should they "dare to do him justice."[22] Modeling for them the optimal response to such a threat, Hopkinson declared himself unaffected by either Cobbett's "recommendation or his censure," having experienced both and having "regarded neither." Cobbett's arrogance and his resentment, Hopkinson represented portended formidable and destructive power that Hopkinson nevertheless discounted as harmless and contemptible. Cobbett, he concluded, was destined to be corrected by the people, whose representatives were to be found on the jury; their duty and their oath would offset Cobbett's black list.

Far from regarding them as worth threatening, Cobbett considered jury members passive puppets in the hands of the judge.[23] The jurors in the Rush case, and by extension American jurors, were for Cobbett no more than sycophantic, easily flattered subjects who deluded themselves into thinking they were more free than their former fellow subjects, the British.[24] Their high opinion of themselves left them open to the influence of the judge whose design, he supposed, was to puff up their pride "to embolden them to gratify you and your private wishes, at the expense of justice." As for the judge, he had capitalized on his prerogative to inform the jury by commenting on the evidence. In Cobbett's view, Shippen forgot his oath to sum up the evidence fairly in his zeal to assist the plaintiff and with an eye to his own hopes of higher office.[25] Not only had defense counsel failed to justify the truth where they might have done so,[26] relying upon whether or not Cobbett's words were malicious and thereby slanderous, but Shippen compounded the error by misrepresenting defense counsel's position on his publications. Shippen had charged the jury, "In what manner do the defendant's counsel repel these proofs? Not by justifying the truth of the matters charged against Dr. Rush, which on the contrary they have repeatedly acknowledged to be false, but by analyzing the several allegations in the newspapers, and from thence drawing a conclusion that no intentional personal malice appears."[27]

Misconstruction of his publications and perversion of the evidence, Cobbett held, gave "cheering encouragement" to the jury, such that the judge telegraphed his intention to certify the jury's verdict "provided they laid on damages enough."[28] As for the judge's instructions on damages—that to order a new trial excessive damages must "be so outrageously disproportionate to the offence as . . . to SHOCK every person who hears of it"—Cobbett mused that such a maxim could only have come from a law book of the French revolutionary Robespierre or, more pointedly, of Pennsylvania.[29] Certainly, Shippen's use of the law would have been "severely reproved" should it have occurred in a British court.[30] Indeed, a British judge would have been stoned to death for applying such a standard—or at least shunned as a hangman's touch would be shunned—whereas a Philadelphia jury will sit before such a judge "submissively as a penitent does to his father confessor."[31]

The judge, Cobbett argued, had dictated to a jury what "no judge ever dared attempt,"[32] so that, having promised "no check upon their rapacity," he provided the pretext for jury conduct based upon "as efficacious an instrument of oppression as ever was devised."[33] Here, the damages called for were intended to "bring down upon the head of the defendant the consequences [both compensatory and exemplary damages] of both a civil and a criminal prosecution!"[34] In this, Cobbett surmised, the judge figuratively both winked and nodded to signal how far the jury might go "without endangering the success of the scheme." Thus, in effect, he told them to ruin the defendant, but to "take care to do it in such a way as will not defeat our intention . . . not to let your malice so far overshoot the mark, as to leave us no excuse for confirming your verdict." Playing the game, the jury followed Shippen's directions "with great exactness."[35]

Cobbett had constructed the judge-jury relationship with a sharp eye to its conformity with American legal practice of the time, whereby judges overinterpreted the law for undereducated and inexperienced common man juries. But Cobbett had gone even further to delineate the larger implications of Shippen's collusion with his fellow countrymen. In allowing this "ruinous verdict," they would not only inoculate republicans like Rush against Cobbett's barbs but they would compensate "also for the negligence of Courts and Juries"[36] that failed to suppress offenses that, as Shippen allowed, had "too much abounded in our city."[37] Cobbett would serve as the part that stood for the whole of all such criminals. Moreover, as a British subject, as an alien, as a foreign correspondent who defended his nation and king when he "exposed the little despots of America,"[38] Cobbett felt he was a target who accounted for three culprits with one blow: the judge's verdict would render mute the voice of the premier antirepublican editor of the period; it would send a message of reform to the litigious American people and their lax courts and juries; and it would put England on warning that the interference of its political agents in American affairs was unwelcome.

Justice Shippen's charge to the jury was not his sole weapon in influencing the jury verdict. His courtroom management of the trial would complement the charge to seal Cobbett's fate.[39] Cobbett's concerns about partiality and prejudice in the judge's crowd control[40] reinforced his critique of Chief Justice McKean's conduct in the Yrujo case to suggest a continuing hostility and arrogance on the part of the court to those brought before it.[41] In the Rush case, Cobbett complained particularly of the difficulty his counsel Rawle and Tilghman had in being heard over the cries of observers in the court. The public had been admitted to an open area in the courtroom where observers stood packed in rows that overflowed to the outside of the building. The jury sat in close proximity to the justices, with jury boxes to the right and left of the room facing the bench on which justices Yeates, Smith, and Shippen sat *en banc*. When defense counsel tried "to repel the abominable aspersions which were cast on [Cobbett's] character and conduct," the crowd hissed and cursed at them from the gallery and around the courthouse. Cobbett not only remarked upon "this most scandalous behavior" but was shocked to discover that it was not met with "any reproof from the Court," which he took to indicate that Shippen refused to control the court when members of the defense were involved.[42] To his lawyer and friend Tilghman, the only member of the defense team in whom he had any confidence, he wrote, "I hear that the rascally sovereign people hissed you while you were pleading on my behalf; you, undoubtedly, understood this as a very high compliment, and trust that the day will yet come when you will have no need to be afraid of such base miscreants."[43]

The Rush camp found itself in more compatible quarters. With the close of the judge's charge to the jury, people in the gallery and the area of the courthouse broke into applause, suggesting that Shippen had played to the crowd.[44] A third outbreak from the "herd," as Cobbett referred to them, occurred when the verdict was delivered and "the joy of the malignant wretches broke out into *loud and repeated acclamations*!"[45] Cobbett reported that "the shouting in the Court-house was the next day recorded by the news-printers, who exulted in this proof of the zeal and *justice* of their *fellow citizens.*"[46] Reactions from Rush's acolytes were no less enthusiastic. Mathew Carey penned a note to Rush on the same day as the verdict to pay his respects, offer his gratitude, and extend "his most sincere congratulations on the very flattering and honorable issue of the laudable attempt to bring a nefarious villain to justice . . . conferring an important benefit on the community."[47] Charles Wharton, writing on the same day, took an even more exhuberant tone in his note, buoyed by the fact that a "Jury of our country have just given you over the Parricidal Cobbett and his coadjutator." Wharton offered Rush his heartfelt joy "on this blessed occasion . . . in removing *Foulmouthed Ben* from bad works to ____ rewards. O! that he may have found Mercy, where he least expects it."[48] Shippen's conduct of the trial in tandem with his charge to the jury, the courtroom's reaction to the verdict, and press and partisan responses help explain not only the climate that informed Cobbett's conviction but the excessive fine that was assigned.

Whereas the partiality of an influential judge would have had a significant effect on a jury, the prosecution's command and control of the trial argument was more likely in this case to have been the tipping point for the jury's mediation of the facts and the law. On one hand, jurors might have seemed passive consumers of counsel's arguments; on the other, juries tended to be less successfully controlled by judges when it came to controversial cases, particularly political ones.[49] Judges had refused to accept verdicts, returned juries with additional instructions, or probed the rationale for their decisions,[50] but such practices had progressively fallen out of favor by the end of the eighteenth century. Indeed, as counsel's greater importance aggregated over the eighteenth century, juries accrued an even greater freedom to avoid judge-directed verdicts should they choose.[51] The gradual reduction of the role of judges gave the jury more options for the performance of its own role, including its ability to down-value or upgrade a crime, and thereby its relative consequence, in order to make an offense less or more serious if it chose.[52] Counsel's ability to address the jury directly led to an even more enhanced appreciation for the role of the "inscrutable" jury as the presumed final decider.[53] The jury was clearly open to the popular appeal of lawyers like Hopkinson, as was the courtroom audience, especially where an audience expressed itself without much control from the bench and exploited the opportunity to turn the court case into theater. Here, the public on the streets and the public in the jury box could speak across the court to each other to inform the verdict along the lines of a jury of neighbors.[54] On the issue of the truthfulness of a statement, for example, so long as it was a matter of interpretation its meaning would be left to the audience of jurors and their courtroom clique, standing in for the potential community of neighbors of which they felt themselves a part.

Negotiating, as it did, the influences of judge, counsel, and the public, and authorized to treat the case generally, and not merely as it related to the facts, this identification with a neighborhood legitimized the jury as members of a common community. The tack taken by the prosecution team was to appeal to just this community. If any one of them was likely to be libeled or to be called a libeler, if anything, true or false, could be called a libel, then no one, the jury might fairly conclude, was safe.[55] Only members of the community, and not a judge, would be sensible of the suffering experienced at the hands of the libeler. They alone could best determine the prospect of a breach of the peace should a libeler escape the judgment of a jury. Who, after all, was best situated to determine the likelihood of the public's response, if not a representative of the public?[56]

The Rush jury, one could argue, was convergent with the crowd that attended the trial. If the brevity of its two-hour deliberation was not all that uncommon for a contemporary jury, the damages it awarded would certainly have been considered excessive in any court of the period. Demonstrating it was creature of its culture, the jury's verdict aligned with the attitudes of spectators in the courtroom and the courtyard, whose politics and local preferences it embodied and expressed. Indeed, the jury played off of a feature of the legal system that had roots in the middle ages: local residents gathered in inquisition to serve as witnesses participating in the disposition of events to which they applied their own prejudices and partialities[57] based on a jury's right to nullify based on community values, customs, traditions, or usage, and the community's own set of norms.[58] As Hamilton in the Zenger case might have argued, Rush's Philadelphia house was on fire; Cobbett the English arsonist ignited the fire; an American jury would put out the flames.

The jury's verdict had much to do as well with the shifting political tide that would punish the federalists and bring in a republican administration in the 1800 elections. Since so many more republicans were, in fact, part of the jury pool, as Cobbett was to complain, and since a stacked jury would have been accommodated by a struck jury process, the likelihood of a republican jury was high. The public preference for free exercise of speech against the state was, at the same time, complicated by the prospect that a new administration might be a republican one. Whereas the public generally might be less attached to the idea of supporting the reputation of a public figure, the public figure in question in this instance was a republican. Moreover, if the public objected to the Alien and Sedition Acts as they were directed against a republican press, here was an opportunity for a republican jury to turn the same acts against a federalist.

The fact that one of the chief architects of the Sedition Act was defending Cobbett would, by this reasoning, have both hurt and helped him. Cobbett would be identified with the much despised Sedition Act, while those defending Cobbett would have had an advantage in interpreting the act or at least in deflecting attacks based upon it. The courts had never arrived at a definition of sedition that would satisfy, persuade, or coerce successful jury verdicts in any numbers,[59] a situation that might have helped Cobbett's case but which also gave juries a free hand to draw up verdicts they thought appropriate,[60] depending upon the public controversy raised by the press or by the public response within the community. In the Rush case, the jury was directed toward sedition by the prosecution and the judge as the most plausible view of the case in terms of its effect on the lives of the jurors themselves as citizens of the community. *Rush v. Cobbett* was, as a result, just the case to empower a jury itching to have its head and to please a crowd roiled by cries of sedition. With the court itself under attack as an elitist institution and republican rhetoric directed against it "as a sort of 'secular jeremiad',"[61] it was, as well, a case capable of redeeming the court, which would profit from being seen as a handmaiden of republican justice.[62]

Under the assumption that the jury in *Rush v. Cobbett* joined with the supreme court justices who presided to constitute a republican courtroom, political issues close to the heart of republicans would have informed the political disposition of the trial. Republicans could hardly have avoided the aftershocks of the XYZ Affair, recognizing that the embarrassment of apologizing for the French and renouncing the Reign of Terror became necessary to republican standing in public opinion. Turning their antipathy toward England as a way of deflecting attacks on pro-French republican sentiments would have provided something of an escape hatch for republican jurors. Equally, the ability to delay the trial until December 1799 aided republican argument in the case. Whereas charges had been filed in 1797 at the height of contentious debate over passage of the Alien and Sedition Acts, the trial itself did not occur until the end of 1799, well after the intense furor over the exposure in May 1798 of the XYZ Affair had blown over, William Cobbett was out of town, and the presidential elections were looming. Cobbett's decided advantage during the federalist period going into the trial was thus diminished. Federalists could be pictured as risking a breach of the peace or a war with France, accusations which the prosecution capitalized on to position federalists as poor citizens or as self-interested parties who took their pleasure at the expense of the public welfare. With themes of patriotism taking center stage, republican jurors could embrace a nativist, defiantly patriotic love of America and reject Europeans of any type. In this way, the jury could celebrate prosecution themes of American independence without being linked to a transatlantic Francophile revolutionary perspective. The jury was freed to arrive at a republican verdict if it so chose.

Colleen Sheehan contends that popular sovereignty, that is, the active participation of citizens in political affairs, was the very basis of republicanism, determining its very character.[63] If so, the jury verdict in the *Rush v. Cobbett* trial was the epitome of republicanism, for it was not rooted so much in the law as it was a statement by citizens endorsing the kind of social system in which they intended to live and which they would serve. The verdict by this account represented not so much a finding in the law as the embrace of a social vision and the ability of its citizens to authorize such a vision in a politically and judicially meaningful way. The verdict might have run the risk of demagoguery (potentially nullifying the law and asserting the priority of the community) and suggested the prospect of civil unrest (represented by the crowd's reaction), but these were the risks republicanism ran historically, trading the prospect of rule by the best for that of rule by those who would be ruled, passion over reason perhaps, but through participation and relative self-governance. If the people's voice became a troublesome issue in the new republic, *Rush v. Cobbett* provided an opportunity for it to work in a legal venue. The people might have spoken as a jury of one's neighbors, but it could do so "inscrutably," that is to say without being held accountable and with relative autonomy with respect to both the law to which it was bound and to the community it presumed to represent. The jury negotiated a conflict between free speech and privacy, between the press and medicine, and between libel and malpractice. It did so by navigating the welfare of the public (which the press held to be its province) and the health of its citizens (which medicine claimed as its), performing its sovereign role as the people's voice and presuming to judge unconstrained by the firm hand of the law but enabled by it.

COBBETT'S COUNSEL

If the judge and the jury presented as problems for Cobbett, they were no more problematic than the defendant's own counsel, Harper in particular and to some extent Rawle. Rawle had difficulty countering Hopkinson's passionate opening; indeed, Rawle implied that the younger lawyer's "extraordinary and unusual manner"[64] interfered with his own ability to address the legal charges made against Cobbett.[65] As for Harper,[66] Cobbett described him in a letter to his friend Edward Thornton in the following terms: "But what think you of the base defence of me by H? Every one is shocked at it. Mr. Shoemaker (Jacob) says I should have done well to give him (H.) a hundred guineas to stay away. While he was pleading, Rush, I am told, leaned over the rail and said to Levy "why did *I* not *fee* Harper!"—Can it be because *he was paid long ago*?"[67] On the verge of launching his self-defense, Cobbett commented further on Rush's presumed remark: "In my pamphlet, I shall endeavour to plead my cause a little better than Mr. *Harper* did it for me. I shall leave Rush no room to exclaim, 'I HAVE NOT GIVEN HIM A FEE.' At any rate, I am sure, I shall not pay my court to the sovereign people by *pouring out nauseous eulogies upon Rush and his followers*, and by *traducing the character of my client*."[68] In support of the reported hearsay, one of Rush's sons penciled a note on a letter from Harper to Rush, referring to Harper in the following terms: "a friend of Dr. R's yet was counsel for Cobbett. He said to Dr. R after the trial: 'I was obliged to say something for him.'"[69]

Cobbett had prepaid the defense team, presumably because his counsel feared that, not being an American citizen, he might leave the country without paying their fee. He considered it a "misfortune to have *paid his counselors beforehand*"[70] and allowed that they had been seduced by the plaintiff and infected by the spirit of republicanism, raising questions of collusion on the one hand and incompetence on the other. By comparison, Cobbett credited Rush's lawyers for an effusion of support for their client, which he attributed to their having been engaged on a conditional fee:

> These impassioned pleaders, who seem to have thought that they heard the sweet chinking of English guineas at the close of every period, not content with representing their client as "*immaculate,*" as the most "*tender*, the most *meek*, the most *unoffending*, and the most *benevolent* of mankind," could not refrain from adding to their vocabulary of superlatives, the most "*patriotic*" and most "*learned.*"[71]

Harper was far too amiable for Cobbett's taste, a fault to which Justice Shippen adverted in his charge when he claimed that the defense failed to justify "the truth of the matters charged against Dr. Rush, which on the contrary they have repeatedly acknowledged to be false."[72] Ingersol, as well, argued that the team had essentially admitted the guilt of their client: "One of his Counsel speaks of Dr. Rush as all but super-natural—another *hints* and insinuates, and damns by faint praise; and a third acknowledges that the publications contain many untruths . . . but he wishes to ease his client from the *legal* consequences."[73] Objecting to Shippen's representation of his defense team, Cobbett nevertheless acknowledged what he regarded as their shameful failure to justify the truth of his attacks on Rush. Directing his remarks to Shippen, he placed his team in the same camp as the judge, Americans, and republicans slavishly serving a government to which they had paid tribute:

> It is true, indeed, that my counsel, to their shame be it spoken, did not justify the truth of the publications laid in the declaration; but that they *might* have justified, every man in America knows well; and you knew, that they *would* have done it, had their client not been an Englishman, and had they not, like you [Shippen], been in fear of M'Kean and of your brother slaves who filled your *tribunes* and crowded round your bench.[74]

Cobbett specified Harper's contribution to the defense as a peculiar brand of sycophancy:

> My counsel, Mr. Harper, who seemed more anxious to find something to commend in every one who gave satisfactory proofs of being my enemy, was kind enough to observe, that the three witnesses (Mease among the rest) were "*gentlemen of great respectability* 'FOR THEIR AGE.'" What he meant by tacking on the phrase "*for their age,*" I cannot think. Did he mean, that they were rendered respectable by their *grey locks*, or that, considering their *beardless chins*, they were very respectable fellows? . . . "*for their age,*" was an unmeaning expletive, clapped in to ward off the charge of having bestowed on these volunteer heroes his *unqualified* approbation.[75]

In truth, Harper appeared to have embraced the prosecution's argument in defense of Rush's virtue. He would not, he contended in court, countenance hazarding "my respectability by standing here to advocate a man who should slander so eminently useful a character as Dr. Rush, or his very respectable wife or family: far be it from me, I should rather have consigned him and his cause to the fate it would deserve. My professional name should never have borne the blot such conduct would justly attach to it."[76] With Tilghman something of a holdout, Harper largely typified the defense strategy. Cobbett critiqued the representation he received at Harper's hands in much the way one might attack opposing counsel. He complained that when he attacked a eulogium delivered by Rush on Dr. Rittenhouse as party-based republicanism, his own counsel impugned his response:

> Mr. Harper (though one of my *advocates*) further observed that it was "very *impertinent* in *me* to express my disapprobation of it, for that I had *no business* with it."—. . . . Mr. Harper does not know everything. . . . Let Mr. Harper learn a little more, before he takes upon him to reprobate and condemn the opinions of those, whose *intentions*, at least, are as good as his own. Let him claim, let him receive and enjoy all the popularity he deserves for his zealous, his great, and efficacious endeavours in support of the government; but, let me conjure him to resolve, before he undertakes another cause, never to seek to preserve that popularity by traducing the character of his client, though that client should have the misfortune to be the subject of a king. . . .[77]

Compared to the prosecution, he suggested, Harper expressed self-interested cowardice and desertion in the face of presumed defeat:

> The conduct of Harper was truly abominable. He engaged in my cause with all apparent alacrity; I have heard him a hundred times reprobate the practice of Rush, and express the utmost contempt for his character. But the fact is the mean wretch thought I was going down, he saw the tide, as he thought, turning against me, and he basely deserted his duty, in order to preserve his popularity. It happened, however, as it ought to happen; for I have the satisfaction to learn, that even in Philadelphia he is universally detested for his treachery.[78]

Faced with what he considered the betrayal of his own defense team, Cobbett was hard put to believe that his trial was not a conspiracy rooted in the Pennsylvania Supreme Court and led by the republican Chief Justice McKean. Cobbett's intemperate language in *The Republican Judge* describing his experience at the hands of McKean suggests just how jaundiced he had become about the legal system in America and the possibility of an alien receiving a fair trial. In a letter to Edward Thornton, Cobbett cited "the flagrant partiality [of *Rush v. Cobbett*], the barefaced illegality of the whole course of proceedings."[79] He considered that as "Base as the conduct and the court and jury must appear, as well as that of all the parties concerned . . . [and] After the aspersions, which the villains, in different parts of the country, have thrown on my character, in order to justify the iniquity of the Philadelphian court and jury," his reader must acknowledge the propriety of a refutation on Cobbett's part, which, indeed, followed in *Rush-Light*. He proceeded to represent presiding judge Shippen, in another letter to Thornton, as an impudent and "Buffle-headed" rascal: "you can have no idea," he told his reader, "of the shocking villainly [sic] that has been practiced from the first to the last."[80] As to the triers of fact of this "most infamous proceeding," Cobbett ranted that "a jury that would find for the plaintiff must be a set of perjured scoundrels."[81]

TRIAL STRATEGY

It is worth noting that the order of presentation in *Rush v. Cobbett*, whereby the six defense and prosecution counsel alternated their addresses to the court, matched the mixed order of the legal arguments that they presented. We might have anticipated that Hopkinson and Rawle (opening for each side) and Tilghman and Ingersol (closing for each side) would have in some sense introduced, on the one hand, or concluded, on the other, by covering the range of arguments for their position. But so did Levy and Harper, respectively, rather than isolate for themselves a discrete role as part of the legal team (whether to clarify the evidence, argue the law, or undermine the other side's argument, for example). The idea of a legal team dividing well-delineated responsibilities in a systematic presentation to create a coherent argument did not play much of a role in the trial. The jury, as a result, would have found it difficult not only to follow the argument either side made but to separate defense from prosecution arguments. Differentiating defense and prosecution positions would have been particularly difficult where the law was not clear, where conflicting interpretations were possible, or even where there were agreements or concessions on a given point. If a clear theme was to emerge and dominate the trial, it would have to be one that was repeated over and again, that was clear and without nuance, one that opposed itself in a forceful way to an alternative way of seeing the same issue, and one that fit comfortably into a self-organizing jury perspective. Under such conditions, the prosecution's positioning—that is, by virtue of opening and closing the trial—would allow it the first word (the initial framing of the case, for a primacy effect) and the last word (the final and concluding statement, for a recency effect) that the jury would hear about the case. That the prosecution was positioned in the middle as well, so that it could interrupt the defense counsel's momentum, interfere in the course of its argument, and side-track it by stepping on its storyline, gave it a discursive advantage in controlling the jury's attention and shaping its responses.

Cobbett's counsel held the view that it was counter-intuitive to argue the facts. Doing so would replay the scandal even should they have chosen to mount a truth defense. Cobbett's apparent instruction to the defense team not to employ American law to make a case for liberty of the press—based on his refusal to acknowledge that the American press was a free press[82]—left his counsel even less to work with. Dodging the prosecution contention that Cobbett was an alien journalist (a contention that catered to the suspicion that Cobbett was a spy for the English government), the defense was still able to stake a position in the press debate to Cobbett's advantage. It did so by couching Cobbett in a protected status under the law by means of which he could claim to have championed the public, guarding the public trust as a member of the fourth estate by accepting a responsibility to come to the defense of an endangered public. Performing this role, Cobbett might inoculate himself against the mischief of which he had been accused, undermining or at least mitigating the charge of malice. Cobbett's venue was presented as that of the free market of ideas. He was thus positioned to operate in a public space, cautioning his readers on an issue of public controversy and invoking the public welfare. The defense strategized that where the public was split and physicians divided, where all had the right to speak their piece, had not Cobbett the right to add his voice to the clamor by way of raising an alarm. How was he to be judged wrong when the entire medical profession and public were divided in their opinions? Who, moreover, was the greater fear-monger: Cobbett or the warring physicians? Why, the defense argued, should he above all others be denied his opinion, unless to suppress the public's right to be informed and to choose freely in an open arena of options so that, as in a true democracy, the people's fate would remain in the people's hands?

This move into the marketplace of ideas compensated for Cobbett's refusal of a liberty of the press defense. It had the advantage as well of avoiding the risk of public disapproval that attacking a great man and a local son would have entailed. Having considered attacking Rush to offset the prosecution's characterization of Cobbett as a suspect alien and potential spy, the defense had in any case determined that the best possible scenario was to concede the ground of Rush's benevolence and altruism and to avoid the contest of opposites into which the prosecution was trying to maneuver it. In a scene in which Rush held the moral high ground of public reputation, where support for the press was waning, and the courts were trying the public's patience (clogged as they were with a backlog of noisome libel cases), the better course appeared to be that of admitting Rush's good faith and intent, acknowledging Cobbett's ignorance of medicine, and sidestepping the prosecution's demand that the defendant propose an alternative system of medicine. Introducing Rush's intemperate language, his feuds with other physicians, his sons' feuds,[83] his disruptive role in the court martial of William Shippen,[84] and suspicion that he associated with a cabal of officers challenging General Washington's leadership in the revolution[85] would have been like stepping into a hornet's nest. Cobbett's own reputation would not sustain the blow-back of such a swarm of negatives. Rather than fight a war he was unlikely to win, the more likely course of action was one of glancing blows aimed at Rush's medical practices, a strategy that stressed the novelty and untested, experimental nature of his cure for yellow fever, the great number of deaths associated with the epidemic, the dissension among physicians, and the inconsistency of treatments for the disease. At best, such a move would displace blame and raise doubts about the prosecution's view of Rush even as it deflected assaults against Cobbett. At worst, it would only demonstrate what the prosecution had feared all along—that Rush was never at much risk from Cobbett's attacks as he was too well established to be injured. Indeed, if Rush's system was so infallible, Cobbett never had much of a chance of destroying either it or Rush's reputation. Cobbett, by this argument, would pose no credible threat to the man of superior reputation as he was not in his league. Elevating Rush in this way, the defense appears to have concluded, could only diminish the threat Cobbett was presumed to have posed.

The prosecution for its part initially announced itself prepared to organize its argument around two central questions: what was Rush's conduct during the calamity (was it beyond reproach and thus aggravated the charges against Cobbett, or did it merit reproach and thereby extenuate Cobbett's actions); and what inducement did Cobbett have for attacking Rush (was his intent to launch a malicious and politically motivated attack on Rush's private character and thus aggravate the charges, or was it to inform the public and thereby extenuate his actions)? The mixed order of presentation and the different styles of counsel arguments exposed systemic cracks and fissures in this plan which, though it was periodically revisited, could not be sustained to create coherence across all three of the prosecution counsels' addresses. In the end, as a result, the prosecution's success depended upon three lines of attack. It appealed to the jury's self-interest; it tried to address its own and the public's love-hate relationship with the press; and it engaged in vilification and oppositionality in its construction of Cobbett. The prosecution framed the jury's roles as those of republicans and citizens, empathizing in particular with one special citizen, Benjamin Rush. Expanded to represent a form of governance rather than a narrow political position or party, republicanism was defined as identification with the republic and entailed resistance to its enemies. Anything that smacked of being anti-American (dependence on or actions on behalf of the primordial villainy of England, for example) or any actor who was alien to an American way of being (an enemy of the city of Philadelphia, for example) would require a response on their part as citizens in defense of the republic. No threat was too great to make them capitulate; no personal risk was too much to undertake. Raising the red herring of a personal threat to the jury from the defendant should the jury refuse to deliver a verdict for him, the prosecution counted on reverse psychology as well as the jury's chauvinism. The pathetic appeal of an old man and his American family at the hands of an alien, army-trained ruffian should be enough to ignite both their patriotic fervor and their desire to come to the aid of their country. The alternative, the risk should the jury not prove up to the challenge, was pictured as disproportionately grave. What was being asked of the jury was small enough, whatever its risk, weighed against the prospects for society should the jury fail to live up to its responsibility. Failed punishment would undermine the court system and risk threatening the peace; citizens without recourse to public justice would revert to a private justice that would rend the very bonds of society.

In order to make this line of reasoning work, the prosecution had, first, to succeed in convincing the jury that Cobbett represented just the kind of threat it warned against and, second, that bringing him down would not destabilize the liberty of the press upon which they and the public at large relied. Representing Cobbett in imagery that spoke to assassinating the honor of one of the nation's great men (a Brutus to Rush's Caesar, a Satan to his saving angel), polluting the land like infesting slime (contaminating the city as a secondary epidemic), running to the ground his helpless prey (a predator on the hunt), and subverting the foundations of a great national institution (tearing down the liberty of the press that stood as the citizenry's great citadel on the hill) constituted a metaphorical level of struggle by means of which the prosecution justified its characterization of the trial as no ordinary case. Indeed, if the trial was to be judged as an unusual case, it thereby required language that might otherwise have been regarded as actionable libel to which the jury might then justifiably take exception.

To make the case that Cobbett was an irremediable danger, not only must the prosecution oppose Cobbett to Rush as an inferior creature from a foreign culture who posed a heightened threat to the city with which the jury and Rush were identified, but it had to expand its characterization of Cobbett as an alien editor to implicate a larger body of meaning beyond himself. Thus, the prosecution reconceptualized Cobbett as an abuser of the press who stood for all abusers of the press. He stood for an entire pack of libelers whom he epitomized, a phenomenon among libelers in a country plagued by them. By the same argument, the prosecution captured in Cobbett an alienated figure whose desire as an Englishman was to reverse Britain's defeat in the American Revolution, a move that would defuse as well any residual pro-English sentiments lingering within the minds of potential holdout jurors. Such jurors would thereby risk framing themselves as antirepublican agents, as spies from within taking part in a threat to reenslave the nation. The very sickness of the city argued against the interests of those who would make it sicker, those who would destabilize the city's confidence in those with the ability to cure it, those informers still suffering from postcolonial anxiety over separation from the home country.

In the last of its three appeals to the jury, the prosecution dealt with a press that had been attacked in its federalist and its republican emanations by conservatives and radicals alike. Threading the needle on freedom of the press would prove the most delicate of the prosecution's tasks. Partisan politics had not merely to be suppressed, they had to be denied. Cobbett might be an English alien and the editor of a federalist and pro-English newspaper, but he could not be attacked as the only editor guilty of abusing the liberty of the press. To make his case, Hopkinson inoculated himself against party motives by, first, acknowledging that he lived in a time when every action was attributable to such motives. He then refuted the implied charge that he was himself guilty of such a bias. Neither denying nor admitting that his politics were opposed to those of Cobbett, he stood, rather, on the grounds of his conscientiousness and the fact that his politics, whatever they were, were not dependent upon Cobbett's approval or disapproval. On the one hand, Hopkinson had left himself free to argue that, by implication, Cobbett's politics, indeed his political character, was open to question, and, on the other, that the prosecution was capable of standing above the fray. Leveraging such a nuanced position was a high stakes gamble, one liable to the charge of being specious and disingenuous, a risk the prosecution was willing to take.

With the ongoing alien and sedition trials against republican journalists and the turnover in political sentiment from a federalist to a republican disposition, the situation in which the press found itself at the time of the trial was, after all, highly ambiguous, which minimized the risk associated with the prosecution's strategy. Knowing which way the political tide was running and appreciating that turnabout was only fair play, the jury was likely to be amenable to punishing a federalist journalist to even the score, so long as it was not forced to admit openly to doing so. The prosecution enabled such a position by arguing that the best defense of the press was to punish all abusers equally. The jury should honor the press when it operated within the proper bounds of liberty, not when it used its liberty as a political shield to hide behind. Guilty of untruths, of malice, and of attacks on personal reputation, having failed to act as part of a public stock of information, the press should have its legal rights constrained. The court (clogged with libels), the city (rife with scurrility), and the country (in which libels had become a national scandal) would all benefit from the courage to restrain such a press, whatever its party affiliation.

As for Rush's standing in the face of press attacks, he would need the cover of privacy and family to inoculate him against those aspects of libel that left public men and public controversies open to public commentary and that assigned to men of the press certain rights to hold figures of high station up to public scrutiny. His counsel would need to capitalize on an appeal to character as the ground on which property was based; reputation (protected as property by law) represented a sign of character so that character was itself protected by law as property. In these terms, an attack on character was an attack on one's livelihood such that a man could be reduced to penury. His counsel would, equally, need to exploit the pathos of the private father and husband, the innocence of whose honor represented the protection of his wife and the legacy of his sons. Strategically, the prosecution had placed private reputation out of bounds even as it privileged character as an issue to make the case opposing Cobbett to Rush. So long as an attack on Rush's character constituted assassination and so long as character was seen as a property right, Cobbett's conviction was within the prosecution's shooting range.

Playing a two-handed game, the prosecution strategized as well that ultimately an individual good such as the right of a private man to his privacy had not only to be understood within the context of the public welfare but had to be trumped by collective rights called into play in a time of public crisis. The trial was not only a question of a civil dispute in which one man's reputation was in jeopardy. It was not only a question of a second man's freedom to raise an alarm or to express himself on a matter of public concern. The case, the prosecution contended, was as much a public as a private prosecution, as much a criminal as a civil case, since a threat to social order was at issue. Recognizing that the privacy argument might not be enough to give Rush the verdict he needed, the prosecution had to cover the risk to collective rights as well. In such a case, as common law implied, it would not be enough to reward an injured party, to make good a harm done, or to ensure the enjoyment of a right denied. The public peace once breached must also be set right, and the state must be satisfied that no hue and cry had been raised that would call forth private revenge or mob action. In this scenario, the young republic was itself at risk, its courts tested, its ability to govern undermined, and the liberty of its press (the means of patrolling abuse of government as well as protecting rights of reputation, conscience, and property) called into question. International unrest, an uncivil contest of party politics in preparation for a presidential election year, a threatened foreign war, and a providential epidemic that ravaged the population of the national capital were all called into play, demanding consideration of threats to the foundation of the country and to the kind of nation to which the jury wished to belong. Only prosecution of the press would protect the press; only punishment of offenders would legitimize the court; only a jury called to arms would ensure the safety of the streets and the public peace. By way of such an argument, the government would not fall into contempt, nor the court into ridicule; the guilty would not go free, and the country would not deny its citizens the justice they applied for.

These were the public protections that outweighed private considerations. They were sealed in lines of argument that extolled the virtues of the republic and expanded upon the responsibility of its citizen jurors in the midst of a noisy clamor of riots and revenge. They were served by clarifying rhetoric that exploited jeremiadic themes of dreadful days and just retribution, a wilderness of disease and death, and a heightened oppositionality of a saint and Satan that elevated the one and cast down the other. Cutting through the confusing mélange of mixed prosecution and defense addresses in a stew of sometimes indistinguishable stories, the jury would identify with overarching themes that resonated with religious sermons and patriotic rhetoric nourishing a developing myth of America.

NOTES

1. Carpenter (1800, 25).
2. Carpenter (1800, 47–48).
3. Carpenter (1800, 50).
4. Carpenter (1800, 52).
5. Carpenter (1800, 51).
6. Carpenter (1800, 55).
7. Carpenter (1800, 54).
8. Carpenter (1800, 66).
9. Carpenter (1800, 20).

10. The Pennsylvania House of Representatives impeached all three justices in 1804 over their performance in another case, although they were not convicted; Rowe (1994, 268, 271).

11. Carpenter (1800, 1).

12. Carpenter (1800, 1).

13. Carpenter (1800, 2).

14. Carpenter (1800, 2).

15. Carpenter (1800, 2).

16. *Rush-Light* IV, March 31, 1800; Cobbett (1801a, 11: 383).

17. Clark (1939, 120, 158–59).

18. December 18, 1799, letter to Edward Tilghman, Historical Society of Pennsylvania, file no. PHI 2129. On the very day the verdict was delivered, a friend of Rush's, Charles Henry Wharton, warned Rush that Cobbett had published notice of "a sale of his furniture, books, and *infamous Press* on some day next week. Tell your Lawyer of this, that an attachment may take place"; Rush Manuscripts, Historical Society of Pennsylvania, vol. 25, letter 39, December 14, 1799. A sheriff's sale interrupted Cobbett's plans and was announced on December 23 for the next day (Clark, 1939, 160), just ten days after the verdict. A notice on the day of the verdict in *Gazette of the United States* indicates that Cobbett intended to pay his debts, if not necessarily the judgment against him: "William Cobbett: Having (in order to avoid the disgrace of living under the Government of McKean) removed from Philadelphia to the City of New York, requests any one in Pennsylvania, who may have a demand against him, to deliver an account thereof to Mr. John Morgan"; Spater (1982, 105). Cobbett nevertheless did try to deal with his property in a way that would avoid the court judgment. In a letter to Edward Thornton, Cobbett revealed that he sent all his goods to New York as early as November 18, 1799, that is, a month before the trial, "so that they are no longer, I hope, within the grasp of the sovereign people of Pennsylvania"; Cole (1924, 21). In a letter to Tilghman (Historical Society of Pennsylvania, December 30, 1799, file no. PHI 2129), he asked if it was not possible to "dispose of that property before the Court meets" (referring presumably to the suit Rush filed immediately after the trial to recover the fine). He even proposed selling his debts to someone in New York, who might then go to Philadelphia and lay claim to Cobbett's property "without accounting for it to anyone."

19. January 20, 1800, letter to Edward Thornton; Cobbett (1937, 36). In response to this threat of a new suit, Cobbett considered Alexander Hamilton to represent him. Hamilton, he claimed, "refused any fee, and . . . told me, that he should think himself honoured in defending me. . . . He behaved with great kindness to me, and assured me that I had nothing to fear from *injustice* in New York"; Rush, (1951, 2: 818, note 6); see March 14, 1800, letter to Edward Thornton; Cobbett (1937, 72). Hamilton had been supported by Cobbett in his newspaper *Porcupine's Gazette*. When Rush was being considered for a position at Columbia University, Hamilton blocked his appointment.

20. April 25, 1800, letter to Edward Thornton; Cobbett (1937, 86–87).

21. See Rush Manuscripts, Historical Society of Pennsylvania, vol. 29, letters 82–90, for letters between Brockholst Livingston and Benjamin Rush; Cobbett (1937,

19-39, 67–89); for letters between Cobbett and Tilghman, Historical Society of Pennsylvania, file no. PHI 2129; Clark (1939, 158-71); Spater, 1: 105–9).

22. Carpenter (1800, 10).

23. See Francis Hopkinson's commentary and poem "A Descant on Adrian's Assertion, that a grand jury is nothing more than a legal machine, subject to the direction and control of the court," in Hopkinson (1792, 1: 194–238); Myrsiades (2008, 167–72). Hopkinson was an admiralty judge and lawyer in Pennsylvania.

24. *Rush-Light* III, March 15, 1800; Cobbett (1801a, 11: 371).

25. *Rush-Light* III, March 15, 1800; Cobbett (1801a, 11: 376).

26. *Rush-Light* III, March 15, 1800; Cobbett (1801a, 11: 374).

27. Carpenter (1800, 1).

28. *Rush-Light* III, March 15, 1800; Cobbett (1801a, 11: 376).

29. *Rush-Light* III, March 15, 1800; Cobbett (1801a, 11: 376).

30. *Rush-Light* III, March 15, 1800; Cobbett (1801a, 11: 373–74).

31. *Rush-Light* III, March 15, 1800; Cobbett (1801a, 11: 377).

32. *Rush-Light* III, March 15, 1800; Cobbett (1801a, 11: 378–79). Cobbett justified his claim by citing at some length British case law.

33. *Rush-Light* III, March 15, 1800; Cobbett (1801a, 11: 377).

34. *Rush-Light* III, March 15, 1800; Cobbett (1801a, 11: 380).

35. *Rush-Light* III, March 15, 1800; Cobbett (1801a, 11: 381).

36. *Rush-Light* III, March 15, 1800; Cobbett (1801a, 11: 381).

37. Carpenter (1800, 2).

38. *Rush-Light* III, March 15, 1800; Cobbett (1801a, 11: 381).

39. In the transcript of the trial, Carpenter did not provide evidence of Shippen's management of the court.

40. *Rush-Light* IV, March 31, 1800, Cobbett (1801a, 11: 374 note, 383 note).

41. See Rowe (1994), who presents the issue of the arrogance of the judiciary as a common complaint that led to popular protests against the justices; 241–42.

42. *Rush-Light* IV, March 31, 1800, Cobbett (1801a, 11: 374 note).

43. December 30, 1799, letter to Edward Tilghman, Historical Society of Pennsylvania, file no. PHI 2129.

44. *Rush-Light* IV, March 31, 1800, Cobbett (1801a, 11: 383).

45. *Rush-Light* IV, March 31, 1800, Cobbett (1801a, 11: 383 note).

46. *Rush-Light* IV, March 31, 1800, Cobbett (1801a, 11: 383 note).

47. December 14, 1799, Rush Manuscripts, Historical Society of Pennsylvania, vol. 29, letter 91.

48. December 14, 1799, Rush Manuscripts, Historical Society of Pennsylvania, vol. 25, letter 39.

49. Langbein (2003, 331–32).

50. Langbein (2003, 336).

51. Clearly where a privilege existed like that allowed by the Pennsylvania Constitution (whereby a jury was endowed with "the right to determine the law and the facts" Section 7), the jury potentially had powers that rivaled those of the judge, even if it infrequently used it. Many juries felt an obligation to follow the court's charge,

suggesting that where a judge's direction was in line with the jury's verdict, it was likely that they were both part of the same political community.

52. Langbein (2003, 6, 58).

53. *Bushel's case* (1670) established that "jurors 'might bring in a verdict, although no proofs were offered on either side' for 'the law supposed[d] them to have sufficient knowledge to try the matters in issue and so they must, though no evidence were given on either side in court.' Furthermore, 'acting upon their own knowledge, [jurors] were at liberty to give a verdict in direct opposition to the evidence if they saw fit'"; as cited in Constable (1994, 132); discussed in Forsyth (1852, 163–64). *Bushel's case* meant that since jurors were not required to accept the judge's version of the facts, but might honestly disagree based on what they had themselves understood the evidence to say, they could not be punished "by the bench for returning a verdict against the trial judge's perception of the weight of the evidence"; Anand (2005, 429). On juries, see Cockburn and Green (1988); Green (1985).

54. Olson (2000, 5).

55. If it was a satire, it could not be strictly true; if merely an opinion, it could not be proved true; if it was false, it was capable of provoking a breach of the peace even if it was free speech; if true and proved true, it risked undermining confidence in a public person or governing body, damage to the polity, and the threat of retribution. With libels like those in the Rush case, jurors were likely to consider that only in the guise of members of the community who located themselves within the same neighborhood would they be able to judge whether libelous writing was capable of inciting their fellows to acts of violence.

56. Olson (2000, 9).

57. They were considered in a manual of Pennsylvania law "to know beforehand the characters of the parties," a convenience nevertheless offset by the unavoidable consequence that they "would be apt to intermix their prejudices and partialities in the trial of the right"; Reed (1831, 3: 331).

58. Friedman (1993, 185).

59. See Smith (1988); Smith (1953a, 3–23); Smith (1953b, 123–55); Olson (2000).

60. Olson (2000, 4–5).

61. Rowe (1994, 243).

62. Its long-standing feud with Cobbett and its inability to make its charges stick in the Yrujo case mean that the court was being tested in *Rush v. Cobbett*. It was in the public eye and could not easily afford to fail in this prosecution, even as a civil case. Moreover, publishers as well as the public were particularly unhappy with the court's British view of libel and contempt, its endorsement of seditious libel laws, and its procedures for punishing judicial contempt; Rowe (1994, 167, 169, 172, 240–42, 252). It had become popular to disapprove publicly of the high court in terms that embarrassed the justices, eventually leading to the impeachment in 1804 of all three of those who had sat on the bench in the Rush case—Shippen, Yeates, and Smith—for their role in what became a politicized case of presumed miscarriage of justice against a shipowner named Thomas Passmore (264–68.)

63. Sheehan (2004, 6).

64. Carpenter (1800, 23).

65. Konkle (1981, 64); Clark (1939, 154).

66. Harper represented Cobbett in an earlier feud with the journalist Mathew Carey; Carey (1799a); Carey (1799b).

67. December 25, 1799, letter to Thornton; Cobbett (1937, 27).

68. *Porcupine's Gazette*, January 13, 1800; Cobbett (1801a, 12: 159). This was Cobbett's farewell issue of *Porcupine's Gazette*.

69. Letter of October 15, 1800, Spater (1982, 1: 269 note 63). William Reitzel (1935, 241 note 34) refers to the date as 1805 (which is unlikely) and to the son as James. See Clark (1939, 162 note 10); Clark and Reitzel cite Rush Manuscripts, Historical Society of Pennsylvania, vol. 21, number 100.

70. *Rush-Light* III, March 15, 1800, Cobbett (1801a, 11: 335note).

71. *Rush-Light* I, February 15, 1800, Cobbett (1801a, 11: 239).

72. Carpenter (1800, 1).

73. Carpenter (1800, 57–58).

74. *Rush-Light* IV, March 31, 1800, Cobbett (1801a, 11: 374).

75. *Rush-Light* I, February 15, 1800, Cobbett (1801a, 11: 246).

76. Carpenter (1800, 35).

77. *Rush-Light* III, March 15, 1800, Cobbett (1801a, 11: 335 note).

78. *Rush-Light* IV, March 31, 1800, Cobbett (1801a, 11: 375 note).

79. December 25, 1799, letter to Edward Thornton, Cobbett (1937, 25).

80. January 20, 1800, letter to Edward Thornton, Cobbett (1937, 33.)

81. January 20, 1800, letter to Edward Thornton, Cobbett (1937, 35).

82. Cobbett took the position that the American press was not as free as the English press—the Grubb Street press of which he felt himself a proud example.

83. Myrsiades (2009, 77–115).

84. Myrsiades (2009, 116–77).

85. Binger (1966, 132–39); Rush (1951, 2: 1197–1208); Goodman (1934, 107–27.)

Afterword

Shippen's carefully crafted charge in the Rush case signaled a jury verdict that, for Cobbett, was the proof of the supreme court's antipress sentiments and a resurgent republicanism that would destroy him as a journalist in America. If Cobbett would not survive the *Rush v. Cobbett* trial with his reputation intact, neither would he flee to England without a few parting shots at his enemies.

COBBETT'S FLIGHT TO ENGLAND

Before he left America, Cobbett penned a tragedy scene and a dialogue that expressed his feelings about the trial. In "A Tragedy Scene," he put his case before his readers in a soliloquy that cast Sangrado in the role of his surrogate, enlisting the fictive master-bleeder to indict the bleeder's real-world counterpart:

A TRAGEDY SCENE

Enter SANGRADO, *with the Rush-Light in his hand. He remains for about half an hour in stupid, sullen silence: and then, starting from his reveries, pours forth, in slow and melancholy accents, the following soliloquy.*

Unthinking Doctor, wherefore did thy rage
Urge thee with printer's prowess to engage?
O, why from puffing to the law retire?
Why for thyself construct the fun'ral fire?
What though an Ingersol before thee stood,
With dangling brush, to paint thee fair and good;

A weeping Hopkinson, dear tender creature,
Sobbing to wail the injuries of Nature;
What though kind-hearted jurors press'd thee round,
And philanthropic judges too were found;
What though the gentle, just, and gen'rous crowd
The verdict sanction'd with applauses loud;
What though five thousand dollars were the prize,
Which, in idea, gratify'd thine eyes?
Say! Could such lenitives relieve thy shame,
Or reunite thee to thy shadow, fame?
Could they kill Peter—whose vindictive art
So well directs his venom to thy art?
Could they prevent exposure and disgrace,
Or change the tincture of an Ethiop's face?
Oh, no! they bade these hellish fires arise,
And bound thee to the stake!—(He dies.)[1]

Chastised for resorting to the law in a matter of honor, Rush was pictured in the hands of a feminized legal team—sobbing, wailing, and weeping, appealing to kind hearts and a gentle crowd. This sentimentalized portrait of plaintiff's counsel figured Rush as a man who had forgotten his honor and failed to relieve his shame. He was a man who could not kill his opponent and who could not thereby avoid disgrace. He was, in effect, posted as a coward. As for Shippen and his panel of justices, they were no more than philanthropic patsies sucked into a sentimental drama.

Lest he prove too indirect, in the same issue of *Rush-Light* Cobbett published "Porcupine's Revenge: A Dialogue Between Rush and Porcupine." Here, Cobbett accused Rush of corruption directly, intimating that the jury was in the doctor's pocket all along, that it was a "struck" jury packed with jurors favoring Rush. Cobbett portrayed Rush seeking advice from Porcupine on how to reward "my twelve sov'reign men . . . now I no longer need them," while Peter's advice constituted his revenge: "Why bleed them, Rush, bleed them," he offered.[2] Just as Rush should reward the jury by venesection, so, Cobbett advised, should he reward Justice Shippen, whose forthcoming appointment as chief justice had left him open to persuasion.[3] Equally, Rush should bleed his successful legal team and Cobbett's colluding counsel, "the mob-courting [Robert Goodloe] Harper," who, Cobbett believed, had catered to his American colleagues and sold out his English client. Rush then asked whether he ought to reward the ambitious physicians James Mease, John Coxe, and William Dewees who, knowing where their best interests lay, "volunteered" to testify for Rush. A complementary reward was to be accorded the good doctors. Peter advised, "purge them, Rush, purge them." Assured that purging and bleeding would kill Rush's benefactors, just as Rush killed his patients, Peter would deny them burial in an honest grave-digger's church yard and treat their corpses to a fate like that of Rush's yellow fever victims:

> Church-yard! honest fellow, my meaning's not such;
> For, where a man's buried it matters not much;
> And the great Dr. Mitchell (of bleeding renown)
> Says, "let all *human carrion* be dragg'd out of town."[4]

Like the trial, Cobbett's flight to England did not go uncelebrated in doggerel. This time it was his old foe Freneau who would see him off, taking up Cobbett's punishment and furtive escape in his poem "On the Departure of Peter Porcupine for England."[5] Flushing him out like a fox from his den, Freneau pictured Cobbett flying across the waters pursued by denizens of the sea delivering his deserved fate. The winds of nature, called upon to join pursuit, made the fugitive howl and snuffed out his "Rush light." Purveyor "of the pension'd pen" in the pay of a foreign power, Freneau's Cobbett so despised the democratic laws of the country that opened its shores to him that "his own projects he defeated." Thus, while "He might have stay'd/And followed here his scribbling trade," Cobbett was launched on his way by Freneau who, like his fellow republican journalists, wished Porcupine a surly farewell:

> O may the sharks enjoy their bait:
> He came such mischief to create
> We wish him not a better fate. . . .
>
> He writ, and writ, and writ so long
> That sheriff came, with writ more strong,
> And he went off, and all went wrong.
>
> May southern gales that vex the main,
> Or Boreas, with his whistling train
> Make Peter howl and howl again. . . .

THE DEATH OF GEORGE WASHINGTON

Whereas Rush's reputation was attacked in the press rather than in a court and he avoided actual charges of medical malpractice, one final outcome of the *Rush v. Cobbett* trial would make an indelible mark on his reputation. Warnings that his reputation would suffer for pursuing publicly his complaint against Cobbett proved prescient, for the controversy that would plague him the remainder of his life arose on the very day the verdict was delivered. George Washington—General, then President, and finally metamorphosed into Father of the Nation—died at ten o'clock on December 14, the second and final day of the trial. One of the physicians attending him, Dr. Elisha Dick, was a student of Rush. Although Dick dissented, the team of physicians attending Washington bled him four times on the last day of his life, contributing to his death that evening. Rush was to pay a price for this heroic treatment, having claimed the practice as his invention, having been the figure most closely associated with extreme bleeding practices in both the press and in the trial, and having lent his name to public advertisements of its efficacy. Until the end of his life in 1813, Rush suffered from conjecture that Washington did not die of a septic throat infection but, rather, of the arrogance of a medical profession that insisted on a grotesque, unproven, and barbaric treatment.[6] Indeed, at the time a potentially lifesaving form of trachoeostomy was available, but it was largely withheld in favor of the better-publicized treatment of choice, bleeding.[7]

Not one to shrink from the spotlight, Cobbett capitalized on the rumors associating Rush with Washington's death, interrupting his farewell to his readers in the final issue of *Porcupine's Gazette* to treat them to the breaking news:

> *a fact* respecting *Rush's practice* . . . has just fallen in my way, and it is a fact of such importance, that I cannot delay mentioning it for a single moment. This fact is, indeed, a most serious one, and must deeply interest the feelings of every American, as being very closely connected with an event which has plunged the whole nation in mourning. The reader will easily perceive, that the event to which I allude, is THE DEATH OF GENERAL WASHINGTON, and, if he has attended to the report of the physicians, he will as easily perceive, that their treatment of the deceased was in precise conformity to *the practice of Rush*.[8]

Cobbett estimated, on the basis of the physicians' report, that the sixty-eight-year-old Washington must have been bled of as much as nine pounds (nine pints in volume) of blood. He compared it to the total blood in the body of a man in the prime of life, which he considered would have been fifteen pounds:

> Thus, on the fatal 14th of December, on the same day, in the same evening, nay, in the very same hour, that a Philadelphia court & jury were laying on me a ruinous fine for having reprobated the practice of Rush, GENERAL WASHINGTON *was expiring while under the operation of that very practice!* On that day the victory of RUSH and of DEATH was complete. . . . General Washington has, I hope, broken the chains of the grim tyrant, Death, and soared into the realms of immortal glory.[9]

The effort to ruin Rush's reputation by attributing the general's death to extreme bleeding practices might have been less successful had Rush not had something of a history with Washington dating back to the revolutionary war.[10] Rush became involved in what came to be called the Conway cabal—a group of officers made up of General Thomas Conway, General Horatio Gates, General Thomas Mifflin, and General Charles Lee—who were critical of Washington during a time in the war when American forces were facing heavy losses.[11] Washington's loss of New York and his failure to protect Philadelphia from British occupation played a large role in his loss of support, as did unsuccessful battles at Brandywine and Germantown.[12] Tom Paine, for one, serving as aide-de-camp to General Nathanael Greene at Fort Lee, was scathing in his judgment of Washington: "the injudicious choice of positions taken by [General Washington] in the campaign of 1776 . . . necessarily produced the losses and misfortunes that marked that gloomy campaign."[13] The *Aurora, General Advertiser*, a republican newspaper run by Benjamin Franklin Bache, was particularly harsh in questioning Washington's leadership. Bache published a letter from John Adams to Brigadier General Samuel Holden Parsons in 1776 essentially condemning the general for incompetence:

> there are strong Marks of Negligence, Indolence, Presumption, and Inadequacy on our Side, by which scandalous Attributes We lost the Island wholly and Manhattan Island nearly . . . for a General to be surprised by an Enemy, just under his nose, in open day and caught in a State of wanton Security, from an overweening presumption in his own Strength, is a crime of so capital a nature as to admit of neither Alleviation nor Pardon.[14]

Adams later supported Washington as the man most fit to head the new nation, but not without considerable reservations about his qualifications to govern and strong feelings about a tendency to idolize the general. He shared his feelings with Rush in 1790:

> The History of our Revolution will be one continued Lye from one end to the other. The essence of the whole will be *that Dr. Franklin's electrical Rod, smote the Earth and out sprung General Washington. That Franklin electrified him with his rod—and thence forward these two conducted all the Policy, Negotiations, Legislatures and War.* These underscored Lines contain the whole Fable Plot and Catastrophy. . . . But this, my friend, to be serious, is the Fate of all ages and Nations . . . No Nation can adore more than one man at a time.[15]

For his part, in 1777 Rush had reported officers' comments to Adams during the war comparing Washington unfavorably to General Gates who, they felt, ran a well-disciplined army:

> The same gentlemen have compared General Washington's imitation of an army to an unformed mob. Look at the characters of both! The one on the pinnacle of

> military glory. . . . See the other outgeneraled and twice beaten. . . . If our Congress can witness these things with composure and suffer them to pass without an inquiry, I shall think we have not shook off monarchical prejudices and that like the Israelites of old we worship the work of our hands.[16]

In the same letter, Rush injudiciously attributed to General Conway a remark, intended to refer to Washington, that would plague Rush in later years: "A great and good God . . . has decreed that America shall be free, or ____ and weak counselors would have ruined her long ago."[17]

Perhaps the most damaging testimony against Rush was an anonymous letter he wrote in 1778 to Patrick Henry in which he encouraged Henry to make the contents public but to destroy the letter itself. The letter treated corruption in the army hospitals, implied a lack of leadership in the middle army—Washington's command—and reported that the army had become a "*mob*. Discipline unknown, or *wholly* neglected."[18] Reminding Henry that "The northern army has shown us what Americans are capable of doing with a GENERAL at their head," the author recommended "A Gates, a Lee, or a Conway" to turn the rabble into "an irresistible body of men." He repeated for Henry's ears the comment attributed to Conway and concluded by asking his reader to protect his anonymity:

> You may rest assured of *each* of the facts related in this letter. The author of it is one of your Philadelphia friends. A hint of his name, if found out by the handwriting, must not be mentioned to your most intimate friend. Even the letter *must* be thrown in the fire. But some of its contents ought to be made public in order to awaken, enlighten, and alarm our country. I rely upon your prudence.[19]

In a letter to John Adams after the war, in 1789, in which he did identify himself, Rush again asked that a letter of his be destroyed. Once more, he made scathing comments like those in his anonymous letter to Patrick Henry.[20]

> At no time after the year 1777 . . . did I believe him to be the "first in war" in our country. In addition to the testimonies of Stephen, Reed, and Mifflin, I had directly or indirectly the testimonies of [General Nathanael] Greene, [Alexander] Hamilton, Colonel [Tench], your son-in-law, and of many of the most intelligent officers who served under him to the contrary. . . . Were I to mention all that I have heard of his "heart," and from some of his friends too, it would appear that he was not possessed of all the divine attributes that have been ascribed to him. But enough of this hateful subject! . . . I earnestly request that you destroy this letter as you read it. I do not wish it to be known that General W. [ashington] was deficient.[21]

Toward the end of his life, in 1804, Rush found himself tearing desperately through his papers to excise his intemperate remarks.[22] He protested against inclusion of parts of the most damaging of his letters in Chief Justice John Marshall's *Life of Washington*, though to little avail. Marshall's only concession, in what can only be taken as an ironic comment on the whole affair, was to suppress the identity of the author.[23]

Of the two potentially most disturbing events of his life—the prosecution of William Cobbett and his relationship with George Washington—Rush's autobiography had little to say. On the day of the trial verdict, December 14, 1799, he neglected to note the successful conclusion of his trial; he did, however, in an understated and clinically cold notice on that day remark upon the passing of George Washington:

> This day died, universally lamented, General Washington. His disease was the Cynanche Trachialis. It proved fatal in 14 hours. He was patient and resigned in his illness. He said his will was made, his private affairs settled, and his public business but two days behind. He wished his physicians to enable him to die easy. Congress instituted public honors to his memory. The whole United States mourned for him as for a father.[24]

Washington was dead and so, apparently, was Rush's reputation. A Pyrrhic victory, having side-stepped a malpractice case and having rescued his honor in his libel trial, Rush would not in his lifetime escape that which he most feared: a stain on his honor that time could not erase.

PETER PORCUPINE V. PAUL POLE-CAT

A final word on the feud between Benjamin Rush and William Cobbett is in order, and that word comes from Hugh Henry Brackenridge, who was appointed to replace Justice Edward Shippen on the Pennsylvania Supreme Court when Shippen was elevated to the position of Chief Justice after the Rush trial. Brackenridge had been following the case on the sidelines from its inception and subsequent to the trial, in the 1804 edition of *Modern Chivalry*, published a satire commenting on it in a tale of Peter Porcupine and Paul Pole-cat. Brackenridge's satire is of particular interest, not only because it provides collateral cultural material by means of which to reflect on the issues raised in *Rush v. Cobbett* but because Brackenridge's extensive musings on the law in his novel and in his law manual *Law Miscellanies*[25] interpret for us a period perspective on courts, judges, juries, and litigants. This perspective gives us new insight into how the law was experienced and understood to offer an important cultural reference for understanding the Rush trial.

Paul Gilmore offers a view of Brackenridge that suggests he was a nuanced critic, a man who cut across the neoclassicism of his times to explore the devolved mechanics of human ambition and failure. Brackenridge defied sentiment and propriety, exposed elitism and professional pomposity, and gave us the worst one could expect from the democratic masses without giving up on them. Here was a robust republicanism that opened up American society and its problems along a continuum that ran from the truly reactionary to the radically democratic. Brackenridge urged his readers away from machine-like republicanism toward an alternative vision that led to a new understanding of the possibilities and the risks of democracy. Steven Watts argues that Brackenridge successfully explored social mores in the early republic with a mixed sense of admiration for foundational republican values and trepidation at the declension of valued traditions. Critical of many liberalizing trends, he was nevertheless in the forefront of those who were encouraged by the accomplishments of the self-made man in the early republic, as indeed he exemplified such a man. Brackenridge's work was broad in its scope, shedding light on the growth of liberal capitalism, republican virtue, civic humanism, and economic and political independence that came to define the last decade of the eighteenth century. At the same time, Brackenridge dealt with problems of identity formation characteristic of the swiftly changing institutions and values of the new republic.[26] Brackenridge thus models for us the struggles we find exemplified in the Rush trial to define Americanism, to navigate conflicting ideologies, and to manage the risks of democracy.

Recalling Cobbett's arrival in Philadelphia in 1794 and his creation of a wildly popular newspaper enjoyed as far away as Boston by President Adams's wife Abigail,[27] Brackenridge's tale of Peter Porcupine and Paul Polecat captured the advent of a new voice in William Cobbett, a voice capable of shocking a community's sensibilities. The tale took place in a culture of journalism that expressed little respect for personal privacy and exploited a period in which juries were loath to convict editors whose newspapers abused freedom of speech. Brackenridge was in good company in his satire of Cobbett's newspaper.[28] Mathew Carey considered *Porcupine's Gazette* a "pestiferous paper"[29] and expressed his hostility to Cobbett's "falsehoods of the most revolting kind—abandoned audacity—atrocious calumny—the most filthy and wretched Billingsgate[30] and buffoonery—cursing, swearing, and blasphemy."[31] He went so far as to assign to Cobbett the title "Director General of the United States,"[32] warning that not even Satan himself had so fierce a thirst for drawing blood.[33] Philip Freneau was no less uncomplimentary in his sentiments, regarding Cobbett as the craftiest of characters, a tool of the English prime minister William Pitt who became obnoxious with all who disagreed with him and his politics. As for Cobbett's *Gazette*, Freneau found it "a despicable Mess of Scurrility"[34] that demeaned Ben Franklin's once noble profession. Its editor's bark, he held, was like nothing so much as "a puppy to snap, or a bull dog to bite."[35] Reduced to doggerel in "On the Departure of Peter Porcupine," Freneau welcomed Cobbett's departure to England with the words: "I hear him screech, I hear him shout!/The storm had put his Rush-light out—/I see him famish'd with sour crout."[36]

Brackenridge's take on Cobbett appeared in the form of a tale of misfortune that struck a village when a printer whose "device was the Porcupine" set up a paper by subscription. Within a month, the printer began lampooning his neighbors, "searching into the secrets of families, and publishing matters of individuals, with which, whether true or false, the public had nothing to do; ridiculing virtue as if it was vice; and this in so low and disorderly a manner, that the more intelligent have disapproved of it; but the bulk read, and it seems to increase rather than curtail his subscribers."[37] One of the townspeople in Brackenridge's tale, Paul Pole-cat, was so offended by Porcupine's version of a free press, that he captured a polecat in the mountains and put it in a cage in an office close to that of the Porcupine. Boys and dogs of the town provoked the cat through the bars, so that Peter and his family were "besprinkled with the effluvia and offended with the odour of the animal."[38] Responding to Peter's justification that he merely practiced freedom of the press, Pole-cat felt himself justified, "that it is but retaliation to the worse than animal odor that proceeds from the press of Porcupine; for, as this affects the organ of smelling, that disgusts the judgment of the mind. . . . The olfactory organ is offended by Paul, but the heart is wounded by Peter."[39]

The protagonist of the novel, a peregrinating gentleman called Captain Farrago, identified the dispute as "a weighty question" and yet "a most delicate thing"[40] and raised questions about its nature: "Is it local or general politics? Is it any disagreement with regard to your corporate interests, or is religion the cause? Has any flagrant instance of moral turpitude, or exceeding knavery in an individual, roused you to this excess of violence and exclamation?"[41] The dispute, he concluded, animated the public in a free government because it concerned a decision about liberty and rights, "The right of conscience, the right of property and the right of reputation."[42]

Brackenridge's queries recalled Cobbett's effort to reframe the case Rush had brought against him by appealing to his right to speak his conscience freely and his rights as an English citizen.[43] Equally, they reflected Rush's concern for his reputation and livelihood, both as forms of property. The trial, like the dispute, considered what areas of law should apply: freedom of the press (the public's right to information), libel by the defendant (the privacy rights of individuals), and the responsibility of public figures (protecting the common welfare). Farrago's juxtaposition of local and general politics was, as well, a concern for the Rush case, albeit with larger, more general implications for the city, for the country as a whole, and for international relations.

In Brackenridge's tale, restraining orders were issued to keep the polecat under a matting as well as to restrain the Porcupine's quills, in spite of which a rumor arose that a fresh cat had been brought in.[44] The Captain anticipated this breach of public order with an announcement that "all annoyances by steam, vapour or effluvia proceeding from a pole-cat shall be suspended during the pendency of this question; and it is an evasion to substitute another badger, and by that means attempt to elude the stipulation."[45] Not only were such violations of restraining orders common fodder for the law, but the recalcitrant Cobbett was repeatedly plagued by recognizances to prevent his continuing attacks and potential breaches of the peace.

Having dealt with the breach of order, Captain Farrago determined that a town meeting should be held in which the dispute could be adjudicated. Making the case for the Porcupine, an advocate claimed "the press is the palladium of liberty," much as if it had fallen from Jupiter. Reciting the popular mantra that "freedom of the press is essential to liberty," the advocate offset the prospect of a finding of libel by arguing that to muzzle the press was to "muzzle the mouth of man." As essential to the amusement of men as chasing the hounds, the press sometimes ascended to "observations on the state of empires, and the characters of great men" and sometimes descended "to the subordinate, affairs of individuals, and private persons." The editor, in sum, had to be all things to all men, for he would find that "Guts and garbage delight bears; and swine will swill the trough in preference to the running stream. Black-guardism is the gout of many. Nay, it is the more prevailing taste; 'The world is naturally averse/To all the Truth it sees or hears;/But swallow nonsense and a lie,/With greediness and gluttony.'"[46] Americans, the advocate concluded, craved indelicacy and like wild beasts "they digest scurrility." He embraced the label of "a blackguard press," for blackguards, like any other men, had rights and, he contended, "while there are blackguards to write, must they not have a press? Is it only men of polished education that have a right to express their sentiments . . . to amuse themselves and others by their lucubrations? You call us the Swinish Multitude, and yet refuse us the food that is natural to us."[47] Porcupine, by implication, spoke for the common herd and for its right to be heard, just as Cobbett had himself contended in his own publications.

Beyond pleasing one's readers and staying in business, the need to address intent was argued by a second advocate. Porcupine, after all, was responsible to a tradition of scurrility, given its considerable utility and its long roots in history as a means of keeping authority honest and speaking truth when the emperor was naked. The tradition reached back to the jester who made certain that royalty gauged correctly the prevailing wind in the kingdom: "Men will hear from the buffoon or the jester, things they would not take from a friend, and scarcely from a confessor . . . even when there was no wit, it was taken for wit; so now, when an editor means to divert, however dull his abuse, it ought to be the mode to laugh, to keep those who know no better in countenance."[48] The press, after all, was to be understood as no less than a form of truth, however witty, vulgar, or abusive that truth might prove, a tack Cobbett's team exploited in his defense, arguing that ridicule, satire, humor were legitimate weapons of the press. Brackenridge himself, however, was less supportive in sections of the novel that he reserved for the author's own commentary on the press. There, Brackenridge established limits on the press's powers. He cast doubt upon the use of scurrilous language that "did harm to the cause which it was thought to serve. . . . An intemperate partisan in public or private life, can never serve any cause." The press might expand what the courts must confine, but this required a greater sensitivity to language than Porcupine allowed, Brackenridge argued: "Even the war of the sword has its laws.—It is not allowable to poison springs, or the means of life. In a paper war nothing is justifiable that does not tend to establish a position, or determine a controversy; that which outrages humanity, is the cruelty of a savage who puts to death with torture, or disfigures, to gratify revenge."[49] In the face of actual objections to Cobbett's Porcupine, Brackenridge nevertheless found himself defending Cobbett, holding "that though occasionally coarse in his language, and gross in his reflections, yet such a spirit and stile of writing, was necessary to counteract the excess of democratic principles; that in fact, it did good."[50] Indeed, nothing so conserved a government, Brackenridge conceded in *Law Miscellanies*, as the press, stressing

> perpetual vigilance, and free discussion of the integrity and wisdom of the administration of affairs, or of the qualifications for official duty in such as are called upon, or offer themselves for office or delegation. The *manner* in which this is done may be *exceptionable*; but the thing is *necessary*, and without which the spirit of liberty could not be preserved. I incline therefore, even in a doubtful construction, to lean to that most favorable to the *freedom of the press*; and the privilege of citizens to be heard on the official conduct of officers, or men in public capacity, or where the matter published is proper for public information.[51]

Given the two extremes, free exercise of the press in Brackenridge's satire needed to be contained or balanced against the enjoyment of one's privileges. Here, Pole-cat's representative spoke against Porcupine touting the need for an antidote to the press and sponsoring the odor of the cat as a candidate for the post. In the spirit of a free and democratic marketplace of odors, he matched the freedom of the press to "the freedom of the express":

> Nay the word *expression* which is common to both institutions, the artificial one of the types, and the natural one of the cat, shews the original to be similar, and

> the comparison to *run on all fours*. . . . Shall the bark of trees made into powder, and this powder into a liquid, impregnated with thought, and put upon paper, and carried to the press, be accounted harmless, notwithstanding the violence of the decoction, yet the wild cats that inhabit those trees, and are denizens of the forest, be prohibited the haunts of men, because of a bag under their tails which contains all unsavory distillation, and may occasionally be spurted upon men?[52]

Pole-cat's advocate argued that a common law right of self-defense should trump nuisance law abating "noisome smells," for the editor's "defamation is more offensive to the feelings of the mind, than the hogo of a civet to the sense of smelling." Retaliation would thereby balance the slander already allowed into people's houses.[53] Reframed by Pole-cat's advocate, nuisance law would be used to address interference with enjoyment of one's property:[54]

> If a man divert a stream from my meadow or obstruct one running through it, so as to dam it up, and drown the grass, have I not a remedy; shall this man at much expence and charge bring a beast from the mountains, tame it, or reduce it under his dominion, and apply it to a purpose in civilized and domestic life, and shall we say that the common law does not protect him in the enjoyment of its musk?[55]

The advocates having exhausted their arguments, the captain sought a precedent to break the tie, asking how the ancients would have heard the case and whether "nature was not then the same as it is now?" Was Aristophanes not "a great blackguard" himself; did not the ancients "call a spade a spade"; and did not the Romans allow for a Saturnalia "to exercise their faculties in all intemperance of language"?[56] In the end, an elder of the town proposed establishing a competitor to break Porcupine's monopoly. Where different family and party interests existed, "To have a printer all on one side, even though he be a dunce, is an inequality."[57] A man of democratic instincts, the captain endorsed the plan and put forward his Irish servant Teague O'Regan, a man of appropriate "low humour, and a sharp tongue; unbounded impudence,"[58] for the task:

> And what may be a restraint upon the licentiousness of his press, should he set up one, he is a most abominable coward; the idea of cudgeling will keep him in bounds; should he over-match Porcupine, and turn upon his employers. . . . What is more, he has been in France, and has a spice of the language, and a tang of Jacobinism in his principles, and conversation, that will match the contrary learning carried to an exorbitant excess in Peter Porcupine. . . . He may call it Mully-Grub, or give it some such title as will bespeak the nature, of the matter it will usually contain.[59]

Brackenridge brought his "allegory," as he called it, to an end when Cobbett ceased publishing. As he acknowledged in a chapter of author's observations that followed the trial scene, he had written the satire "while an editor of the name of Cobbet, published a paper under the title of 'Porcupine.' But the breaking up of that paper in a manner similar to that just stated, prevented the going on with the allegory, or the handing to the public by way of the press, in some shape, the pamphlet begun."[60] In the novel, the tale ended when Porcupine "decamped in the night,"[61] much as Cobbett himself had precipitously left Philadelphia for New York when his libel trial was about to begin and then fled to England following the verdict, leaving Rush's agents behind to seize his holdings. Brackenridge had Porcupine flee the town either out of fear of competition and loss of reputation or "what is more likely, the constables were after him for debt, his press and types having been seized the day before, and sold for rent . . . fines and penalties also hanging over him for libels; and damages recoverable in actions of defamation."[62] Although he considered resuming his satire at some later time, Brackenridge thought better of it when he heard of the fate of James Thomson Callender who, tried and found guilty under the Alien and Sedition Acts in 1800, drowned while bathing in the Potomac, an apparent suicide. To continue with the Cobbett satire, Brackenridge contended "would be like throwing water on a dead, or as the proverb is, a drowned rat."[63]

In the tale of Peter Porcupine and Paul Pole-cat, Brackenridge had produced what he called a vehicle to his thinking, like the ancients who "moralized in parables and feigned cases, a way of reasoning"[64] capable of providing "immediate and direct instruction."[65] Like Aesop, Brackenridge reached for a common understanding and was unafraid of finding in man his bestial origins. Like a good republican and a good Platonist, he treated matters of "maintaining and enlightening a republic,"[66] producing a tale of the "national character."[67] America, he warned, would get the press it deserved rather than the one it needed unless it took an interest in the conduct of the press. Toward that end, the tale represented an opportunity to correct the excesses of the press, most directly the "black-guardism"[68] of Cobbett's *Porcupine's Gazette* and his use of "Billingsgate" language.[69] That a gentleman like Rush would have to bring himself down to respond to a slanderer might be necessary to offset press attacks, particularly given the general vulgarity of the reading audience of the press and its demand that it had a right to a press of its own "party," that is, a blackguard press.[70] The greater risk, however, was the presumed infectiousness of Cobbett's work, reflected in the tale by children running home carrying the odor of the cat through the town[71] as well as in Brackenridge's comment that a leading editor in a great city who distinguishes himself "in any way" was imitated by editors in smaller towns so that "one black sheep, gives the rot to the herd."[72] Thus, while a man who has been slandered might not hope to correct his adversary, he ought to improve, as Brackenridge's tale intended, the judgment of the people. Not to do so, to allow the circulation of press scurrility, was to tolerate "a disgrace to a people." The press was far too useful to society in a free government and the dignity of its editor "too elevated in his own regard of its honor"[73] to allow its abuse, to allow it to escape censure.

Brackenridge placed the press in the company of the Scriptures and the courts, one of three great means of protecting and improving the republic. Whereas morality and justice were the respective provinces of its companions, its duty was "as sacred as the priesthood"[74] and its sphere of action greater than the law. As America was beyond all governments in the freedom it granted the press, Brackenridge's concern for its honor was matched only by his strong sense that its abuses constituted a form of assassination. The press, after all, was the shield of liberty, preserving the essential rights of conscience, reputation, and property.[75] As it was essential to liberty and thereby protected by the state and federal constitutions, the press must be free, Brackenridge argued.[76] Even its scurrility as a means of correcting foibles had been time-tested from antiquity. The press thus acted as a safety valve, a means of public reform, and a restraint upon the powerful. Indeed, as in the tale, festivals, court fools, and comic poets constituted precedent: what, he asked, would the ancients have said or done.[77]

Even in this context, however, Brackenridge regarded Cobbett as a figure of monstrous proportions. Linking the journalist to the republican editor Callender, and through Callender to the alien-sedition trials, Brackenridge was unwilling to see the press further degraded: "the example of the two monsters mentioned, has had the effect to disgust the public, and lead to a reform of . . . imitations of their blackguard personalities."[78] By calling Callender into play, Brackenridge reminded his readers to take an evenhanded approach to the tale. It was not merely a question of Cobbett the porcupine, the federalist, stirring the rabble for his own amusement and profit, not merely a question of catering to the delight of the rabble[79] by endorsing their desire to exercise a right of free expression that ought not to be restricted to their masters alone.[80] Rather, it was a question of porcupines (federalists) and polecats (republicans) both agitating their factions; it was a generic question of the press at large as an institution. Asked to recall the American and French Revolutions, Brackenridge's audience was reminded that the press might have served a useful and purposeful agitation and propaganda role in the past, having indulged the "stirrings of men's minds with a potential convulsion."[81] Now, however, "deliberate reason, and prudent temperament are necessary, to preserve what is gained, and to turn it to advantage."[82] Brackenridge's initial resolution of Porcupine's altercation with Pole-cat might have called for a balance of rights whereby a monopoly of expressive rights was busted and rabble on each side would be provided with a party press of their own. His ultimate and preferred solution, in the end, would be a "chaste and pure paper containing solid information, and strictures useful to the republic,"[83] a paper that would protect the liberty of the press and the attendant rights of its public equally. We need not, then, Brackenridge reminded his readers, "buff at a bear when there is no bear to buff at."[84] Indeed, once Porcupine decamped in the night[85] and Callender drowned, the prospect of just such a pristine press allowed Brackenridge himself to decamp from his tale.

The tale, as we have seen, raised issues central to an eighteenth-century preoccupation with the order of the new nation and threats to both its self-governance and its sustainability. The potential of mob violence, for example,[86] represented a hue and cry form of assembly that responded to the self-organization and contentious issues that typified the early democracy. Captain Farrago decried such madness as an act of violence invoked by a lack of law in the western Pennsylvania territories of the novel. It was the same kind of unrest threatened by failed law incapable of resolving conflicts between a man libeled and the libeling press. Farrago called for an orderly assembly under the advice of a judgelike figure to exert the "virtues of temperance and moderation,"[87] a role for which he was himself nominated by a fellow townsman. The qualifications offered were those Brackenridge had recommended in a jurist throughout *Modern Chivalry*: a man experienced by travel, possessing learning and humanity, with the skill to resolve differences, and with the reputation of one who studied to do good and by whom none had ever been injured.[88] The assembly was meant to be the very prototype of an orderly court, one that would capitalize on men of the robes to preserve decorum and assign times of speaking,[89] a transitional form arising out of ad hoc proceedings and leading to formal adversarial litigation.[90] To ensure the public's acceptance of the assembly and its legitimacy as a deliberative body, so that its rules would be respected, the captain maintained that men must put away their swords and adjourn to cool their tempers before the issues could be engaged.[91] In the meantime, the author teased out the issues over which the assembly should have jurisdiction, as opposed to those that were a matter of municipal regulation and thereby required a form of legislative consensus.[92] Invoking a cross-section of community interests, the issues served as a reminder of essential questions for founding a social order, from questions of politics to those of corporate interests, religion, and morality.[93] The town thus resolved jurisdiction, venue, and standing before the court: what authority should this body have and over what issues; did one body trump another; was there a separation and balancing of authority? An incorporated borough could regulate a new trade by an executive or legislative function whereas common law on nuisance and freedom of speech would invoke a judicial decision.[94] Modes of analysis would differ as well. Common law represented general reason applied to a particular case and relied upon precedents of different types—custom, usage, tradition, and prior judicial decisions. Borough regulation was case specific, particular, and regulatory as a form of "police," or public welfare and security.

Beyond such foundational questions, the law had to be specifically applied in the case of *Porcupine v. Pole-cat*, requiring legal tests, reasoning, and principles. How in Brackenridge's faux court would one identify what was a right and what was not; how were rights to be balanced against one another; what weight should be assigned to one relative to others? Relating liberty of the press, public security, and private reputation meant that government repression, press abuse, and an individual's public role would have to be added to the mix. Reasoning by applying a principle to an individual instance would differ from reasoning by analogy, so that comparable outcomes would be difficult to anticipate over time. Brackenridge's central focus was the balance of rights, which weighed whether one's enjoyment of a right interfered with another's enjoyment of that right or conflicted with enjoyment of yet another right. Enjoining one's enjoyment to enforce a common superseding right or simply enjoining temporarily to resolve an issue became a means of enforcing or regulating rights. What, in sum, marked the limit or boundary of a right and who had the greater right to enjoyment? Was it a question of individual as opposed to collective enjoyment, of voluntary as opposed to involuntary enjoyment, or enjoyment only to the point that one transgressed another's enjoyment? The odor of the civet, it could be argued, trespassed the rights of others not to have to smell the cat. On the other hand, the civet's noisome smell constituted by analogy an "expression" commensurate to that of Porcupine's press. It was, after all, a noisome smell, an offensive stink that freely expressed the party from which it emanated. Both the press and the cat represented potentially abatable nuisances or protected liberties. On the one hand, they were a statement, a form of speech; on the other, they were acts of retribution or self-defense. Whether they were symbols, acts, or expressions, the common laws of nuisance and speech were made to apply to the "express" (the smell) and the press (the statement) equally. In one sense, the cat's odor reified the effect of speech, translating the "rot" represented by the abuse of free speech into physiological terms. The spread of the odor translated into Porcupine's infectious influence upon other presses. At the same time, Brackenridge questioned whether the emissions of the cat and the slander of the press were commensurate as nuisances. Did the slander of the press wound the heart just as the cat's smell offended the olfactory organs and was it thereby an equal nuisance? If express and press, smell and slander made for poor logic as analogies in terms of the common law of nuisance, did they make any better an analogy as they applied to the common law of free speech? One might or might not choose to read a newspaper, whereas an odor was less a matter of choice. By contrast, even if there was no saving oneself from the exhalation of the cat, volition as it applied to the press was less successfully argued when a newspaper held a monopoly and other opinions were thereby prevented from being heard. In terms of protection, free speech was protected as a social good, whereas odor was not so protected. Even so, one could argue, the cat's smell might enjoy as great a protection as a course of water that none may divert. As weak as they were, the analogies nevertheless held long enough, whether as nuisance or as free speech, that an injunction was applied to subject the effusions of both press and express. The cat was caged and Porcupine's quills restrained, although Porcupine breached the peace by violating the injunction, just as in *Rush v. Cobbett*, which encouraged Pole-cat to do the same.

Brackenridge's use of balanced rights and common law analogies structured not only the debate over the contested rights claimed by Porcupine and Pole-cat, but the verdict delivered by the assembly. The verdict expressed again an equality between the body and the mind, holding that "the licentiousness of the press is not more a nuisance in the moral, than offensive smells are in the physical world,"[95] as a college man who contributed to the verdict was to say. The verdict generally agreed-upon was, in fact, the work of four experienced figures: an elderly inhabitant, the captain, a college man, and a principal of an academy. A laughing man encouraged them to create a Judas-goat, from whom their purpose might be concealed, to act as a stalking horse. Along that line, the four found merit in the idea of a comic solution to deflate the situation by means of a counterpress of the same ilk as Porcupine's. The captain advised calling it the "Mully-Grub."[96] "[W]hen the useful is mixed with the jest, I count every point gained," added the college man; "It is only by an appeal to feeling that the mind sometimes can be awakened."[97]

Thus, in a preliminary solution, those offended by the press should enjoy an equal right to offend, that different interests might survive and none experience a hardship. In this resolve, blackguardism might match its counterpart or at the very least burlesque it: "He must out Herod Herod in all that is scurrilous,"[98] the captain's Scottish servant M'Dougal added, irritating his master by his excess in proposing "Rams Horn" for its name, that it might all the better, on the analogy of Jericho, knock down Porcupine's press.[99] Brackenridge's parable of the Porcupine was just such a ploy. Agitating his own readers by his comic treatment of the contemporaneous feud between Rush and Cobbett, Brackenridge amused and instructed, pleased that with the death of Callender and the departure of Cobbett the scurrility of the press in America had, he believed, abated. *Porcupine v. Pole-Cat* would serve as Brackenridge's pulpit, his court of judicature, and his press in one to enlighten the new republic, serving reason much like the ancient poets, philosophers, and fools he so admired.

As a Pennsylvania Supreme Court justice appointed immediately after the *Rush v. Cobbett* case, and who would sit in other cases with the very justices who heard *Rush v. Cobbett*, Brackenridge reflected legal thinking on the press and the courts that was comparable to that of the justices who had heard the Rush case and that clearly would have been informed by those justices' reflections on the case. Brackenridge's take placed the press and the courts on a continuum whereby the one was accessory to the other, such that a publisher venting in a gazette might well preserve society from "battery and bloodshed."[100] But whereas some thought it better "to argue all matters of meum, or tuum, in the public papers,"[101] Brackenridge found the press was more likely to spread a controversy and give fighting words greater permanence than otherwise. Law, by this argument, needed to check the press, both by standing between it and those would cudgel a publisher and by preventing the press from persecuting judges.[102] Brackenridge conceded that, without the correction of the courts, a runaway editor who did not libel "could threaten to libel, and compel a submission"[103] which would itself carry the threat of despotism.[104] At the same time, a public man need not be so fearful of the press in personal matters, for "I should not think," he contended, "the public had any interest in their amours, their costumes, as for instance the cut of their pantaloons, of the colour of their breeches; or peccadillos, even in the breaches of decorum."[105] On this argument, personal libel reduced itself for Brackenridge to a question of "exasperated vanity" or "irritated pride."[106] Men were not hurt as much as they thought, he claimed, given "that every character has a natural station, from which it cannot be effectively degraded."[107]

This argument was made by Cobbett's defense, although its effect on Justice Shippen is questionable given the judge's addiction to the need to restrain offences of this kind and to the suppression of "so great an evil."[108] Certainly Rush's counsel felt that suppression of the press was a risky notion and one reason why the doctor was advised against suing the journalist. Addressing himself to Philadelphians, Brackenridge acknowledged the state of litigiousness in the city, the excesses of the press in writing a man down, and the need for reform of the law to protect against a state of affairs in which the entire press was tarred with the same brush. In particular, he cited Cobbett who, he claimed, "had done good service indirectly in bringing into disrepute the language of what the English call Billingsgate; and that abuse which knows no restraint of decency, delicacy, or refinement."[109] Although he left prosecution open as a potential check on such abuse,[110] Brackenridge nevertheless saw little in Cobbett's "coarse language" and "gross reflections"[111] to justify the kind of attack on "the excess of democratic principles" that prosecution of Cobbett would have entailed, as Cobbett did more than enough harm to his own cause by his intemperate partisanship.

On the question of determining whether Rush should have been considered a public figure, and thereby vulnerable to press attacks without effective recourse to a libel prosecution, Brackenridge applied Blackstone to the effect that only those "who endeavor to pursue, in humble life,—The noiseless tenor of their way"[112] were truly entitled to their privacy. Rush's counsel might have argued that Rush was entitled both to protection of his privacy as a private figure and to protection under the public peace as a public servant in a time of a great health emergency, but such double-dipping would have been unlikely to appeal to Brackenridge who preferred the clarity of the public-private distinctions he borrowed from Blackstone. If Brackenridge's standard was that those whose conduct did not concern the community should not be dragged from their private abodes into the public light,[113] Rush was not a good fit. Considering the controversy arising from the doctors' wars over Rush's treatments,[114] neither did he fit Brackenridge's standard that a matter be considered private if it was vexatious rather than infamous.

Having chosen a satiric novel as an avenue for comment, Brackenridge found himself without quite so large a readership as a trial by press and without the authority to resolve a conflict in as determinative a way as a court case. Whereas the gentlemanly Rush would not have chosen to have his case called and heard before his neighbors in such a middle class venue as a novel, Brackenridge made good use of the medium to ground the law in the lives of his audience, to mold a law more responsive to those whose affairs it regulated, and to model giving common people greater access to the law. The author, in any case, provided a warning, lest one go too easily into the dark night of such law: "For what man without indignation and bitter resentment, can bear the touch of the slanderer, more especially if that slander is of a private, and domestic nature and alludes to what cannot be explained or defended. Not that it is true, but a man in the just pride of standing in society, would scorn to appeal to the public or bring it to court!"[115] As he considered retaliation against the kind of press Cobbett operated, Brackenridge raised and answered his own question: "But what could [one] do? The same language was unbecoming a gentleman. The like strictures of foibles or of faults on the part of an adversary, could only become the characters of a subordinate."[116] In the Rush case, comparable advice was provided to the plaintiff, and duly ignored. Brackenridge's summary judgment on Porcupine v. Pole-cat was thus to declare that the case ought never to have gone to trial. That it did spoke volumes about the litigiousness of Philadelphians that Shippen, McKean, Hopkinson, and Brackenridge had all condemned and little to the credit of either party in the case. Brackenridge's last word in *Rush v. Cobbett*, it appeared, would be that, for all the fire and storm it provoked, the case ended in *Modern Chivalry* where it began in *Porcupine's Gazette*, as a fit subject for satire.

NOTES

1. *Rush-Light* IV, March 31, 1800; Cobbett (1801a, 11: 385–86.)
2. *Rush-Light* IV, March 31, 1800; Cobbett (1801a, 11: 385); the poem reads:

A DIALOGUE BETWEEN RUSH AND PORCUPINE

Rush: Master Peter, you see, with my twelve sov'reign men,
I have tipp'd you a squeeze for the strokes of your pen.
These twelve sov'reign men, now I no longer need them,
How shall I reward?

Peter: Why bleed them, Rush, bleed them.

Rush: But to the Judge on the bench, so just and humane,
(The worthy successor and tool of M'Kean);
To my lawyers who bellow'd so loudly against you,
To Hopkinson, Ingersol, Levi the Jew,
The half-quaker Lewis (who once was a carter),
And your faithful counsel, the mob-courting Harper;
To my volunteer witnesses, grateful young Mease,
To the poor Dr. Coxe, and poor granny Dewees,
(Who gen'rously came, with no duty to urge them),
What return shall I make?

Peter: Why, purge them, Rush, purge them.

Enter Grave Digger.

Grav. Dig: By my soul; Master Peter, I think it too hard,
That with such folks as these I must fill my church yard.

Peter: Church-yard! honest fellow, my meaning's not such;
For, where a man's buried it matters not much;
And the great Dr. Mitchell (of bleeding renown)
Says, "let all human carrion be dragg'd out of town."

3. *Rush-Light* IV, March 31, 1800; Cobbett (1801a, 11: 366).
4. *Rush-Light* IV, March 31, 1800; Cobbett (1801a, 11: 385).
5. Freneau (1963, 3: 240–41). The rest of the poem reads:

A bird of might attends the sail
That now towards us turns her tail
With Porcupine, escaped from jail. . . .

This hero of the pension'd pen
Has left our shores, and left his den
To write *at home* for English men.

Five thousand dollars, we may guess,
Hath made his pension something less—
So, Peter left us,—in distress. . . .

I hear him screech, I hear him shout!—
The storm has put his *Rush light* out—
I see him famish'd with *sour crout*.

May on the groaning vessel's side
All Neptune's ruffian strength be try'd
Till every seam is gaping wide.

And while the waves about him swell
May not one triton blow the shell
(A sign at sea of doing well):

But should he reach the british shore,
(The land that englishmen adore)
One trouble will he find and more:

His pen will run at such a rate,
His malice so provoke *the great*,
They soon will drive him out of date.

With broken heart and blunted pen
He'll sink among the *little* men
Or scribble in some Newgate den.

Alack, alack! he might have stay'd
And followed *here* the *scribbling* trade,
And lived without the royal aid.

But democratic laws he hated,
Our government he so be-rated
That his own projects he defeated.

He took his leave from Sandy Hook,
And parted with a surly look,
That all observed and few mistook.

Freneau (1815, 1: 76–79).

6. Neilson and Neilson (1958, 178).

7. On the death of Washington, see Davies, Davies, and Sanders (February 18, 1983, 912–15); Wallenborn (September 23, 2004); Butterfield (1951b, 2: 1197–1208).

8. *Porcupine's Gazette*, January 13, 1800; Cobbett (1801a, 12: 146–47).

9. *Porcupine's Gazette,* January 13, 1800; Cobbett (1801a, 12: 150).

10. Binger (1966, 132–39); Goodman (1934, 107–27); Butterfield (1951b, 2: 1197–1208).

11. Butterfield (1951b, 2: 1201).
12. Goodman (1934, 108).
13. *Aurora*, November 21, 1776; Rosenfeld (1997, 301–2).
14. *Aurora*, October 2, 1776; Rosenfeld (1997, 297).
15. April 4, 1790, letter from John Adams; Butterfield (1951b, 2: 1207).
16. October 21, 1777, letter to John Adams; Rush (1951, 1: 159–60).
17. October 21, 1777, letter to John Adams; Rush (1951, 1: 161).
18. January 12, 1778, letter to Patrick Henry; Rush (1951, 1: 183).
19. January 12, 1778, letter to Patrick Henry; Rush (1951, 1: 183).
20. Goodman (1934, 118); Butterfield (1951b, 2: 1206–7); Corner (1948, 4–9).
21. April 6, 1789, letter to John Adams; Rosenfeld (1997, 345).
22. Corner (1948, 6).
23. Butterfield (1951b 2: 1206–7). Butterfield characterizes Rush's letter to John Marshall as agitated and a set of letters to Marshall's intermediary Bushrod Washington, nephew of the deceased president, as "urgent pleas"; Rush (1951, 2: 889 note 1). Rush requested the suppression of comments in a letter from Washington to Henry (March 28, 1778) in which Washington had indicated that Rush had played the hypocrite by using "the most elaborate and studious professions of regard" (as quoted by Rush in his September 5, 1804 letter to John Marshall (2: 887) long after Rush had written his letter to Henry. In his September 5, 1804, letter to Marshall, Rush denied any association with those military officers who doubted General Washington's abilities and criticized Washington's conduct: "I declare I neither conversed with nor corresponded with the gentlemen who were publicly said to be hostile to General Washington. . . . The private anecdotes alluded to, with the names of the persons who related them, I have always intended should descend to the grave with me" (2: 888).
24. Rush (1948, 248–49).
25. Brackenridge (1814).
26. Watts (1986, 128, 144).
27. Mitchell (April 18, 1945–October 17, 1945, 347). Karen K. List (1983, 8–9) quotes Abigail Adams in the following terms: that Cobbett's "shafts are always typt with wit, and his humor is such as frequently to excite more of good than ill"; Wilson (1994, 37) quotes her as well: "He can write very handsomely and he can descend and be as low and vulgar as a fishwoman," a combination she found a "strange mixture." Cobbett spoke of *Porcupine's Gazette* "surpassing in extent of numbers, any [paper] ever known in America . . . by the year 1800, I might safely have asserted, that there was not in the whole country, one single family, in which some part or the other of my writings had not been read"; *Political Register* IV (1804, 150-51), as quoted in Reitzel (1935, 242).
28. Cobbett's most publicized altercations were with Benjamin Franklin Bache and Matthew Carey; see Burns (2006, 338–50); Carey (1942, 30); see also, Clark (1939); Cole (1924); Rosenfeld (1997); Smith (1953a); Smith (1953b); Woodbury (1919-1920); List (1983); Reitzel (1935).
29. Carey (1799b, v).
30. The term "Billingsgate" originated in the seventeenth century to refer to one of the gates of London where a fish market was located and where rhetoric of abusive

language was common fare. The term was used to refer to Cobbett by the pseudonymous Paul Hedgehog, a pseudonym for Mathew Carey's brother James, in the *Aurora*, accusing him of "Billingsgate rhetoric"; Cobbett (1797, v).

31. Carey (1799b, v).
32. Carey (1799b, 22).
33. Carey (1799b, v, 13).
34. *Time-Piece*, September 13, 1797.
35. *Time-Piece*, September 13, 1797.
36. Freneau (1963, 3: 240).
37. Brackenridge (1965, 334).
38. Brackenridge (1965, 332).
39. Brackenridge (1965, 334).
40. Brackenridge (1965, 335).
41. Brackenridge (1965, 333).
42. Brackenridge (1965, 335).
43. *Rush-Light* IV, March 31, 1800; Cobbett (1801a, 11: 355–59, 364).
44. Having indeed brought a new badger to town, Pole-cat defended his violation of the restraining order as a preemptive move against Porcupine's hire of more journeymen to enlarge his sheet. As he argued, "I thought it not amiss to extend the scale of my vapour and employ two conduits instead of one . . . not to have regress, or egress, until this assembly shall dissolve, nor for a reasonable time after, that enudo, and reenudo, or going as well as coming you may be safe let what will be the issue of the controversy; whether I am to break up stock, or be suffered to go on"; Brackenridge (1965, 340).
45. Brackenridge (1965, 339).
46. Brackenridge (1965, 337).
47. Brackenridge (1965, 340).
48. Brackenridge (1965, 340).
49. Brackenridge (1965, 351).
50. Brackenridge (1965, 445).
51. Brackenridge (1814, 226).
52. Brackenridge (1965, 338).
53. Brackenridge (1965, 338).
54. Brackenridge's analogies described the townspeople's application of legal principles in terms of nuisance law and the right to enjoyment of one's property. Under the maxim of *sic utere*, one was prevented from using one's own property so as to harm others' enjoyment of their property, while under the maxim of *salus populi* the welfare of the public required the elimination of nuisances. By extension, one had the ability to prevent others from interfering with one's use of one's own land, as well as the ability to constrain one's neighbor from using his land in a way that conflicted with one's enjoyment. Not only did such principles prevent the development of land use, but they reflected deeply held prerogatives related to private property in the face of both protecting the health and welfare of the public and making use of the land for the good of the public (*pro bono publico*). In the context of the Porcupine and Pole-cat feud, such arguments reinforced the importance of both press freedom and

private reputation as fungible forms of property, the one a public right and the other private, that needed balancing for the sake of the public good. See Novak (1996, 42–50, 60–62, 74).

55. Brackenridge (1965, 339).
56. Brackenridge (1965, 341–42).
57. Brackenridge (1965, 342).
58. Brackenridge (1965, 343).
59. Brackenridge (1965, 343–44).
60. Brackenridge (1965, 350).
61. Brackenridge (1965, 347).
62. Brackenridge (1965, 347–48).
63. Brackenridge (1965, 350). See *U.S. v. Callender* (1800); Stewart (1969, 482–84).
64. Brackenridge (1965, 350).
65. Brackenridge (1965, 351).
66. Brackenridge (1965, 351).
67. Brackenridge (1965, 352).
68. Brackenridge (1965, 331).
69. Brackenridge (1965, 352).
70. Brackenridge (1965, 340).
71. Brackenridge (1965, 332).
72. Brackenridge (1965, 345).
73. Brackenridge (1965, 350–51).
74. Brackenridge (1965, 352).
75. Brackenridge (1965, 335).
76. Brackenridge (1965, 337).
77. Brackenridge (1965, 340–42).
78. Brackenridge (1965, 351).
79. Brackenridge (1965, 337, 340).
80. Brackenridge (1965, 340).
81. Brackenridge (1965, 348).
82. Brackenridge (1965, 348).
83. Brackenridge (1965, 348).
84. Brackenridge (1965, 350).
85. Brackenridge (1965, 347).
86. Brackenridge (1965, 332).
87. Brackenridge (1965, 333).
88. Brackenridge (1965, 333).
89. Brackenridge (1965, 335).
90. Brackenridge (1965, 335).
91. Brackenridge (1965, 336).
92. Brackenridge (1965, 335).
93. Brackenridge (1965, 333).
94. Brackenridge (1965, 338).
95. Brackenridge (1965, 344).

96. Brackenridge (1965, 343).
97. Brackenridge (1965, 343–44).
98. Brackenridge (1965, 346).
99. Brackenridge (1965, 345).
100. Brackenridge (1965, 549).
101. Brackenridge (1965, 395).
102. Brackenridge (1965, 397).
103. Brackenridge (1965, 397).
104. Brackenridge (1965, 559).
105. In this regard, Brackenridge might have been, as he put it, "laying an anchor to windward" (1965, 560) in speaking contrary to the rhetoric of the times, for the great danger, as he saw it, was in the very areas in which the press was most protected, that is, on issues of the principles and constitution of government where the press could in his view be a virtual poison.
106. Brackenridge (1965, 444).
107. Brackenridge (1965, 444).
108. Carpenter (1800, 2).
109. Brackenridge (1814, 232).
110. Brackenridge (1965, 445).
111. Brackenridge (1965, 445).
112. Brackenridge (1814, 234).
113. Brackenridge (1814, 234).
114. If infamous, introducing the truth of the matter was justified; if merely vexatious, "*the greater the truth, the greater the libel*" on the grounds that without justification for hearing the truth, the community had a responsibility "that *the peace be preserved*"; Brackenridge (1814, 234–35).
115. Brackenridge (1965, 331–32).
116. Brackenridge (1965, 332).

Bibliography

PRIMARY SOURCES

Newspapers

Constitutional Diary and Philadelphia Evening Advertiser. 1799–1800. Ed. James Carey.

Federal Gazette (Philadelphia Gazette and Universal Daily Advertiser). 1788–1823. Eds. Andrew Brown; Andrew Brown (the son).

Freeman's Journal or The North American Intelligencer. 1781–1792. Ed. Francis Bailey.

Gazette of the United States. 1790–1800. Eds. John Fenno; John Ward Fenno.

General Advertiser (Aurora General Advertiser). 1790–1800. Eds. Benjamin Franklin Bache; William Duane.

Independent Gazeteer. 1782–1799. Eds. Eleazer Oswald; Joseph Gales.

National Gazette. 1791–1793. Ed. Philip Freneau.

Pennsylvania Journal and Weekly Advertiser. 1742–1797. Eds. William Bradford; Thomas Bradford.

Pennsylvania Packet and Daily Advertiser. 1771–1839. Eds. John Dunlap; David Claypoole.

Pennsylvania Gazette. 1766–1805. Eds. David Hall; William Sellers.

Porcupine's Gazette. 1797–1800. Ed. William Cobbett.

Rush–Light. 1800. Ed. William Cobbett.

Time–Piece. 1797. Philip Freneau.

Other Sources

Addison, Alexander. 1800. *Reports of Cases in the County Courts of the Fifth Circuit, and in the High Court of Errors and Appeals, of the State of Pennsylvania*. Philadelphia: John Colerick.

Alexander, James. 1963. *A Brief Narrative of the Case and Trial of John Peter Zenger, Printer of the New York Weekly Journal*. Ed. Stanley Nider Katz. 1736. Reprint. Cambridge: Harvard University Press.

Allen Richard. 1960. *The Life Experience and Gospel Labors of the Rt. Rev. Richard Allen To Which is Annexed The Rise and Progress of the African Methodist Episcopal Church in the United States of America*. 1794. Reprint. Nashville: Abingdon Press.

———. 1801. *A Collection of Hymns and Spiritual Songs*. Philadelphia: T. L. Plowman.

Bates, William. [1788]. *Gil Blas; Or, the Fool of Fortune. A New Pantomimic Eetertainment [sic], in Two Parts*. London.

Baugh, Albert Ellery, ed. 1905. *The Writings of Thomas Jefferson*. Vol. 10. Washington, D. C.

Beattie, James. 1777. *An Essay on the Nature and Immutability of Truth, in Opposition to Sophistry and Scepticism*. 6th ed. Edinburgh.

Belknap, Jeremy. 1796. *The Foresters, an American Tale; Being a Sequel to the History of John Bull the Clothier*. 2nd ed. Boston.

Binns, John. 1851. *Binns' Justice, or Magistrate's Daily Companion. A Treatise on the Office and Duties of Aldermen and Justices of the Peace in the Commonwealth of Pennsylvania*. Ed. Frederick C. Brightly. 4th ed. Philadelphia: James Kay, Jun. & Brother.

Blackstone, William. 1774. *Commentaries on the Laws of England. In Four Books*. 6th ed. 4 vols. London: T. Cadell.

———. 1794. *Commentaries on the Laws of England. In Four Books*. 12th ed. 4 vols. Dublin.

Brackenridge, Hugh Henry. 1814. *Law Miscellanies: Containing an Introduction to the Study of the Law, Notes on Blackstone's Commentaries, Shewing the Law of Pennsylvania from the Law of England and What Acts of Assembly Might Require to be Repealed or Modified*. Philadelphia: P. Sterne.

———. 1937. *Modern Chivalry*. Ed. Claude M. Newlin. 1815. Reprint. New York: American Book Company.

———. 1965. *Modern Chivalry, Containing the Adventures of Captain John Farrago and Teague O'Regan, His Servant*. Ed. Lewis Leary. 1792, 1793, 1797. Reprint. Albany: New College and University Press, Inc.

———. 1970. *A Hugh Henry Brackenridge Reader, 1770–1815*. Ed. Daniel Marder. Pittsburgh: University of Pittsburgh.

———. 1971. *The Life and Writings of Hugh Henry Brackenridge*. Ed. Claude Milton Newlin. Mamaroneck: Paul P. Appel.

Braunberger v. Cleis. 1865. *Medical and Surgical Reporter* 12.36: 555–58, 569–73.

Bronner, Edwin B. 1962. "Letter from a Yellow Fever Victim: Philadelphia, 1793." *The Pennsylvania Magazine of History and Biography* 86.2: 204–7.

Brown, Charles Brockden. 1943. *The Rhapsodist and Other Uncollected Writings*. Ed. Harry R. Warfel. NewYork: Scholars' Facsimiles and Reprints.

———. 1999a. *Arthur Merwyn or, Memoirs of the Year 1793—A Romance*. 1799. Reprint. New York: The Library of America.

———. 1999b. *Ormond; Or, The Secret Witness*. Ed. Mary Chapman. 1799. Reprint. Orchard Park: Broadview Literary Texts.

Brown, Thaddeus. 1798. *An Address in Christian Love, to the Inhabitants of Philadelphia; on the Awful Dispensation of the Yellow Fever, in 1798*. Philadelphia: R. Aitken.

Butterfield, Lyman H. 1954. "Further Letters of Benjamin Rush." *Pennsylvania Magazine of History and Biography* 78.1: 3–44.

Caldwell, Charles. 1968. *Autobiography of Charles Caldwell, M.D.* Ed. Harriot W. Warner. 1855. Reprint. New York: Da Capo Press.

Carey, James. 1797. *A Pill for Porcupine, Anticipation! Peter Porcupine's Descent into Hell*. Philadelphia: James Carey.

Carey, Mathew. 1786. *The Plagi–Scurriliad: A Hudibrastic Poem Dedicated to Colonel Eleazer Oswald*. Philadelphia: Mathew Carey.

———. 1793. *Observations on Dr. Rush's Enquiry into the Origins of the Late Epidemic Fever in Philadelphia*. Philadelphia: Mathew Carey.

———. 1794. *A Short Account of the Malignant Fever Lately Prevalent in Philadelphia: With a Statement of the Proceedings That Took Place on the Subject, in Different Parts of the United States*. 4th ed. Philadelphia: Mathew Carey.

———. 1799a. *Plumb Pudding for the Humane, Chaste, Valiant, Enlightened Peter Porcupine by His Obliged Friend Mathew Carey*. 2nd ed. Philadelphia: Mathew Carey.

———. 1799b. *The Porcupiniad: A Hudibrastic Poem in Three Cantos Addressed to William Cobbett*. Philadelphia: Mathew Carey.

———. 1942. *Mathew Carey: Autobiography*. 1837. Reprint. Brooklyn: Research Classics.

Carpenter, T. 1800. *A Report of an Action for a Libel Brought by Dr. Benjamin Rush against William Cobbett in the Supreme Court of Pennsylvania, December Term, 1799, for Certain Defamatory Publications in a Newspaper Entitled Porcupine's Gazette*. Philadelphia: W. W. Woodward.

Citizen. 1799. *Fever; An Elegiac Poem Dedicated to the Citizens of Philadelphia by a Citizen*. Philadelphia: John Ormrod.

Cobbett, William. 1797. *The Life and Adventures of Peter Porcupine, with a Full and Fair Account of All His Authoring Transactions; Being a Sure and Infallible Guide for All Enterprising Young Men Who Wish to Make a Fortune by Writing*. Philadelphia: William Cobbett.

———. 1798a. *The Democratic Judge: or, The Equal Liberty of the Press, as Exhibited, Explained, and Exposed, in the Prosecution of William Cobbett, for a Pretended Libel Against the King of Spain and his Embassador, before Thomas McKean, Chief Justice of the State of Pennsylvania*. Philadelphia: William Cobbett.

———. 1798b. *The Republican Judge: or the American Liberty of the Press, as Exhibited, Explained, and Exposed, in the Base and Partial Prosecution of William Cobbett, for a Pretended Libel against the King of Spain and his Embassador, before the Supreme Court of Pennsylvania*. London: J. Wright.

———. 1800. *The American Rush–Light; by the Help of Which Wayward and Disaffected Britons May See a Complete Specimen of the Baseness, Dishonesty, Ingratitude, and Perfidy of Republicans, and of the Profligacy, Injustice, and Tyranny of Republican Governments*. London: J. Wright.

———. 1801a. *Porcupine's Works; Containing Various Writings and Selections, Exhibiting a Faithful Picture of the United States of America; of Their Governments, Laws, Politics, and Resources; of the Characters of Their Presidents, Governors, Legislators, Magistrates, and Military Men; and of the Customs, Manners, Morals, Religion, Virtues and Vices of the People*. 12 vols. London: Cobbett and Morgan.

———. 1801b. "Remarks on the Pamphlets Late Published Against Peter Porcupine. September, 1796, *The Political Censor*." In *Porcupine's Works; Containing Various Writings and Selections, Exhibiting a Faithful Picture of the United States of America; of Their Governments, Laws, Politics, and Resources; of the Characters of Their Presidents, Governors, Legislators, Magistrates, and Military Men; and of the Customs, Manners, Morals, Religion, Virtues and Vices of the People*. Vol. 2. 54–57. London: Cobbett and Morgan.

———. 1937. *Letters from William Cobbett to Edward Thornton Written in the Years 1797 to 1800*. Ed. G. D. H. Cole. London: Oxford University Press.

———. 1994. *Peter Porcupine in America: Pamphlets on Republicanism and Revolution*. Ed. David A. Wilson. Ithaca: Cornell University Press.

———. 1998. *Collected Social and Political Works of William Cobbett*. Ed. Noel Thompson. London: Routledge.

College of Physicians of Philadelphia. 1798. *Proceedings of the College of Physicians of Philadelphia, Relative to the Prevention of the Introduction and Spreading of Contagious Diseases*. Philadelphia: Thomas Dobson.

———. 1799. *Facts and Observations Relative to the Nature and Origin of the Pestilential Fever, Which Prevailed in the City of Philadelphia, in 1793, 1797, and 1798*. Philadelphia: James Philips & Son.

Cooper, Thomas. 1800. *An Account of the Trial of Thomas Cooper, of Northumberland; on a Charge of Libel against the President of the United States*. Philadelphia: John Bioren.

Cresson, Joshua. 1803. *Meditations Written During the Prevalence of the Yellow Fever in the City of Philadelphia in the Year 1793*. London: W. Phillips.

Currie, William. 1793. *A Description of the Malignant, Infectious Fever Prevailing at Present in Philadelphia: With an Account of the Means to Prevent Infection, and the Remedies and Method of Treatment, Which Have Been Found Most Successful*. Philadelphia: Dobson.

———. 1794. *An Impartial Review of that Part of Dr. Rush's Late Publication Entitled "An Account of the Bilious Remitting Yellow Fever, as it Appeared in the City of Philadelphia*." Philadelphia: Dobson.

———. 1798. *Memoirs of the Yellow Fever, Which Prevailed in Philadelphia, and Other Parts of the United States of America, in the Summer and Autumn of the Present Year, 1798*. Philadelphia: John Bioren.

Dallas, Alexander J. 1790. *Reports of Cases Ruled and Adjudged in the Courts of Pennsylvania, Before and Since the Revolution*. Philadelphia: T. Bradford.

———. 1905. *Reports of Cases Ruled and Adjudged in the Several Courts of the United States and of Pennsylvania, Held at the Seat of the Federal Government*. Vol. 3. New York: Banks Law Publishing Company.

Dennie, Joseph. 1796. *The Lay Preacher; or Short Sermons, for Idle Readers*. Walpole, Newhampshire.

Deveze, Jean. 1794. *An Enquiry into and Observation Upon the Causes and Effects of the Epidemic Disease, Which Raged in Philadelphia From the Month of August Till Towards the Middle of December, 1793*. Philadelphia: Parent.

Elwell, John J. 1860. *A Medico-Legal Treatise on Medical Malpractice and Medical Evidence*. New York: John S. Voorhis.

Faugeres, Margaretta V. 1797. *The Ghost of John Young, the Homicide, Who Was Executed the 17th of August Last, for the Murder of Robert Barwick, a Sheriff's Officer*. New York.

Fielding, Henry. 1793. *The Adventures of Joseph Andrews, and His Friend Mr. Abraham Adams*. 1742. Reprint. 2 vols. London.

———. 1988. *An Enquiry Into the Causes of the Late Increase of Robbers and Related Writings*. Ed. Malvin R. Zirker. 1751. Reprint. Middletown: Wesleyan University Press.

Fitzpatrick, John C., ed. 1940. *The Writings of George Washington from the Original Manuscript Sources, 1745–1799*. Vol. 33. Washington: U.S. Government Printing Office.

The Foretokens of the Pestilence and Sickness Which Befel the Philadelphians, as It Was Warned to a Pious Inhabitant of the State, Many Years Ago, and Rewarned Again Some Time Past: Also, Signs and Tokens of Its Awful Approach, to Which is Added, a List of the Daily Burials. [1794]. Philadelphia: Ormrod and Conrad.

Franklin, Benjamin. 1954. *Some Account of the Pennsylvania Hospital*. 1817. Reprint. Baltimore: Johns Hopkins University Press.

Freneau, Philip Morin. 1795. *Poems Written Between the Years 1768 & 1794 by Philip Freneau, of New Jersey*. Monmouth.

———. 1809. *Poems Written and Published During the American Revolutionary War and Now Republished from the Original Manuscripts, Interspersed with Translations from the Ancients, and Other Pieces Not Heretofore in Print.* 2 vols. Philadelphia: Lydia R. Bailey.

———. 1815. *A Collection of Poems, on American Affairs, and a Variety of Other Subjects, Chiefly Moral and Political; Written between the Year 1797 and the Present Time*. 2 vols. New York: Daniel Longworth.

———. 1963. *The Poems of Philip Freneau: Poet of the American Revolution*. Ed. Fred Lewis Pattee. 3 vols. New York: Russell and Russell, Inc.

———. 1986. *Newspaper Verse of Philip Freneau: An Edition and Bibliography*. Ed. Judith R. Hiltner. Troy: Whitston Pub.

[Green, Ashbel]. 1799. *A Pastoral Letter, from a Minister in the Country, to Those of His Flock Who Remained in the City of Philadelphia During the Pestilence of 1798*. Philadelphia: John Ormrod.

Greene, Nathanael. 1919. "Letter of Nathanael Greene to Dr. John Morgan, 1779." *Pennsylvania Magazine of History and Biography* 43: 77–80.

Hall, John, and Samuel Clarkson, eds. 1890. *Memoirs of Matthew Clarkson of Philadelphia, 1735–1800*. Philadelphia.

Heald, William Margetson. 1789. *The Brunoniad: An Heroic Poem. In Six Cantos, by Julius Juniper*. London.

Helmuth, J. Henry C. 1794. *A Short Account of the Yellow Fever in Philadelphia for the Reflecting Christian*. Philadelphia: Jones, Hoff, & Derrick.

Historical Record of the Bethel African Methodist Episcopal Church. 1864. New York: Carlton and Porter.

Hopkinson, Francis. 1792. *Miscellaneous Essays and Occasional Writings*. 3 vols. Philadelphia: T. Dobson.

"The Infallible Doctor, a New Song. Sung in the Character of a Merry Andrew." 1783. In *The Charms of Cheerfulness; Or, Merry Songster's Companion: Containing a Collection of Songs, Cantadas, and Genuine Pieces of Wit and Humour*. 23. London.

Jones, Absolom. 1999. "A Thanksgiving Sermon." 1808. Reprint. In *American Sermons: The Pilgrims to Martin Luther King, Jr.* 538–45. New York: The Library of America.

Jones, Absalom, and Richard Allen. 1993. *A Narrative of the Proceedings of the Black People, During the Late Awful Calamity in Philadelphia, in the Year 1793 and a Refutation of Some Censures Thrown Upon Them in Some Late Publications*. 1794. Reprint. *The Life Experience and Gospel Labors*. Richard Allen. 1831. Reprint. Philadelphia: Independence National Historical Park.

La Roche, R. 1855. *Yellow Fever Considered in its Historical, Pathological and Therapeutical Relations Including a Sketch of the Disease as It Has Occurred in Philadelphia from 1699 to 1854*. 2 vols. Philadelphia: Blanchard & Lea.

La Rochefoucauld-Liancourt, Francois de. 1800. *Travels through the United States of North America*. Vol 1. London.

Latrobe, Benjamin Henry. 1799. *View of the Practicality and Means of Supplying the City of Philadelphia with Wholesome Water*. Philadelphia: Zachariah Poulson, Jr.

Le Sage, Alain Rene. n.d. *The Adventures of Gil Blas of Santillane*. Trans. Tobias Smollett. 1749. Reprint. Chicago: Belford, Clarke & Co.

Lee, Richard Henry. May 1860. "Selections and Excerpts from the Lee Papers." *The Southern Literary Messenger* 30: 344–346.

Linn, William. 1795. *A Discourse, Delivered on the 26th of November, 1795; Being the Day Recommended by the Governor of the State of New York To Be Observed as a Day of Thanksgiving and Prayer, On Account of the Removal of an Epidemic Fever, and for Other National Blessings*. New York: T. and J. Swords.

Lowell, Charles. 1825. *Authentic Report of a Trial before the Supreme Judicial Court of Maine for the County of Washington. June 1824*. Portland: C. Lowell.

M. September 1788. "The Republic of Beasts, A Fable." *Columbian Magazine* 2: 538–39; 602–5.

Marshall, William. 1799. *A Theological Dissertation on the Propriety of Removing from the Seat of Pestilence*. Philadelphia: David Hogan.

Mason, John Mitchel. 1793. *A Sermon, Preached September 20th, 1793: A Day Set Apart, in the City of New York, for Public Fasting, Humiliation and Prayer, on Account of a Malignant and Mortal Fever Prevailing in the City of Philadelphia*. New York: Samuel Loudon & Son.

McClelland, Milo A. 1877. *Civil Malpractice: A Treatise on Surgical Jurisprudence*. New York: Hurd and Houghton.

Melville, Lewis. 1913. *The Life and Letters of William Cobbett in England and America*. 2 vols. London: John Lane.

Minutes of the Proceedings of the Committee, Appointed on the 14th September, 1793, by the Citizens of Philadelphia, the Northern Liberties, and the District of Southwark, To Attend to and Alleviate the Sufferings of the Afflicted with the Malignant Fever Prevalent in the City and Its Vicinity. 1848. Philadelphia: City of Philadelphia.

Mitchell, Stewart, ed. April 18, 1945–October 17, 1945. "New Letters of Abigail Adams." *American Antiquarian Society* 55: 347.

Moreau de St.-Mery, M. L. E. 1947. *Moreau de St.-Mery's American Journey, 1793–1798*. Trans. Kenneth Roberts and Anna M. Roberts. Garden City: Doubleday and Co., Inc.

Morgan, John. 1765. *A Discourse Upon the Institution of Medical Schools in America; Delivered at a Public Anniversary Commencement, Held in the College of Philadelphia May 30 and 31, 1765*. Philadelphia: William Bradford.

———. 1777. *A Vindication of His Public Character in the Station of Director-General of the Military Hospitals, and Physician in Chief of the American Army*. Boston: Powars and Willis.

Nassy, David. 1793. *Observations on the Cause, Nature, and Treatment of the Epidemic Disease, Prevalent in Philadelphia*. Philadelphia: Mathew Carey.

"On the Multitude of Lawyers." December 1789. *Massachusetts Magazine* 1: 792.

Peterson, Merrill D., ed. 1984. *Thomas Jefferson: Writings*. New York: The Library of America.

Plain Truth. 1803. *A View of the Absurd Practice, in the Yellow, or Bilious Fever, Addressed to the Inhabitants of Philadelphia*. Philadelphia: John Bioren.

Reed, John. 1831. *A Modification of the Commentaries of Sir William Blackstone With Numerous Alterations and Additions, Designed to Present an Elementary Exposition of the Entire Laws of Pennsylvania*. 3 vols. Carlisle: George Fleming.

Rosenfeld, Richard N. 1997. *American Aurora, a Democratic-Republican Returns: The Suppressed History of Our Nation's Beginnings and the Heroic Newspaper That Tried to Report It*. New York: St. Martin's Press.

Rowlandson, Thomas. 1971. *Thomas Rowlandson; Medical Caricatures*. New York: Editions Medicine Rara Ltd.

Rush, Benjamin. 1773. *An Address on the Slavery of the Negroes in America*. Philadelphia: John Dunlap.

———. 1778. *Directions for Preserving the Health of Soldiers, Recommended to the Consideration of the Officers of the Army of the United States*. Lancaster: John Dunlap.

———. 1791. *Observations and Reasoning in Medicine*. Philadelphia.

———. 1794. *An Account of the Bilious Remitting Yellow Fever, as It Appeared in the City of Philadelphia, in the Year 1793*. Edinburgh: John Moir.

———. 1811. *Sixteen Introductory Lectures to Courses of Lectures Upon the Institutes and Practice of Medicine, With a Syllabus of the Latter*. Philadelphia: Bradford and Innskeep.

———. 1815. *Medical Inquiries and Observations*. 4th ed. 3 vols. Philadelphia: Johnson & Warner.

———. 1947. *The Selected Writings of Benjamin Rush*. Ed. Dagobert D. Runes. New York: Philosophical Library.

———. 1948. *An Autobiography of Benjamin Rush: His Travels Through Life Together with His Commonplace Book*. Ed. George W. Corner. Princeton: Princeton University Press.

———. 1951. *Letters of Benjamin Rush*. Ed. L. H. Butterfield. 2 vols. Princeton: Princeton University Press.

Smith, Horace Wemyss. 1880. *Life and Correspondence of the Rev. William Smith, D. D.* Vol. 1. Philadelphia: Ferguson Brothers & Co.

Smollett, Tobias George. 1794. *The Adventures of Peregrine Pickle. In Which are Included, Memoirs of a Lady of Quality*. 1751. Reprint. 4 vols. London.

Spring, Samuel. 1798. *A Thanksgiving Sermon Preached November 29, 1798*. Newburyport: Angier.

Stearns, Samuel. 1794. *An Account of the Terrible Effects of the Pestilential Infection in the City of Philadelphia, with an Elegy on the Deaths of the People*. 1793. Reprint. New York.

Thomson, Samuel. 1843. *Learned Quackery Exposed; Or, Theory According to Art, As Exemplified in the Practice of the Fashionable Doctors of the Present Day*. Syracuse: Lathrop and Dean.

U.S. v. Callender. 1800. No. 14, 709. Circuit Court, D. Virginia.

Warton, Joseph. 1756. *An Essay on the Writings and Genius of Pope*. London.

Washington, H. A., ed. 1854. *The Writings of Thomas Jefferson, Being his Autobiography, Correspondence, Reports, Messages, Addresses, and Other Writings, Official and Private*. 4 vols. New York: John C. Riker, Taylor & Maury.

Webster, Noah. 1947. *Letters on Yellow Fever Addressed to Dr. William Currie*. 1797. Reprint. Baltimore: Johns Hopkins University Press.

———. 1970. *A Brief History of Epidemic and Pestilential Diseases With the Principal Phenomena of the Physical World, Which Precede and Accompany Them and Observations Deduced From the Facts Stated*. 1799. Reprint. 2 vols. New York: Burt Franklin.

Whitworth, M. April 27, 1767. "To the Public." *The Boston Gazette and County Journal.*

Winchester, Elhanan. 1795. *Wisdom Taught by Man's Mortality; Or the Shortness and Uncertainty of Life, the Certainty and Suddenness of Death, Considered a Discourse Adapted to the Awful Visitation of the City of Philadelphia, by the Yellow Fever, in the Year 1793*. Philadelphia: R. Fowell.

Woodruff, Hezekiah. 1779. *To the Publick*. Trenton.

Wright, Henry. 1794. *A Sermon, Delivered October 9, 1793 at Bristol, at a Time Set Apart for Public Prayer and Humiliation by Several Christian Churches in the State of Rhode–Island, etc., On Account of the Distressing Sickness in the City of Philadelphia*. Warren: Nathaniel Phillips.

Yeates, Jasper. 1871. *Reports of Cases Adjudged in the Supreme Court of Pennsylvania: With Some Select Cases at Nisi Prius and in the Circuit Courts*. 1818. Reprint. Vol. 3. Philadelphia: Jno. Campbell.

SECONDARY SOURCES

Amsterdam, Anthony G., and Jerome Bruner. 2000. *Minding the Law*. Cambridge: Harvard University Press.

Anand, Sanjeez. 2005. "The Origins, Early History and Evolution of the English Criminal Trial Jury." *The Alberta Law Review* 43: 407–32.

Applegate, Howard Lewis. 1961. "The Medical Administrators of the American Revolutionary Army." *Military Affairs* 25.1: 1–10.

Arnebeck, Bob. 2004. *Destroying Angel: Benjamin Rush, Yellow Fever and the Birth of Modern Medicine. http://www.geocities.com/bobarnebeck/fever1793.html. 2004.*

Axelrad, Jacob. 1967. *Philip Freneau, Champion of Democracy*. Austin: University of Texas Press.

Bacon, Jacqueline. 1998. "'Do You Understand Your Own Language?' Revolutionary 'Topoi' in the Rhetoric of African-American Abolitionists." *Rhetoric Society Quarterly* 28.2: 55–75.

———. 2001. "Rhetoric and Identity in Absalom Jones and Richard Allen's *Narrative of the Proceedings of the Black People, during the Late Awful Calamity in Philadelphia*." *The Pennsylvania Magazine of History and Biography* 125.1/2: 61–90.

Baron, Jane. 1999. "Storytelling and Legal Legitimacy." In *Un-Disciplining Literature: Literature, Law, and Culture*, eds. Kostas Myrsiades and Linda Myrsiades. 13–27. New York: Peter Lang.

Baron, Jane, and Julia Epstein. 1997. "Is Law Narrative?" *Buffalo Law Review* 45.1: 141–87.

Becker, Ann M. 2004. "Smallpox in Washington's Army: Strategic Implications of the Disease During the American Revolutionary War." *Journal of Military History* 68.2: 381–430.

Beeman, Richard R. 1992. "Deference, Republicanism, and the Emergence of Popular Politics in Eighteenth-Century America." *The William and Mary Quarterly* 49.3: 401–30.

Bell, Whitfield J., Jr. 1964. "The Court Martial of Dr. William Shippen, Jr., 1780." *Journal of the History of Medicine and Allied Sciences* 19: 218–38.

———. 1965. *John Morgan Continental Doctor*. Philadelphia: University of Pennsylvania Press.

Bender, John, and Michael Marrinan, eds. 2005. *Regimes of Description in the Archive of the Eighteenth Century*. Stanford: Stanford University Press.

Bercovitch, Sacvan. 1978. *The American Jeremiad*. Madison: The University of Wisconsin Press.

Bewell, Alan. 1999. *Romanticism and Colonial Disease*. Baltimore: Johns Hopkins University Press.

Binder, Guyora, and Robert Weisberg. 2000. *Literary Criticisms of Law*. Princeton: Princeton University Press.

Binger, Carl A. L. 1966. *Revolutionary Doctor: Benjamin Rush, 1746–1813*. New York: Norton.

Blake, John B. 1959. *Public Health in the Town of Boston, 1630–1822*. Cambridge: Harvard University Press.

Bloch, Ruth. 1985. *Visionary Republic: Millennial Themes in American Thought, 1756–1800*. Cambridge: Cambridge University Press.

Bloomfield, Maxwell. 1976. *American Lawyers in a Changing Society, 1776–1876*. Cambridge: Harvard University Press.

Bourdieu, Pierre. 1977. *Outline of a Theory of Practice*. Trans. Richard Nice. Cambridge: Cambridge University Press.

———. 1987. "The Force of Law: Toward a Sociology of the Juridical Field." *Hastings Law Journal* 38: 805–53.

Brock, Helen. 1990. "North America, a Western Outpost of European Medicine." In *The Medical Enlightenment of the Eighteenth Century*, eds. Andrew Cunningham and Roger French. 194–216. Cambridge: Cambridge University Press.

Brodsky, Alyn. 2004. *Benjamin Rush: Patriot and Physician*. New York: St. Martin's Press.

Brooks, Peter. 1996. "The Law as Narrative and Rhetoric." In *Law's Stories: Narrative and Rhetoric in the Law*, eds. Peter Brooks and Paul Gewirtz. 14–22. New Haven: Yale University Press.

———. 2005. "Narrative in and out of the Law." In *A Companion to Narrative Theory*, eds. James Phelan and Peter J. Rabinowitz. 415–26. Oxford: Blackwell Publishing.

Brooks, Peter, and Paul Gewirtz, eds. 1996. *Law's Stories: Narrative and Rhetoric in the Law* New Haven: Yale University Press.

Burns, Chester R. 1969a. "Malpractice Suits in American Medicine before the Civil War." *Bulletin of the History of Medicine* 43.1: 41–56.

———. 1969b. *Medical Ethics in the U.S. before the Civil War*. Ph.D. Diss. Johns Hopkins University.

———. 1980. "Medical Ethics and Jurisprudence." *The Education of American Physicians*, ed. Ronald L. Numbers. 273–89. Berkeley: University of California Press.

Burns, Eric. 2006. *Infamous Scribblers: The Founding Fathers and the Rowdy Beginnings of American Journalism*. New York: Public Affairs.

Butterfield, L. H. 1951a. "The Cobbett–Rush Feud." In *Letters of Benjamin Rush*, ed. L. H. Butterfield. Vol. 2. 1213–18. Princeton: Princeton University Press.

———. 1951b. "Rush and Washington." In *Letters of Benjamin Rush*, ed. L. H. Butterfield. Vol. 2. 1197–1208. Princeton: Princeton University Press.

Cash, Philip. 1980. "The Professionalization of Boston Medicine, 1760–1803." In *Medicine in Colonial Massachusetts, 1620–1820*, eds. Philip Cash, Eric H. Christianson, and J. Worth Estes. 69–94. Boston: Colonial Society of Massachusetts.

Cash, Philip, Eric H. Christianson, and J. Worth Estes. 1980a. "Eighteenth-Century Medicine and the Modern Physician." In *Medicine in Colonial Massachusetts, 1620–1820*, eds. Philip Cash, Eric H. Christianson, and J. Worth Estes. 26–32. Boston: Colonial Society of Massachusetts.

———, eds. 1980b. *Medicine in Colonial Massachusetts, 1620–1820*. Boston: Colonial Society of Massachusetts.

Chaden, Caryn. 1991. "Dress and Undress in Brackenridge's *Modern Chivalry*." *Early American Literature* 26.1: 55–72.

Chinard, Gilbert. 1947. "Eighteenth-Century Theories on America as a Human Habitat." *Proceedings of the American Philosophical Society* 91: 45–52.

Clark, Mary Elizabeth. 1939. *Peter Porcupine in America: The Career of William Cobbett, 1792–1800*. Philadelphia: Ph.D. Diss. University of Pennsylvania.

Clark, Randall Baldwin. 2008. "Bleedings, Purges, and Vomits: Dr. Benjamin Rush's Republican Medicine, the Bilious Remitting Yellow-Fever Epidemic of 1793, and the Non-Origin of the Law of Informed Consent." *Journal of Contemporary Health, Law, and Policy* 24: 209–50.

Cockburn, J. S., and Thomas S. Green, eds. 1988. *Twelve Good Men and True: The Criminal Trial Jury in England, 1200–1800*. Princeton: Princeton University Press.

Cohen, Daniel A. 1993. *Pillars of Salt, Monuments of Grace: New England Crime Literature and the Origins of American Popular Culture, 1674–1860*. New York: Oxford University Press.

Cohen, Dov, and Joe Vandello. 1988. "Social Norms, Social Meaning, and the Economic Analysis of Law: Meanings of Violence." *Journal of Legal Studies* 27: 567–84.

Cole, G. D. H. 1924. *Life of William Cobbett*. New York.

Conrad, Lawrence L, Michael Neve, Vivian Nutton, Roy Porter, and Andrew Wear, eds. 1995. *The Western Medical Tradition: 800 BC to AD 1800*. Cambridge: Cambridge University Press.

Constable, Marianne. *The Law of the Other: The Mixed Jury and Changing Conceptions of Citizenship, Law, and Knowledge*. Chicago: U of Chicago P, 1994.

Cooter, Roger. 2004. "'Framing' the End of the Social History of Medicine." In *Locating Medical History: The Stories and Their Meanings*, eds. Frank Huisman and John Harley Warner. 309–37. Baltimore: Johns Hopkins University Press.

Corner, Betsy Copping. 1951. *William Shippen, Jr.: Pioneer in American Medical Education*. Philadelphia: American Philosophical Society.

Corner, George. 1948. "Introduction." In *An Autobiography of Benjamin Rush: His "Travels Through Life" Together with His Commonplace Book*, ed. George W. Corner. 4–9. Princeton: Princeton University Press.

Cunningham, Andrew, and Roger French, eds. 1990. *The Medical Enlightenment of the Eighteenth Century*. Cambridge: Cambridge University Press.

Davidson, Cathy. 1986. *Revolution and the Word: The Rise of the Novel in America*. New York: Oxford University Press.

Davies, N. E., G. H. Davies, and E. D. Sanders. February 18, 1983. "William Cobbett, Benjamin Rush, and the Death of George Washington." *JAMA* 249: 912–15.

Davies, Terence C. 1976. "American Medicine During the Revolutionary Era." *Journal of the Medical Association of the State of Alabama* 6: 34–36.

Davis, Audrey P. 1981. *Medicine and Its Technology: An Introduction to the History of Medical Instrumentation*. Westport: Greenwood Press.

Dawes, James. 2004. "Fictional Feeling: Philosophy, Cognitive Science, and the American Gothic." *American Literature* 76.3: 437–66.

De Certeau, Michel. 1984. *The Practice of Everyday Life*. Trans. Steven Rendall. Berkeley: University of California Press.

Delgado, Richard. 1989. "Storytelling for Oppositionists and Others: A Plea for Narrative." *Michigan Law Review* 87: 2411–41.

Dershowitz, Alan M. 1996. "Life is Not a Dramatic Narrative." In *Law's Stories: Narrative and Rhetoric in the Law*, eds. Peter Brooks and Paul Gewirtz. 99–105. New Haven: Yale University Press.

De Ville, Kenneth Allen. 1990. *Medical Malpractice in Nineteenth Century America: Origins and Legacy*. New York: New York University Press.

Doyle, William. 1990. *Oxford History of the French Revolution.* Oxford: Oxford University Press.

Duffy, John. 1953. *Epidemics in Colonial America.* Baton Rouge: Louisiana State University Press.

———. 1990. *The Sanitarians: A History of American Public Health.* Urbana: University of Illinois Press.

Eckert, Jack. 1993. "In the Days of the Epidemic: The 1793 Yellow Fever Outbreak in Philadelphia as Seen by Physicians." *Transactions & Studies of the College of Physicians of Philadelphia* ser 5, 15: 31–38.

Edwards, Linden F. 1951. "Resurrection Roots During the Heroic Age of Anatomy in America." *Bulletin of the History of Medicine* 25: 178–84.

Eisenberg, Leon. 2007. "*Furor Therapeuticus*: Benjamin Rush and the Philadelphia Yellow Fever Epidemic." *American Journal of Psychiatry* 164.4: 552–55.

Ellickson, Robert C. 1991. *Order Without Law: How Neighbors Settle Disputes.* Cambridge: Harvard University Press.

Elliott, Emory. 1986. *Revolutionary Writers: Literature and Authority in the New Republic, 1725–1810.* New York: Oxford University Press.

Ellis, Joseph J. 2000. *Founding Brothers: The Revolutionary Generation.* New York: Vintage Books.

Ellis, R. 1971. *The Jeffersonian Crisis: Courts and Politics in the Young Republic.* New York: Oxford University Press.

Engell, John. 1987. "Brackenridge, *Modern Chivalry*, and American Humor." *Early American Literature* 22.1: 43–62.

Estes, J. Worth. 1980. "Therapeutic Practice in Colonial New England." In *Medicine in Colonial Massachusetts, 1620–1820*, eds. Philip Cash, Eric H. Christianson, and J. Worth Estes. 289–383. Boston: Colonial Society of Massachusetts.

Estes, J. Worth, and Billy G. Smith, eds. 1997. *A Melancholy Scene of Devastation: The Public Response to the 1793 Philadelphia Yellow Fever Epidemic.* Philadelphia: College of Physicians of Philadelphia.

Etting, Frank Marx. 1891. *An Historical Account of the Old State House of Pennsylvania Now Known as the Hall of Independence.* Philadelphia: Porter and Coates.

Feeney, Joseph J. 1982. "Modernized by 1800: The Portrait of Urban America, Especially Philadelphia, in the Novels of Charles Brockden Brown." *American Studies* 23. 2: 25–38.

Ferguson, Robert A. 1979–1980. "Yellow Fever and Charles Brockden Brown: Context of the Emerging Novelist." *Early American Literature* 14: 293–305.

———. 1984. *Law and Letters in American Culture.* Cambridge: Harvard University Press.

———. 1996. "Untold Stories in the Law." In *Law's Stories: Narrative and Rhetoric in the Law*, eds. Peter Brooks and Paul Gewirtz. 84–98. New Haven: Yale University Press.

———. 2004. *Reading the Early Republic*. Cambridge: Harvard University Press.

Finger, Simon. 2010. "An Indissoluble Union: How the American War for Independence Transformed Philadelphia's Medical Community and Created a Public Health Establishment." *Pennsylvania History* 77.1: 37–72.

Fissel, Mary E. 1991. *Patients, Power, and the Poor in Eighteenth–Century Bristol*. Cambridge: Cambridge University Press.

———. 2004. "Making Meaning from the Margins: The New Cultural History of Medicine." In *Locating Medical History: The Stories and Their Meanings*, ed. Frank Huisman and John Harley Warner. 364–85. Baltimore: Johns Hopkins University Press.

Forsyth, William. 1852. *The History of Trial by Jury*. London: L. W. Parker.

Fortune, Brandon Brame, and Deborah J. Warner. 1999. *Franklin and His Friends: Portraying the Man of Science in Eighteenth–Century America*. Washington, D.C.: Smithsonian.

Fox, Claire G., Gordon L. Miller, and Jacquelyn C. Miller, eds. 1996. *Benjamin Rush, M.D.: A Bibliographic Guide*. Westport: Greenwood Press.

Fox, Nick J. 1997. "Is There Life After Foucault? Texts, Frames and Differends." In *Foucault, Health and Medicine*, eds. Alan Peterson and Bryan S. Turner. 31–50. London: Routledge.

Friedman, Lawrence M. 1993. *Crime and Punishment in American History*. New York: Basic Books.

Garner, Bryan A., ed. 1999. *Black's Law Dictionary*. 7th ed. St. Paul: West Group.

Gewirtz, Paul. 1996. "Narrative and Rhetoric in the Law." In *Law's Stories: Narrative and Rhetoric in the Law*, eds. Peter Brooks and Paul Gewirtz. 2–13. New Haven: Yale University Press.

Gibson, James E. 1937. *Dr. Bobo Otto and the Medical Background of the American Revolution*. Springfield: Charles C. Thomas.

Gieskes, Edward. 2006. *Representing the Professions: Administration, Law, and Theater in Early Modern England*. Newark: University of Delaware Press.

Gilman, C.M. 1960. "Military Surgery in the American Revolution." *The Journal of the Medical Society of New Jersey* 57: 491–96.

Gilmore, Michael T. 1978. "Eighteenth-Century Oppositional Ideology and Hugh Henry Brackenridge's *Modern Chivalry*." *Early American Literature* 13: 181–92.

Gilmore, Paul. 2004. "Republican Machines and Brackenridge's Cave: Aesthetics and Models of Machinery in the Early Republic." *American Literature* 39.2: 299–322.

Goodman, Nathan. 1934. *Benjamin Rush: Physician and Citizen, 1746–1813*. Philadelphia: University of Pennsylvania Press.

Gough, Hugh. 1998. *The Terror in the French Revolution*. New York: Palgrave Macmillan.

Gould, Philip. 2000. "Race, Commerce, and the Literature of Yellow Fever in Early National Philadelphia." *Early American Literature* 35.2: 157–86.

Gramsci, Antonio. 1985. *Selections from Cultural Writings*. Trans. William Boelhower. Cambridge: Harvard University Press.

Green, Daniel. 1983. *Great Cobbett: The Noblest Agitator*. London: Hodder and Stoughton.

Green, Thomas Andrew.1985. *Verdict According to Conscience: Perspectives on the English Criminal Trial Jury 1200–1800*. Chicago: University of Chicago Press.

Greene, John C. 1984. *American Science in the Age of Jefferson*. Ames: University of Iowa Press.

Greenhouse, Carol J. 1982. "Nature is to Culture as Praying is to Suing: Legal Pluralism in an American Suburb." *Journal of Legal Pluralism* 20: 17–35.

Griffith, Sally F. 1997. "'A Total Dissolution of the Bonds of Society': Community, Death and Regeneration in Mathew Carey's *Short Account of the Malignant Fever*." In *A Melancholy Scene of Devastation: The Public Response to the 1793 Philadelphia Yellow Fever Epidemic*, eds. J. Worth Estes and Billy G. Smith. 45–60. Philadelphia: College of Physicians of Philadelphia.

Gustafson, Sandra M. 2000. *Eloquence is Power: Oratory and Performance in Early America*. Chapel Hill: North Carolina University Press.

Hale, Matthew Rainbow. 2003. "Many Who Wandered in Darkness: The Contest over American National Identity, 1795–1798." *Early American Studies* 1.1: 127–75.

Hall, Kermit L. 1989. *The Magic Mirror: Law in American History*. New York: Oxford University Press.

Harkey, Joseph H. "The *Don Quixote* of the Frontier: Brackenridge's *Modern Chivalry*." *Early American Literature* 8 (1973): 193–203.

Harley, David. 1990. "Honour and Property: The Structure of Professional Disputes in Eighteenth-Century English Medicine." In *The Medical Enlightenment of the Eighteenth Century*, ed. Andrew Cunningham and Roger French. 138–64. Cambridge: Cambridge University Press.

Harrell, Willie J. Jr. 2006. "A Call to Consciousness and Action: Mapping the African-American Jeremiad." *Canadian Review of American Studies* 36.2: 149–80.

Harris, Jonathan Gil. 2004. *Sick Economies: Drama, Mercantilism, and Disease in Shakespeare's England*. Philadelphia: University of Pennsylvania Press.

Hartog, Hendrik. 1995. "Abigail Bailey's Coverture: Law in a Married Woman's Consciousness." In *Law in Everyday Life*, eds. Austin Sarat and Thomas R. Kearns. 63–108. Ann Arbor: The University of Michigan Press.

Hastings, George Everett. 1926. *The Life and Works of Francis Hopkinson*. New York: Russell & Russell.

Hedges, William L. 1973. "Benjamin Rush, Charles Brockden Brown, and the American Plague Year." *Early American Literature* 7: 295–311.

———. 1981. "The Old World Yet: Writers and Writing in Post-Revolutionary America." *Early American Literature* 16.1: 3–18.

Heinzelman, Susan Sage. 1994. "Guilty in Law, Implausible in Fiction: Jurisprudential and Literary Narratives in the Case of Mary Blandy, Parricide, 1752." In *Representing Women: Law, Literature, and Feminism*, eds. Susan Sage Heinzelman and Zipporah Batshaw Wiseman. 309–36. Durham: Duke University Press.

Helfand, William H. 1978. *Medicine and Pharmacy in American Political Prints (1765–1870)*. Madison: American Institute of the History of Pharmacy.

Higginbotham, A. Leon. 1978. *In the Matter of Color, Race and the American Legal Process: The Colonial Period*. Oxford: Oxford University Press.

Hogan, Paul. 1999. "Fictive Tales, Real Lives: Problems with Reading Law as Literature." In *Un–Disciplining Literature: Literature, Law, and Culture*, eds. Kostas Myrsiades and Linda Myrsiades. 271–88. New York: Peter Lang.

Holifield, E. Brooks. 2003. *Theology in America: Christian Thought from the Age of the Puritans to the Civil War*. New Haven: Yale University Press.

Holmes, Chris. 1966. "Benjamin Rush and the Yellow Fever." *Bulletin of the History of Medicine* 40: 246–63.

Horwitz, Morton J. 1977. *The Transformation of American Law, 1780–1860*. Cambridge, Harvard University Press.

Howard-Pitney, David. 1990. *The Afro-American Jeremiad: Appeals for Justice in America*. Philadelphia: Temple University Press.

Howell, Scott M. 2001. "William Cobbett and American Society in the Age of the French Revolution." Ph.D. Diss. University of California, Riverside.

Jameson, Fredric. 1981. *The Political Unconscious: Narrative as a Socially Symbolic Act*. Ithaca: Cornell University Press.

Jelenko, C. 1982. "Emergency Medicine in Colonial America: Revolutionary War Casualties." *Annals of Emergency Medicine* 11.1: 40–43.

Jones, Colin. 1996. "Plague and Its Metaphors in Early Modern France." *Representations* 53: 97–127.

Jordanova, Ludmilla. 2004. "The Social Construction of Medical Knowledge." In *Locating Medical History: The Stories and Their Meanings,* eds. Frank Huisman and John Harley Warner. 338–58. Baltimore: Johns Hopkins University Press.

Kafer, Peter. 1992. "Charles Brockden Brown and Revolutionary Philadelphia: An Imagination in Context." *Pennsylvania Magazine of History and Biography* 116.4: 467–92.

Kahn, Paul W. 1999. *The Cultural Study of Law: Reconstructing Legal Scholarship*. Chicago: The University of Chicago Press.

Katz, Stanley Nider. 1963. "Introduction." In *A Brief Narrative of the Case and Trial of John Peter Zenger, Printer of the New York Weekly Journal*, ed. Stanley Katz Nider. 1–35. Cambridge: Harvard University Press.

Kilpatrick, Robert. 1990. "'Living in the Light': Dispensaries, Philanthropy, and Medical Reform in Late-Eighteenth-Century London." In *The Medical Enlightenment of the Eighteenth Century*, eds. Andrew Cunningham and Roger French. 254–80. Cambridge: Cambridge University Press.

Kirschenbaum, Alan. 2004. *Chaos Organization and Disaster Management*. New York: Marcel Dekker, Inc.

Kirschner, Ann. 2003. "'Tending to Edify, Astonish, and Instruct': Published Narratives of Spiritual Dreams and Visions in the Early Republic." *Early American Studies* 1.1: 198–229.

Klepp, Susan E. 1997. "How Many Precious Souls Are Fled?: The Magnitude of the 1793 Yellow Fever Epidemic." In *A Melancholy Scene of Devastation: The Public Response to the 1793 Philadelphia Yellow Fever Epidemic*, eds. J. Worth Estes and Billy G. Smith. 163–82. Philadelphia: College of Physicians of Philadelphia.

Konkle, Burton Alva. 1981. *Joseph Hopkinson, 1770–1842: Jurist, Scholar, Inspirer of the Arts*. Philadelphia: University of Pennsylvania Press.

Kopperman, Paul E. 2004. "'Venerate the Lancet': Benjamin Rush's Yellow Fever Therapy in Context." *Bulletin of the History of Medicine* 78: 539–74.

Kornfeld, Eve. 1984. "Crisis in the Capital: The Cultural Significance of Philadelphia's Great Yellow Fever Epidemic." *Pennsylvania History* 51: 189–205.

Landsman, Stephan. 1990. "The Rise of the Contentious Spirit: Adversary Procedure in Eighteenth Century England." *Cornell Law Review* 75: 497–606.

Lane, John. 1936. "Jean Deveze (1753–1826? [sic]): Notes on the Yellow Fever Epidemic at Philadelphia in 1793." *Annals of Medical History* n.s. 8: 202–26.

Langbein, John H. 1978. "The Criminal Trial Before the Lawyers." *University of Chicago Law Review* 45: 263–316.

———. 1983. "Shaping the Eighteenth-Century Criminal Trial: A View from the Ryder Sources." *University of Chicago Law Review* 50: 1–136.

———. 1994. "The Historical Origins of the Privilege against Self-Incrimination at Common Law." *Michigan Law Review* 92: 1047–85.

———. 2003. *The Origins of Adversary Criminal Trial*. Oxford: Oxford University Press.

Lapansky, Phillip. 1997. "'Abigail, a Negress': The Role and Legacy of African Americans in the Yellow Fever Epidemic." In *A Melancholy Scene of Devastation: The Public Response to the 1793 Philadelphia Yellow Fever Epidemic*, eds. J. Worth Estes and Billy G. Smith. 61–78. Philadelphia: College of Physicians of Philadelphia.

Laracey, Mel. 2008. "The Presidential Newspaper as an Engine of Early American Political Development: The Case of Thomas Jefferson and the Election of 1800." *Rhetoric and Public Affairs* 11.1: 7–46.

Latour, Bruno. 1988. *The Pasteurization of France*. Trans. Alan Sheridan and John Law. Cambridge: Harvard University Press.

Leary, Lewis. 1941. *That Rascal Freneau: A Study in Literary Failure*. New Brunswick: Rutgers University Press.

———. 1965. "Editor's Introduction." In *Modern Chivalry, Containing the Adventures of Captain John Farrago and Teague O'Regan, His Servant*, ed. Lewis Leary. 7–19. Albany: New College and University Press, Inc.

Lerner, Renee Lettow. 2000. "The Transformation of the American Civil Trial: The Silent Judge." *William and Mary Law Review* 42: 195–263.

Lettow, Rene B. 1996. "New Trial for Verdict Against Law: Judge-Jury Relations in Early Nineteenth-Century America." *Notre Dame Law Review* 71: 505–64.

List, Karen K. 1983. "The Role of William Cobbett in Philadelphia Party Press, 1794–1799." *Journalism Monographs* 82: 1–41.

Lupton, Deborah. 1997. "Foucault and the Medicalisation Critique." In *Foucault, Health and Medicine*, eds. Alan Peterson and Bryan S. Turner. 94–110. London: Routledge.

Lyotard, Jean Francois. 1984. *The Postmodern Condition: A Report on Knowledge*. Trans. Geoff Bennington and Brian Massumi. Minneapolis: University of Minnesota Press.

———. 1988a. *The Differend: Phrases in Dispute*. Trans. G. Van Den Abbeele. Minneapolis; University of Minnesota Press.

———. 1988b. *Peregrinations: Law, Form, Event*. Trans. Cecile Lindsay. New York: Columbia University Press.

Lyotard, Jean Francois and Jean Loup Thebaud. 1985. *Just Gaming*. Trans. Wald Godzich. Minneapolis: University of Minnesota Press.

Madden, Etta. 2006. "'To Make a Figure': Benjamin Rush's Rhetorical Self-Construction and Scientific Authorship." *Early American Literature* 41.2: 241–72.

Maier, Pauline. 1970. "Popular Uprisings and Civil Authority in Eighteenth-Century America." *William and Mary Quarterly* 3rd ser. 27: 3–35.

Malone, Wex. 1986. *Essays on Torts*. Baton Rouge: Paul M. Herbert Law Center, Louisiana State University Press.

Martin, Julian. 1990. "Sauvages's Nosology: Medical Enlightenment in Montpellier." In *The Medical Enlightenment of the Eighteenth Century*, eds. Andrew Cunningham and Roger French. 111–37. Cambridge: Cambridge University Press.

Martin, Wendy. 1971. "On the Road with the Philosopher and the Profiteer: A Study of Hugh Henry Brackenridge's *Modern Chivalry*." *Eighteenth-Century Studies* 4: 241–56.

———. 1973. "The Rogue and the Rational Man: Hugh Henry Brackenridge's Study of a Con Man in *Modern Chivalry*." *Early American Literature* 8:179–92.

McAuley, Louis Kirk. 2007. "'Periodical Visitations': Yellow Fever as Yellow Journalism in Charles Brockden Brown's *Arthur Mervyn*." *Eighteenth-Century Fiction* 19.3: 307–40.

McFarland, Joseph. 1929. "The Epidemic of Yellow Fever in Philadelphia in 1793 and Its Influence upon Dr. Benjamin Rush." *Medical Review of Reviews* 25: 627–74.

Meehan, Thomas R. 1967. "Courts, Cases, and Counselors in Revolutionary and Post-Revolutionary Pennsylvania." *Pennsylvania Magazine of History and Biography* 91.1: 3–34.

Miller, Jacquelyn C. 1996. "An 'Uncommon Tranquility of Mind': Emotional Self-Control and the Construction of a Middle-Class Identity in Eighteenth-Century Philadelphia." *Journal of Social History* 30.1: 129–47.

———. 1997. "Passions and Politics: The Multiple Meanings of Benjamin Rush's Treatment for Yellow Fever." In *A Melancholy Scene of Devastation: The Public Response to the 1793 Philadelphia Yellow Fever Epidemic*, eds. J. Worth Estes and Billy G. Smith. 79–96. Philadelphia: College of Physicians of Philadelphia.

———. 2001. "The Body Politic and the Body Somatic: Benjamin Rush's Fear of Social Disorder." In *A Centre of Wonders: The Body in Early America*, eds. Janet Moore Lindeman and Michelle Lise Tarter. 61–74. Ithaca: Cornell University Press.

Miller, John C. 1951. *Crisis in Freedom: The Alien and Sedition Acts*. Boston: Little, Brown.

———. 1960. *The Federalist Era, 1789–1801*. New York: Harper.

Mitchell, Stewart. April 18, 1945–October 17, 1945. "New Letters of Abigail Adams." *American Antiquarian Society* 55: 347.

Mires, Charlene. 2002. *Independence Hall in American Memory*. Philadelphia: University of Pennsylvania Press.

Modlin, Charles E. 1975. "The Folly of Ambition in *Modern Chivalry*." *Proceedings of the American Antiquarian Society* 85: 310–13.

Mohr, James C. 1993. *Doctors and the Law: Medical Jurisprudence in Nineteenth-Century America*. Oxford: Oxford University Press.

Moody, Richard, ed. 1966. *Dramas from the American Theatre, 1762–1909*. Cleveland: World Publishing Co.

Morrison, Tony, ed. 1992. *Race-ing Justice, En-Gendering Power*. New York: Pantheon Books.

Moss, Stephanie, and Kaara L. Peterson. 2004. *Disease, Diagnosis, and Cure on the Early Modern Stage*. Burlington: Ashgate.

Myrsiades, Linda. 1998. "A Language Game Approach to Narrative Analysis of Sexual Harassment Law in *Meritor v. Vinson*." *College Literature* 25.1: 200–30.

———. 2008. "Grand Juries, Legal Machines, and the Common Man Jury." *College Literature* 35.3: 158–78.

———. 2009. *Medical Culture in Revolutionary America: Feuds, Duels, and a Court-Martial*. Madison: Fairleigh Dickinson University Press.

Myrsiades, Kostas, and Linda Myrsiades, eds. 1999. *Un-Disciplining Literature: Literature, Law, and Culture*. New York: Peter Lang.

Mullen, Fitzhugh, Ellen Ficklen, and Kyna Rubin, eds. 2006. *Narrative Matters: The Power of the Personal Essay in Health Policy*. Baltimore: Johns Hopkins University Press.

Nance, William. 1967. "Satiric Elements in Brackenridge's *Modern Chivalry*." *Texas Studies in Language and Literature* 9: 381–89.

Nash, Gary B. 1988. *Forging Freedom: The Formation of Philadelphia's Black Community, 1720–1820*. Cambridge: Harvard University Press.

———. 1989. "New Light on Richard Allen: The Early Years of Freedom." *William and Mary Quarterly* 3rd ser. 46: 332–40.

———. 1997. "Poverty and Poor Relief in Pre–Revolutionary Philadelphia." *William and Mary Quarterly* 33.1: 3–30.

Nathans, Heather S. 2003. *Early American Theatre from the Revolution to Thomas Jefferson: Into the Hands of the People*. Cambridge: Cambridge University Press.

Nattrass, Leonora. 1995. *William Cobbett: The Politics of Style*. Cambridge: Cambridge University Press.

Neilson, Winthrop, and Neilson, Frances. 1958. *Verdict for the Doctor: The Case of Benjamin Rush*. New York: Hastings House.

Nelson, Dana D. 2002. "'Indications of the Public Will': *Modern Chivalry*'s Theory of Democratic Representation." *ANQ* 15.1: 23–39.

Nelson, Richard. 1989. "Liberalism, Republicanism and the Politics of Therapy: John Locke's Legacy of Medicine and Reform." *The Review of Politics* 51.1: 29–54.

Nelson, William E. 1967. "Emerging Notions of Modern Criminal Law in the Revolutionary Era: An Historical Perspective." *New York University Law Review* 42: 450–82.

———. 1975. *Americanization of the Common Law: The Impact of Legal Change on Massachusetts Society, 1760–1830*. Cambridge: Harvard University Press.

Novak, William J. 1996. *The People's Welfare: Law and Regulation in Nineteenth Century America*. Chapel Hill: University of North Carolina Press.

O'Day, Rosemary. 1987. "The Anatomy of a Profession: The Clergy of the Church of England." In *The Professions in Early Modern England*, ed. Wilfrid Prest. 25–63. London: Croom Helm.

———. 2000. *The Professions in Early Modern England, 1450–1800: Servants of the Commonweal*. London: Longman.

Olson, Alison. 2000. "The Zenger Case Revisited: Satire, Sedition, and Political Debate in Eighteenth-Century America." *Early American Literature* 35.3: 223–45.

Onuf, Peter. 2000. *Jefferson's Empire: The Language of American Nationhood*. Charlottesville: University of Virginia Press.

Papke, David Ray, ed. 1991. *Narrative and Legal Discourse: A Reader in Storytelling and the Law*. Indianapolis: Deborah Charles Publications.

Paster, Gail Kern. 1993. *The Body Embarrassed: Drama and the Disciplines of Shame in Early Modern England*. Ithaca: Cornell University Press.

Pelling, Margaret. 1987. "Medical Practice in Early Modern England: Trade or Profession?" In *The Professions in Early Modern England*, ed. Wilfrid Prest. 90–128. London: Croom Helm.

Pernick, Martin S. 1997. "Politics, Parties, and Pestilence: Epidemic Yellow Fever in Philadelphia and the Rise of the First Party System." In *A Melancholy Scene of Devastation: The Public Response to the 1793 Philadelphia Yellow Fever Epidemic*, eds. J. Worth Estes and Billy G. Smith. 119–46. Philadelphia: College of Physicians of Philadelphia.

Phelan, James, and Peter J. Rabinowitz, eds. 2005. *A Companion to Narrative Theory*. Oxford: Blackwell Publishing.

Philip, Eric H. Christianson, and J. Worth Estes, eds. 1980. *Medicine in Colonial Massachusetts, 1620–1820*. Boston: Colonial Society of Massachusetts.

Porter, Roy. 1989. *Health for Sale: Quackery in England 1660–1850*. Manchester: Manchester University Press.

———. 1995. "The Eighteenth Century." In *The Western Medical Tradition: 800 BC to AD 1800*, eds. Lawrence I. Conrad, Michael Neve, Vivian Nutton, Roy Porter, and Andrew Wear. 371–475. Cambridge: Cambridge University Press.

Posner, Eric A. 2000. *Law and Social Norms*. Cambridge: Harvard University Press.

Powell, John H. 1965. *Bring Out the Dead*. 1949. Reprint. Philadelphia: University of Pennsylvania Press.

Prest, Wilfrid. 1987a. "The Professions and Society in Early Modern England." In *The Professions in Early Modern England*, ed. Wilfrid Prest. 1–24. London: Croom Helm.

———. 1987b. "Lawyers." In *The Professions in Early Modern England*, ed. Wilfrid Prest. 64–89. London: Croom Helm.

———, ed. 1987c. *The Professions in Early Modern England*. London: Croom Helm.

Ranger, Terence and Paul Slack, eds. 1992. *Epidemics and Ideas: Essays on the Historical Perception of Pestilence*. Cambridge: Cambridge University Press.

Readings, Bill. 1991. *Introducing Lyotard: Art and Politics*. New York: Routledge.

Reiss, Oscar. 1998. *Medicine and the American Revolution: How Diseases and Their Treatments Affected the Colonial Army*. Jefferson: McFarland & Co.

Reiter, Paula Jean. 1999. "Husbands, Wives, and Lawyers: Gender Roles and Professional Representations in Trollope and the Adelaide Bartlett Case." In *Un-Disciplining Literature: Literature, Law, and Culture*, eds. Kostas Myrsiades and Linda Myrsiades. 246–70. New York: Peter Lang.

Reitzel, William. 1935. "William Cobbett and Philadelphia Journalism: 1794–1800." *The Pennsylvania Magazine of History and Biography* 59.3: 223–44.

Rice, Grantland S. 1995. "*Modern Chivalry* and the Resistance to Textual Authority." *American Literature* 67.2: 257–81.

Richards, Louis. 1915. " Hon. Jacob Rush of the Pennsylvania Judiciary." *The Pennsylvania Magazine of History and Biography* 39.1: 53–68.

Richardson, Ruth. 1987. *Death, Dissection, and the Destitute*. London: Routledge and Kegan Paul.

Richman, Irwin. 1967. *The Brightest Ornament: A Biography of Nathaniel Chapman, M.D.* Bellefonte: Pennsylvania Heritage, Inc.

Robinson, Arthur Thomas. 1993. *Third Horseman of the Apocalypse: A Multidisciplinary Social History of the 1793 Yellow Fever Epidemic in Philadelphia*. Ph.D. Diss. Washington State University.

Roeber, A. G. 1997. "J.H.C. Helmuth, Evangelical Charity and the Public Sphere in Pennsylvania, 1793–1800." *The Pennsylvania Magazine of History and Biography* 121: 79–100.

Rosen, George. 1952. "Political Order and Human Health in Jeffersonian Thought." *Bulletin of the History of Medicine* 26: 32–54.

———. 1957. "The Fate of the Concept of Medical Police, 1780–1890." *Centaurus* 5.1: 97–113.

———. 1974. *From Medical Police to Social Medicine: Essays on the History of Health Care*. New York: Science History Publications.

Rosenberg, Charles E. 1987. *The Cholera Years: The United States in 1831, 1849, and 1866*. Chicago: University of Chicago Press.

———. 1992. *Explaining Epidemics and Other Studies in the History of Medicine*. New York: Cambridge University Press.

———. 1998. *"Every Man his Own Doctor": Popular Medicine in Early America, an Exhibition Drawn from the Collections of Charles E. Rosenberg, William H. Helfand, and the Library Company of Philadelphia*. Philadelphia: Library Company of Philadelphia.

Rosenberg, Charles E., and Janet Golden, eds. 1992. *Framing Disease: Studies in Cultural History*. New Brunswick: Rutgers University Press.

Rosenberg, Norman L. 1986. *Protecting the Best Men: An Interpretive History of the Law of Libel*. Chapel Hill: University of North Carolina Press.

Rowe, G. S. 1978. *Thomas McKean: The Shaping of an American Republicanism*. Boulder: Colorado Associated University Press.

———. 1994. *Embattled Bench: The Pennsylvania Supreme Court and the Forging of a Democratic Society, 1684–1809*. Newark: University of Delaware Press.

Ryken, Leland. 1998. *Dictionary of Biblical Imagery*. Leicester: Inter Varsity Press.

Sambrook, James. 1973. *William Cobbett*. London: Routledge & Kegan Paul.

Samuels, Shirley. 1985. "Plague and Politics in 1793: *Arthur Merwyn*." *Criticism* 27.3: 225–46.

———. 1987. "Infidelity and Contagion: The Rhetoric of Revolution." *Early American Literature* 22.2: 183–91.

Sappol, Michael. 2002. *A Traffic of Dead Bodies: Anatomy and Embodied Social Identity in Nineteenth-Century America*. Princeton: Princeton University Press.

Satire and Caricature in Medical History. [1924]. Yonkers: New York Pharmacal Association,

Scherr, Arthur. 2003. "'Sambos' and 'Black Cut-Throats': Peter Porcupine on Slavery and Race in the 1790s." *American Periodicals: A Journal of History, Criticism, and Bibliography* 13: 4–30.

Schor, Esther. 1994. *Bearing the Dead: The British Culture of Mourning from the Enlightenment to Victoria*. Princeton: Princeton University Press.

Schultz, Lucille. 1979–1980. "Uncovering the Significance of the Animal Imagery in *Modern Chivalry*: An Application of Scottish Common Sense Realism." *Early American Literature* 14: 306–11.

Schwartz, Warren F., Keith Baxter, and David Ryan. 1984. "The Duel: Can These Gentlemen Be Acting Efficiently." *Journal of Legal Studies* 13: 321–55.

Shapiro, Barbara. 1991. *'Beyond Reasonable Doubt' and 'Probable Cause': Historical Perspectives on the Anglo–American Law of Evidence*. Berkeley: University of California Press.

Sharp, James Roger. 1993. *American Politics in the Early Republic: The New Nation in Crisis*. New Haven: Yale University Press.

Sheehan, Colleen A. 2004. "Madison v. Hamilton: The Battle over Republicanism and the Role of Public Opinion." *The American Political Science Review* 98.3: 405–24.

Shryock, Richard Harrison. 1960. *Medicine and Society in America, 1660–1860*. New York: New York University Press.

———. 1966. *Medicine in America: Historical Essays*. Baltimore: Johns Hopkins University Press.

———. 1967. *Medical Licensing in America, 1650–1965*. Baltimore: Johns Hopkins University Press.

Silvette, Herbert. 1967. *Doctor on the Stage: Medicine and Medical Men in Seventeenth-Century England*. Nashville: University of Tennessee Press.

Sloane, David Charles. 1991. *The Last Great Necessity: Cemeteries in American History*. Baltimore: Johns Hopkins University Press.

Smith, Billy G. 1990. *The "Lower Sort": Philadelphia's Laboring People, 1750–1800*. Ithaca: Cornell University Press.

Smith, James Morton. 1953a. "The Aurora and the Alien and Sedition Laws, Part I: The Editorship of Benjamin Franklin Bache." *Pennsylvania Magazine of History and Biography* 77.1: 3–23.

———. 1953b. "The Aurora and the Alien and Sedition Laws, Part II: The Editorship of William Duane." *Pennsylvania Magazine of History and Biography* 77.2: 123–55.

Smith, Jeffery A. 1988. *Printers and Press Freedom: The Ideology of Early American Journalism*. New York: Oxford University Press.

Smith, Olivia. 1984. *The Politics of Language*. Oxford: Oxford University Press.

Spater, George. 1982. *William Cobbett: The Poor Man's Friend*. Vol 1. Cambridge: Cambridge University Press.

Specter, Benjamin. 1947. "Noah Webster: His Contribution to American Medical Thought and Progress." In *Letters on Yellow Fever Addressed to Dr. William Currie*. 1–18. Baltimore: Johns Hopkins University Press.

Starr, Paul. 1982. *The Social Transformation of American Medicine: The Rise of a Sovereign Profession and the Making of a Vast Industry*. New York: Basic Books.

Stewart, Donald H. 1969. *The Opposition Press of the Federalist Period*. Albany: SUNY Press.

Surrency, Erwin C. 1976. "The Development of the Appellate Function: The Pennsylvania Experience." *The American Journal of Legal History* 20.3: 173–91.

———. 1981. "Law Reports in the United States." *The American Journal of Legal History* 25.1: 48–66.

Terrell, Colleen E. 2003. "'Republican Machines': Franklin, Rush, and the Manufacture of Civic Virtue in the Early Republic." *Early American Studies* 1.2: 101–32.

Tompkins, Jane. 1985. *Sensational Designs: The Cultural Work of American Fiction 1790–1860*. New York: Oxford University Press.

Tucker, E. F. J. 1984. *Intruder into Eden: Representations of the Common Lawyer in English Literature 1350–1750*. Camden House.

———. 1986. *Corum Paribus: Images of the Common Lawyer in Romantic and Victorian Literature*. Charleston: Citadel.

Wald, Patricia. 1995. *Constituting Americans: Cultural Anxiety and Narrative Form*. Durham: Duke University Press.

———. 2008. *Contagious: Cultures, Carriers, and the Outbreak Narrative*. Durham: Duke University Press.

Wallenborn, White McKenzie. September 23, 2004. "George Washington's Terminal Illness: A Modern Medical Analysis of the Last Illness and Death of George Washington." *The Papers of George Washington. http://gwpapers.virginia.edu/articles/wallenborn/index.html. 9/23/04.*

Warden, G. B. 1980. "The Medical Profession in Colonial Boston." In *Medicine in Colonial Massachusetts, 1620–1820*, eds. Philip Cash, Eric H. Christianson, and J. Worth Estes. 145–57. Boston: Colonial Society of Massachusetts.

Warner, John Harley. 1986. *The Therapeutic Perspective: Medical Practice, Knowledge, and Identity in America, 1820–1885*. Cambridge: Harvard University Press.

Watson, Patricia A. 1991. *The Angelic Conjunction: Preacher Physicians of Colonial New England*. Knoxville: University of Tennessee Press.

Watts, Steven. 1986. "Masks, Morals, and the Market: American Literature and Early Capitalist Culture. 1790–1820." *Journal of the Early Republic* 6.2: 127–50.

———. 1994. *The Romance of Real Life: Charles Brockden Brown and the Origins of American Culture*. Baltimore: Johns Hopkins University Press.

Webster, Richard. 1976. *Philadelphia Preserved: Catalog of the Historic American Buildings Survey*. Philadelphia: Temple University Press.

Weisberg, Robert. 1996. "Proclaiming Trials as Narratives: Premises and Pretenses." *Law's Stories: Narrative and Rhetoric in the Law*, eds. Peter Brooks and Paul Gewirtz. 61–83. New Haven: Yale University Press.

White, Hayden. 1987. *The Content of the Form: Narrative Discourse and Historical Representation.* Baltimore: Johns Hopkins University Press.

White, James Boyd. 1984. *When Words Lose Their Meaning: Constitutions and Reconstitutions of Language, Character, and Community*. Chicago: University of Chicago Press.

———. 1985. *Heracles' Bow: Essays on the Rhetoric and Poetics of the Law*. Madison: University of Wisconsin Press.

———. 1990. *Justice as Translation: An Essay in Cultural and Legal Criticism*. Chicago: University of Chicago Press.

———. 1994. *Acts of Hope: Creating Authority in Literature, Law, and Politics*. Chicago: University of Chicago Press.

Whittle, Amberys R. 1971 "*Modern Chivalry*: The Frontier Crucible." *Early American Literature* 6: 263–70.

Will, Thomas. 2002. "Liberalism, Republicanism, and Philadelphia's Black Elite in the Early Republic: The Social Thought of Absalom Jones and Richard Allen." *Pennsylvania History* 69.4: 558–76.

Williams, Daniel E. 1990. "Gadding About Quack Like: The Science of Deception and the Practice of Physic in the Narrative of Henry Tufts." In *The Body and the Text: Comparative Essays in Literature and Medicine*, eds. Bruce Clarke and Wendell Aycock. 77–89. Lubbock: Texas Tech University Press.

Williams, Joan. 1987. "Critical Legal Studies: The Death of Transcendence & The Rise of the New Langdells." *New York University Law Review* 62: 429–96.

Williams, Wade. 2000. "Religion, Science and Rhetoric in Revolutionary America: The Case of Dr. Benjamin Rush." *Rhetoric Society Quarterly* 30.3: 55–72.

Williams, William H. 1976. *American's First Hospital: The Pennsylvania Hospital, 1751–1841*. Wayne: Haverford House.

Wilson, David A. 1994. "Introduction." In *Peter Porcupine in America: Pamphlets on Republicanism and Revolution*, ed. David A. Wilson. 1–49. Ithaca: Cornell University Press.

Woodbury, Margaret. 1919–1920. "Public Opinion in Philadelphia, 1789–1801." *Smith College Studies in History* 5.1–2: 1–138.

Index

www.ingramcontent.com/pod-product-compliance
Lightning Source LLC
LaVergne TN
LVHW011524200926
848484LV00001B/146
9781611461022